Aristocratic Vice

DONNA T. ANDREW

Aristocratic Vice

THE ATTACK ON DUELLING, SUICIDE, ADULTERY, AND GAMBLING IN EIGHTEENTH-CENTURY ENGLAND

Yale UNIVERSITY PRESS
New Haven &
London

Published with assistance from the Annie Burr Lewis Fund.

Published with assistance from the foundation established in memory of Philip Hamilton McMillan of the Class of 1894, Yale College.

Yale University Press books may be purchased in quantity for educational, business, or promotional use. For information, please e-mail sales.press@yale.edu (U.S. office) or sales@yaleup.co.uk (U.K. office).

Set in Postscript Sabon type by IDS Infotech Ltd.
Printed in the United States of America.

Library of Congress Cataloging-in-Publication Data

Andrew, Donna T., 1945–. Aristocratic vice : the attack on duelling, suicide, adultery, and gambling in eighteenth-century England / Donna T. Andrew.
   pages   cm
Includes bibliographical references and index.
ISBN 978-0-300-18433-4 (cloth : alk. paper) 1. Great Britain—Moral conditions. 2. England—Social life and customs—18th century.
3. Upper class—England—Conduct of life—History—18th century.
4. Vices—History—18th century. I. Title.
HN400.M6A53 2013
305.5'20941—dc23

                                                        2012041362

A catalogue record for this book is available from the British Library.

This paper meets the requirements of ANSI/NISO Z39.48–1992 (Permanence of Paper).
10 9 8 7 6 5 4 3 2 1

This book is dedicated to the memory of my father,
Bernhard Trembowelski

Contents

Acknowledgments

This book has been in the works for more than three decades. And of course, there are numerous people and institutions to thank for having discussed ideas with me, sponsored me for stays, or invited me to present papers. So after all this time, if I've forgotten anyone, please just put it down to creeping senility.

First and foremost, I would like to note my gratitude to my friend and mentor, John Beattie, who has enormously helped me over the years, most importantly by giving me a sterling model of both intellectual integrity and hard work. And then to my friends and colleagues on both sides of the Atlantic and Pacific, John Brewer, Margot Finn, Joanna Innes, Sarah Lloyd, Randall McGowen, Danny O'Quinn, Mark Phillips, Nicholas Rogers, and Gillian Russell, more thanks for all your help, advice, and patience.

Next I would like to express my appreciation for the opportunity for both scholarly research and intellectual conversation that the following institutions afforded me during my stays: to the Humanities Research Centre at the Australian National University under its then-head, Iain McCalman, and later also in Australia as a Visiting Research Fellow at the Law School of the University of Adelaide and to my friends in both History and Law, and finally thanks to Emmanuel College, Cambridge, for awarding me a Fellowship for a wonderful semester there.

In Canada I would like to thank following institutes for inviting me to give a paper: the Early Modern Studies Programme at Dalhousie University, Green College at the University of British Columbia, the History Department of the University of Prince Edward Island, the Law School at the University of Toronto, and the Graduate-Faculty Colloquium at York University, Toronto.

In Britain my thanks both to the Department of History at the University of Warwick, and to the "Women and Luxury" conference held there, the Institute of Historical Research at the University of London, the Cambridge University Restoration to Reform Seminar, the Centre for Eighteenth Century Studies at the University of York, the Department of History at the University of Edinburgh, and for the opportunity to give a paper at my home away from home, Clare Hall College, Cambridge.

In Australia, I received feedback and friendship at the Law School of Griffith University, and the Departments of History of the University of Newcastle, Perth, and Queensland.

I would also like to express my deep appreciation to all the staff at the Microtext Center of the University of Toronto for their unfailing good humour and assistance. In addition I must commend the attention and extraordinary patience of my fine copyeditor, Katherine Scheuer.

And last, but certainly not least, I wish to thank the History Department of the University of Oregon at Eugene.

I would also like to express my indebtedness to the Social Sciences and Humanities Research Council of Canada for funding my research for many years. Also I would like to thank the Lewis Walpole Foundation for aiding in the publication of this volume.

Though it is rather obligatory to thank one's spouse for support and assurance, for fellowship and intellectual dispute, I gladly do likewise; I would, in addition, like to thank mine for ceaseless nagging, without which I probably never would have finished this book.

Introduction:
The Middle Way: Cultural Skirmishes

It was a commonplace in eighteenth-century England that in terms of importance, both fiscally and morally, the middling sort occupied a significant position. It was they who were "the sinews and strength of a nation . . ." This was thought to be so not only because "out of their Labour, Industry and Skill the greatest Part of all our Taxes are raised . . ." but also since in terms of national moral stability "the middling People are certainly more happy in the married State, than Persons of a more elevated Dignity . . ."[1] In contrast, both the upper and lower orders were chastised for their improvidence and immorality:

> Cast but a single glance of the eye on the Great Vulgar, all devoted to Pleasure and Extravagance, even in a Christian Country; and then look again at the Little Vulgar, and you'll find 'em all aping the Great ones, even to ruin and destruction . . . What! is to be Great and Good, a Meanness of Spirit? and all Order and Decency become the Scorn of the People? . . . the Great neither see, nor hear, nor regard any of these Things: but the Country Gentleman, and the middling sort of People, both hear and see, and feel it too.[2]

Still, some recognized that this middle sort were not exempt from vice, that they, like their betters, enjoyed prodigious and unnecessary spending.

> this Vice [is not] confined to those alone who affect a Prodigality beyond the real Profusion of their Plenty: But the same with glorious Extravagance, that

drains off so much more than the Superfluities of the Affluent in high Life, is no less frequent among the middling sort of people.

Even here, however, the implication was that such middling irresponsibility was more a matter of imitation than an innate tendency. For it seemed obvious to many, as one newspaper reported, without any need for explication or justification, that "so much more honest and incorrupt are the Middling people than the Great, as they are vulgarly nick-named!"[3]

However, while many historians have noticed "a deep ambivalence among trading people" in eighteenth-century England "toward upper-class mores—as middling people defined them, at any rate"—few have considered such ambivalence in detail; "It was commoner by far," notes one, for contemporaries "to dwell on the superior moral credentials and industry of the middle class than to analyse its make-up." And yet very little historical analysis exists about this clichéd and much-repeated trope.

Surely this lack of engagement can be explained by the sanctimonious and perhaps hypocritical quality of such self-applause: a fine example of which can be found, early in the century, in *Robinson Crusoe*. Crusoe's "middle station," his father noted, spared him not only from the poverty of "the lower orders," but equally, and as fatally, from the "vicious living, luxury, and extravagancies" of the upper ranks. While, then as now, no segment of society was free of fault, no group pure of failings, whatever its qualities, perhaps the reiterative and insistent repetition of such comments through the eighteenth century can tell us something important about the society from which they sprang. That is the underlying premise of this study.

We get some sense of the significance of frequent praise for the moral middle when we recall the purpose of the Societies for the Reformation of Manners of the late seventeenth and early eighteenth centuries, and the similar aims of the Proclamation Society, formed almost a hundred years later, i.e. the reformation of the manners and morals of the lower classes. By the late eighteenth century, however, there were expressions of disquietude that such reform was aimed only downwards. Thus one letter-writer, addressing "the Noblemen and Gentlemen" of the Proclamation Society, noted that:

> You must also be sensible that you will with great difficulty obtain, what appears to be the peculiar object of your Association, the reformation of the inferior branches of the community, while the grossest abuses prevail uncensored, at least unreformed, in the higher orders.[4]

The desire of the letter-writer, Theophilus, to improve the morals and manners of *both* the lower *and* upper orders was perhaps the less self-congratulatory side of the common assertion of middling virtue, and it is this element in the development of the social understanding of the period that has largely been neglected. This book seeks to examine some of this vast body of disapproval to see whether, and in which ways, these critiques of their superiors served some positive function. By considering four practices which contemporaries saw both as linked to each other, and as largely identified with the upper classes, we can perhaps gain some insight into why upper-class vices were thought by many to be pernicious, and what could, should, and must be done to ameliorate them, to guard Britain's national prosperity and internal unity of purpose.

A Constellation of Corruption

There is much in the structure of this book that needs explanation, and it will illuminate some of my central themes to consider the decisions that have gone into its adoption. First is the notion that, in the very long eighteenth century, there was an attack on something that might be called 'aristocratic vice.' Second is the question of why I have called it 'aristocratic' since many of its practitioners were not noble men or women. And why is Vice singular?— for surely, whoever they were, they indulged in more than one. And why Vice? why not Sin or Crime?

On the one hand there are good reasons for seeing the repeated attempts to curb certain forms of elite immorality as parts of an ongoing movement, as a sort of extended conversation, or an argument, between a social elite and its critics about the best ways to promote a powerful and healthy polity. On the other hand, it would be wrong to see these efforts as part of a concerted and organized movement by a united group of campaigners, entirely aware of well-defined goals and conjoined in their efforts. These critics of fashionable vice, who tended to be neither aristocrats nor working people, formed at best a very loose alliance, brought together at specific times and places, but as yet with no abiding and distinct group identity. Sociologically, in so far as they produced and read a wide variety of printed material, they tended to belong to the middle strata of society, with few aristocrats and even fewer working people represented. Not surprisingly many of these critics were clerics. But in matters of belief, the entire group was very diverse, separated not only in time but by general outlook, by political allegiance and vehemence of concern. This movement then can be seen as both one and multiple—an issue to which we will return throughout the following chapters.

Vice, Sin, and Crime

Almost as disparate a group as their critics, the habitués of the world of aristocratic vice, although they all required and possessed some measure of wealth and birth, were defined by other qualities. We get some clue to their essential attributes when we consider the names frequently used to describe them. Tags such as "the Great" or "the better sort" situated them on the social ladder; others such as the *beau monde*, "people of fashion," the *ton, haut ton*, or *bon ton*, or most inclusively, "the polite world" delineated their manner of living. These were the trend-setters, the arbiters of style, the celebrities of eighteenth-century Britain.[5] And many of them, at least in the popular imagination, were practitioners of the multiple modes of aristocratic vice, ranging from minor follies to major sins.

However, there were four activities singled out by eighteenth-century contemporaries as belonging to a system of vice, as being archetypical immoralities, as constituting a sort of constellation of corruption. These practices were duelling, suicide, adultery, and gambling.[6] These four, it was said, owed their origin to the besetting failing of the upper class—pride. And though it was claimed that all these vices originated with society's elite, a great danger of their practice, as we have already noticed, was in their effects upon the rest of society. Not only would social inferiors inevitably imitate their superiors, but also, in the commission of illegal acts for which they escaped punishment and in the engagement in sinful activity which met only with mild censure, aristocrats would fatally weaken the force of the laws of Man and God. For Vice was something that not only hurt individuals but also harmed the public weal. To be overly schematic (for often eighteenth-century writers used vice, sin, and crime interchangeably), sin is that which corrodes the individual soul, while vice, like crime, corrupts public life. While there were many attempts to criminalize the vices of duelling, gambling, suicide, and adultery, most thought that the law would continue to turn a blind eye until public opinion raised the awareness of juries to the gravity of aristocratic transgressions. Crime was to be dealt with by the heavy hand of the law, but since vice was sustained or attacked by "opinion," only a concomitant change in opinion would resolve the problem.

What sorts of specific vices made up the general category, what constituted the acts that composed prideful vice? Vices could be minor ill-acts, like over-drinking or ingratitude, or major and serious breaches of morals, like gaming, adultery, or duelling, but most were seen as damaging the nation, as directly and harmfully weakening its moral stamina. When Thomas Erskine asked, "Of what consequence is the finest system of laws, if the morals of the people that are to obey and to defend them, are contaminated and lost; their dictates will be despised, and their execution cannot long continue,"[7] he was only repeating a widely held notion, the primacy of morality to the nation's welfare and the fatal effects of vice on its continuing vitality. In sum, a vice was a breach of morality, an act which had consequences far beyond the harm it did to the private world of the vicious person.

On occasion, all three terms—sin, vice, and crime—were used more or less interchangeably. Even so, there were four particular sets of actions in which this sort of confused and multiple description was common and which are the subjects of this book. All were called vices, all were against both God and man's law, and none was punished, at least by the courts, if the offenders were well-born.

Let us first consider contemporaries' descriptions of adultery, duelling, gaming, and suicide as sins and crimes. In Henry Fielding's *Amelia*, Dr. Harrison wondered whether "in the great sin of Adultery, for instance, hath the Government provided any law to punish it . . . ." while in his *Covent Garden Journal* Fielding thundered: "By what means our Laws are induced to consider this atrocious *Vice* as no Crime, I shall not attempt to determine. Such however is the Fact . . ."[8] The rector of Waltham Parva preached a sermon at St. Paul's Cathedral in 1727, entitled "The Obliquity of the Sin of Duelling" while the *London Chronicle* noted that "Through the inefficacy of our boasted laws, does not the fell aggressor in a duel commit a most atrocious crime with impunity; while the meek and injured person is exposed to general contempt."[9] A letter signed 'Francisco Grimaldi' sent to the *Public Advertiser* in 1765 concluded that "card-playing is unfortunately a sin that cannot be practiced alone" while a correspondent to the *Gazetteer* argued that "it appears on the whole that gaming is the particular crime to which the destruction of this country (if ever it happen) will be ascribed."[10] A mid-century tract against suicide, entitled *A Discourse Upon Self-Murder*, concluded that "if a Man, through the Habit of Sin, and the long Government of the Devil, should at last become thereby disorder'd in his Senses, or a Lunatick, and then kill himself, his Madness in that Case would be no more Excuse than Drunkenness would be." Thirty years later, a *Times* correspondent lamented, "That self-murder has become a crime frequent among us is a truth too generally and too justly lamented; and the ill forbearance of the Coroner's juries of late perhaps have not a little contributed to its frequency."[11] For these four misdeeds, the terms vice, crime, and sin were used interchangeably.

One of the main reasons for such denunciatory descriptions of these four activities was, as I have already suggested, the inability or unwillingness of the Church or the State to tackle them practically. Neither seemed to punish miscreants of fashion, men and women of the upper orders, in the same manner that they punished less well-connected folk. The law's partiality, its failure to bring the well-born to condign punishment, was recognized to be a special and especially dangerous quality in relation to these upper-class immoralities. It is clear that for many, these four transgressions were vices, sins, and crimes simultaneously. While sins broke divine law, and crimes human law, vice, while often breaking both of these, also had clear damaging practical effects on the nation.

Having considered vice, let us look at another central concern of this book, that of "cultural skirmishes." Given its complexity, it will be necessary to disassemble the notion, and consider its individual parts. First, I will explain what I mean by culture, and why a cultural conflict might be significant and worthy of attention. Second, I will discuss why the phrase "cultural skirmishes" is used to describe the waves of criticism which are the subject of this book. And finally I will examine where, in what venues or sites, and under what conditions such skirmishes occurred.

Cultural history is a relatively new and diverse sub-genre in British historiography. One strand of this new history of culture considers the creation and dissemination of what we often call High Culture. To oversimplify somewhat, this sort of cultural history describes the world of works and objects whose artistic or intellectual worth transcends the period in which they were created. Recently, this sort of study has also been enhanced by a consideration of delivery and reception: who read novels in family circles, and how this could lead to different sorts of experiences for the hearers or how readers could find notions within literature which were totally unintended by its creators.[12] Another sort of cultural history is more influenced, perhaps, by anthropology, and considers as its subject for investigation "how people live." These histories are informed by Geertzian notions of culture as a web of significance, a study of the largely unconscious *habitus* of lives, the roadmap or diagram of strategies available to people in particular times and places.[13] I cite these two predominant types to distinguish the sort of history considered in this study from its better-known and more well-worked relations. Unlike histories of high culture, this study looks at culture more widely considered. That is not to say that works of drama, of art, of thought will not be examined, but that, on the whole, they will be considered for what they say as part of the ongoing arguments of the day and not for their atemporal insights into the human condition. And unlike histories of the unthinking structures and codes by which most people conducted themselves most of the time, this study will focus specifically on conscious or semi-conscious arguments. As we shall see, these arguments and those who propounded them were often confused or held contradictory opinions, lacking the clarity of grand concepts and the venerability of received wisdom. They formed a changing body of musings on that society of which they were a part. This sort of cultural history can be called the "history of opinion." There is no better recommendation for, or explication of, this sort of study than David Hume's well-known analysis of the force of opinion in the upholding and sustaining of social order:

> Nothing is more suprizing to those who, consider human affairs with a philo-
> sophical eye, than to see the easiness with which the *many* will be governed
> by the *few*; and to observe the implicit submission with which men resign
> their own sentiments and passions to those of their rulers. When we enquire
> by what means this wonder is brought about, we shall find that as FORCE is
> always on the side of the governed, the governors have nothing to support
> them but opinion. 'Tis therefore, on opinion only that government is founded;
> and this maxim extends to the most despotic and military governments, as
> well as to the most free and most popular.[14]

Sometimes, as Hume pointed out, such opinion sustained elite control. At other times, however, it challenged elite authority, claiming either that the governors themselves were not abiding by their own rules, or that those rules were wrong, wicked, or outmoded. On important practical issues of social principles or correct morals, these sorts of arguments were especially significant. In an age where political opposition was still seen as dangerously divisive, where economic and military strength resided in the hands of a relatively small cadre, where religious argumentation still smacked of "the world turned upside down," discussions and disagreements about morals and manners were in no way so tainted. Concerning themselves with something to which everyone paid lip service, the moralists and critics of improper behavior could safely and public-spiritedly speak their minds. Thus, if we can come to some understanding of these diffusive and sprawling sets of views and arguments, if we can use them as the largest frame of reference or box in which arguments about politics, religion, or economics might "sit," we might recover an important though misunderstood strand of the history of the period, and also construct a framework in which older sub-genres of research could reveal insights.

Though meant ironically, the entry in the *Gentleman's Magazine* for 1752, under the heading of "A Modern Glossary," which defined "virtue and vice" as "subjects of discourse"[15] captured this freedom of expression. This book is informed by a consideration of such discourse, not only as "discourse" (that is to say, ideas or notions without particular anchors in the everyday world) but as constitutive elements in a world of discourse/practice. For often discourses about virtues or vices were not only about what was correct and proper, but about what particular persons had done in specific circumstances that was immoral and improper. Such discourses not only criticized actual actions, but also recommended actual solutions to habitual indecencies. In this way, the history of opinion seeks to combine the methods of studying high culture with the objectives of anthropological history.

The *Oxford English Dictionary* gives as its first definition of "skirmish"–"to engage in a skirmish or irregular encounter; to fight in small parties."[16] The irregular, inconclusive, hit-and-miss small scale of the term "skirmish" seems to fit perfectly the outbursts of criticism that characterized the attack on aristocratic vice. Whereas a war, even a cultural war, presupposes a coherent body of like-minded forces fighting a well-defined foe, the skirmishes I will be analyzing contain no such definition. Indeed, the very diversity of the opponents is one of the things that testifies to the significance and strength of these encounters. However, it does complicate the shape of the narrative, since it is hard to gather like-minded types together in these critical engagements. Thus, for example, we find both Enlightenment thinkers and Methodist preachers agreeing about the pernicious influence of custom, the authority for such vice; both the progressive feminist Mary Wollstonecraft and the conservative philanthropist Jonas Hanway seeing eye-to-eye on the world of fashion, the scene of such vice; both Thomas Erskine, supporter of radical causes, and Hannah More, defender of the old order, chastising the spurious honor of the Great, the cause for such vice. Coming together from different parts of the political and ideological spectrum, such folk found few things they could agree on beyond the need to purify social mores and eradicate genteel vices.[17]

This analysis, then, depends upon an investigation of both discourse and practice, and attempts to trace outbreaks of largely negative commentary about four aristocratic practices over a period of almost two hundred years, the "long" eighteenth century. It is grounded in and relies for its main methodological impetus on the use and investigation of all genres of writing on these vices, to see what difference different forms made, to consider continuities and changes between and within genres, and to get a sense of both dominant and minor contemporary evaluations, as well as to contrast "real life" with its various representations. It is the history of notions, swirling in the air, never entirely forgotten, but still periodically rediscovered and reinvigorated. It is the history of the activities that these notions combated (the duel unpunished, the adultery implicitly allowed) as well as those recommended as prophylactic (a raft of proposed new laws, new institutions, and new punishments).

But where did people come to share these swirling notions, how and where did they imbibe this charged "air"? The answer to this, is, of course, diffuse.

A summary of some of the sites for such interchange reveals, in fact, the sources for this volume. Of course, there is much that history and historians can never recover; the important though unrecorded conversations at breakfast tables, at coffeehouses, doing the shopping, or chatting with the postman. But there is a world of communication and interchange that is available to us, which allows us partial insights into this larger lost world. I have already mentioned some of these in my discussion of culture, though I rely more on really evanescent novels, plays, and poetry than I do on great artistic achievements, since it is in these transient literary forms that repeated segments of condemnation of aristocratic vice emerge. Not surprisingly, perhaps, aristocratic vice offered just the sort of spectacle that eighteenth-century consumers (like their modern descendants) seemed to be unable to resist—beautifully clothed, often physically attractive rich people doing bad things publicly. Whether on the stage, in a book or newspaper, or even in a poem or satire, the scandalous doings of the wicked and well-born, offered as objects of vicarious pleasure under the guise of information and condemnation, were a clichéd though popular trope. In addition to these ambiguous portrayals, an enormous number of serious pamphlets, which often originated as sermons, were available and cheaply priced. There were even a number of defences of various aristocratic activities, some quite sober, and others more ironic or satiric. Most of the memoirs and collections of letters of the day contain references to recent outrages or reflections on the causes of such improprieties. London's popular debating societies also discussed the frequency and seriousness of such sins, and their debates were reported in the newspapers of the day.[18]

This brings us to what is perhaps the most significant, and until recently, most understudied form of popular discussion, the British periodical press.[19] Although not the first European nation to have newspapers, England was unusual for the size and nature of its press. With the lapse of the Licensing Acts in 1697 and even before the permission to print Parliamentary proceedings was granted in 1774, England had an extraordinary range of periodical publications. Magazines of various types flourished, ranging from essay-journals, like the *Athenian Mercury*, to the better-known works of Steele and Addison in the *Spectator* and *Tatler*, through England's first storehouse of information, the *Gentleman's Magazine*, and including such notable and influential works as Johnson's *Rambler* and Thornton's *Connoisseur* and the less reputable but equally popular *Town and Country Magazine* or the *Bon Ton Magazine*. An important feature of all these journals was the opportunities they offered not only for moralists to broadcast their complaints to a wide and growing reading public, but also for that public to respond with letters to the editor. Such letters as often took exception to as agreed with the pieces to which they were responding. Here then was yet another forum for debate, a forum more anonymous and perhaps more "open" than even the debating clubs. In the many newspapers of the day, in the weeklies, tri-weeklies, and dailies that proliferated in extraordinary numbers, the letters-to-the-editor section was often one of the liveliest features. As significant as its function as a communicative site was the press's growing willingness to publicize and excoriate instances of upper-class misdeeds. Newspaper editors soon realized that aristocrats hated to see their names and follies spread over three-penny sheets, abhorred the thought that butchers and watermen might know of their personal lives and sins. It is said that suppression or omission fees were signifi-cant sources of income to early eighteenth-century newspapers.[20] But by the early 1760s, newspaper editors had realized that much more could be made from selling such items, by publishing such deeds in their papers, than they could ever hope to make by suppressing them. Opponents of such tell-all journalism were shocked by such publicity. Other commentators, however, were delighted, and argued that the press and publicity were the only means by which a thoroughgoing reform of the upper classes could be achieved.

One can see how attractive a tool this press must have seemed to critics of the upper classes. Finding existing legal recourse to be too ineffectual in preventing or punishing vicious acts, the opponents of aristocratic vice, while seeking to stiffen existing statues and make enforcement both more depend-able and resolute, turned largely to that quasi-legal moral force, the "court of public opinion," and attempted to educate, convince, and mobilize the power of that opinion as the best, perhaps the only moral social regenerator. For the power of the law against aristocratic offences seemed puny and ineffective when contrasted with the refusal of juries to punish, and with the loyalties of the Great themselves sworn to another code than the Law of the Land.

While historians and others have, in recent decades, written fine books on a number of the topics covered in this volume—on honor, duelling, gaming, suicide, and adultery[21]—no one, to my knowledge, has considered the vices over such a very long period of time, or as an ensemble, as a "constellation of corruption," neither for Britain, nor for any other of the countries of Europe. I aim to demonstrate that this sort of endeavor is possible for eighteenth-century Britain, in large part because of the relative development and sophis-tication of the British newspaper and periodical press, a press which, I shall argue, did more to familiarize its readers with, and promote popular objection to, aristocratic vices than any other written form. In a population that was largely literate, such daily and reiterative broadcast of fashionable immorality unpunished by the law must have acted as a constant irritant, and convinced those who did not belong to "Society" that its code was deleterious to the well-being of the nation's polity and welfare.

When Thomas Erskine noted the need for virtue for a successful polity, he used two phrases interchangeably which we might hesitate to see as equivalents. For Erskine, however, "general manners" and "morals" stood for the same sort of actions and beliefs. In contrast to these necessary and positive attributes, Erskine selected "the vices of the times," introducing, if only by implication, a third positive synonym for manners and morals, and that was virtue. For the modern historian, and perhaps the modern reader, these three notions, so closely allied in Erskine, have come to have three rather different inflections, if not meanings. For us manners are accomplishments that can be learned and taught. They vary with time, place, and circumstance. They are matters of accommodation and sociability, making it easier to get along in the company of strangers and even of friends. They have, even now, a faint flavor of arbitrariness about them, of form without substance. Morals on the other hand have come to carry a weightier load. Morals cannot be acquired as manners can, but are the outcome of early education, of inward belief or faith, or of the mandates of conscience. Often they are seen as the teachings of particular religious systems or ethical codes. If present, they regulate life's significant decisions and hard choices. Morality is unconcerned with gracefulness, with social amity, considering only what is correct belief or action, important. It is uncompromising, stern, and usually forbidding. And the third term, virtue, sits perhaps most uncomfortably in modern parlance. It is remote and faintly chilly, not involved in the messiness of everyday life and everyday decisions.

What does it matter what these words meant then and what they might mean now? I have taken time with terminology since this is a book about manners, morals, virtue, and vice, and about a series of attempts made over a long time to redefine, to rehabilitate, and to control their meanings. This is a book about a series of contestations, of challenges over moral authority, of symbolic struggles over who gets to decide what manners, morals, and virtue should be. And, because, in practice, such contests are always undertaken piecemeal, holus-bolus as it were, it is not at all surprising that, at their most effective, these challenges were not so much in favor of a new system of morals or a new code of manners, as against immoral activities; against current vices, against current outrages, against current evils. That is not to say that gradually, and in a semi-submerged manner, such a new code of conduct did not come to be, as we shall see. But rather what I wish to argue is that for most of the period under investigation, such attacks remained negative, inconclusive, and oppositional.[22]

Structure and Themes

Having considered the argument of this book, let us discuss its structure and its themes. Structurally, after a general introduction to that system of unwritten though pervasive rules that some called "the code of honor," and to which others took grave exception (chapter 1), each of the vices (duelling, suicide, adultery, and gambling) will be examined in turn, with contemporary criticisms of such misconduct drawn from a wide range of sources, detailing continuities and changes in thought and practice over the "long eighteenth century." Finally, Chapter 6 will sketch the fate of these vices in the first several decades of the nineteenth century. Though the history of each of these vices has received scholarly attention, this study considers them as a combined moral (or rather immoral) complex. When they are brought thus together, it will become evident that an examination of this knot of miscreancy reveals more than the consideration of its parts would suggest.

While gender is an important theme of this volume, it perhaps should be noted that although some of these vices, like duelling, were only or mainly practiced by men, others found practitioners among members of both sexes. Chapter 1 examines various desired masculine and feminine attributes in the early eighteenth century, and briefly considers the effects of the new code of politeness. Chapter 3 features a micro-history of the suicide of a very prominent man, casting some light on the ongoing debate on manly virtue, while chapter 5 contains a similar micro-history of a gaming woman, whose story, told throughout the century, became an exemplar of the old saw about the wages of sin, especially for women.

An animating theme is the effect, broadly considered, of press coverage, specifically the publication of the vices under consideration, on the reading public. For the newspaper and magazine press of the eighteenth century did not just provide news and views to its readers, but also exposed their audiences to immoral acts they might never have personally "seen," and gave them repeated instances of such acts that they may have thought infrequent or unusual.[23] Though most of the papers and magazines examined were metropolitan, their influence, though no doubt greatest in London, surely spread throughout the realm.

Second only to the press in the extent of its appeal was the topical and lively theatrical scene. From the plebs who sat in the "heavens" to the patricians who occupied grand boxes, eighteenth-century drama appealed to all classes, though perhaps in very different ways. Plays feature in both chapters 4 and 5; in the former the reception of a single play over a period of time discloses important changes in the understanding of adultery; in the latter, a succession of plays on the same topic reveals changes in attitudes toward gambling, while chapter 2 examines plays in the context of other literary commentary on duelling and chapter 3 looks at changes in plays in which suicide was the central leitmotif.

Finally, a central theme of this book is the ways in which contemporaries thought the vices of the *haut ton* weakened and threatened to overthrow the Law—both human and divine. In their campaign against aristocratic vice, critics argued for the necessity of thorough legislative reform and the passage of more punitive and more enforceable laws against the misdeeds of the Great. In this way legal sanctions would not only be, but would be seen to be, operating equally against the powerful and the powerless; men and women of the *ton* were not exempt from penalties that were enforced against those of the town.[24]

In studying these reiterative attacks we will chart the growth of a consciousness, an understanding that "we" were not vicious like "them" and through this growing awareness the development of what might be called proto–class consciousness. For, as E. P. Thompson, echoing Marx, noted: "class happens when some men, as a result of common experiences (inherited or shared), feel and articulate the identity of their interests as between themselves, and as against other men whose interests are different from (and usually opposed to) theirs." And, by the early nineteenth century, we can see the beginnings of such a consciousness: "What a state should we be in . . . if we had, as was the case with France, only two classes—great nobles and the common people! Happily we have another class, the middle class—a class, the glory and characteristic feature of England—a middle class more intelligent, more educated and more virtuous than either of the extremes."[25] While this view was by no means universal, it did express the sense and the hope that many must have shared that a new and much better, more moral and virtuous age was dawning.

But before we can arrive at the end of our story, we must begin in the "bad old days" when the code of honor and the behavior it gave rise to was beginning to come under attack.

Contesting Cultural Authority:
The Code of Honor and Its Critics

Whatever the form the principles of honor may take, they serve to relate the ideal values of a society to its social structure and to reconcile the world as its members would see it with the world as it is.[1]

Definitions and Usages

"What is Honour?" asked George Stanhope, dean of Canterbury, early in the eighteenth century. His answer was swift and clear. It was, he explained, "but a greatness of mind which scorns to descend to an ill or base thing." This view of honor had, however, already been pondered, questioned, and redefined for a great while. Yet at the same time the desire for honor, however debated it might have been, was still held up as the guiding ideal, if not the actual principle, which governed the lives of England's upper classes.[2]

Who possessed such honor? Since social commentators rarely were precise in their descriptions of this group, I will adopt a rather inexact and capacious definition for this sort of person. Most, when they bothered to think about what constituted this set, described their qualities as long pedigree, lineage, or "birth."[3] However, the term "honor" also had an older and less exalted usage. Thus the much-translated French author Antoine Courtin wrote of different sorts of honor for different occupational and gender groups; the honor of the noble was his courage, the merchant his honesty, the laborer his industriousness, the cleric his purity, and women their chastity.[4] The ubiquity of this usage can be seen in a variety of titles published from the Restoration through the early years of the eighteenth century: *"The Clergies Honour"* [1682], *"The Honour of the Clothworking Trade"* [1680], *"The Honour of a London 'Prentice"* [1701], and even *"The Duty and Honour of Aged Women"* [1711]. In this sense then, honor consisted of the proper fulfilment of one's occupation or situation. States, both relational and civic, could also have "honor": *"The Honour of Bristol"* [1695], *"England's Path to Wealth and Honour"* [1700], or *"The Wedding Garment, or the Honourable State of Matrimony"* [1692]. Thus in this more inclusive definition, everyone, whether individual or corporate, whatever his or her situation, could act honorably and receive honor, or esteem, for so doing. However, over time, this sort of expansive understanding of honor was increasingly narrowed and redefined so that it usually referred to the code of behavior of Britain's upper classes. Thus Bishop Berkeley ironically described this code as "the mark of a great and fine soul, and [it] is to be found among persons of rank and breeding."[5] By the eighteenth century, this reinterpretation was well in place. And the code of honor, like the English constitution itself, was an unwritten but powerful organizing structure, repeatedly attacked by its opponents, which seemed to weather the many criticisms made of it, and continued to influence its adherents, and to a degree, all of society, to accede to its rules and mandates.

This chapter will outline the "state of play" of expressed opinions on the nature, usefulness, and difficulties of both the principle of honor and the code in which it was embodied, beginning late in the seventeenth century and covering the first half the eighteenth, along with a brief consideration of what was responsible for subsequent expansions of contestation. Of course, as will become almost immediately obvious, it is chimerical and almost entirely arbitrary to think that such dates have an intrinsic merit. They have been chosen in part to fill a historiographical "hole" and in part to serve as an introduction to, and background for, similar though more charged discussions later in the century. And, as will become equally clear, this chapter deals largely with the concept of honor as it applied to men, who, by and large, and with one important exception, were thought to be the only possessors of such an attribute. Male aristocratic hauteur was to be exhibited in a variety of venues, evinced as an easy negligence about the loss of money, and even and especially about the loss of life itself. Traditionally the great exception, of course, to the monopoly of honor by men was the sole attribute of female honor, to be displayed by women in the proper defence of their chastity, which we shall consider only in passing here, but will look at in more detail later. Finally, it is important to be clear about the sources for the views under consideration. Many of the works cited, insofar as we can determine (for several were anonymous), were written by clerical opponents of the principles of honor, or of various parts of the honor code. Only rarely do we hear a contemporary defending honor; usually we have to infer such a defence, or find it within the attacks themselves. This perhaps is unsurprising: when a social code is strong and confident, it shrugs off and ignores, but feels no need to reply to the paltry attacks of those outside its domain. These clerical diatribes will be contrasted with more general moral and philosophical writing of the period, and with popular printed sources. But rather than consensus, even among the clerics themselves, we shall hear several views and viewpoints, sometimes forcefully articulated, and other times contested and even self-contradictory. When people ponder difficult questions, the results are likely to be messy.

True Honor and False: Virtue or Vice?

Exponents and practitioners of aristocratic honor had always linked it to the glory of their "house," to pride in their lineage and its history. Thus, when counseling his sons not to game, Lord Herbert of Cherbury warned them that by gambling, a man "loseth very often his patrimonie, wherewith hee should continue the honour of his house and name, and maintaine his own person, wife, children and familie, with that splendour and decencie which the memorie of his Auncestours, and the worth of his state deserve and require." By the early eighteenth century, this identification, this possession of honor by the nobility seemed stronger than ever. Thus John Mackqueen argued that "Honour is the Fuel of the Emulation of Nobles, the Whetstone of the Valour of Heroes."[6] The exercise of this aristocratic quality had, it was proposed, several desirable effects. Lord Herbert was proud of the fact that he had several times challenged and fought with those who "I conceiued had Iniured Ladyes and Gentlewomen. . . ." This obligation to defend the weak would also lead honorable men of family to rule the state with a generous, patriarchal care: "There is something in Men of *high Birth, Fortune and Distinction*, which makes them think it a Diminution of their own Characters to oppress and insult over those beneath them. . . ."[7] Not only were such men better in domestic government, it was said, but it was they who protected the nation from foreign domination. "The Principle of Honour, then, so far as it consists in doing more . . . it seems inseparably connected with that Valour which is essential to the other great End of Society, the Defence of its Members from external Attacks." Finally, there were those who believed that a concern for family honor and repute, the honor of the well-born, would lead not only to lives of public service but to virtue. "BIRTH and *Nobility* are a stronger Obligation and Incitement to Virtue than what are laid upon meaner Persons."[8]

Why was it felt that aristocratic honor would have these desirable consequences? First, because of the power of the desire for recognition, esteem, and reputation which the well-born shared with mankind in general, though they alone possessed it in superabundance, and second, because of their possession of that attribute, courage, which most wins and maintains this universally desired esteem. Of the desire for esteem, John Mackqueen commented, "let a generous Ambition after a high Reputation or desire of Fame be reckon'd, and justly too, as one of the most considerable Springs of magnanimous Deeds." The *Tatler* concurred: ". . . every man living has more or less of this incentive which urges . . . men to attempt what may tend to their reputations."[9]

This acknowledgment of the power of the desire for esteem was surprising, for, from the time of Hobbes onward, all social commentators agreed that mankind's strongest passion, the first law of nature, was the desire for self-preservation, and mankind's greatest fear that of personal annihilation. Before we can consider the centrality of courage to aristocratic honor, therefore, we must briefly look into this position.

Though the notion of self-preservation was not absent in pre-modern and early modern thought, it is really only after the mid-seventeenth century that the concept became widespread, not only amongst moralists and philosophers, but also in poetry and popular writing. It was humorously employed by Robert Heath in a poem arguing against excessive tooth-pulling:

> . . . I'm sure
> That self-preservation Nature
> Commands: what should we more preserve
> Than teeth . . . .

In a post-Restoration sermon, the clergyman explained that upon "self-preserving Principles, Submission may sometimes be yielded to the lawful Commands of an unlawful . . . Power."[10] All living things, asserted John Prince, obeyed this law. "There is no animate Creature, how contemptible soever, down to the meanest Worm, but is careful of Self-preservation."[11]

Since this prime directive was thought to be innate and equal in all ranks of men, the ability to face death with equanimity was even more exalted than it had been earlier, when courage was presented as part of the nature of the aristocratic military male. Thus an "Officer," celebrating this ability, noted:

> A Brave *Contempt* of what is so *dreadful*, and cannot therefore be *natural*; but must be produced in us by some Motive stronger than the Fear of what

we so *abhor*: And this is a *Vast* Desire of *Honour*, and *Love* of doing *Good*, which only some *noble and diffusive Minds* are *inspired* with.[12]

Mandeville concurred: "The Passion [that Courage] has to struggle with, is the most violent and stubborn, and consequently the hardest to be conquer'd, the Fear of Death: The least Conflict with it is harsh Work, and a difficult Task." Thus many late seventeenth- and eighteenth-century commentators would have agreed with Defoe that "*Contempt of Death* is in itself justly esteem'd the most *exalted* of all *Virtues.*"[13]

By the early eighteenth century, then, the aristocratic male quality par excellence was courage. "Courage and Intrepidity," Mandeville remarked, "always were, and ever will be the grand Characteristick of a Man of Honour." And this quality was considered essential to a martial nation and to military leaders. "A Soldier is of no Esteem, if he does not sacrifice all Considerations to his Honour."[14] This view was a restatement of Courtin's earlier notion that courage was the particular excellence of noblemen: ". . . all Noblemen and Gentlemen . . . are naturally, as it were, a Body of Reserve for the Defence of the Prince and State, [and the nobleman] ought principally to be a Man of *Courage*, this being *his Point of Honour.*"[15] Though not a "natural" attribute, this sort of ability was essential for national power, though only resident in the nation's elite.

> Since there had never been any Thing . . . invented before, that was half so effectual to create artificial Courage among Military Men [as the principle of Honour] . . . it was the Interest of all Politicians . . . to cultivate these Notions of Honour with the utmost Care, and . . . to make Every body believe the Existence and Reality of such a Principle, not among Mechanicks, or any of the Vulgar, but in Persons of high Rank, Knights and others of Heroick Spirit and exalted Nature.[16]

But courage was not only a quality reserved for the battlefield, and honor was not only a principle active among military men. A man without courage would not stand up for what he knew to be true or just because of his fear of rebuke or chastisement:

> . . . to be Knavish and Cowardly are Properties that never part; Knaves are generally Cowards, but Cowards are always Knaves, for a Coward cannot be an Honest Man—How should he be Honest? He has not Courage, and he that dares not look Danger in the Face, dares not to be Honest.[17]

By the early eighteenth century, however, those applauding the values embodied in the aristocratic code of honor were facing attack, for a tide of criticism, aimed not only against its inevitable abuses, but at some of the central tenets of the code, was becoming common, and its proponents scarcer. Of course, the force of these objections may be more seeming than actual. For as we have seen, when a system of social practices is widely accepted, there is little need to applaud or defend it. Criticism therefore may be an inverse measure of the entrenchedness of a system. But on the discursive level, at least, between the second and the sixth decades of the eighteenth century, a vigorous debate raged about the nature and value of aristocratic mores, about the relation of honor and honesty, and about the role of honor in a well-ordered civil polity.

The single quality that most defined aristocratic practice and behavior was pride: pride of birth, of breeding, of position. At its best, pride, it was said, could lead noblemen to lives of "noblesse oblige," of service without recompense, except of recognition and esteem. At its worst, pride was condemned as the source of sin, of pollution and lawlessness. Pride was that aristocratic quality earliest attacked by opponents. Not surprisingly, pride had many critics; more surprisingly perhaps, pride also had its champions. Thus Archibald Campbell saw pride as a laudable emotion, and asked whether it was "a piece of Weakness, or any Thing blameable in a finite Creature, to pursue after Happiness, or to desire the good Opinion and Applauses of *God*, and of all the rational Creation, through all the several Stages of our Eternal Existence?" Similarly, in the notes to his poem "The Universe," Henry Baker argued that

> As Self-Love is the inborn Principle of Mankind, so is Pride, its first-begotten, their general Passion . . . Nor is this Passion useless, or to be blamed . . .: for the Mind is hereby excited to emulate and rise above its Fellows, to gain and to deserve Esteem. The Love and the Respect of Others are the just as well as the wished Reward of every good Action: but, without this Passion, they both would be disregarded, and we should want the strongest Motive to encourage Us onward in the Pursuit of Virtue.[18]

Insofar as it was a spur to right action, then, pride could be tolerated and even encouraged. However, most commentators presented pride as the primal sin, in which Adam's fall was only a repetition of Lucifer's.

> The Original and Primitive Source and Rise of the *Luciferian* Faction, against their Supream Monarch, and Omnipotent Creator, was Pride: the Punishment of which Rebellion, was everlasting Banishment from the Regions of Bliss, and unexhausted Felicity, and Confinement to the black and dreadful Kingdoms of Endless Darkness and Obscurity.

Led to violence, unruliness, and rebellion by pride, mankind, like Lucifer, would be embroiled in endless acts of injustice and anarchy unless they overcame its allure. The effects of such pride "would if possible, remove the very Foundations of the Universe, confound the Order of Nature, and convert all to the Subjection of Ambition."[19] Even that urbane teacher of civility, Courtin, criticized pride, which, he remarked, "exercises a kind of tyranny in the world." And who more than aristocrats were likely to be so tyrannous or so liable to that sort of vain-glory that Hobbes described as a result of the misguided opinion that "difference of worth were an effect of their wit, or riches, or blood, or some other natural quality. . . ."[20] This line of reasoning was made obvious in a tale reprinted in the *Gentleman's Magazine* of 1736. As a result of his attack on a lowly-born neighbor, a gentleman "of Rank and Distinction" is marooned, along with the man whom he has mistreated, on a barbarous island. Like "the admirable Crichton," the injured laborer saves the life of his tormentor, and the gentleman finally learns that "the Superiority of his Blood was imaginary." The tale concludes with the proper moral: "It continues a Custom in that Island, to DEGRADE ALL GENTLEMEN, who can not give a better Reason for their Pride, than they were born, to do no thing. . . ."[21]

Pride was seen not only as the usual vice of the well-born and thoughtless, but also as the central attribute of that code or system which governed their lives. "The Honour, with which these Persons greatly bluster, with whom my Argument is concerned," remarked the Anglican divine Anthony Holbrook, "seems to me, to be Pride and Vanity, Fury and Revenge; mad Passion for their own Humour, regardless of social Decency and Reason." Attempting to save the principle of honor, Holbrook distinguished what others would call true or ancient honor, from the false or modern sort. For, by the early eighteenth century, the phrase "a man of honour" or "a modern man of honour" often denoted a libertine miscreant. Thus the protagonist of Ned Ward's tale "The Dignified Adulterer or the Libertine of Title," married by his parents to a woman he dislikes, takes up with other women, "till at last, he becomes famous, for a Man of Honour, among all the intriguing fair Ladies of Quality. . . ." Ward could not resist ending the tale with its moral; his hero "notwithstanding he is so sinful a Drudge to his own Vices . . . yet Honour and Estate to a Libertine of Quality . . . are so effectual a Skreen from the Reproaches of the Publick, and the Punishments of the law, that [he] may whore on, without Danger or Reflection . . . ."[22]

For some, what distinguished true and false honor was that the latter implied that the honor-code was just a screen to hide what was really at stake—the desire for power and domination. Francis Hutcheson called the benign desire for honor, ambition, but noted that "custom [had] joined some evil ideas to that word, making it denote a violent desire of Honour, and of Power also, as will make us stop at no base means to obtain them." While Hobbes had simply stated that "the acknowledgement of power is called HONOUR,"[23] others saw in the swaggering courage of the man of honor only the desire to domineer and intimidate his fellows.[24]

Men who exercised this power-hunger, who used honor as their excuse to browbeat others, were not truly possessed of honor, but were a sort of ravening animal, seeking prey. Abraham Clerke noted how, "under the influence of that false principle of honour . . . it becomes unequal and unsteady, not like the courage of a man, but the fierceness of a beast." Practitioners of this false honor and courage were not fit for the society of civilized men and women, but only for the "Conversation of barbarous *Indians*, or the Company of Out-laws and *Banditti*."[25] In contrast, true courage was hailed as "Parent of Virtue! Daughter of Benevolence! Prop of Nations! Guardian of the Publick Good!" This distinction between true and false courage and honor was an attempt to save the good points of the system from some of the abuses that critics felt it had fallen into.[26]

The use of the term "a man of honour" as an ironic device to indicate true honor's absence, was given an interesting turn in a 1741 essay on honor. Its author argued that there were two sorts of honorable types: the man of honor, who displays his superiority by a "Firmness of Mind, improved by a Train of wise and religious Reflections, and generous Actions, in which personal virtue and real Merit truly consist" and the person of honor, who "may be a prophane, irreligious Libertine, a penurious, proud, revengeful Coward, may insult his Inferiors, oppress his Tenants and Servants, debauch his Neighbours Wives or Daughters, defraud his Creditors, and prostitute his publick Faith for a Protection, may associate with Sots and Drunkards, Sharpers and Gamesters, in order to increase his Fortune. . . ." Unfortunately, most people mistook the second for the first, since for them, "noise and Shew, Title and Equipage, Glitter and Grandeur constitute the whole Idea of Honour. . . ." Many argued that true honor, honesty, and justice were synonymous; that only virtuous conduct could really be considered worthy of honor. Libertines, it was said, "scorn to take up with the old-fashioned Notions of *Virtue* and its *Beauty*, and in their Room have substituted *Honour*."[27] In the *beau monde*, the characters of the men of honor were "so very singular" and deformed because "the Laws of Fashion and Custom prevail over those of Justice and Morality." But most would have agreed with Mackqueen that the truly virtuous "count nothing Great, but what is Just; nothing Glorious, but what is Virtuous; nothing Honourable, but what springs from a good Principle; is carried on by fair Means, and terminates in noble Ends. . . ."[28]

"Outward Honour," argued Antoine Courtin, is just the reflection of inner virtue; it "attracts the Heart of Men; for 'tis the Property of Virtue to make it self esteemed, applauded and believ'd." But honor could be used as a guise for evil practices, and this misuse would "prove a universal evil, a general deluge, a common combustion over the world."[29] Some compared this virtue-less honor to a fiction; the person of honor is a "fictitious character," remarked Timothy Hooker. Others, like Anthony Holbrook, thought it an illusion, describing it as "that Bubble which is called Honour."[30] For contemporaries, calling honor a bubble would have immediately called to mind the scandal and corruption of that other bubble which had occurred less than a decade before, the South Sea Bubble, and which brought the nation to its knees. Perhaps the strongest and most damning description, however, of the mere seemingness of such honor came from the pen of an aristocrat himself. In distinction to honesty, the Duke of Wharton was cited as characterizing honor as "a rotten Carcass in Brocade and gilded Chariot." According to him, while honesty is scrupulous in its companions and constant in its virtues, honor "is as easy in Consort with Vice as with Virtue . . . wholly external and loves to be taken notice of, [and] is a perpetual Courtier." For this reason, the French writer on civility François Troussaint noted that "All the Men of Honour together are less worth than one virtuous Man."[31]

How had false honor replaced virtue in the behavior of the upper classes? In what ways was the code of honor systematic, and how was it seen as relating to other, competing moral systems? Mandeville, often called "Man-devil" by his opponents, of course had answers to these questions, but they were not ones that most contemporaries wished to hear, or could accept. According to him, the code of honor was devised after the fall of Rome by politicians and clerics who wished both to control and to channel aristocratic violence. And so they invented a code of honor.[32]

But despite the unpalatably radical cynicism and irony of Mandeville's depiction of its origins, many contemporaries agreed with his assessment of how such modern honor functioned; "Honour signifies likewise a Principle of Courage, Virtue and Fidelity, which some Men are said to act from, and to be aw'd by, as others are by *Religion*" [emphasis mine]. Bishop Berkeley, in most respects Mandeville's opponent, agreed with him in his assessment of the religion of honor among people of fashion. Matching Mandeville's ironic tone, he remarked that for them, "Honour is a noble unpolluted source of virtue, without the least mixture of fear, interest or superstition. It hath all the advantages without the evils, which attend religion."[33] Some even went so far as to compare the vices of fashionable persons of honor to rites carried on in worship of a deity.[34] So, for example, an opponent of the practice of duelling argued that the upper classes "make *Honour* a *Cannibal*, or *Horseleach*, hungry for want of *Mans flesh*, and thirsting after *blood*; and intimate to the World that there is a *God* of *Honour* so incensed that nothing will apease him but *Human Sacrifice.*" The system of aristocratic honor appeared to many critics as an alternate to the teaching of Christ, as the private religion of society's elite.[35]

Perhaps of equal concern were the deleterious effects that a privileged code of behavior would have on all of civil society. For when the law of honor and the law of the land clashed, it was imperative for the formal judicial system to come out the victor. This was often not the case. "A virtuous Man thinks himself obliged to obey the Laws of his Country," commented Mandeville, "but a Man of Honour acts from a Principle which he is bound to believe Superiour to all Laws." Yet from Courtin onwards, while many commentators remarked on the corrosive effects that the laws of honor would have on the nation and the law, they seemed unable to recommend simple and effective alternatives. By disobeying the laws of the polity, men of honor flaunted the commands of their sovereign, and thus were guilty of treason of sorts.[36] Obeying no law but that of his own making, a man of honor thought himself "infinitely above the Restraints which the Laws of God or Man lay upon vulgar Minds, and knows no other Ties but those of Honour." But few thought it proper that any group decide that the laws of the polity were only for lesser men, and that they were guiltless if they obeyed their own private code. Most believed that for "the profligate Party, who . . . look upon . . . all the *Laws of Religion*, and *Morality* as *Shackles* to their *Liberty*, 'tis fit that they should be brought under some *Rules*, as well for their particular Reformation, as for the general Interest of the Kingdom." The only question was how this could be done.[37]

Some suggested that men of great mind and magnanimity should fly in the face of opinion, shun the dictates of an immoral honor, and act as good Christians and true gentlemen. In his dialogue-essay against duelling, Jeremy Collier had his man of the world question whether refusing a challenge would not result in loss of reputation and of good company. Collier's alter-ego, Philalethes, assured the questioner that this would not be the case, that "there are not a few of good Extraction, of another Opinion." Thomas Comber, dean of Durham, also assured the wary reader that such virtuous conduct would not be condemned but publicly lauded. No man, he argued, should worry about his reputation if he refused to duel; this "expresses a great Reverence for the Laws of the Land, and a mighty Aversion to do anything that is Evil." This will ever be "Honourable among considering Men, and the Opinion of all others . . . is to be despis'd."[38] However this line of resolute virtue in the face of public opinion seems to have disappeared by the beginning of the eighteenth century.[39]

That aristocratic misbehavior would have grave national consequences was never challenged. For it seemed almost the universal consensus that mores and manners depended on example. Children learned virtue (or vice), it was said, from their parents and instructors; society learned these lessons from the behavior of its leaders, its patriarchal figures, the upper classes. When vicious, they were the font of corruption. This sentiment explains, said one pre–civil war commentator, why gambling had spread through the nation. "And were it not for the common example of great ones, whose continuall practice, may seeme to enact a law for it, & proclaim it apparently both just and fitting . . . who would not abhorre it as a most dangerous and sinful employment. . . ." Forty years later, an opponent of the practice of duelling explained its prevalence upon this same evil example. "Noblemen cannot but discern how Gentlemen of *less quality throng* and *croud* to come as *neer* them as is possible, imitating them according to (nay beyond) their *Abilities*, in their *Habit, Carriage*, and all pieces of *Gallantry*: Nay, even in their *Vices*; esteeming all things *Lawful*, or at least *Creditable* which are worthy of their pursuit. And were it not an easie matter for them to bring this foolish and rash way of *Duelling* into contempt, by being neither *examples* nor *countenancers* of it."[40]

By the late 1730s it was said that this corruption of the leaders of society would have two grave consequences. The first was the inevitable spread of viciousness through the entire polity. The elite man of honor "not only immediately corrupts his own circle of acquaintance, but the contagion spreads itself to infinity. To such practice, and such examples in higher life, may justly be imputed the general corruption and immortality which prevail thro' this kingdom." Most agreed that the upper classes were not what they should be, and, even worse, that despite this, they seemed to be immune from all punishment. Thus, at mid-century, John Brown wondered: "It may seem strange that such Excesses should be allow'd in a free State: But it is yet more strange, that such Excesses should be allow'd and practised among the *Great*, at a Time when there are Laws in force against them."[41] Several writers pointed out the incongruous behavior of men who served as Members of Parliament and as magistrates, behaving in ways that broke the laws of the land. If those among the Great who "act the Part of Magistrates, of Legislators, or Patriots wantonly set at Defiance the very Laws which themselves have made or recommended" what could be expected but a tidal wave, an overwhelming deluge of vice, from the actions of their inferiors?[42] Thus, Erasmus Mumford warned the aristocratic habitués of Whites' gambling club:

> The forms of Government should be carefully preser'ved . . . [therefore] to practice it [gaming] in Defiance of all Order, in the very Sight, as it were of

the Government, and against the Spirit and the letter of the Laws which you made yourselves, is entirely inconsistent with the Character of Patriots, Nobles, Senators, Great Men, or whatever name of public Honour you would chuse to call yourselves by.[43]

The lower orders, it was said, would inevitably follow their superiors in either virtue or vice, through the lures of fashion or from a natural subordination. Thus Alexander Jephson commented that he was "sensible, indeed, that nothing hath contributed so much to the quick and extensive Propagation of these accursed Vices, as that so many Persons of the greatest Fashion and Distinction . . . have given so much Countenance to them by their own Example."[44] If this were not a worrying enough prognostication, the critics of aristocratic behavior also pointed out that an invariable consequence of the degeneracy of the upper classes was the decline of the nation. ". . . the united Voices of all Ages and Nations do proclaim this Truth, That a general and open Contempt of establish'd Laws among the *higher Ranks* of Men, hath always been a preceding Symptom, a certain Indication, of the approaching Dissolution of a State—."[45]

However, it was in the fact of emulation, that all of society imitated the manners and ways of the Great, that hope for the rehabilitation of the moral fabric of the nation resided. If the noble and fashionable could be convinced of their responsibility to the nation, could understand that their vice would inevitably lead to widespread social decay, they would also see that their virtue would as naturally rehabilitate and revivify the manners of the whole. "Since then People of Distinction are the perpetual Objects of Imitation . . . they cannot be good or bad themselves without being the Cause of Piety or Wickedness in others. . . ." Even that old cynic Mandeville agreed that the power of fashion could lead to virtue as well as vice. "When a Reformation of Manners is once set on Foot, and strict Morality is well spoken of, and countenanc'd by the better Sort of People, the very Fashion will make Proselytes to Virtue."[46] And, from the mid-century, some critics started to call for a strict enforcement of existing laws, especially where the offenders were people of station and condition. "The greater the Offender the greater the Criminal, and the more notorious the Punishment the more Benefit will the Publick receive from the Prosecution," said the author of *Reflexions on Gaming*. Without such exemplary punishment, "without punishment meted out to the great and little alike, the bonds of civil society would be weakened."[47] However, as we shall see, it was easier to analyze the problem and make recommendations for its mitigation than to convince aristocrats to live more uprightly or to more equitably enforce the law when the offenders were high-born.

Thus, by the mid-century, we see the honor code still in existence, despite more than a half-century of attack. We also have noted the growing weight of criticism against the code, though at the same time, of an appreciation for some of its side effects. Yet while most recognized the value of hierarchy, and esteemed the institution of the peerage and their role as martial leaders, the value of courage, and that of hereditary titles themselves were coming under attack. It is perhaps in these last criticisms, as well as in the faint praise one occasionally hears for the conduct of those in the middle station, that one can most clearly see the depths of opposition to the code of honor.

We have already noted the wavering admiration of courage among most writers on manners. Thus, when the author of a piece titled "On Bravery and Cowardice" rhetorically asked "Is not Courage an Infallible Mark of greatness of Soul?" his immediate answer was "Granted." However, he went on to note that "we are apt to mistake the Effects of Cowardice for Instances of Valour. Duels are of this sort; for 'tis the most consummate Cowardice for a Man to be afraid of following the Rules of Reason and Humanity." A decade later, Timothy Hooker denied even this ambiguous claim, noting that "when I consider the Bulk of Military Heroes, the Conquerors of Nations who stand foremost in the Lists of Fame, I esteem them no better than so many *glorious Robbers*, and *illustrious Plunderers*, born to be the Scourges and Plagues of Mankind . . . ."[48]

From the 1730s onwards we see a rather remarkable attack not only on the value of courage but also on the nature and value of noble titles. In a piece entitled "The Vanity of Titles" its author argued that "In Athens and Rome, there were no Titles of Honour. Some Author has observed, that when true Merit began to cease, Titles of Honour were invented in its Room. . . ." Only three years later, another article, "Titles of Honour Prostituted," went through a long historical account of European villains who "have advanced themselves to the first Honours of their Country" and been ennobled through their villainy.[49] In the 1740s Hooker pointed out that a foolish man's title would only make his lack of accomplishments more public and visible, and by the 1750s several went even further. Thus William Webster chastised the proud, noble miscreant:

> Many of those whom we call *great* Men have very *bad*, and very *little* Souls; and the *Greatness of Mind*, which usually begets *Anger*, is no better than one of the very worst of *Vices*, and that is *Pride*: And when this *Tumor* of the Mind, arising from *Self-love*, is swell'd beyond its natural Size, by *Riches*, *Titles and Places*, by the habitual Adulation of *Creatures*, and *Syncophants*, it grows *enormous*, and *intolerable*.[50]

With a haughty and slightly supercilious tone, *The Man* announced that "A pride founded upon birth, title, estate, or other things no way essential to our nature, is but a childish vanity. Whoever would think nobly of himself, must drop this silly pretension to regard; whose just reproof is the pitying smile of men." And yet, only a year later, an essay appeared in *The Gentleman's Magazine* which seemed a direct denial of the former argument, entitled "The Advantages of Ancestry demonstrated." The author of this piece made no bones of the fact that he thought the value of pedigree was now under severe and unprecedented attack: "In this refined and innovating age, when 'tis the mode to profess a licentiousness of sentiment, even in the most sacred and important concerns; 'tis not so much to be wondered at, that there are a set of men, who from a levelling disposition, speak evil of dignities and distinctions, and have in particular aimed at extirpating the deference heretofore paid to birth." Even, and perhaps especially, at this late date, its author argued that the virtues of birth and breeding needed to be honored. A salutary national spirit of emulation and a desire to bequeath an unsullied reputation to one's posterity depended on the preservation and support of what he called "family honour."[51]

It is clear, however, that the author realized that his position was not the popular one, that it was under attack by "innovating" and "levelling" opinion. We get small hints of the nature and perhaps the direction of such attacks. I do not wish to overemphasize the importance of these, but merely to point out that a few critics of aristocratic manners, as early as the 1730s, were comparing them unfavorably with those of the middle station or rank. Thus in explaining the spread of free-thinking and irreligion amongst people of fashion, Bishop Berkeley had a character, Lysicles, a flashy unreflective young libertine, admit that "while the principles of free-thinking do [find easy admission] among ingenious men and people of fashion, . . . you will sometimes meet with strong prejudices against them in the middle sort, an effect of ordinary talents and mean breeding." Even stronger was the comment in *The Man* of 1755: "We see, by daily experience, that men of a higher rank are more frequently guilty of cruelty and injustice, than those of a middling station; because their power is greater, and their fear of punishment less."[52] Here we see some quiet, tentative assertions of the virtue of the "middling sort."

Components of the Code of Honor

We have seen modern or false honor several times referred to as a glittering garb, a misleading external costume. In part this was an attack on the "inauthenticity," the artificiality of modern honor, in part it was the observation that this honor consisted as much in manner, in outward show, as in anything else. What were the key elements of this manner of honor? Early in the eighteenth century, John Mackqueen argued that the man of honor and valor "must march, and go on among all the cruel Instruments and frightful Circumstances . . . undauntedly, with a stately pace, serene Countenance and a stout Heart; as if he were making a Pastime of Dangers, a May-game of Terrors; as if he counted hard Trials and fierce Skirmishes but his Playfellows." A certain coolness, an elaborate *je ne sais quoi*, were reckoned one of its chief qualities. People of honor, it was said, knew this manner almost instinctively, and therefore it did not need to be explained or codified. "There is a *Quintessence* called *Honour*, for the use of the *Nobility, Gentry,—but No Other*. . . . As to defining it, I shall not set about it . . . it being a thing much easier to be felt than understood."[53] Others were more condemnatory; integral to the character of the man of honor, one article noted, was the necessity for there to "be a Haughtiness and Insolence in his Deportment, which is supposed to result from conscious Honour." Haughtiness was probably the most frequently used English term to describe this sort of bearing. The French writer François-Vincent Toussaint was lighter in his characterization of the man of honor: "A confident and assuming Air, an easy Fortune, with the Vices in Fashion, are what constitutes the *Man of Honour*." Both English and French writers agreed, however, that the finishing touches to the complete man of honor were certain fashionable failings, arguing that a certain seasoning of the "genteelest Vices" was required to fit a gentlemen for this exalted station.[54]

What were these genteel vices, these requisites for membership in the *beau monde?* A wide variety were cited at different times by different writers, though a fair amount of overlap also existed. Of course, then as now, vices were thought to be multitudinous, ranging from swearing to drinking to not paying tradesmen's bills. However, it is the four vices most commonly lamented, most commonly thought to be interrelated and to form a vast cluster of aristocratic misconduct, that are the subject of this book and this chapter. These four were duelling, suicide, adultery, and gaming. And all were thought to be directly inspired by the Devil and, in some macabre way, acts of Devil-worship. It was a well-known and accepted fact that suicide, or self-murder as it was usually called through the first half of the eighteenth century, was a result of the Devil's incitement: "For without the Instigation and Influence of that Evil, Envious and Malicious Spirit, it cannot be supposed, that Men of themselves, even left to themselves, could be transported to such detestable Things. . . ." And a decade later, in a pamphlet entitled *Self-Murther and Duelling the Effects of Cowardice and Atheism*, its author asserted that both vices were "a tame and dishonourable submitting and yielding to our grand Adversary the Devil . . . [for these sins are] owing to a direct Assault of the Devil. . . ."[55] Much earlier, the author of *Timely Advice* presented adultery as one of the first lures of Satan: "Many are the temptations of the devill, whose beginning are Idolatry,

Adulterie, Theft, Rapine. . . ." He added, as well, that anyone who gambled and played at dice "doth sacrifice to the devill, and rather deserveth the name of a Pagan than a Christian." And, at mid-century, in a magazine named after his infernal Highness, the Devil reveled in the "practice of which I am the supreme head and director, namely that fashionable delight GAMING."[56] Thus, one strand tying together these four vices was that all were seen as inspired, though perhaps only rhetorically, by satanic influences.

Second, and more important perhaps, these vices constituted the "dark side" of fashionable life; they were the acts that the great and not-so-good could indulge in without feeling the full weight of the law. They were examples of the governing principles that controlled and policed the genteel world of honor. If the men and women of the *ton* obeyed its rules, they could flaunt those governing the polity. Men could duel, though duelling was against the law, and by extension could kill themselves when tired of life.[57] Aristocratic men and women could commit adultery and annul unsuccessful marriages. And the only debts that the inhabitants of the *beau monde* needed to worry about quickly paying were "debts of honour," i.e., gambling debts, due to other members of their world. By the mid-century, all these vices were coming, individually and collectively, under significant attack. Thus, *The Man* linked gaming and suicide as natural consequences of a misspent life:

> Voluptuaries, who spend their days in company, gallantry, and gaming . . . A constant round of moral dreaming brings some of this class into such distresses, as rouse them, at length, to their confusion, and drive them, in a frighted, cowardly desperate state, to put a violent and unnatural period to their lives. They shamefully steal away from the sight of men, and rush audaciously into the more immediate and awful presence of God.

The author of *The Whole Art and Mystery of Modern Gaming*, in describing the vice, also pointed out the class of its chief participants/victims. It is, he noted, "the most fatal and epidemical Folly and Madness, especially among the Persons of superior Degree, and Quality."[58] Both adultery and suicide were also presented as acts pre-eminently committed by the *beau monde* or men and women "of honour." The *Connoisseur* of 1755, describing the latest affectation of genteel rakes and men of mode, noted that "Suicide is the most gallant exploit by which our modern heroes chuse to signalize themselves." And Alexander Jephson pointed out the unlikely connection of honor and adultery; "And yet these [adulterers] frequently affect to call themselves men of honour! . . . A horrid prostitution of terms! The guilt of the highwayman, and even the murderer, is, in many cases, much inferior." How upsetting it must have been to such critics to confront the mitigating words of John

Oldmixon, after his friend General McCartney's involvement in an infamous duel. Oldmixon asserted, as a matter of widely recognized truth, that "No Man of Honour can avoid a Duel, or refuse being a Second. . . . Legislatures of Europe have not been able to find a Remedy for this Evil, nor no way of making injured Honour an ample Reparation, then a Man of Honour has no other recourse but to a Duel, or live under a Blemish'd Reputation." Therefore, he concluded, a man had to do what a man had to do, and "the Law should wink at such Misfortunes it can't with Justice prevent or repair."[59] But such comments were rare, such suggestions unusual. While, in practice, many were willing to "wink" or turn a blind eye to the evil practices of the self-indulgent Great, few were willing to defend or discuss the oversight. A frank admission of the law's inadequacies, of the actual as opposed to the ideal administration of criminal justice, might have provided the fuel for massive social unrest and resistance. Most preferred to deride the particular vices, to attempt to convince the men and women of the *ton* that they must be good Christians and good citizens, and to leave it at that.

And, after all, what more could they have done? For, while many denounced elite vice, while clerics thundered against it from pulpits and print, English society at large remained committed to notions of honor as essential to the sort of nation they wished to be. And the law refused to intervene. Few attacked the principle of honor itself, or the traditional understanding of what it meant to be a gentleman. "To be a fine gentleman," Steele insisted, "is to be a generous and brave man." While calling for an end to duelling, they reaffirmed the importance of the passion for honor and its centrality in the well-ordered state:

> The innate Desire of Honour and the general Disposition to esteem those that are Worthy are from God. . . . For this is a Curb to Rashness, a Restraint to Licentiousness, and a Spur to Industry. It rouses up from Laziness and puts one upon the Search, Study and Practice of what is good and commendable. . . . The innate Desire of Honour and of what doth merit it is a better Security of one's good Behavior than either private and personal Obligations.

Freed from its fashionable misinterpretations and restored to its original purity, the pursuit of honor would result in a society characterized by quality and magnanimity.[60]

Honor: Male and Female

In his *Journal* of 1738 John Wesley recounted a meeting with a felon whom he visited in prison, where the prisoner was awaiting execution:

He attempted twice or thrice to shoot himself; but it [the gun] would not go off. Upon his laying it down, one took it up and blew out the priming. He was very angry, went and got fresh primer, came in again, sat down, beat the flint with his key and . . ., pulling off his hat and wig, said he would die like a gentleman, and shot himself through the head.[61]

This short parable of the prisoner wishing to be thought a gentleman sheds some light on popular eighteenth-century notions of both masculinity and gentility. By taking his own life, the nameless felon declared not only that he faced extinction with equanimity and disdain, but also that he, and he alone, was to be the ultimate judge and executioner in his case and his life. By the cool resoluteness of his endeavor he clearly hoped to make good his claim to be a man of standing and fortitude.

In this chapter we have considered the evolution of, and support and opposition for, a code of honor, a set of social practices governing what was considered as the exclusive law of men and women of rank, and of the sorts of activities that that code forbade and allowed. Now we must look more closely at the gender specifications of that regimen. The code of honor was seen as both defining and separating genders in the upper classes, for a series of masculine and feminine practices were sanctioned by its principles.

For men and women of the *beau monde*, as we have seen, whose lives were governed by the code of honor, this gender difference was equally, though particularly, present. Addison neatly encapsulated these differences when he noted that "The great point of honour in men is courage, and in women chastity." In comparing women with men, *The Man* argued that since "courage, intrepidity and valour, being virtues suited to the make of a man," these qualities "are justly expected from him."[62] But for women, few mentioned any other female honor but chastity. While many may have agreed with this articulation of the essence of male and female honor, fewer would have followed Mandeville's entirely logical conclusion that, in consequence, "Gallantry with Women, is no Discredit to the Men, any more than Want of Courage is a Reproach to the Ladies." But many surely would have, in their hearts, and in their practices, agreed. For the "double standard," though already (and perhaps always) venerable by the early eighteenth century, was one that was usually implicitly held without being spoken of.[63] Though philandering, both before and after, without and within marriage, was clearly a Christian sin, it was one usually that was tolerated in upper-class men, though deemed heinous, or at least actionable, in women. But despite the fact of dissimilarity of virtues between the genders, one slip from gender-appropriate behavior was said to be fatal for both men and women:

he that has Religion and good Sense enough to refuse a Challenge, is in danger of being kick'd out of the fashionable World for a Scoundrel and a Coward; and every Woman who has once been so unhappy as to offend in point of Chastity, cannot by the most sincere Repentance, by all the merciful Abatements that ought to be made for human Frailty, and a thousand amiable Qualities besides, thrown into the Balance, be ever able to wipe off an indelible Mark of Infamy fixed upon her by all the ill-natur'd Prudes and Coquets about Town.

Of course, in practice, it was possible for a man to regain his honor, either by bravery in battle or by accepting the next challenge, and to a smaller degree, it was possible for some, if not all, women to avoid the public notoriety of their loss of honor, through their indulgence in amorous infidelity.[64]

Even accepting these limitations to the perceived innate virtues of men and women, if we consider courage and chastity as two component aspects of a larger understanding of the essential differences between men and women rather than the entirety of their honor, we may be able to see other ways in which the character of the two genders was different, though intertwined. For if courage, intrepidity, or valor were understood as elements of the basic male qualities of determination, self-control, and steely resoluteness, and in contrast, chastity was seen as part of the female virtues of compliance, sensitivity, and modesty, the honor of each gender rested on a wider, and perhaps more significant base than on either the willingness to duel or the refusal to have lovers. Women, in fact, by the preservation of their innate delicacy, could influence men and effect a modification in their natural aggressiveness and incivility. We will come back to this aspect of their gendered roles later.

As we have seen, male honor, or virtue, consisted for many primarily of courage. Mandeville made explicit the connection between such masculine virtue and valor. "This makes me think, that *Virtus*, in its first Acceptation, might, with great Justice and Propriety, be in *English* render'd *Manliness*; which fully expresses the Original Meaning of it. . . ." However, increasingly, most commentators thought that courage, while the beginning, was not the end of male honor, that men needed other qualities in conjunction with valor to be useful and reputable leaders of their nation. The man of noble stature was a man of power, of self-direction and self-control. He was recognizable by the "easiness" of his demeanor; his behavior was cool though courteous, and his word was his bond. Courage was neither the highest virtue, nor one that was most difficult to acquire.[65] Even before the publication of the *Spectator* and the *Tatler* or Shaftesbury's evocation of polished society had influenced social thought, critics of courage as the main virtue of the man of honor realized that mere brute valor might be wrong-headed and harmful, describing it as a "mistaken and unmanly Courage." As Anthony Holbrook noted, "Good Men preserve the Masculine under Provocations; whereas habitual Passions are ruffled by every Storm they meet, and made the Sport of the Indiscretions and Infirmities of Men."[66] The ability to remain calm when challenged or insulted, the element of control, this mental and psychological steadfastness, came to be seen as at least as important as physical bravery. Which polished man of the world would wish his main virtue, it was asked, to be that in which a brute beast might well outstrip him? The anonymous author of the two-volume work *The Gentleman instructed in the Conduct of a Virtuous and Happy Life* [1755], warned his readers: "be not deceived in the Notion of Honour; some seat it on the Sword's Point, and persuade themselves it consists in slaughter; as if there were no difference between Honour and Savageness, between a Gentleman and a Butcher." Of such men of "honour" *The Man* noted that "Some are so savage as to thirst for blood; . . . Their actions shew no signs of humanity. Few brutes, even in a fever, are so mischevious and outragious as such desperados, resembling mad dogs more than men."[67]

We can see this endeavor to "tame" courage, to make it act as the arm of civility, rather than the muscle of savagery, when we look at that sort of male vocation for which the man of breeding was pre-eminently intended, and consider attitudes toward the requisites of soldiers. Mandeville had argued that the code of honor was created because of the need for a cadre of men who were willing to fight and die at their country's call. This "itch," as Prince dubbed it, "to be thought brave and gallant," though useful in motivating young bucks and gallants, would often cause them to waste their own lives and those of their acquaintance thoughtlessly and uselessly.[68] Good soldiers needed to rely on intelligence, not anger, needed to win in conflict while shedding as little blood as possible. "Conduct as well as Courage is the Souldiers Character; and his Conduct may be really shewn in extricating himself dextrously from a Personal Rencounter, as well as from Superior Numbers, or an Ambush in the Field." And, in an article entitled "*Of Honour*" in the urbane *Gentleman's Magazine*, which reads more like a sermon than a tea-table essay, the writer proposed that only men of religion and probity, men who believed in salvation and redemption, could have the sort of cool and deliberate courage that made the best fighting military men. "He only is truely Valiant, because he knows his Protector, the Justice of his Cause, and considers what is he to expect hereafter; he encounters Dangers with Calmness of Thought and Presence of Mind; which is true Courage; while wicked Men are both Fools and Cowards."[69] And in his sermon of 1751, "True Religion the only Foundation of true Courage," Joshua Kyte gives us the fully formed picture of the genteel soldier, the true Christian hero as one who is "early accustomed to endure difficulties and inconveniences . . . calling into action every generous and manly Virtue."[70]

What qualities would make up this refined and modern soldier? In addition to that self-possession already discussed, he would need a certain panache, a careless generosity, an easy refinement, and a well-developed though modest eloquence. Like all true gentlemen, the polished soldier needed to be able to get on in civilian life as well as on the battlefield. Like all true gentlemen, the soldier needed to be "well-bred"; breeding in this sense had much more to do with nurture than lineage. Such well-bred, gentlemanly soldiers would have had their tempers softened so that "they may bend in compliance and accommodate themselves to those they have to do with." And the English soldier really needed this sort of amendment because of the innate "Rudeness of our Northern Genius."[71]

Thus all gentlemen, but especially military men, needed to become "polite" members of a new sort of refined social order. Of course, a great deal could be done by rearing. Yet even more central to the creation of a polished, gentle man of honor, was his interaction, the smoothing of his rough edges, by genteel yet delicate, well-educated though modest women. Thus, as male honor was interpreted to mean more than brute courage, but to imply qualities of resoluteness and self-command, female honor, resting on a natural compliance and softness, perhaps became as valued as, though in no sense replaced, the older and narrower virtue of female chastity.[72]

The importance of women's *mission civilatrice* made it only more imperative that they retain their natural characteristics, that they guard their femininity, which consisted of both chastity and modesty. For, if they approached the masculine, whether in temper, dress, or vice, they lost their influence, their ability to improve. It was they and they alone, for example, who could "discountenance rakes" and banish male sexual predators from fashionable assemblies, making them pariahs rather than favored guests. As much for the sake of social refinement as for their polishing of men, women were urged to preserve their demure characters. Thus, the author of *The Essay On Modern Gallantry*, in an open letter to the young women of Great Britain, advised them

> that you would not think it wholly unnecessary to take some Care of your Reputations, by retrenching some of those masculine Arts, and rampant Liberties, which have been so much in Fashion of late . . . .[73]

Of course, in committing adultery, a woman not only gave up all potential for influence but, by implicitly denying the absolute property her husband had in her person, threatened all property relationships. "Nothing," said Addison, "besides chastity, with its collateral attendants, truth, fidelity, and constancy, gives the man a property in the person he loves, and consequently endears her to him in all things." Still it was thought, as we have already seen, that many aristocratic women, under the cover of marriage, were able to get away with such adultery and even with illegitimacy, as ladies "of gallantry and fashion."[74] But by mid-century, there is some evidence that the toleration of adultery in both men and women was coming under attack.

In a sermon entitled *The heinous sins of* ADULTERY *and* FORNICATION, *considered and represented, in a* SERMON, Alexander Jephson spoke of the mutual need for men and women to be true to their marriage vows: "And therefore, whenever a married Man or Woman forsakes each other's Company, thro' their Love and Affection to a Stranger, they are not only false in their own Word and Promise, . . . but are guilty also of the very worst kind of Lying and Perjury."[75] Clearly illicit private acts, even when complicity or toleration between the couple involved was present, had effects beyond the marriage bed. Lying and especially perjury were general practices that were both worrisome and socially deleterious.

With the view that male virtue was not merely harsh bravery, but polished and genteel fortitude, and with the usefulness of female influence in this refining process, came concomitantly a strengthening of the notion that while men of honor must shine in the public world, they must also exhibit virtues of a private and domestic sort. The Christian hero must be exemplary not only on the field of battle but in the parlor.

That politeness was much talked of and usually recommended in early eighteenth-century English writings is now an accepted, understood, and important strand of the prescriptive literature of the period.[76] Whether the practice of these forms of polite civility, which would have meant the restraint of pride and violence and the avoidance of illicit forms of sociability, was as widespread as its discourse, is another matter. Of course, the daily lives of men and women of wealth and standing often did not conform to even their own notions of propriety and good behavior. But in the continuance, and perhaps even in the growth, of aristocratic vice through the century, we can see the rift that existed between polite ideals and unmannerly practices.

While it is a matter of conjecture whether or not the members of the *ton* would, at any point in the latter eighteenth century, have reformed their ways, eschewing aristocratic honor for the more solid and prosaic virtues, it is clear that a great impetus to such a change was provided by the growth and nature of the press.

"The greatest FACT *of our times" or the* *"News-paper Moralists"*[77]

When, in 1785, George Crabbe in his poem "The Newspaper" lamented that it was to this printed form that "all readers turn, and they look/ Pleased on a paper, who abhor a book," he was going against the tide.[78] Most contemporaries not only very much enjoyed the daily dose of news and gossip, opinion and vituperation, advertisement and advice that the papers offered, but also saw the (reasonably) free press as a great "palladium of liberty," which, along with the jury system, differentiated England from the despotic regimes of the continent, and provided a forum for peaceful, general debate and discussion. For many, the press taken collectively was a sort of Parliament out-of-doors, a representative of varied opinions and beliefs, an anonymous and protected public space where men and women could exchange information and points of view. In addition to serious sites like the pulpit and the floor of Parliament, and frivolous ones like the theater, the press was a collective commercial endeavor whose role were to educate, to amuse, and to improve the public weal. "We live in an age" said a noted late-century attorney, "in which the most important questions were decided by the newspapers."[79]

Though news sheets and various forms of news-letters had flourished in the seventeenth century, and a variety of magazines and newspapers had come into being after the Restoration, it was only in 1702 that England's first daily paper, *The Daily Courant*, began. Like most dailies of the first half of the eighteenth century, the *Daily Courant* was very short (it consisted only of one single-sided page) and was almost entirely devoted to foreign news.[80] However, the early eighteenth century saw the growth and development of an important and powerful type of periodical press, the essay-journal, the most famous examples of which were, of course, the *Tatler*, the *Spectator*, and the *Guardian*. These (tri-weeklies) were largely composed of articles and letters, with occasional comments on newsworthy items, theatrical reviews, and advertisements. In addition to providing their readers with entertainment and improvement, these journals devoted themselves to identifying and satirizing what they saw to be the failings, or to use an eighteenth-century term, the vices, of their society. Eschewing partisan politics, they criticized fashionable faults, endeavoring simultaneously to re-create their readers, that is, to amuse them while ameliorating public and private morality. For morality could not be accused of belonging to a party or a faction; promoting virtue through the ridicule of vice could not be considered as anything but salutary. For most of the rest of the century, the essays published in these periodicals would be reread, recopied, and repeated as authoritative statements of virtuous maxims.[81]

By the 1730s, however, the world of London periodical publishing had been significantly diversified. Essay-journals, resembling both news-sheets and the older general tri-weeklies, proliferated, now in weekly format, though it was the appearance of new monthly magazines in the 1730s that was to have the most long-term impact. These storehouses of miscellaneous information, like the pioneering *Gentleman's Magazine*, provided something for every taste, never hiding the fact that, initially, much of their contents was excerpted from other journals or papers. Including essays on history, on manners, or on travel, the *Gentleman's* also included lists of bankruptcies, a monthly historical chronicle, and a list of births, deaths, marriages, and promotions. The new monthlies also continued and increased the practice of including letters from their readers, begun in the earlier periodicals. Between 1731 and 1769, seven such monthlies appeared, the majority of which continued to be published for a decade or more.[82] Both in these publications, and in the proliferation of the newspapers in the second half of the century, an overlooked but important circulation of items occurred; books were often excerpted as items in the papers, and books were created of especially interesting items from the press. And, as we have seen with both the *Gentleman's* and the *London*, the press circulated stories and essays internally. The enormous expansion of print enabled both a growth and a concentration of available information of wide public interest.

It was, however, with the appearance of the new daily papers of the 1760s and 1770s that the nature of the relationship between what might be called "the news," the press, and its readership became transformed in several ways. Throughout the eighteenth century, the press was centrally involved as a partisan player in the political struggles of the day, on both the international and the domestic stage. Some papers, like the *Daily Gazetteer*, owed their very inception to a particular political stance. This involvement continued to be true of many of the papers begun during the Seven Years' War, which, for most part, were oppositional and Wilkite.[83] However, what made the daily press of the 1770s different from that of the 1730s and 1740s, was its size and the variety of its concerns. Appearing 6 days a week meant that 96 paper columns needed to be filled. Of course, much of this space could be and was filled with advertisements, but, even so, much more space was now available for commentary, sometimes lengthy and sometimes brief, on a variety of issues formerly less featured. Thus, the *Daily Courant* of January 1, 1735, a paper of only two pages with three columns on each page, had only one advertisement on the bottom of page 2; the rest of that day's coverage was taken up by the continuation of "A Dissertation on Parties." In contrast, forty years later, the *Gazetteer* of January 1, 1775, a paper of four pages, each with four columns, or 16 columns in total, had advertisements covering more than half (51.5 percent) its pages, letters to the printer accounting for one fifth (20.3 percent) of its column lines, with news from home and abroad, notes from other papers, and miscellaneous items filling the remaining almost one third of the columns. And as its historian, Robert Haig, has noted, "The *Gazetteer* of the sixties, there can be no doubt, owed a great deal of its increased popularity to the letters it printed." He cites the paper's own figures on its receipt and publication of such letters: "From the first day of January [1764] to this day [four months later], we have received 861 letters: of which 560 have been inserted at length: 262 have been taken notice of . . . and 39 now remain in hand. . . ."[84] Since most of these letters were signed by a pseudonym, it is impossible to know how many were written by journalist-hacks, by interested parties, or by the editor himself. Still, it is undoubtedly the case that whatever their actual parentage, "letters to the press gave the impression of the newspaper as a national forum, open to all. . . ." Such letters perhaps also enabled editors, and now allow us, to catch "a useful insight into the preoccupations of their readers."[85]

In order to properly assess the impact of the press, however, we must briefly consider how and where it was read, and the nature of its content. In many ways, the growth of the press and that of the coffee-house were integrally connected. The latter afforded the venue and lured in customers by providing a selection of many of the most popular papers of the day. In turn, the papers' readers ordered coffee or tea, making possible and sustaining the proliferation of this sort of public forum for reading and discussion. Reading the papers of the day was often not a solitary or domestic activity, but for many occurred as part of a neighborly consideration of what was happening in the locale, the nation, or even the world.[86] And for much of the century, the nature of press layout, with many news items arranged quite helter-skelter, did not encourage or allow for introspection or sustained attention. Only late in the period do "stories" really appear, enclosed in boxes, and with headlines. Before then, a wide variety of "items" of various lengths and subject matter filled the many papers of the day. And much of the body of these pages was filled with advertisements for both goods and services, as well as communicative public (and private) notices. Catering to a multiplicity of tastes and views through the eighteenth century, a huge number of monthly, weekly, tri-weekly, and daily newspapers and magazines offered their readers, "the public," a cornucopia of items both serious and trivial.

And, like the owners of the *Gazetteer*, who claimed that theirs was "the best family News-paper ever yet published,"[87] the other competing journals wished to capture, however they could, a share of this new "niche" in the market for news. Fashion, especially the fashion of the court, sports, and amusements, as well as accounts of foreign travels, found an enlarged place in the press of the second half of the century. In addition, newsmen soon found that scandal, served hot and frequently, seemed an irresistible lure to many readers. The establishment of the *Morning Post* in 1772, under its first and most daring editor, the swashbuckling Rev. Henry Bate, set the pattern for, and forced its competitors to copy, the wholesale purveyance of this steamy commodity. But the *Post* was only serving daily what the innocently named *Town and Country Magazine* had begun to dish up monthly for a grander audience—frank discussions of the various goings-on of the denizens of the world of fashion. In their commercially successful and much-copied revelations about the doings and mis-doings of the great and not-so-good, these journals appealed to that combination of prurience and outrage which allowed a hungry public simultaneously to both desire and deplore the reports they consumed.

In addition to affording more room for letters, the expanded dailies also allowed for more playful experimentation with various forms of satirical content, as well as an increased commentary aimed at what were perceived to be current immoralities. Thus, after the publication and popularity of Laurence Sterne's *Tristram Shandy*, some papers not only used its characters in dialogues designed to gently mock specific vices, but even adopted Shandean punctuation to carry the joke, and the lesson, even further. Mock advertisements and dictionaries appeared which, while employing well-known forms, surprised by putting those forms in the service of ridiculing fashionable improprieties. And, of course, the tri-weeklies, the weeklies, and the monthlies all borrowed from, and expanded on these popular concerns. Thus the *Connoisseur* praised the efforts of the daily press, noting that he knew of nothing "which would give posterity so clear an idea of the taste and morals of the present age, as a bundle of our daily papers."[88]

And, in ways which are central to the topics under investigation in this book, the press changed the nature of its coverage of such issues through the century. While, as we shall see, they had excoriated immorality and ridiculed improper behavior during the period's first six decades, newspaper editors rarely descended to personalities, rarely "named names," especially if those involved were members of the upper classes. Pushed by the cut-throat competition between the large number of papers, propelled by their growing political and moral fearlessness, the press, and especially the daily press, increasingly indulged in exposés of aristocratic wrong-doing and calls for general and specific reformation and legislation. And, as an eminent biographer has noted of a later period, "Society scandals which got into the newspapers were the tip of the iceberg . . . [however] if nothing was said or read, nothing had happened."[89] Such scandal was made "real" and easily available through this burgeoning press. Perhaps because the advocacy of moral reform could not be called partisan, perhaps because newspaper editors were both reflecting and helping to shape public opinion, we will see how such commentary increased in scope, became more specific in its coverage, and created repeated demands for positive action. For in publicizing, that is in publishing, the misdeeds and mal-conduct of the Great, the press informed its readership, made them armchair witnesses to much more upper-class immorality than most would have known about from personal experience, and more than many could otherwise have imagined. Like the crime reporting which heightened popular fears and concerns about lawlessness, the reporting by the press of upper-class faux pas created and gave public voice to waves of moral anxieties. In such reporting the press erased the insecure boundary between the "private" and the "public," allowing readers a keyhole into the lives of the political and social leaders of society. For how else could most people know about the private vices of the better sort? And these keyhole views, these scandalous insights, fostered a growing sense of resentment and irritation among the public, a feeling that the lives of the great and powerful were not what they should be, and that reformation was necessary.

"The Sinister (or Left-Handed) Theatrical Duel." *The Town and Country Magazine*, March 1770. Courtesy of the Lewis Walpole Library, Yale University

2

"That Wild Decision of the Private Sword"

it is a Scandal, that our Nation only has not made sufficient Provision against this Crime, but that we may have the Liberty of Killing one another, and yet be reckon'd good Subjects, and be as much commended for Destroying as Propagating one of our Species.[1]

This comment, coming after the murderous Mohun-Hamilton duel of 1712, the duel, as Victor Stater has dubbed it, "that shook Stuart Society,"[2] was part of an appeal to Parliament to pass legislation that would finally end the practice.[3] This demand, many times repeated in the eighteenth century, was never satisfied, and many doubted legislative efficacy in combating such an entrenched custom. While duelling continued into the nineteenth century, a variety of alternate remedies were put forward for its cessation, yet none were adopted. Though men and women of all sorts, clerics, novelists, poets, and playwrights, presented, and mainly censured, the duel as an outmoded relic of a bygone age, it continued to be practiced and to go unpunished. And then, after more than a century of debate, duels ceased to be fought in England. This chapter seeks to explore the confused welter of representations, attitudes, and acts surrounding this persistent vice through the eighteenth century and then to suggest some reasons why, in England alone of European nations, men of honor turned away from this fearsome custom.

"That Bubble which is called Honour":[4] *Duelling to* 1760

The eighteenth-century debate on duelling grew naturally from and repeated many of the earlier complaints and criticisms of the practice. While some continued to describe the act as devilish, seeing Satan and his minions as still active in the world,[5] more common in the explanations for this wide-spread vice was the influence and force of custom, and the deformation that this inertia caused to notions and practices of virtue and honor. Thus in Fielding's *Amelia*, when the voice of reason and religion, Dr. Harrison, attempted to answer Amelia's plaint that her husband's honor as well as his life must be preserved, he noted:

> Can Honour dictate to him to disobey the express Commands of his Maker, in Compliance with a Custom established by a Set of Blockheads, founded on false Principles of Virtue, in direct Opposition to the plain and positive Precepts of Religion and tending manifestly to give a Sanction to Ruffians, and to protect them in all the Ways of Impudence and Villainy?[6]

Here, in the guise of the Doctor, Fielding was gesturing to a connection that would become clearer in the last third of the century: that between an uncivilized gothic inheritance and the practice of duelling, the distance between a savage practice smacking of the Vandals and the acquisition of gentility and politeness so valued by contemporary society.[7] How else could this powerful, deadly compulsion be explained but by the irrational but potent force of custom?

"That, to let any thing grow into Custom, which is against Law, is owing to the Inadvertency, Negligence, or Guilt of Princes."[8] This quote, from the *Spectator*, served as the opening line of a letter on duelling in a mid-eighteenth-century newspaper. Three-quarters of a century later, in a survey of persuasives against the practice, the anonymous author of *The Duellist* quoted from the same magazine, the *Spectator*, for Addison's articulation of the nature of false honor. The continuing appeal of the writings of Addison and Steele are examples of what Philip Carter has noted: "that would-be polite men continued to consult seminal guides to polite conduct like the *Spectator* throughout the [eighteenth] century."[9] By the mid-century such guides, along with various sorts of didactic and literary material and newspaper accounts and comments, both formed and informed contemporary opinion about the nature, prevalence, and undesirability of the practice of duelling.

Of course, while the attack on stultifying, savage custom was at the forefront of anti-duelling rhetoric, the most traditional sort of criticisms of the practice came from clergymen, sometimes delivered as sermons and other times as tracts and pamphlets denouncing this unchristian vice. However, at the end of the day, neither military men, moved by the exigencies of their profession, nor gentlemen, persuaded by their own code of propriety, heeded any of these, and felt they could avoid the duel. So whatever ministers and preachers might have taught, whatever Addison and Steele advised, many would surely have agreed with the Lieutenant's comment to Tom Jones:

> My dear boy, be a good Christian as long as you live: but be a man of honour too, and never put up an affront; not all the books, nor all the parsons in the world, shall ever persuade me to that. I love my religion very well, but I love my honour more. There must be some mistake in the wording of the text, or in the translation, or in the understanding of it, or somewhere or other. But however that be, a man must run the risk, for he must preserve, his honour![10]

In fact, the presentation of the duel in the literature and drama of the first half of the eighteenth century was largely favorable, and only very occasionally condemnatory. Many of the period's most popular plays, ranging from Centlivre's *The Beau's Duel* to Popple's *Double Deceit*, had their heroes cheerfully and without censure so engaged.[11] Neither the heroes of Haywood's novels nor Fielding's celebrated the duel, but nevertheless they engaged in them when required by the demands of honor and public shame. While Richardson's exemplary aristocrat, Sir Charles Grandison, not only refused to fight duels himself, but expatiated at some length upon their criminality, Richardson had, in an earlier work, presented Colonel Morden, the greatly beloved and highly virtuous cousin of Clarissa, challenging and killing Lovelace in such an encounter.[12] So while religious men condemned the duel, few authors or dramatists issued strong denunciations of the practice.

Duelling in the Press to 1760

Duelling was an illicit activity. What this meant, of course, is that most people who duelled tried to evade detection, tried to conduct their encounters at out-of-the-way spots and at odd hours of the day. If the meetings did not result in fatal wounds, it is possible that they entirely escaped notice, and so were lost both to contemporaries and to historians. Though we can never recover the totality of duelling for the eighteenth century, we do have a great deal of contemporary evidence that allows us partially to reconstruct what ordinary men and women of the time might have read and consequently thought about this practice. One of the best of these sources is the growing newspaper press.

However, we must first pause a moment to consider what constituted a duel. On the whole, we assume that we know what a duel was. Ideally, the duel, like the minuet, was above all a formal and well-mannered event. It was supposed to contain and give shape to the passions which generated and animated it. By giving these passions a limited mode of expression, duelling, at least in theory, substituted a conventionalized, well-demarcated conflict for a potentially endless state of war. "Casual or irregular violence," the assassination and the vendetta, were replaced, it was frequently claimed, by the recognized rules of the field of honor. What this meant was that, following an affront, the parties were expected to approach seconds to represent them, who would attempt peacefully to resolve the conflict, but, if this proved impossible, would assist their principals at the event, would try "to see that all was upon the square, and make a faithful report of the whole combat."[13] They would secure weapons, transportation, and medical assistance; they would discuss duelling procedures and would attend the duel to make sure that only honorable conduct would occur. However, in practice, as far as we can tell, these requirements were often ignored, especially before mid-century. In each of the major reported duels and in several of the minor ones before the late 1760s, one or more of these necessities was often missing. The Mohun-Hamilton duel was notorious for the involvement of the seconds in the conflict itself; in neither the Deering-Thornhill, the Walpole-Chetwynd, nor the Clarke-Innes duels were seconds present, and in the last, the opponents fought with weapons of vastly different sizes. Both the Dalton-Paul and Byron-Chaworth duels took place in darkened rooms with no witnesses.[14] For these decades, then, what made an encounter a duel, at least in so far as the press and the public were concerned, was the use of weapons, i.e., swords or pistols, sometimes the testimony and forgiveness of the injured or dying duellist, and the social class of the participants. The rather hit-and-miss, unregulated quality of these early eighteenth-century duels can be seen in the press accounts of four rather commonplace matches reported during the reigns of the first two Georges. It should also be noted that, on the whole, these reports were brief and almost never commented directly on the duel itself.

The first, a fatal duel between two young men who lodged in the same house, is a good example of the rather hot blood and lack of preparation that typified the reports we have of the conflicts of this period. After fighting on the evening of their quarrel, they parted when the sword of one of the men was broken. Next day, Mr. Andrews, an ensign in a regiment of foot, came to his opponent, Lee's, room, and challenged him to fight again. The two young men left the house, procured swords along the way, and walked deep into Kensington Gardens where "on a sudden Mr. Andrews bid the other draw, and after a short Engagement," Andrews was fatally wounded. Similarly unstructured and un-seconded was the meeting between two Irish friends, who one evening exchanged "some words." Despite the attempts of one to apologize for having caused offence, the two men renewed their quarrel; "Here no third Person being present, they were heated into Passion, and a Case of Pistols lying in the Window, they engag'd in a Duel" in which one was fatally shot. A similar affray between two young friends during a walk, arguing philosophical questions this time, led to a sword fight, and to the death of one.[15] Finally, the affair between a Captain Gray of the Guards and Lord Lempster was also resolved without prior challenge, seconds, or ceremony. The duel, occasioned by a quarrel over a gambling match, was insisted on the next morning by the Captain, and the two men went into Marybone fields, where the Captain died of a sword wound.[16] The pattern seems clear; though some duels were more formal, many were reported as occurring without the regularity or control that seconds and rules afforded and that the manuals insisted they required.

Between 1680 and 1750, the press reported 356 duels or inquests and trials of duelling offences. Through these seventy years, the great majority of these reports were only one sentence long and gave no reason for the contretemps. The weapons employed in these contests consisted for the most part of the sword, or the sword and pistol. While much remained constant in such accounts, two changes of emphasis did occur. The first was the steady growth in the reports stating the weapons employed; the second was the declining number of named duellists, and the replacement of names with either their occupations or their status. Thus, by the 1740s, a common description of a duellist was "a person of distinction" or "of honour."[17]

It is unclear why newspaper accounts of duels were so abbreviated, seldom mentioning details or outcomes. Part of the explanation undoubtedly lies with the small size of the early eighteenth-century newspaper itself, and the few pages available for news of all sorts. It may be that editors just did not consider such items to be "news-worthy." Perhaps they were intimidated by the possibilities of prosecution, or even violence, if they reported such events. Or it may be that the widespread use of "omission fees" made it both safer and more profitable for newspapermen not to write about such conflicts. This is certainly what occurred in one eighteenth-century novel, *The Woman of Honour* [1768]. In a letter to a female correspondent, the novel's protagonist, Lady Harriet, explained that after her brother's duel "their steward did a very sensible thing: considering the pain which the publication of the incident would give to all parties, he sent round to the editors of the news-papers to have it suppressed."[18] Clearly many of the upper classes felt demeaned and sullied by having their private affairs made public. Commenting in the aftermath of Lord Byron's trial of 1765, for killing his neighbor in a duel, Horace Walpole, though openly unsympathetic to the man and his cause, still noted that though Byron "escaped with his life and recovered some portion of honour, if that can comfort him" it must have been a terrible ordeal "after the publicity made of his character."[19]

It was in the 1750s that the press response to and reportage of duels deepened. In the accounts of one of these, the duel between Captains Innes and Clarke of the Navy, we can observe both the rhetorical and intellectual reliance on older sorts of criticism and some of the newer arguments coming to the fore, as well as a certain hesitant reluctance to acknowledge the difficulties, for military men at any rate, in retaining their most prized possession, their honor and reputation.

Briefly to recapitulate the events leading up to this duel: in 1749, Admiral Knowles, commander of the British Navy in the Caribbean, was court-martialed for what some thought naval mismanagement or negligence. During the trial, one of the Captains under his command, Captain Clarke, was called by the court to testify and gave evidence which mitigated the culpability of his Admiral. The Admiral was reprimanded, though not condemned, and the trial's outcome led to a series of challenges and duels, most notably between Knowles and several of his Captains, but also between Innes, another naval officer, and Clarke. Innes himself was court-martialed by Knowles, found guilty of not obeying orders, and suspended from command for three months. Innes, however, asserted that Clarke had perjured himself at the trial, giving false evidence on the Admiral's behalf; as a consequence Innes proceeded to taunt and heckle Clarke until he agreed to meet him in a duel. The event was totally unregulated, without any seconds present and each using his own weapons. Clarke fired first, with a gun twice as long as Innes's, from a range of five or six yards, and gave his opponent a mortal wound. It is unclear whether Innes ever got a chance to return the shot. Despite some contradictory evidence about Innes's last words, when the jury, rather unwillingly, found Clarke guilty of murder, the foreman remarked that "the provocation given by the Deceased to the Prisoner, was so extraordinary, that they begg'd the Court would please to recommend him to his Majesty's Mercy." This was accordingly done, and Clarke was pardoned and freed.[20]

Unlike the duels of the preceding two decades, this duel provoked more newspaper coverage and commentary. Waiting, perhaps, until the outcome of Clarke's trial and sentencing was announced, an interesting front page letter about this affair appeared in the *Whitehall Evening Post* on April 19, 1750. A little more than a month later another account was featured on the front page of *Old England*, which was edited and copied as an item in the *Gentleman's Magazine* of the same month. Both of these essays cited the criticisms of duelling made almost forty years before in the *Spectator*. This reliance on the received wisdom of moral arbiters, like the *Spectator*, was joined with a comment in *Old England*, which connected the outcome of this event with that of the infamous Mahon-Hamilton conflict, and even with the Pulteney-Harvey duel. It also noted that while the *Spectator's* virtuous king, Pharamond, had, in his Edicts, "parted with a branch of his prerogative," i.e., his power to pardon duellists, England's George had not.[21]

The discussion of this duel not only relied on earlier analyses, but came up with new proposals. The first, made by *Old England*, was that words, as well as blows, be seen as sufficient legal provocation to mitigate the severity of the offence of duelling. The second critical remark stressed the private evil of the duel, invoking a language of sentiment and domesticity that connected the transgression of the duel with an attack on the sanctity of the family and its members. Finally, the commentary on this duel again raised the question, which was a central one in this century in which England was intermittently, but almost constantly at war, of the difficulty of being both a military officer and a man who wished to obey the law, and thus not duel. So *Whitehall's* noted, as a matter of fact, that "should an Officer in the Army or Navy, in Reverence of the Law, either of God or Man, refuse a Challenge, his Commission shall be taken from him!" Yet, it went on to argue that the duellist, in regarding only the purity of his personal honor, ignored the demands of his position, and by endangering his life, shirked his duties "of doing Service to his King and Country." *Old England* on the other hand, saw the revival of duelling as "prevailing after a bad Peace." Unlike *Whitehall's*, *Old England* asserted the centrality of honor to the military man, arguing that "to be traduced and vilify'd . . . are more than Man can bear, or indeed what ought to be borne by a Gentleman; more especially, by one who holds his Commission by the Tenure of his Sword, as Obedience to the Laws of the Land in such a Case would render him contemptible by those of Honor." What could a man do who must either fight a duel or lose his job or his honor, or both?[22] After the mid-century, then, both the volume and detail in press reporting of duels increased significantly, and many of these involved military men, or, in the wake of the insurgent anti-Scots sentiments egged on by the *North Britain*, duels between Englishmen and Scots.[23] Since for the six decades from 1680, it was quite apparent from the newspaper reports that a sizeable percentage of duellists were military or naval men, it is clear why they were seen as most under the tyrannous sway of this barbarous ritual.

"that most barbarous and cowardly custom of duelling":[24] The Byron-Chaworth Affair

Yet, despite the visibility of duelling among military men, the duel which received the greatest coverage at this time was fought for quite different reasons by men of quite a different sort. This was the encounter between William, Lord Byron and William Chaworth, his neighbor and relation, which occurred at the Star and Garter tavern in Pall Mall on January 26, 1765. This was a duel fought because of a quarrel which occurred at a London club-meeting of Nottinghamshire gentlemen. One account claimed that the men fought over which of them had the best method for promoting game on his estate, another, that Chaworth resented Byron's guests hunting on the land of his tenants. Whatever the argument, Byron and Chaworth fought within minutes of the dispute, in a dark room without any seconds. After securing medical care for Chaworth, mortally wounded in the combat, Byron went into hiding, eventually giving himself up for trial. Undoubtedly the fact that Byron chose to be tried by *his* peers, i.e., by the House of Lords, and that this was the first such serious trial since Earl Ferrers had been tried and found guilty of murder, did much to enhance its notoriety. To give some sense of the widespread nature of its coverage: from the date of the duel through the subsequent trial, which took place on April 16th of the same year, that is, in almost a three-month period, at least sixty-eight items related to the duel appeared in six of London's newspapers, as well as in most of her periodical press. It is true that most of these notices were either very short, or virtually identical with stories printed elsewhere, but it is hard to think that anyone reading the press in London (and much of the kingdom received London periodicals) in those months could be ignorant of the duel or not have an opinion about its outcome. While the spectacular nature of the trial as well as the differing versions of the duel itself made the event a media "happening," equally interesting, perhaps, was the number of letters that the duel evoked, and the dialogue that began within the press through such letters, about this particular duel, but more about the practice of duelling in general. While three of the eleven letters published in the six months after the duel were concerned with the costs of the trial to the public,[25] all of the others were on matters of principle, and several appeared on the front pages of their papers. While one of these letters argued that, for a man reviled "in the most bitter and biting terms of contumely," there was no recourse but the duel, more typical was that which asserted that duelling could only be stopped by insisting that "the Legislature must forbid all (save military) men from wearing swords; and a decree for this purpose, I am certain, can be of no injury to this nation, as I am sure that the advantages resulting from wearing swords, are far short of countervailing the various mischiefs that attend the use of them."[26] Perhaps most interesting of the eleven letters that appeared following this engagement was the last, which purported to be, and was perhaps, a "genuine Letter" from one Alexander Robinson to a Walter Smith, refusing to accept a challenge to engage in a duel. In this note, Robinson made three interesting points. The first was an answer, of sorts, to the "silence of our Legislature with regard to Duelling"; Robinson pointed out that in the ancient world, laws against parricide were also thought unnecessary "because they thought it a Crime the worst of Villains would be incapable of." Second, he argued against the duel on traditional Christian grounds, and finally concluded by reminding Smith that as a furious duellist, he, Smith, was a slave "to the Tyranny of your Passions," while he, Robinson, "remain Master of my own." This final argument, which recalls the earlier comments that those truly manly can rise above their passions, and display cool control, was perhaps the lowest blow of all.[27]

Despite these public condemnations, both the well-respected *Gentleman's Magazine* and its younger but prestigious rival, the *Annual Register*, published as their concluding comments on the affair, an article entitled "An authentic Narrative of the Duel between Lord Byron and Wm Chaworth." This essay, glossing over the impropriety of an unwitnessed, unregulated duel fought in the dark by two men who had spent the evening drinking and quarrelling, determined that

> it should seem that neither Mr. Chaworth nor any of his friends could blame Lord Byron for the part he had in his death. Mr. Chaworth it is manifest, was under the apprehensions of having mortally wounded Lord B and Lord B being still engaged, had a right to avail himself of this mistake for the preservation of his own life. His lordship himself, no doubt, may wish that he had, in that situation, disabled him only; but in the heat of duelling who can always be collected?[28]

Thus, while duelling became more frequently featured and more negatively portrayed in the press, there still seemed to be a basic incapacity to come to terms with the vice. For the *Gentleman's* in 1765, as for Steele in 1709, the enigma, the inability forcefully to find and recommend an antidote remained:

> It is confessed, I have writ against Duels with some Warmth; but in all my Discourses, I have not ever said, that I knew how a Gentleman could avoid a Duel If he were provoked to it . . . .[29]

For most of the eighteenth century, whatever being a gentleman meant in the everyday, it was a commonplace that, if demeaned physically by a blow, or verbally by being called a liar or coward, every gentleman, whatever his situation, station, or occupation, had to "resent so gross an insult" "in the manner [in which] such indignity ought to be resented," i.e. cudgelling non-gentle and duelling with gentle antagonists.[30]

From *"Wilkes will fight" to Pitt's "amende honourable"*:[31] *Duelling and Politics*

In the early eighteenth century contemporary commentators frequently characterized duels as having arisen from political disagreements. Both the Mohun-Hamilton and the Hervey-Pulteney duels fit this model. Both of these, it was said, were connived to settle long-standing scores. Other duels, like the one between Lord Walpole and Walter Chetwynd, erupted both from older grievances, and from words spoken in anger in Parliamentary debate.[32] In these, neither man was hurt, and no more was heard of the quarrel. Little more was published about John Wilkes's first duel of 1762. Most of the press reports of this meeting were equivocal and did not name the antagonists.[33] A year later, however, Wilkes's next duel received much more press notice, and in fact might be seen as the beginning of an epoch in which the political duel, and duelling more generally, became a sought-for news item and one commonly found in the daily and periodical press. While the duels of notable political figures were most prominently featured in the press, there was also an increase in stories of others whose duels were described as resulting from political disputes.[34]

What was considered so noteworthy about this second duel of Wilkes? First, while in France, Wilkes had been repeatedly challenged to fight by a young Scot, Forbes, and had evaded that encounter. Furthermore, the political situation in the House of Commons was electric, as the Ministry had done every thing in its power to find ways of silencing Wilkes. After the failure of General Warrants, and Wilkes's triumph over the Ministry, he must have felt invulnerable. So, in November 1763, he called out his fellow Member of Parliament, Samuel Martin, and, in the resulting duel, Wilkes suffered what might well have been a fatal wound. Early press accounts presented Wilkes as going out of his way to be a magnanimous opponent, urging Martin to flee after wounding him; later stories gloried in the polish that Wilkes's tarnished reputation had received. "The Affair effectually wipes off all Aspersions of Cowardice, which the Scots attempted to fix upon him [Wilkes] by the Scheme of Capt. Forbes."[35] Within two weeks of the duel, at least five letters were published about it. Only one, the earliest, lamented its occurrence, though it did not condemn it. All the rest reflected on the degree of honor that each of the contestants had won through his actions.[36]

The next decade, however, saw the first full flowering of political duels, with a number of very prominent public men fighting about things said or done in public, usually in Parliament, which, they felt, impugned their honor, and could only be eradicated by blood. Newspapers also became much more important for the proper conduct of the duel, with participants and seconds often sending in their accounts, to inform the public that things had gone properly and in an honorable fashion. Rather than paying editors *not* to publish such stories, public men who duelled increasingly seemed to feel that it was imperative that their story be correctly told, and that the public be informed of its true circumstances. Increasingly the public were invited to view the duel, to see how coolly and fairly it had been conducted, and how all the rules of honor had been obeyed.

The first of these political duels, which ended happily, was between Governor Johnstone and Lord George Germaine. Germaine, who had been court-martialed after the battle of Minden, had, like Wilkes after Forbes's challenges, publicly duelled to regain his honor, which the encounter completely accomplished. Thus the *Gazetteer* recounted the story of "a witty gentleman" who maintained that the duel was "the greatest act of grace that L[ord] G[ermaine] could have received. "When his companion asked 'why is that,' the wit replied 'because the G[overnor] has thoroughly whitewashed him.'" Many of the papers repeated the words or sentiments of the *Lady's Magazine* that Lord Germaine "behaved with much cool and real courage." Horace Walpole seems to have captured the general mood when, in a letter to Mann, he wrote: ". . . whatever Lord George Sackville was, Lord George Germaine is a hero."[37] The gentility and honor of both men was proved not only by their duel, but by their subsequent behavior. The press noted that "Lord G- G- and Gov. J- are now entirely reconciled: a few mornings since they walked together near an hour in St. James's park, and conversed the whole time seemingly in the most friendly manner."[38]

Undoubtedly, however, two of the most famous political duels of the 1770s and '80s were the meetings between Charles James Fox and William Adam in November 1779 and that between the Earl of Shelburne and William Fullerton, fought about four months later. Both these duels were widely reported, with accounts from the seconds as well as letters between the duellists published in the press. In addition, a poem, in French, praising Fox, a satirical ballad entitled "Paradise regained, or the Battle of Adam and the Fox," was published on this occasion.[39] Both duels were fought with Scots, both resulted in minor injuries to their English participants, and both were the talk of the day. Of the four letters to the printer written on this affair, two applauded Fox's behavior as "manly, determined and liberal" while one took strong exception to this encomium. Arguing that words were wounds, "JB" wrote about the impropriety of Parliamentary privilege for unfettered speech. For "JB," the very publicness of the offence required the possibility of the duel to keep "political incendiaries" in check. Only "Right" argued against both the practice of, and praise for, *any* political or other sort of duellists; "I believe," he said, "it to be bigoted and rank cowardice and very high presumption to give or accept a challenge."[40] While duelling for men out-of-doors, though still practiced, was increasingly condemned, opinion about the propriety of public men duelling was less clear.

The letters following the second duel, between the Earl of Shelburne and William Fullerton, were more generally negative, though employing a wide range of condemnatory tropes. That old chestnut, that duelling was the result of custom, that it was "astonishing that fashion should so darken the mind and pervert the understanding, as to annex *honour* to the most unreasonable and dishonourable thing in the world" was joined in the same letter to violent anti-Scots sentiment, and to the accusation that Fullerton was an assassin hired by the Ministry. Another letter, while claiming no acquaintance with either combatant, offered to "satisfy" either of the duellists by a martial engagement. A third extraordinarily long missive, which took up almost a whole newspaper page, after arguing at great length for the need for unchecked Parliamentary free speech, concluded by noting that it took Fullerton two weeks from the time of Shelburne's original comments to decide that these had injured his reputation, and needed to be atoned for by a duel. Though the bulk of these letters, and of most of the press comments, were both partial and congratulatory, we do see views publicly expressed, not only by newspaper writers, but also by their readers and correspondents, which raised serious questions about the role of duelling amongst public men. By the early 1780s there was some sense that such behavior demeaned the political process and was inappropriate in a "certain Assembly, where good manners and politeness should form the basis of all debates which are there agitated."[41]

The question of duelling in general, and especially of political duels, was taken up by the many debating societies in London from the mid-1770s onwards. From 1773 through 1779 ten such debates took place at different venues. Of the three debates for which we have the audience vote, we know that, in each case, the practice of duelling was condemned. Thus, for example, in 1778, when the Robin Hood Society asked "Whether the observation of the general rule of appealing to arms upon particular affronts or personal insults, deserves greater censure than a deviation therefrom?" the answer was unambiguous: it was "determined that giving into the practice of duelling on any account deserved greater censure than avoiding the same upon any provocation."[42] And, in the March and April following the Shelburne/Fullerton duel, five debates were held on the propriety of duelling in general, and three on the specific situation of political duels. Thus, on March 25, 1780, the University for Rational Amusements raised the question of whether "challenging a Member of Parliament for any freedom he may take in debate, was contrary to any principles of the Constitution?" and two weeks later, the Carlisle House School of Eloquence wondered whether it was "consistent with the necessary freedom of Parliamentary debate, that the gentlemen should not be accountable in a private capacity, for any expression they may use as members of the Senate?"[43] Though we do not have the result of either of these questions, that they were raised at non-elite fora shows the level of popular interest in and concern about this phenomenon. Yet perhaps popular opinion was already more condemnatory of such practice than that found within the House of Commons. Following a debate on political duels in the wake of the Wilkes, Fox, and Shelburne affairs, one MP, "high in office," argued in Parliament that "No means, nor no authority could prevent gentlemen, who felt or who thought their honour injured, from seeking and obtaining redress in the customary mode. In talking of the recent affairs he said, they were matters which every man must lament, but which no man, nor no set of men, were able to put a stop to."[44] The argument was made that only in private conversation did every man have a duty "to be on his guard, and to take care, that he let no expression slip, which might either give offence to any individual, or to disturb the harmony of the whole. In public debate, the case was widely and essentially different."[45] Here we see the beginning of a new doctrine: gentlemen "in private life" were to be governed by the code of politeness and refrain from wounding words, but men in public roles were not only allowed, but obliged to speak freely and without restraint, and act on the consequences, be they what they might.

The last major duel of the eighteenth century to arise because of words spoken during debate occurred during the Napoleonic wars, with George Tierney, leader of the opposition, the challenger, and William Pitt the younger, the offender. The cause of the conflict was itself very slight. When, during Friday's debate, Tierney had demanded more time to discuss a Navy bill, Pitt implied that Tierney did not wish to properly defend his country, and then refused to explain or apologize for his remarks when this was called for. Later that night, Tierney sent Pitt a challenge, and the duel, which took place on Whitsunday afternoon, passed without injury, the two men firing simultaneously and missing, then Tierney firing and missing, and Pitt shooting above his head. It may well have seemed an odd time for such a rencounter; England was fighting a desperate war against the forces of republican France on the continent, while, closer to home, Ireland was, yet again, in flames, torn by civil strife. And Pitt was still the great hope of the rising Evangelical party in Parliament, a party devoted to ending the slave trade, the lottery, and the practice of duelling. This cadre of dedicated and religious men and women saw themselves as the vanguard of a movement of social and political rehabilitation through moral and religious reform. And, for most of these ventures, Pitt proved an ally and, if not a leader, at least a willing fellow-traveller. Though they few in numbers, the influence of the Evangelicals, both within Parliament and without, was to prove tremendously important in organizing and focussing public attention, and leading a national campaign to return English men and women to a purer, primitive Protestantism, a creed of both faith and action. While this movement was not without its critics, it did manage to capture the moral "high ground," to present its goals and agenda as perhaps the only, and undoubtedly the best, program for national amelioration. Only a year before the duel, William Wilberforce, the most prominent Evangelical in Parliament and a close friend of Pitt's, had published his widely read and influential *Practical View of the Prevailing Religious System of Professed Christians* in which he forcefully denounced those contemporaries who thought that "to covet wealth is base and sordid but to covet honour is treated as a mark of a generous and exalted nature."[46] And by the 1790s, even secular writers were arguing that what was said by Members in the Houses of Parliament should not be considered either personally dishonoring or publicly disreputable; "the law can not take cognizance of what is there said, be it ever so treasonable." If Parliamentarians were held back from freely expressing their views by fear of challenge and the necessity to fight, real debate would be fatally constricted. "What passes in the Senate is not subject matter of personality that any man out of Parliament" or even within it "can take up as an individual offence."[47] However, by their duel, both Tierney and Pitt demonstrated that not everyone agreed. The Evangelicals and the King were horrified, Wilberforce going so far as to draft a piece of legislation which, if passed, would have prevented any Parliamentarian who fought a duel from sitting in the House.

But how was this duel presented to the public by the press? Of course, much of what was printed was prompted as much by political alliance as by conviction; various newspapers tended to be either pro-Ministry or pro-Opposition. Given that, however, they still had to present arguments rather than blatant slurs, and it is in the careful consideration of such stances that we can discern differences or nuances of principle, not just of political expediency. Several papers remarked on the potential disaster that might have resulted from such a duel; the Prime Minister, it was said, was too important to the future of England and to the freedom of Europe to endanger his life in such a way, however honorable; "it is now become a doubt whether he [Pitt] was justifiable, having the business of the Empire on his head, to try the precarious direction of a bullet."[48] The opposition papers, not surprisingly, stressed Pitt's highhanded refusal to explain or apologize for his language, and took great delight in the discomfort that Pitt's duel had given to his Evangelical friends.[49] What gave these papers especial glee was the fact that the duel had occurred on a Sunday, and the pain this had caused Wilberforce and his associates. "Mr. Wilberforce is highly displeased with his friend, Mr. Pitt, for his late *unchristianlike* conduct, in *fighting a duel* on the *Sabbath*," remarked the *London Packet*. "The Premier hath much offended his best friends, by going out on such a profane business as a duel during *Divine Service*," quipped the *Morning Chronicle*; "Indeed this is so much worse than *dining* on a *fast day*, that nothing short of an *octavo* can apologize for it." And, after Wilberforce's withdrawal of his censuring motion, the *Morning Herald* snickered that "at the particular request of Mr. Pitt's friends, the *meek and pious Member* does not mean to persist in his determination to bring the subject before the House [emphasis mine]."[50]

But, at the end of the day, almost none of the newspapers took a legal, moral, or religious stance; only one said that duelling was illegal or unchristian, or that the tacit complicity of the Law condoned acts in Parliamentarians that would have been condemned in lesser men.[51] In all the to-ing and fro-ing, only one voice was heard to make these sorts of comments, and that belonged to a mocking member of the Common Council of London, Mr. Hodgson. If "two carmen, or carcass butchers had met in a field to fight on a Sunday," he noted, "the Lord Mayor, or any other Magistrate, would have sent them to the Comptor, where both these Gentlemen should have gone for disregarding the Sabbath, and giving such an example to the different orders of society." In contrast, the *Morning Herald* applauded the late duel, seeing in the resort to gentlemanly violence a method of promoting Parliamentary propriety.

> One good effect may result from a late Duel; it will probably teach every *Prime Minister*, that however he may find himself entrenched under a covering majority in a certain House, it will not protect him from those *explanations* in the *open air*, which every Gentleman there may *freely* demand of another by the common courtesy of *English honour!*[52]

Whatever their political position, all the papers agreed "that that nothing could be more honourable than the conduct of all parties upon the occasion," and that since firing in the air "is considered as an *apology*; or, as an Irish

Gentleman said, a *tacit* acknowledgement of error. In this view Mr. Pitt may be said to have made the *amende honorable* to Mr. Tierney, by the *shot explanatory.*"[53] And after rounds of shots had been fired, Pitt and Tierney's seconds retired to consult together on what should next be done. During this time, the two duellists, who, moments before, had fought on the field of honor, were left by their friends, "in conversation together." They then shook hands and left the field. Next day, the *Morning Chronicle* reported, "Mr. Tierney called on Mr. Pitt, and left his card; and Mr. Pitt returned the compliment to Mr. Tierney. This was the *etiquette* of expressed satisfaction."[54] However unexpected and troublesome to some, if prominent public men fought over slurs to their political honor, and did so in an ordered, regulated, and approved fashion, neither the state nor the Church, nor the voice of public opinion, the press, was willing wholeheartedly to condemn it.

"Courage is so essential to the character of a soldier":[55] *Military Men Duelling*

If the 1770s were pre-eminently the era of the political duel, the 1780s saw a great many military duels and some spectacular military cases which received much publicity and caused continual discussion about the role of honor and duelling in the armed forces.[56] We have seen how, through the first half of the eighteenth century, most critics of duelling still recognized that military men had a particular problem with loss of face, with courage, and with public displays of honor. Though the percentage of duels involving military men was probably no greater in the 1780s than it had been a decade before, they seemed, in several instances, to have taken on a new ferocity and, perhaps for that reason, to have evoked a much greater public response. "X.Y." whose front page letter was published in *Lloyd's Evening Post*, blamed "arrant custom" for the continuance of this practice "in an age so polished and refined as the present." And, he noted, "those who contribute to the making this custom fashionable, are the military gentlemen who are so absurdly tenacious of (what they are pleased to call) their *Honour*"[57] that they will fight a duel on the slightest pretext. And, as though to concentrate the public's attention, three fatal military duels occurred in one year, 1783. Perhaps the commentator in *Old England* who had remarked that a rise in duelling was the result of a bad peace had some real insight, for that year, at least.

The first of these, between two young men who came from military families and who had served together some years before, may have begun in a quarrel over gambling debts; the newspapers were largely silent on the origins of the enmity. Most of the information about it came either from the seconds or from the father of one of the young men, Sir James Riddell, and almost every account started with an explanation to the reader of the need to make the events entirely clear: "When it is considered how many erroneous accounts are generally fabricated on similar occasions, to answer private purposes, we trust an impartial narrative in the present unfortunate instance, will be considered as a faithful discharge of the important duty we owe the public." The *Morning Herald* underlined this necessity by claiming that "various reports [were] being circulated of a late duel, which might be prejudicial to the honor of both men. . . ." and that only an unbiased account, signed jointly by both seconds, and published above their names, could be trusted.[58] Contrast this view with that we have already noted in the *Prompter*, almost half a century before, which claimed that duelling was a private matter, not to be discussed in a public communication. Because of pressure, perhaps stemming from the need to demonstrate the fairness and well-ordered nature of this affair, the very privateness which had been so valued was deliberately put aside and the public invited to sit in judgment.

There are several elements in this tale that made it particularly chilling and melodramatic, and perhaps explained the public's strong interest. First, though there were various versions of the conflict in the press, was the fact that the duel seemed to have been necessitated, not by the men themselves, but by the regiments to which they belonged.[59] Second, the father of one of the duellists, Sir James Riddell, had not only recently lost his only other son in fighting in the Mediterranean, but having received the challenge in his son's absence, had read it, resealed it, and done nothing other than ensure that adequate medical care be present at the confrontation. "The situation of Sir James Riddell, as a parent, is truly pitiable." Third was the fact that, while the younger Riddell fired the first shot, which pierced his opponent Cunningham's chest, and though Cunningham said he was mortally wounded, he still insisted on taking his shot, "declar[ing] that he would not be taken off the field until he fired at his adversary,"[60] thus inflicting the deadly wound that took Riddell's life. Finally, Riddell's funeral, which occurred with magnificence in his family's vault in Westminster Abbey, was also reported in great detail. While a full-blown military procession had been planned to accompany the body, this was "prohibited by a special order," though the next day various aristocrats and generals, along with seventy officers, attended the interment. The *General Evening Post* gave details of the dress and order of the ceremony, and named most of the well-born pall-bearers and mourners. The *Morning Chronicle* noted that Purcell's service was movingly sung, and that a young man in the procession "wept bitterly."[61] The duel also occasioned many remarks in the press, in the form both of letters and of editorial comment, and all, unsurprisingly, were hostile to the practice of duelling. The first, published in the *Morning Chronicle* less than a week after the event, began by noting that "In the whole code of penal laws, no one perhaps is more unequivocally established, than that against *duelling*," and at the same time no one less enforced. Its author addressed himself to the "giddy unthinking Gentlemen of the army" and urged them to "look upon the catastrophe of [Cunningham and Riddell's] bloody temerity, with silent awe and horror." Another very pointed and very condemnatory letter, signed "A.O.W.," criticized the actions of both Sir James Riddell, who by forwarding the challenge, made himself "an accessory to his [son's] fate," and Cunningham, whose "very unusual and shocking thirst for blood" caused him to insist on returning Riddell's fire "when every claim even of honour would have been more generally applauded by discharging his pistol in the air." Finally, this correspondent bemoaned the "pomp and pageantry" of the funeral itself, which "could with propriety only be exercised at the funeral of warriors and conquerors."[62] Other correspondents suggested a number of expedients to reduce the practice: the *London Packet* noted that one proposal, "an efficacious law, if every person who returned from the field without a wound, should be *hanged* for cowardice, . . . it would probably induce men to reflect cooly before they went into the field." The threat of Gustavus Adolphus to the officers of his army was recommended—that the victor of a duel would be hanged by the neck and his opponent by the heels—and it was claimed this punishment was presently being employed in Holland.[63] Furthermore, another claimed (and in 1783, with the great rise in crime of all sorts, this was a potent threat) that the proliferation of duelling would lead to a general increased incidence of violent crime.[64] Satire was also employed against the practice. A columnist for the *Morning Chronicle* gave two (perhaps) mock responses to challenges which employed wit rather than the sword to encounter foolish opponents. But perhaps the most interesting response came in the form of a letter-essay on the front page of the *London Packet* of May 14, 1783. The first part of this essay on duelling examined in detail why "the usual excuse" for the practice, that it "*is for the preservation of honour*," was incorrect. All the claims of religion, of duty, and of self-worth were explored, with the now-common appeals to humanity as well. "View the bleeding body of a newly killed duellist—view his parents—his frantic father—and speechless mother—view their grey hairs brought with sorrow to an untimely grave." But remarkably, this essay concluded with a comparison between the guilt of parallel pairs; the one who coolly and deliberately engaged in a duel, in which "the survivor is pronounced a *man of honour*, and his crime *manslaughter*;"

while the other pair who, "in a drunken brawl, through no premeditation and in hot blood, engage in a scuffle in which one is killed, is adjudged guilty of murder and hanged at the gallows." The relative guilt was clear: coolness made the crime worse, not better; there was nothing honorable or distinctive in a well-regulated and orchestrated butchery. Even if one did not wish to go so far, to see hot-blooded killing as better somehow than cool encounters, one could still deprecate the relative public odium attached to those who refused, as compared to those who accepted challenges: "Thus they who obey the law are scorned and indeed punished; while we see those who act in direct contradiction to these wise, humane institutions (not to mention anything of divine ones) honoured and respected either in life or death."[65] About a month after this duel, the debating society which met at the Coachmakers' Hall argued the question "Can duelling be justified upon the principles of reason and true courage?" probably in response to the enormous publicity and public discussion that the duel had evoked.[66]

In another duel that took place later the same year, both the officers were considerably older, the reason for the duel much graver, and in this case the coroner's jury found the survivor guilty of murder, not manslaughter, though he, like Captain Clarke, was also later pardoned. The conflict between Colonel Cosmo Gordon and Lieutenant Colonel Frederick Thomas, both of the Guards, went back to the American war, during which Thomas had accused Gordon of mismanagement and had him brought before a court-martial tribunal. After Gordon was found not guilty at his trial, he repeatedly challenged Thomas to a duel until such a meeting was arranged for the morning of September 5, 1783. There were several odd things about this meeting. First, for whatever reasons, it was clear from the testimony of Thomas's manservant that for almost a year Thomas had evaded Gordon's repeated demands for a duel. Second, after the first round of bullet shots, in which Gordon was slightly injured, there were no reports that the seconds had attempted mediation, but instead they had re-loaded the pistols, which enabled Gordon to fire the fatal bullet. Lest the public be prejudiced by these reports, however, within a week of the duel, an anonymous correspondent, impelled, he argued, by the 'very unfair state" of the event as reported, presented a description of it much more sympathetic toward the survivor, Gordon. "Col. G," he reported "gave Col. T. every advantage" and the whole "business was conducted in a manner every way satisfactory to the two gentlemen present."[67] In the weeks that followed, this duel, like the last, also generated a great deal of comment and many letters. One correspondent remarked (yet again) about the need to have legislative changes, like those proposed in Pharamond's edict, while others thought some Parliamentary action, and perhaps even a bill to be introduced by the Bishop of London, to be imminent. This, of course, was a hope that had been expressed several times before and that was to be yet again disappointed.[68]

In the five front-page letters on the topic sent after this duel, a number of themes we have already seen emerging were repeated even more forcefully, while others were brought up for the first time.[69] A frequent trope, that of the sorrow of the bereaved wife, deprived of a husband by the demands of honor, was brought forward, yet again, here. Another reflection, which we have already seen raised in the letter following the Riddell-Cunningham duel, but which was even more powerfully stated here, was against the coolness, and by implication the barbarity, of the modern duel. Thus "A Constant Reader," though deprecating duels in general, insisted that "If it should unfortunately so happen, that two men should quarrel, let them at the time (if justifiable at any) take upon them to avenge their cause, not go home, cool, and appoint meeting, the event of which may be fatal to both." But it is the last letter of this group, signed "Scrutator," which is in many ways the most interesting. Again, like "Constant Reader," this author maintained that while some conflicts may in fact be unavoidable, that "if we would submit to be governed by common sense, duels would rarely, or, perhaps, never happen." "Scrutator" then proceeded to discuss those occasions in which duelling was inappropriate, or the methods by which it was currently practiced, were unwarranted. "No man who has distinguished himself in the service, or otherwise, by his valour is under the least obligation to send or accept a challenge"; he further noted that "no man need challenge another on account of words spoken in a Court of Law." Finally, "Scrutator" argued that "the practice of duelling should be regulated with some regard to the preservation of life, and the seconds should never allow it to become a matter of mere butchery." These dicta, clearly influenced by reflection on the spate of military duels of the decade, concluded a letter which began with a quote from the *Mirror:* "He was a man of that extraordinary courage, that he dared not to fight."

The third fatal military duel of the year, in some ways the most tawdry and dishonorable, arose over a squabble over seats at the theater which led to two duels (one of which was fatal) and a third stopped only by the interposition of the magistrates.[70] The cumulative effect of these three fatal episodes, though significant, was by no means fatal to the practice of military duelling. However, by the mid-1780s, even for those who saw the inevitability of some duelling, it was an activity not to be admired, but to be regulated and kept within the strictest check, even for military men.[71]

"Established Etiquette" or *"A Change in Public Opinion"*:[72] The Debate in Words and Deeds, 1775–1814

Early in the eighteenth century, Swift had made a sort of modest proposal, warning Parliament not to make laws against duelling, since "the methods are easy, and many, for a wise man to avoid a quarrel with honour, or engage in it with innocence." And, he added, he could "discover no political evil in suffering bullies, sharpers and rakes to rid the world of each other by a method of their own, where the law hath not been able to find an expedient." In contrast, through the first three-quarters of the century, almost all writers on the subject condemned the practice and the false honor on which it was based. In fact the only exception I have been able to find is an anonymous *Hint on Duelling* of 1752, whose basic message was "that the Mischiefs attending this Practice are Inconsiderable; the resulting Advantages Important; the Enormities that will ensue its attempted Abolition Terrible; and that we much more want a Regulation, than a severer Prohibition, of it."[73] By the mid-1770s, however, not only were there a spate of defences of the practice, but these began appearing in the daily press, to be consumed with breakfast or afternoon tea. Before we consider these arguments, however, we must look briefly at the perceived relationship between duelling and its press coverage.

First, it is important to get a sense of the increased breadth of press reporting of duels. For, when a duel had occurred, and was noted in the press, it was usual by the 1760s for some account of the event to appear in several papers, usually within a week of the meeting itself. This meant that it was likely that whatever paper a reader favored, he or she would generally get an account of whichever duels any of the press reported. Though the most famous duels were reported, usually multiply, in all the papers, even quite minor events could get significant press space. Five of London's major newspapers, for example, included an account of two unnamed men, a Mr. S and a Mr. G, who fought a duel near Kensington in a dispute over a lady, and fired at each other with no harm to either; twenty years later another, similar duel, this one taking place in Hyde Park, was reported in three of the metropolis's major newspapers.[74] This coverage not only testifies to the depth of public interest in duelling, but to its availability to an eager readership.

Second, as we have seen, the volume and nature of newspaper accounts of duels changed from the mid-century. By its third quarter, it was more and more common for the seconds to send their accounts of the incident to the press, for reports of the coroners' inquests to appear, for letters to the printer to be published, and for a wide variety of other sorts of items about recent duels to find their way into print. However, the willingness of the press to publish these accounts was condemned by both supporters and opponents of the practice of duelling. In a letter signed "Truth," a correspondent to the *Morning Post* bemoaned what he claimed had been an incorrect and scurrilous account of a duel that had just taken place; such improper and insulting accounts were, in his opinion, the best reason for finding an alternative to the duel: "it were only to be wished that another mode of deciding differences of this sort between gentlemen was to be adopted, not only for their own peace of mind, but also to prevent their being publicly abused by every insignificant garretwriter." Only a few agreed. Others thought the growing practice of including the testimony of seconds scandalous: "It is the height of impudence and ignorance, . . . to obtrude their cases upon the public—that published within these few days by a half-payofficer, should be noticed by the Magistrates, as being an insult upon the law and police of the country."[75] Still others argued that when the opponents were military men, whose "courage is not only a professional but essential qualification, it may be sometimes necessary that the persons attendant on the issue of their quarrel should give a public statement of the manner in which it was conducted," but that this sort of coverage should never be accorded to conflicts involving "lawyers' clerks, petty gamblers or any similar characters." Such accounts, "A Friend to true Honour" continued, "really make men of honour ashamed of the weapons they wear" and which, he concluded, they cannot help employing in duels now and again. On the other side, most argued that only satirical or ridiculous stories of duels should appear in the press, only stories which mocked the practice and its participants. Furthermore, said one, "let no accounts appear as written by the parties, for it is a thousand to one that a little *newspaper fame* was all the combatants had in view, when they pretended to quarrel."[76] A good example of the "proper" sort of story was published in the *Universal Register*. Signed by the two seconds, a hairdresser and a chimney sweep, the account exactly copied the structure and language of other duelling accounts, except that the quarrel was between characters at the very bottom of the social scale, and that fists, rather than swords or pistols, were used. While such satires increasingly appeared, press coverage of duels and their circumstances grew even more quickly.[77] Excusing themselves, the *Times* noted that they had only "entered into this detail" in publishing a minute-by-minute account of a duel between two military captains, "in hopes that PRIVATE COMMENTS may effect a PUBLIC GOOD, and be the means in time, of suppressing this irrational mode of Gentlemanlike satisfaction." While these hopes may have been sincere, equally important to the paper's editor and owners was the draw that these sorts of accounts had for the public, and the number of papers sold by including such details.[78]

In addition to this increased coverage also came a spate of pamphlets and press items which, if they did not all support the practice of duelling, at least saw it as an ineradicable part of the social world, a practice which was less damaging than its alternatives. It is not clear why these opinions began to be publicly expressed at this time. For much of the earlier eighteenth century, supporters of the code of duelling did not feel the need to appear in print to defend the custom; duellists did what they had to do, sure that all those who mattered would understand and condone their actions. So perhaps the appearance of defences of duelling in print is evidence of some loss of confidence, some perceived need to explain and convince the wider newspaper readership of the legitimacy and value of their honorable intent and necessary practice.

Those engaged in this debate took one of three positions: that duelling was "a good thing," that it was a bad though necessary thing, or that it not only could be but must be ended. The first defence I have found is actually contained in an anti-duelling pamphlet, the *Thoughts on Duelling* of 1773. Its anonymous author, noting that the arguments he was presenting are in "the high Stile in which the Practice of duelling is usually stated and defended," maintained that supporters held that when the law of the land could not give satisfaction to individuals, those persons reverted to the state of nature, in which they "may take the matter, in their own case, into their own cognizance, and redress it themselves; for, '*The law of nature is the law of God.*'" And, according to these defenders of duelling, "*Affronts of Honor* are actually such cases, which it is not in the nature of human Laws to redress or take cognizance of; yet are they grievous and intolerable to noble and generous minds: and, if suffered to pass uncontrouled, would soon remove all order, decency, and good manners from human Society." An item in the *Morning Post* five years later seemed to be using a slightly modified version of this defence; duelling was necessary, it said, for the preservation of natural right and good order, "but in no one instance where the laws have secured the subject from violence, and oppression." Thus, this view held that the Law could not adequately punish breaches of certain kinds of interpersonal hostility, and that the impulse and justification of duelling was "something antecedent and stronger than any law." Even more eloquent was the essay which appeared in the *Gazetteer* in December 1784, simply entitled "Duelling." Its author argued that

> Duelling is a topic of general and unjust reprehension. It has its uses, and is a corrector in society, without which we should have no security against the petulancies of the proud, and all the nameless transgressions of breeding, which would render our lives unpleasant.

He continued that certain offences, when committed by or against people of "breeding," were necessarily outside the reach of the Law, though Law was fully applicable to less well-bred folk. Giving several mock accounts of such duels involving shoemakers, haberdashers, and the like, he asserted that if "[m]atters of bargain and traffic" became "duel-able" subjects, such bouts "would be ridiculous as well as incompatible" with true honor.[79]

The clearest expression of this view, that the Law could only take cognizance of certain kinds of offences, was most strongly stated in the response to a judgment by Lord Ashurst, who had fined a Mr. Johnson £60 for challenging a Mr. Toovey to a duel. While Ashurst had asserted that "duelling was not to be tolerated in a country governed by laws, and where redress might be had for every injury that had been sustained," the *Times* noted that "advocates for duelling, however, differ a little from his Lordship." They, it went on to say, and to repeat in print the next day as well, knew that "a Gentleman might be grossly insulted in various ways, without being able to make out an actionable case."[80] For these proponents of the duelling code, then, the Law was not properly sensitive to the noble and delicate feelings of men of quality, and had to be complemented by extralegal means.

Not only was duelling necessary, but, some thought, even desirable. Thus, in a letter to the *Town and Country Magazine* "J.C." gave five reasons why the practice was admirably justifiable: it was an alternative to nations fighting; it was more above-board than assassination—the other way that personal honor could be avenged; it ended animosities between men; it was necessary to preserve the "courageous and generous spirit of the nation"; and it was the best defence "from the assaults of power, pride and brutality, and . . . promote[d] that reciprocality of good offices and attentions which constitute true politeness. . . ." That this was a not uncommon view among supporters received confirmation from the comment found in *A Short Treatise upon the Propriety and Necessity of Duelling*, published the same year as this letter. Though its author argued against duelling, he noted that the "Government makes a point of extending their indulgence and lenity to the criminal," since they maintained the practice made "people *civil*, and *polite* to each other, and that of many evils which would arise from insult, a duel is the least."[81] Several letters and comments in the press suggested that, for some people, the connection between duelling and politeness was a causal one.[82] But perhaps the clearest articulation of this point of view appeared in a pamphlet, *The Principles of Duelling*, published in 1790 by a military man, Lieutenant Samuel Stanton. Arguing that duelling was both necessary and salutary, Stanton not only bemoaned the fact that duelling was "now daily resorted to by the lowest classes of society" but also urged gentlemen to engage only with others of their own sort; "were such instances [of inter-class duelling] frequent," he noted, "they would entirely do away with all distinction of person, and render the name, gentleman, a nothing, a nonentity." But Stanton also remarked that the practice could be defended on the "grounds of general utility": "it affords *satisfaction*, where nothing but that, and that alone, could do so; and independent of the law's delay, of money, superiority in rank, power, birth, or interest, points out a very proper and necessary mode of redress."[83]

In between these advocates for duelling and their vociferous opponents were those who thought duelling to be a regrettable, but inescapable practice. While admitting that such engagements were only justified by prejudice, passion, custom, and the fear of shame, the penal reformer William Eden noted that neither the law nor the fear of punishment could cause their cessation. While admitting that men who refused challenges were often braver than those that accepted them, an "Old Officer" noted that those military men who refused challenges were often broken. Similarly "Scrutator," whose letter to the *Morning Chronicle* was printed in a coveted first-page position, expressed his hope "to mitigate, and in some degree regulate what it seems impossible to prevent entirely." The tone of a contemporary article in the *Gazetteer* was more pessimistic, noting that men the world over obtained what revenge they could whenever they felt themselves to have been misused. "So strong is the desire of redress for injuries received, that for an offence of which the law takes no cognizance, we appeal to the pistol or the sword, in defiance of the laws of God as well as of man."[84]

In contrast to the novelty of defences of duelling by the first group, and to the resigned acceptance of the practice by the second, the arguments of its opponents, while most vocal and most prominent, were least original. Repeated yet again, this time in direct opposition to its proponents, was the claim that duelling, rather than being a mark of a polite society or an agent of the civilizing process, was a sure feature of barbarism.[85] Another argument, not new but given a more insistent tone and wider coverage, was the deleterious effects of private vice on the public weal. Noting as a commonplace that the very foundation of politics was morality, the *London Packet* contended that "[t]he first object of a legislature should be the manners of the people; permit them to become profligate, and they will by degrees overturn the Constitution, without knowing the mischief they are working." The great bulwark of the Constitution was, of course, the law, applied uniformly and equally. If men could not get the satisfaction they desired from its operations, this did not, however, justify their illicit activity:

if a man does suffer in any case, for want of an established Law to redress him, such evil is unavoidable: the State must not be thrown into confusion, nor the Laws already established infringed, that his wrongs may be redressed in that instance: he must be content with the enjoyment of the many other valuable blessings and privileges which Society affords him . . . .[86]

Of course, both the stability of society and the power of the law depended on Parliament's monopoly of punishment, on the exclusive control by the legislature of the authority to punish wrongdoers. By allowing duellists to go free and unpunished, though they broke the law, the government not only turned a blind eye, but "they really tacitly encourage murder." As an alternative to duelling, these opponents repeated the old suggestion that men become soldiers, and spill their blood for their nation's sake. And, with the outbreak of the French Revolution and the war against the traditional enemy needing dedicated soldiers, a clear role existed for those desiring conflict. However, countering the argument that duelling kept a martial nation in "fighting-trim," Jonas Hanway, employing the comparison yet again between the duellist and the highwayman, argued that both illegal activities, the second as well as the first, could be commended on these (false) grounds.[87]

Perhaps of most interest in this debate was the point on which all agreed: that, while duelling had previously been the preserve of only the upper classes, it was becoming more widely indulged in by commoners. "Was duelling confined to *Lords* and *Commoners*, there would be no cause of complaint, but the nation suffers by permitting *manufacturers* to blow out each others' brains."[88] It is not entirely clear what is being complained of here; but perhaps that is part of the message. On the one hand is the implication that manufacturers, unlike Lords and Commons, were productive citizens whose loss would impoverish the nation, on the other the fear that violence had been generally unleashed, and that murder and rapine would surely follow.

In addition to the newspaper and pamphlet contributions to the debate about duelling, a variety of popular literary works also appeared, which almost exclusively argued, one way or another, against the custom. Thus, in *The Duel*, a play translated from the French by the actor William O'Brien, the father of a young man about to fight a duel tries to persuade him against it, by arguing that it takes more courage to pardon than to fight: "A coward, Sir, may fight—nay, cowards have fought—a coward too may conquer, but 'tis the truly brave only can forgive!"[89] In a pair of poems of 1775, both called "Duelling," their authors repeat the charge that "As murder first arose by Satan's means/So Duelling, tho' he the falsehood screens/By names or reasons wrongly understood,/But fully open to the wise or good." Both saw that the claims of outraged honor as the motive to duel was only an excuse "to autho-rize infernal Crimes . . . [which] subvert the high decree of Heav'n/And cancel ev'ry bond 'twixt Man and Man." And in a slight piece of fluff entitled "Modern Honour, or the Barber Duellist," published in the same year, the plot revolves around two tradesmen, a barber and a tailor, who almost come to a duel. At its end, the story's hero, young Steady, remarks, in a joking tone befitting light comedy, "Well, I hope since Barbers have caught the spirit of duelling, all real gentlemen will despise it in future."[90] Though the manner of the rebuke differed, the message, that duelling was spreading outwards and becoming a resource to the ungentle as well as their betters, was the same.

By the next decade, at least in theatrical comedies, when male protagonists/heroes accepted challenges to duel, they did so in a very modified form, a form which in fact stopped the duel from occurring, but without a subsequent loss of honor. So, in both Miles Peter Andrews's *The Reparation* of 1784 and John Burgoyne's *The Heiress*, performed two years later, when the central figures meet at the duelling assignation, one of the two drops his weapon and "exposes his breast." In Andrews's play, its hero, Loveless (an ominous name for eighteenth-century theater-goers and readers) had, in his misspent youth, seduced a virtuous but poor young woman by staging a false marriage and then marrying another, richer lady. The father of the abandoned woman, a retired soldier, believing her to be "a wanton," abandoned her to what he thought was her deserved infamy. Finding out years later about the "pretended solemnization of [the] marriage," he challenged Loveless to a duel. Though Loveless was advised by his best friend, Belcour, that such "a meeting would be impossible" for not only would it be comply[ing] with the false idea which that world calls honour" but wicked and unjust "to raise your arm against a man already too much injured," Loveless answered: "Mistake me not—I have no such intention—I have been the aggressor; and 'tis proper, if such is the reparation he wishes, that I shou'd abide its consequence—yes, I will meet him—but without resistance—I shall offer myself a willing victim to his resent-ment." Needless to say, the duel does not occur, everyone is reconciled, and the past forgotten and forgiven. Similarly in *The Heiress*, the play's two heroes, Lord Gayville and Clifford, agree to fight a duel due to a complex misunder-standing; Gayville thinks Clifford, his closest friend, has stolen his true love, Harriet, not knowing that she is Clifford's sister, whom he is merely trying to protect. When they meet at the duelling grounds, Clifford, "[a]fter a struggle with himself" drops his sword and invites Gayville to do his worst: "You said nothing but my life wou'd satisfy you, take it, and remember me." After the inevitable denouement, of course, no blood is shed, and both heroes honor-ably unite with the women they love. In these two plays we can see the combination of anti-duelling rhetoric with a new, sentimental male hero, one who, while not completely abjuring the duel, renounces the murderous and revengeful impulse which was its signature.[91] Duelling on the stage was no longer a laughing matter.

"The approbation of every good man, and every person of real honour":[92] *Taking Duelling to Court*

When, on March 16, 1792, the elderly Earl of Coventry rose in the House of Lords, asking for action against a Mr. Cooksey for a breach of privilege in sending him a challenge to a duel, the *Times*, in the words above, applauded his stance, noting that this response was the correct one and merited popular approval. More than twenty years before, another Member of Parliament, Sir William Meredith, had made a similar request when challenged, and also had his opponent, Miles Burton Allen, committed to Newgate. Unlike the Coventry case however, the earlier appeal received less newspaper coverage.[93] Perhaps little should be made of the similarity and differences in these two cases. Yet by the time of Coventry's appeal, and its wide newspaper coverage, the London press had enormously expanded its reporting not only of cases brought against challenges but also of various types of legal recourse available to men who refused to duel. If historians of the law are correct, if eighteenth-century courts were stages on which the power of the state was performed, then newspapers, in their reporting of these legal challenges to the code of honor, acted as amplifying devices for the dissemination of alterations in the stance of the state toward duelling. When news of such cases was published, readers could see that there were honorable alternatives to the duel, or at least that men of family, lineage, and propriety were willing to use legal means to avoid bloodshed. It is to these uses of the law that we must now turn.

It may have been much more common than the press record suggests for men facing duels to resort to the law.[94] There were two major methods by which this could have been effected; the first, a warrant sworn before a magistrate, which would cause the impending conflict to be broken up, and the antagonists bailed for good behavior, or the second, an action brought before a court, for the offence of sending a challenge. In the first sort of interference, while there were many press reports of duels stopped by magistrates, by Army guards, or by sentinels, no indication was given that these were initiated by either of the duellists. The only examples of such practice, that is, of voluntary resort to the law in the first half of the century which was described by the press, were cases brought against the challengers by reluctant duellists.

According to newspaper accounts, there were just a trickle of such cases before the mid-century; and the only clue given in the papers about the source of magistrates' knowledge of impending duels before 1786 was that "information" had been received.[95]

However, in the years between 1780 and the end of the first decade of the nineteenth century, newspaper stories of men taking challengers to court or going to magistrates increased dramatically; in fact in these thirty years there were at least 164 such reports. Nearly ninety percent told of men who were challenged to a duel and took their opponents to court rather than accepting the meeting. Included in this number were the interesting cases in which the prosecutors claimed that the defendants, by their words and deeds, had attempted to provoke them to either issue or accept a challenge.[96]

Most of these reported cases occurred at the Court of King's Bench, and some received multiple reports at various stages of the proceedings.[97] Furthermore, while there were many press stories which told of duels either stopped or interrupted by the exertions of London's magistrates, most often those who were employed at Bow Street, in at least 18 cases we know that the challenged person brought this to the attention of the magistrate, and himself initiated a charge against his challenger.[98] In addition to these two main sorts of duelling-related reports were a variety of other kinds of stories of interrupted affairs; accounts of duels that were compromised at the last moment by friends or family, by Scottish courts, or by an apology from the offending party.[99] These not uncommon stories meant that newspaper readers could see not only that legal alternatives to the duel existed, but also that people of name and position were employing these avenues, and perhaps that the vaunted inevitability of the duel was fallacious.

This supposition is supported by a letter from a reader, addressed to an aristocrat who, instead of fighting, sued his challenger in court. On February 1, 1800, a story appeared in the press, that Thomas Erskine, acting for Lord George Henry Cavendish, was taking a criminal information against John Bembric for attempting to provoke Cavendish into an armed conflict by insulting him at the Opera, and widely posting him as a "poltroon, a coward and a scoundrel." Less than two weeks later, an anonymous correspondent, who signed his letter "Anti-Duellist," commended Cavendish's action, noting that he:

> can only wish your Lordship to enjoy such thanks as mine, which I am sure must also be the wish of every rational man, who looks with horror at the system of duelling. I trust your Lordship will *ascertain* how far the Law will protect a Gentleman against abuse; and I consider your appeal to the laws as a more effectual means of preventing this detestable alternative of duelling, than all the logic that can be used.[100]

In the past an aristocrat like Cavendish might simply have refused to meet Bembric, a man of lower station, or have caned him in self-protection. The status inequalities, as well as the legal recourse sought by a man of rank, made this case unusual. However, newspaper accounts both of actions of the courts and the activities of the magistrates made it clear that many men of family and wealth were taking the same action against others of their own rank and circle. Members of Parliament, challenged for words spoken or letters sent, now sometimes took their opponents to court rather than fight them; aristocrats sometimes took embattled relations to court, or were themselves taken there by former friends or neighbors.[101]

Even less dignified than these court appearances, however, were the reports of the increased activities of the London magistrates and the peace officers working for them, in breaking up or preventing duels from occurring in "high life." Thus, on June 30, 1795, when Earl Fitzwilliam and Mr. Beresford came to the duelling fields, their seconds could not, though they tried, effect a reconciliation and end the threat of violence. When the magistrate, however, intervened, and as the *Times* reported it, "threatened to take them into custody" unless they gave "their words of honour that nothing further should pass between them . . . to this they at length consented."[102] How gratifying must have been the sense of the middling reader, seeing these great men humbled by the power of the Law. Some aristocrats, like Lord Craven, were actually summoned to the magistrate's office, to explain and apologize for having sent a challenge; others, even grander, like Lord St. Vincent, commander of the Mediterranean fleet, and his second-in-command, Sir John Orde, were arrested on the way to their duel, and had to give hefty recognizances to keep the peace.[103] Members of Parliament also featured in newspaper accounts of challenges or interrupted duels in this period; thus when James Brogden, M.P., challenged a Mr. Brown, a warrant was taken at Bow Street, and like commoner miscreants, Brogden had to be bailed.[104] The appearance of such men both in the magistrates' offices and in the more prestigious courts like King's Bench would have given readers a sense that, at least in some instances, the Great were as liable to prosecution for breaking the peace as the small.

A second impact of this increased coverage was to familiarize the reading public with the hefty fines paid for such law-breaking. Duellists or challengers potentially faced serious fines, though sometimes, if they were willing to be reconciled and go in peace, such fiscal punishment could be waived. Thus, when two members of the Opera corps, Didelot and Onarati, having "agreed to settle some difference in Hyde Park," were apprehended and taken before Justice Addington at Bow Street, he "persuaded [them] to shake hands in good fellowship" and let them leave. When, after being arrested and imprisoned in a roundhouse overnight on a warrant, two prospective duellists, John Newbon, an attorney's clerk, and Thomas Gibbons, a nightman, came before Justice Bond, "they said they were perfectly reconciled, they were reprimanded and discharged."[105] At King's Bench, we also sometimes see such an attempt at mediation. When the Rev. James Beevor took a Major Payne to King's Bench for attempting to provoke him to a duel, Thomas Erskine, Payne's attorney, said he thought he could resolve the dispute between the two men outside the court, and Lord Kenyon, addressing Beevor, commented that "he would leave it to the Prosecutor as a Gentleman, and hoped that Mr. Beever would think, on recollecting what was past, that there was more dignity in overlooking the offence than in punishing it."[106] On the other hand, when such peacemaking either was not attempted, or proved impossible to effect, the financial penalties were significant. Of the twenty-one such cases seen by the magistrates in the period 1795–1815, for which the press reported the sureties demanded, in about one-third of the cases the bail was one to two hundred pounds for each potential duellist (with additional smaller sums payable by third parties), in another third between four and five hundred pounds, and in a final third between one thousand and five thousand pounds. It was even whispered that the violent and combative aristocrat Lord Camelford, after he challenged Captain Vancouver to a duel, was "sworn in a private room at the House of Lords before the Lord Chancellor to keep the peace, under a penalty of *Ten thousand pounds!*"[107] By the first years of the new century, not only were duellists themselves forced to enter into recognizances for future good behavior, but seconds also sometimes had to find such guarantees, ranging, in the cases for which we have evidence, from two hundred to five hundred pounds.[108] The wages of sin were not only being seen to be charged, at least some of the time, but to be sizeable and punitive.

And, though the fines and sureties demanded at King's Bench were, on the whole, less hefty, as part of the court decision the challenger might well face time in gaol, time ranging from three weeks to a year, incarcerated for an event that, in the end, never took place. Furthermore, when two unnamed men decided to duel, after having given the court one thousand pounds each as their recognizance to keep the peace, the *Times* reported that "The Court, however, with its accustomed impartiality and justice, have ordered the recognizance to be sent in to his Majesty's Exchequer, to be estreated, and the sum to be levied by the sale of their effects, or their persons to be imprisoned." This "exemplary punishment," the *Times* commented, "will not only be a means of enforcing a due obedience to the laws, but of checking that rage for duelling, which has too long reflected a stigma on the civilization of mankind."[109]

Newspaper readers could not only witness upper-class malefactors appearing in the press, along with "common" criminals, and observe them punished by having to serve prison time or pay large sureties, but could read, often at great length, the views of some of England's greatest judges about the heinousness of duelling, delivered at their trials, and made widely available through press coverage. The comments of the judges in these cases were, on the whole, more often published, and at far greater length, than in most other sorts of King's Bench cases. In almost one-third of these cases, we have a published statement of principle by the judge; in one case this ran to more than 2,000 words, or more than one-quarter of all the news published that day.[110] And the press recognized that a significant portion of the court's work was dealing with provocations to duel or challenges sent. By 1794, under the general title "Law Reports" the *Times* on occasion had a subcategory simply labeled "Challenges."[111]

We can get some notion of the flavor of these long judicial decisions by considering four such trials that occurred between the beginning of February 1798 and the end of that month one year later. The first was a case which the *Times* itself tagged as "highly worthy of the attention of all men of rank and fashion." In his summary, Kenyon, a well-known enemy to duelling, noted that "the Laws of Honour have been alluded to" in the course of the proceedings, but that he knew "of no law which ought to bind the honour of people, except prompt obedience to the Law of the Country in which they live," and he went on to argue that "in this particular case it is become absolutely necessary that this Court should not acquiesce in those supposed Laws of Honour." He then laid down rules which he felt must govern all judges in like circumstances: "A Judge, who should fritter away the law in such a case, would but ill deserve to continue on the seat of Justice . . . they fail in their duty, when cases of this kind come before them, and they decide according to the notions of honour, in opposition to the Law of the Land."[112] Kenyon also officiated at the second case, a trial in which the bearer of the challenge, an attorney, rather than the challenger himself, was the defendant. Characterized as "the officious minister of mischief" by the prosecutor's lawyer, the defendant was admonished by Kenyon to apologize. "The Defendant," he noted, "who was of the Profession of the Law, should not have been induced to do what he had done. His Lordship supposed he was a man of liberal education, and, on reflecting on his conduct for a moment, he must feel he was in the wrong; and if so, it was no degradation of him to ask pardon."[113] The third defendant, a clergyman who had libeled the prosecutor, "one of the commanding Officers of the light troop of Yeomanry Cavalry for the Country of Somerset" in his attempt to incite the officer to fight a duel with him, was chastised by Justice Grose. After castigating the challenger-libeler for acting in a most unchristian and particularly un-clerical fashion, Grose commented, "By your example, I trust every man will see, whether he be of your profession or in any other situation of life, that the laws of the land are not to be infringed with impunity; and the higher the station of the offender is, the greater ought to be his punishment."[114] Kenyon was once again the acting judge in the last case under consideration, a case in which the prosecutor's lawyer, Thomas Erskine, described the goal of Kenyon's legal career, "to make the justice that was administered in that Court an improvement on the morals of the public, and beneficial to the public comfort and tranquillity." Erskine was not wrong in this characterization; speaking of himself in an earlier challenge case, Kenyon described his function to be "a Minister of Law and Morality." This case was one in which the defendant had severely assaulted and battered the prosecutor in an attempt to provoke him to a duel. After giving a very long discourse on the history of duelling in the ancient world and on the barbarity and gross irreligion of the practice in the modern world, Kenyon bemoaned the fact that the defendant "had harboured in his mind too long the thought of duelling. . . . A man must never lay down upon his pillow with such a thought. The Law of England did not grant so much indulgence." His conclusion was significant; this case, he commented "is of importance to the public. . . . It is addressed to the minds of gentlemen of the higher orders of society and you, as gentlemen and as jurymen, will give such damages as you shall think fit." Unsurprisingly, the jury found for the defendant, awarding him a handsome sum.[115]

Together these three elements in reports of duels ended or challenges brought to the court may well have created a sense of possibility, that duelling was not the only or even the most desirable recourse for the insulted or injured gentleman. As important, perhaps, as this general sense that such reports gave the reading public of available alternatives to the duel, was the large number of military men who, as either challengers or prosecutors, figured in both the magistrates' and court reports. In approximately two-fifths of all the reports we have been looking at, of duels interrupted or challenges brought to court, at least one of the major actors was described by a military title. Not surprisingly, perhaps, most but not all of these military men were the challengers. Here too the reported comments of the judges were important in creating new attitudes even to these most vulnerable victims of the challenge. Erskine, involved in both defending and prosecuting military men for challenging or attempting to provoke, often used the service record of the defendant as exculpatory; for example, when speaking of a naval defendant whom he was representing, Erskine exclaimed, "I am quite overpowered and disabled by my own sensation, when I reflect that the honour and safety of a brave and glorious British seaman is committed to my care and protection." When appearing for the prosecution, however, Erskine argued that military men were in this respect under the auspices of civil law; he said he "could not compromise that offense at all by any judgment that could be given by military men, because he [the defendant] had offended against the law of the land, which all military men were bound to see observed."[116] The judges, in these cases, were generally, though not always, given to a strict construction and application of the law to military men, whether they were defendant-challengers or prosecuting-challenged. In a case where a clergyman had attempted to provoke a soldier to a duel, the judge, addressing the minister, noted that his

> behaviour to the Prosecutor has been atrocious, and much aggravated by his situation. That situation as to the Public, has been exceedingly meritorious, in protecting and really serving the country in the moment of rebellion and war; and his particular conduct now before the Court, is a proof that that merit is increased. Some men in his situation would have erroneously imagined, that to have recourse to the laws for protection, would betray pusillanimity and cowardice. But such men should learn, that true courage consists in daring to be void of offence; in daring to obey the law of the land, and spurning at those notions of honour, as they are falsely called . . . .[117]

In another case, the judge commended the prosecutor, an army general, for bringing the suit, which, the *Times* noted, "was of great importance to the public, and particularly to the army." By refusing the challenge, General Coote had "bid defiance to those laws of BARBARISM which some men forgetful of morals and their obligations to society have deemed laws of honour." To a military challenger in a third case, the judge remarked that "it was the duty of military men not only to fight the battles of their country, but to abstain from wanton and unnecessary violence and insolence to individuals."[118]

However, before we leave the courts and the judges we must acknowledge that even they thought that military men deserved special respect and treatment, and that the lack of such consideration could mitigate, if not excuse, challenges to the duel. Thus, for example, when the Mayor of Tiverton, in having to find billeting for a corps of military men, attempted to put officers and soldiers in one room, and in response to a complaint that these were inappropriate facilities for gentlemen, the Mayor responded that "he was not talking of room for a gentleman, but for an officer," Kenyon discharged the rule, indignantly commenting that "the putting of the officers and men together in the same room was not to be endured" and that the Mayor "was bound to call the officers gentlemen." Similarly in another case also involving Erskine for the defence, Kenyon refused to overlook both the military and status distinctions of the challenger. On the grounds that the prosecutor had given "very strong provocation" before the challenge had been sent, combined with the unacknowledged effect that Erskine's characterization of the defendant as one of "the heroes of the British Navy" had had on the judges, Kenyon declared that he was "glad that the evidence of the transaction enables us to pronounce a nominal Judgment upon so meritorious an officer."[119] Everyone, even judges of the high court, it seems, loved a military man.

"To maintain my character and station, I must be respected":[120] *Duelling During the Napoleonic Wars*

As we have seen, at the beginning of the eighteenth century, any man who, by reason of birth, wealth, and education, was acknowledged by his contemporaries to be a gentleman, was both the possible subject and object of the code of duelling. If he was insulted by another such as he, he could demand that satisfaction to which he had a right, i.e., to face his antagonist in a duel; if he was the offender, the injured party also had the right to demand a duel, a duty which he was equally obliged to fulfil. While, in theory, this duty and privilege continued to hold through the eighteenth and a good bit of the nineteenth century for all who were recognized to be gentle, in practice the field in which a man might feel constrained either to challenge an opponent or himself accept a challenge became narrower, or at least less clear and binding. Perhaps as "new men" themselves began duelling, began to adopt what Lord Justice Ellenborough dismissively characterized as the "spurious chivalry of the compting house and the counter,"[121] the cachet of the duel faded somewhat. Or perhaps it was only in those two occupations in which one's personal character, one's honesty and courage, were thought essential to its proper fulfilment, i.e., in political and military life, that the force of the *code duello* was slowest to wane.

We have already noted the rash of political duels of the late 1760s and 1770s, and considered the extraordinary reaction to Pitt's duel while Prime Minister in 1798. While politically motivated duelling was not nearly as rampant during the wars as it had been in previous decades, it still occurred every now and then. We know of at least three such duels that occurred in

the 1790s: one between the Earl of Lauderdale and the renegade
Benedict Arnold for words spoken in Parliament, the second in which the
Duke of Norfolk challenged Lord Malden for what he took to be derogatory
language in a letter that Malden had sent to the electors of Leominster, and
the third between two Irish politicians in "consequence of a dispute which
occurred on the late election for the County of Donegal.[122] However, we know
of at least two instances in these same years when Members of Parliament,
challenged for political statements or views, either refused to duel or talked
their way out of a meeting. Thus, in 1792, an MP refused a challenge to duel
with someone upset at his comments about Ireland; just three months later,
it looked very much as though the Duke of Richmond and the Earl of
Lauderdale would meet because of words uttered by the two during debate
in the Lords. However, when Lauderdale explained that "the expressions used
by him, applied solely to the Duke of Richmond's public conduct, and that
he meant nothing in any respect personal to his Grace's private character,"
the Duke graciously replied that "he did not persist in the term he used to
Lord Lauderdale, those expressions having been suggested solely by the idea
of his private character having been attacked"[123] and they both went away
with honor intact.

In the first fifteen years of the new century, I have come across only two
major political duels. The first, in June 1800, received only brief press coverage,
and was between the Earl of Ormond and the brother of the Marquis of
Drogheda, Sir Robert Moore; "The duel originated in a dispute relative to the
Union." The second, much more widely reported, was the duel between George
Canning and Lord Castlereagh, which took place in September 1809. Both
men were cabinet ministers, and the duel arose from a challenge Castlereagh
sent to Canning, because he thought that Canning had been plotting to have
him expelled from his position. The two men met, two sets of shots were fired,
and after the second, Canning was wounded in the thigh, and the duel
concluded. What is remarkable about the coverage of this incident is
while the press gave a great deal of space to reflections on the political propri-
eties and consequences of such a conflict, virtually no attention was
paid to the duel itself, to the fact that duelling was illegal. I have been able to
find only one press notice, in the *Morning Advertiser*, that made any sort of
disparaging comment on the spectacle, but one that deserves to be quoted
in full:

> The practice of Duelling requires some direct and legal check. The example
> of Cabinet Councillors is dangerous in the extreme—it leads to corrupt public
> opinion, and even, by a very natural and intelligible influence, to soften down

the interpretation of the Law, as it actually stands.—With what reluctance must a Judge declare Duelling murder—and a Minister recommend the execution of the consequent sentence in Council, when the Minister himself is a Duellist.[124]

In comparison with political duels, however, military duels during the Wars received much attention. Perhaps this is because they appeared so much more frequently in the press. In a rather rough-and-ready count made of duels which appeared in the London newspapers between 1793 and 1806, in 63 of these reports both participants were in the military services, in 45 at least one of the duellists was a military or naval officer, and 42 incidents were between civilians. Thus, the great majority (72 percent) of the cases found involved at least one such officer.[125]

One of the recurring features of all the reports was the rather petty motives for which they were fought. The most famous military duel of this period, which we will look at shortly, occurred because the Newfoundland dog of one of the antagonists snarled at the other. Another meeting, between a young lieutenant and a military surgeon's mate, in which the former died on the spot, arose from a quarrel at the billiard table. A third, between an aristocratic naval Captain and another member of Society, was fought because the Captain addressed the other, a Mr. Powell, by an inappropriately familiar nickname. The last instance, between two young officers described as the "most intimate friends," which resulted in the death of one, arose from a quarrel "concerning a female with whom both were intimate."[126]

But more worrying perhaps, in a time of all-out war, were the duels and challenges that seemed to have stemmed from failures of military discipline. One early example of this was the infamous duel between Lt. Col. Roper and the man whose court-martial he had ordered, and whom he had cashiered, Ensign Thomas Purefoy, for challenging him to a duel. Though the initial incident occurred in St. Vincent's in 1787, Purefoy pursued Roper to England, and posted him as a coward. He finally persuaded Roper to fight; the two met in December of 1788, and Roper was killed. Purefoy fled the country, only to return in 1793, to stand trial. William Garrow, the prosecuting attorney, after noting that even if Purefoy were found guilty, he would never be executed, informed the jury that "it was also material to consider, that the conduct of the unfortunate gentleman at the bar was such, as if not legally punished, precluded all idea of due discipline and subordination in the army." Though the judge and the jury overruled Garrow's concern (the judge, Baron Hotham, instructed the jury that an acquittal "may trench on the rigid rules of law, yet the verdict will be lovely in the sight of God and man"), the same anxiety surfaced in several of the challenges we have already considered. For Purefoy's case, challenge and dismissal were not unheard of; the armed forces took a very dim view of subordinates challenging their superiors to duels for any reason.[127] When one disgruntled Major, angered by the required testimony of his superior officer at his court-martial, challenged his commander to a duel, the King himself intervened, and ordered his Adjutant-General to send a letter praising the conduct of the senior officer in bringing the case to court. This letter, which Erskine, the prosecuting attorney, read, noted that "his Majesty had seen this matter in so serious a light towards the Army" that his commendation was to be sent to and read aloud in every military camp in the country. Direct monarchical involvement and publicity in such affairs was surely very unusual, and gave newspaper readers some sense of what their ruler thought about military duelling.[128]

Even before the war's end, contemporaries had already noted the changes that had occurred among this group, who remained, perhaps longer than any other, susceptible to the pressures of "honor" and the requisites of the duel. How could good citizens risk their lives on such foolishness, asked Rowland Ingram in 1804; "Call him not a Briton, who, in this time of unparalleled emergency, would relinquish his post—the post of efficient duty and real fortitude—to exhibit such a pitiful display of brute hardihood. . . ." In response to Erskine's hyperbolic whitewashing of a military-client challenger, Samuel Romilly, speaking for the prosecution, claimed that "there is more courage in resisting the custom of duelling, in such a situation, than in marching up to the mouth of a cannon, or exposing the individual to the utmost degree of personal danger." And, in a prize-winning Oxford essay, John Taylor Allen argued that modern military strategy made individual courage inessential: "The fortune of the field does not now depend on exertions of individual prowess, or the valour and hardihood of an individual chieftain; it is from the concentrated efforts of a well-disciplined army; from the bravery and firmness of united battalions, that the fate of battles and of empires must now be decided."[129]

While duelling did not end during the Napoleonic conflict, or with the war's end, despite such optimists as the Rev. William Butler Odell ("The officers of the army do not often fight duels"[130]), much had changed, in a piecemeal and unplanned fashion, over the previous hundred years. Duels were now no longer private, but public affairs, thanks to the ubiquity of the newspaper press, and the appetite of its readers for reports of these sorts of affairs. Duelling, from being the obligation and privilege of every gentleman, had increasingly been recognized as appropriate only for public men, whose professions depended on their veracity and courage, i.e., political and military figures. And, by the end of the Napoleonic wars, again thanks to the publicity afforded by press coverage, more and more of even such men were using the Law, the magistracy, and the courts, as alternative venues to the fighting field. Duelling had not ended, but its imperative, its power, had waned and could be, though it not always was, resisted.[131]

"Bankhead, let me fall upon your arm. 'Tis all over." Frontispiece of *The Strange Death of Lord Castlereagh*, from a drawing, George Cruikshank, by H. Montgomery Hyde (London: Heinemann, 1959)

3

Against "Nature, Religion and Good Manners":
Debating Suicide

Amongst all the crimes that were ever produced in the world, never any yet was born equal to the horrid one of suicide; and nothing can be so shocking a prospect to men of a common sensibility, as the alarming progress and havock it has made, and is still making.[1]

This condemnation of suicide as the worst of crimes may perhaps be surprising to the modern ear.[2] Yet many in the seventeenth and eighteenth centuries would have quickly and completely agreed with it. How could perfectly intelligent and thoughtful people, in a world filled then (as now) with horrific cruelties and unspeakable deeds, consider suicide to be in the first rank of offences? A central reason was surely the widespread belief that the first law of Nature, "the first Lesson taught in Nature's schools," was the law of self-preservation. Poets and playwrights, philosophers, clerics, and moralists of all persuasions agreed on this, though they could agree on little else. The "Fundamental, Sacred, and unalterable Law of *Self-Preservation*" was the foundation of John Locke's political thought.[3] The anonymous author of *Populousness with Economy* of 1757 declared that "Self preservation is the voice of reason and first law of nature." The playwright David Mallet presented it as an obvious truth: "Self-preservation is heaven's eldest law,/ Imprest upon our nature with our life," and the popular cleric John Herries,

83

in an *Address to the Public* in 1781, proclaimed that suicide was "contrary to the strongest law of nature, SELF-PRESERVATION." The strength of this primal urge was so thoroughly accepted that, by the late eighteenth century, a long-running advertisement for a popular skin cream had as its opening headline, "Self preservation the first Law of Nature."[4]

Given the widespread belief in the force of this drive, how was it possible for people either to kill themselves or to fight duels? For, in many ways, as we shall see, the campaigns to understand the reasons for and to end the practice of self-murder were strikingly similar to those employed by the critics of duelling. From the late seventeenth century, it was common for opponents of suicide to see it as the other face of duelling, or duelling "as a kind of Self-Murder." Both duellists and suicides, claimed John Jeffery in a sermon of 1702, by their practices, attempt to revive "the obsolete knight errantry of barbarous antiquity in our enlightened days." The conjunction of these vices furnished the title of a tract of the late 1720s, *Self-Murther and Duelling the Effects of Cowardice and Atheism*. In it, its author claimed that these activities were sacrifices "to some of the meanest Vices and Passions that belong to Human Nature, viz., the Rage of Resentment, a cloudy Discontent, and a profane Tempting and Distrusting of Providence."[5] In addition, both duellists and well-born suicides seemed to avoid the penalties of the law, and, as MacDonald and Murphy point out, "suicide could serve the same function as the duel among men of honour."[6] Therefore most thought that only through a total abrogation of the normal human equilibrium, brought about by insanity in some cases, by decadent indulgence in the case of the suicide, or by a willful giving-in to the basest and least human passions, in duelling, could this imperative be overcome. This often unspoken, but underlying belief in the centrality of self-preservation would give shape to much of the discussions and debates of the eighteenth century about these two related vices.

Having considered why so much attention was given to this act, this chapter will examine the sorts of evidence that we have of what people thought about suicide during the long eighteenth century. This will begin with a survey of the notions and representations of suicide during the reign of the first two Georges, before considering the extent, nature, and impact of press accounts of such events. We will attempt to canvas the many popular opinions expressed in the press about the motives for suicide. Finally we will look at two important bodies of writing that dealt with such acts—the body of medical thought on the relation of suicide, insanity, and medical competence, and an equally important mass of legal views of suicide, of its legal ramifications and general consequences for the polity. Following a consideration of proposed changes in punishments for suicide at the century's end, we will conclude with a case study, the press responses to the suicides of some prominent early nineteenth-century men, and with changes in the law governing suicide.

"We are not Masters of Ourselves":[7] *Arguments about Suicide in England to* 1760

2nd clown: "Will you ha'the truth on't—if this had not been a gentlewoman, she should have been buried out o' christian burial."

1st clown: "Why, there thou say'st: and the more pity, that great folk should have countenance in this world to drown or hang themselves more than their even Christians."[8]

When a person was found to have died in surprising or mysterious circumstances, a coroner's jury was supposed to be called to decide on the cause of death. Though there were several possible inquest verdicts on the death of someone found dead unnaturally, ranging from accident to visitation of God, the two most common at the beginning of the eighteenth century were *felo de se* or conscious and willful self-murder, self-murder in cold blood we might say, and lunacy, *non compos mentis*, an unintended act which occurred when the person was deranged, with blood and brains boiling. If one were adjudged *felo de se* one could not obtain Christian burial, and, depending on the circumstances, the burial might be degrading and shameful to friends and relations. Also, as in other cases judged felonious, the possibility remained that the estate of the deceased might be forfeit to the Crown. Yet, throughout the late seventeenth and eighteenth centuries, most suicides (and all such deaths of "great folk") were declared lunatic, and given Christian burial. As with the vice of duelling, to which suicide was often compared and conjoined, eighteenth-century juries not only refused to impose the full weight of the law against these, but seemed, by never finding them criminally culpable, to exculpate the self-destruction of the Great.

Nevertheless, through this period, a prolific and overwhelmingly negative outpouring of printed materials condemned the practice on a number of grounds. The excoriation of the act of self-murder rested on three "planks" which resembled, not surprisingly, the criticisms of duelling. The first, and most obvious perhaps, was that by killing oneself one brought woe and disgrace upon one's family, one's aged parents and innocent children. Even if one were alone and entirely solitary, many reasons still remained for not committing this final outrage. For, in several ways, suicide was seen as weakening the polity in which one lived, in depleting the cohesiveness and attacking the principles on which it rested. Suicide, it was said, was "contagious," and if unpunished, would lead to copycat acts. Only the fear of a frightful punishment could deter others from following such fatal example. When a juror refused to find the proper harsh verdict in a case of self-murder, he had not only committed perjury, but "the doing what in him lies toward the incouraging *Self-Murder* in Others also." Only by punishing such acts with "a Mark of Infamy" was it possible to "deter others from the like inhuman and detestable Practices."⁹ Second, suicide weakened the bonds of civil society by denying the very grounds of, and reasons for, its existence, i.e., the preservation of life. Therefore, according to the popular pulpit-thumper "Orator" Henley:

> for if we may murder ourselves, we may soon be induc'd to think that of others is not unlawful; it defeats the Force of human Laws; for where is legal Punishment, if Self-Murder be warrantable? it opposes the Reasons for which the Murder of others is forbidden, as the having no Authority, depriving the State of a Subject, the Impossibility of making an equivalent Satisfaction.

If each was left to "judge his cause and redress his fancied wrongs," argued a Norwich clergyman, "anarchy the consequence would be." The danger that unpunished suicide posed to civil society was so great and so widely felt, that even a letter in the *London Journal* which argued against the common notion that self-murder was an act of cowardice still agreed that it was "highly suitable, and in political Societies, absolutely necessary, to oppose and discourage all we can"¹⁰ this fearsome practice.

However, the strongest and most enduring criticism of the practice throughout the period was based, not surprisingly, on religious grounds. Now, it should be pointed out that no one condemned those who, plagued by obdurate insanity, killed themselves under their afflictions. While these sorts of death were regrettable and cause for sorrow, they were part of the ills the flesh was heir to, and thus not culpable. Neither were such deaths thought to constitute the greatest part of all self-murders. Only people "who rid themselves of their Being, as a perfectly reasonable Action . . . and as simply preferring, in their Circumstances, Death to Life" were considered to be particularly heinous, particularly dangerous and sinful. Thus a late seventeenth-century writer thought the prevalence of suicide was "a great Proof of the Degeneracy of the Age," especially since "there are so many *Christians* who do such Violence to themselves." Zachary Pearce, Bishop of Rochester, in a sermon against suicide, took as his text the injunction "that it is our Duty *to receive Evil as well as Good, at the hand of God*."¹¹ Many religious writers argued that people's lives were not their property, to dispose of as they liked. Either men and women were to consider themselves as "so many hir'd Servants, set on Work by our Great Master Above, who hath set out our labour to us . . . ."

or, even more strongly, that only God was the absolute proprietor of men's lives, and therefore a man has "a Right of Use over it, not of Propriety; a Power to employ it to that End for which he receiv'd it, and may therefore hazard, but not himself destroy it."[12] God's property in human lives and destinies could not, in this view, ever be superseded or set aside. To protect his property, God implanted in all peoples what we have already seen described as "the first law of Nature," i.e., the desire for self-preservation. Thus, willful self-murder was seen to be not only ungodly but unnatural.

If suicide was such an atrocious act, how could some men and women bring themselves to commit it? In addition to the moral contagion we have already considered, a number of other reasons were adduced to explain how this could happen. Despite MacDonald and Murphy's view that, in an increasingly secular age, suicide (like duelling) was explained by natural, physical causes rather than by supernatural temptations, many contemporaries still argued that the Devil and his minions were active in seductions to suicide.[13] There were, of course, some few in the first six decades of the eighteenth century who thought that the act of suicide always arose from illness; a correspondent to the *London Magazine* noted, in his "Reflections on Suicide" that, like many other illnesses, the melancholy leading to suicide was due not to demonic possession, but to physical disorder; "many diseases, which were formerly ascribed to super-natural causes, and regarded with a superstitious reverence, are now found to submit to the powers of medicine." The weight of opinion, however, seemed otherwise, the anonymous author of the *Occasional Paper*, for example, arguing that if the suicide "was at that Instant beside himself," this did not "take away the Guilt of it. . . . For he ought to have been otherwise, and to have restrain'd his Passions in time, e're they brought him into that Fury."[14]

Most writers on suicide held that the act had always been most common "precisely in those periods, and in those communities in which impiety and profligacy were most prevalent." Modern, like ancient suicides, were due to "Impotence of Mind and Dissoluteness of Manners, together with a general Ignorance or Disregard of the Law of Nature."[15] But the relation between irreligion and self-murder was complex, and a variety of connections were discussed. Most dismissed the influence of English weather on suicide rates, but some thought that an English love of freedom and equality were indeed to blame. A much-copied essay, for example, explaining why "the English are more liable to this Crime than other People," attributed it to the fact that all ranks of English men and women, believing themselves "equal and free," could not cheerfully bear either subservience or the reversals of fortune. Others thought that the moderns, misled by an exaltation of Roman suicide, were fooled into the practice. The devil, claimed the author of the *Occasional*

Poems, "will stir up some subtile Instrument/That Crime of *Suicide* to represent/As if it were a *Roman*, Manly Fact/A daring, brave, and a courageous Act." And especially after the success of Addison's play *Cato*, with its sympathetic portrayal of heroic self-sacrifice and self-destruction, most opponents of suicide argued against this example. Even a decade after its first performance, this play was thought to have had a powerful, negative influence.

> Those Authors who have wrote either directly or indirectly in favour of *Self-Murther*, have (as 'tis to be feared) contributed not a little to the Frequency of this horrid Fact. Among the latter I am sorry that I'm obliged to place the ingenious Author of the celebrated Play call'd *Cato* . . . .[16]

And, regardless of the play, when the facts of Cato's life were considered, observed the editor of the *Universal Spectator*, it would be seen that he "acted on false Principles, deceiv'd himself with a mistaken Notion of Honour, and that which is celebrated for an *Heroic Virtue*, was nothing but the Effects of *Fear* and a *sullen Pride*."[17] But most laid the blame squarely on two interrelated moral flaws or sins, on overweening pride and an overreliance on the power and veracity of human reason.

"Pride," said Thomas Knaggs, "is the predominant Vice that Reigns among us, and it is so radicated by Time and Custom, that I am afraid, it lies too deep in the Hearts of many to be easily swept away." And, in 1756, in an article in the *Gentleman's Magazine* (a magazine which MacDonald and Murphy characterize as polite society's *arbiter elegantiae*) entitled "Pride the chief Inducement to Suicide," the same theme was spelled out at length.[18] Thus, through the first half of the eighteenth century, this sinful pride was often connected with the fallacious notion that a man could properly conduct his life by the light of his reason alone. "O Reason," apostrophized one correspondent, "false, delusive, specious Name! What art thou, but Ignorance, Pride, Fancy, Whim and Chance." The failure of ancient Stoicism, argued John Jeffery, proved the weakness of unaided human reason against the pressures and passions of life; by itself reason could not deter the commission of suicide, and thus needed legislative assistance "to press the duty a feared conscience will not see." One writer went so far as to suggest that this overvalued reason was, "amongst the learned and thinking part of mankind," the chief inducement to suicide: "It is the groundless conception, that man, by his natural powers, is able to sustain himself in the most trying circumstances, and even to work out his own salvation, that is the cause of vast misery to human creatures."[19]

In an age when deistic writings were not uncommon, but were much feared for their corrosive impact on what were perceived to be virtues supported by religious sanctions and faith, the obvious ensemble of relationships among intellect, pride, irreligion, and suicide were often drawn. Two cases especially provided instances or examples of such connections. The first, and one of the most widely written-about suicides of the entire eighteenth century, was the disturbing deaths of Richard and Bridget Smith, who killed themselves after dispatching their sleeping infant. Richard Smith was a bookbinder by trade and clearly a literate, philosophically engaged person. He was confined with his family in King's Bench debtor's prison. Neither the fact of the incarceration, nor even of the self-murders could have been so unusual as to merit the judgment of the *Gentleman's Magazine*, that their deaths were "the most melancholy Affair . . . heard of for many Years." In fact, what made this such a cause célèbre were the letters that the Smiths left behind, both as practical requests and a sort of testament to the loftiness of their minds. Even today, reading these, one can sense both their enormous pain in the life they were leaving and their proud resolution in the face of adversity. Proclaiming a belief in a wise and good first-mover, they noted, however, that "this Belief of ours is not an Implicit Faith, but deduced from the Nature and Reason of Things" and because it was their opinion that since such a benevolent being could not possibly "Delight in the Misery of his Creatures" they felt justified in killing themselves "without any Terrible Apprehensions." Not surprisingly, "the Coroner's Jury found them both guilty of Self-Murder . . . and they were both buried in the Cross-Way near Newington Turnpike."[20] Many years later Voltaire referred to this case in his *Philosophic Dictionary*, as did Richard Hey, more than half a century later, in his *Dissertation on Suicide*. It was this case, and the suicide of Eustace Budgell in 1737, that were probably responsible for the outpouring of articles in the journals and newspapers of the decade on this topic.[21]

In her book on Victorian suicide, Barbara Gates has called the Budgell affair "one of the most notorious suicides of the eighteenth century." Budgell, a cousin of Addison's, and a contributor to the *Spectator*, took his life in 1737. The causes for his suicide are unclear; all we know is that he left a note on his desk that read "What Cato did/And Addison approved/Cannot be wrong," and drowned himself. He was widely held to have been a free-thinker, and his death was described as of the same sort as those of earlier deists, Charles Blount and Thomas Creech. His sad end was referred to not only a few months after his death in the journals of the day, but by the great Cham himself, Samuel Johnson. When Johnson discussed suicide with Goldsmith and Boswell, he noted that once a man had resolved to kill himself, there was nothing to stop him from doing *any* harm or evil. Thus, he argued, when "Eustace Budgel was walking down to the Thames, determined to drown himself, he might, if he pleased, without any apprehension of danger, have turned aside and first set fire to St. James's Palace."[22]

Suicide in the Press

The phenomenal growth of the periodical press and the continuing spread of literacy after 1700 transformed the hermeneutics of suicide, just as they affected almost every other aspect of social and cultural life. . . . [The press] also carried news of suicides to a vast audience of readers and enabled them to form their own judgments about them.[23]

These two dramatic cases, however, were quite unlike the run-of-the-mill press reports of self-inflicted deaths through the first six decades of the eighteenth century. When we get such accounts, they tend to be both very brief and cryptic, neither condemnatory nor exculpatory, usually emotionless statements of fact.[24] Two such reports, both coming from *Fog's Weekly Journal*, are good illustrations of the brevity and flatness of tone so common in the press notices of this period. The first and longer of the two, is an account of the death of

Hugh Hunter, who keeps the Crown Inn or Livery Stables, in Coleman Street for many Years, being reduc'd in his Circumstances, it caused such disorder in his senses that he hanged himself last Thursday se-'nnight in the morning at his Bed's Feet. The Coroner's Jury sate upon his body and brought him in a Lunatick.

The second story was of "one Clarke, a broker in Shoe lane, [who] upon some Discontent, shot himself in the Belly and dy'd soon after. There was a Woman in the Room when he did it." Sometimes the press gave a reason for the act, such as the belief that Woolaston Shelton, "the youngest cashier of the Bank," had killed himself because of "some concerns he had with Messrs. Woodwards, the Bankers." Most, however, were explained merely with the phrase "some Discontent of Mind."[25] And, as far as I have been able to find, no newspapers reported the *felo de se* of anyone of "family" (with one exception, which we will discuss in chapter 5); such deaths were, and continued for a long while to be, glossed over and misrepresented. Thus, for example, when the Duke of Bolton killed himself in 1765, the *London Evening Post* merely reported that "Yesterday . . . after a short illness, his Grace, the Duke of Bolton" died at his house. Only in Horace Walpole's letters do we get the real story. In a letter to his friend Mann, Walpole remarked, "The Duke of Bolton t'other morning, nobody knows why or wherefore, except that there is a good deal of madness in the blood, sat himself down upon the floor in his dressing room, and shot himself through the head." Walpole then went on, "What is more remarkable is, that it is the same house and the same chamber in which Lord Scarborough performed the same exploit." According to Walpole, Richard Lumley, Earl Scarborough had also shot himself in 1740: however, the press at the time merely noted that he had "died suddenly . . . of an apoplexy." Walpole commented that "*Suddenly*, in this country, is always at first construed to mean, *by a pistol*."[26] However, by the 1760s, though the Great were still being shielded in this way, press reporting of ordinary suicides, as of duels, was becoming more frequent and fuller.

One of the lengthiest and most curious of all these articles was the lead story in the *Gentleman's Magazine* of September 1760, entitled "Some Account of Francis David Stirn." This story, which ran six full pages, told of the life and death of a talented young German, who, coming to England around 1758 in pursuit of employment, ran into a variety of difficulties, largely because of "his jealous and ungovernable temper." Conceiving a deadly hatred for his last employer, a Mr. Matthews, he first challenged him to a duel, and then when Matthews refused to fight, shot him point blank. Stirn was tried and found guilty of murder, but defeated the hangman by taking poison and killing himself. This tale was told with a great deal of circumstantial detail, and with considerable sympathy for Stirn's situation as a very bright and able man forced to swallow his pride and accept (at least in his own mind) insult and rejection from his employer. It ended, however, with a moral and a warning to those like Stirn, "whose keen sensibility, and violence of temper" might lead them to murder and suicide: "If, by this mournful example, some of these shall be warned gradually to weaken their vehemence of temper by restraint . . . neither *Stirn*" nor his employer "will have died in vain." Here is a fine example of the contrarieties of eighteenth-century thinking about suicide—sympathy for the man, but not the deed, and a firm belief that passion and temper could be brought under control by the force of habit and God's mercy.[27]

With few exceptions, the newspaper accounts of suicides of this period did not give the victims' names, even if they were not of the *ton*. And, although this is more a "hunch" than a fact, it certainly seems as though, through the 1760s, those suicides that had some interesting personal appeal or some eccentricity had a better chance of being featured in the press. In 1765 alone we have six reports of suicides, of which five had some unusual feature or human-interest element. One of these, the death of a gentleman who had previously served as high sheriff of "a certain county," was unusual because he was reported to have been found *felo de se*; the second concerned a gentleman who killed himself on the eve before his marriage "to a very amiable young lady of 10,000l. fortune"; the third was about "a young lady, elegantly dressed, [who] threw herself from a boat into the *Thames*" because of a step-mother's cruelty; the fourth described a woman harshly treated by her husband who, after passing a sociable evening at cards with a party of friends, "shot herself thro' the head," and the last, a Scot fleeing his creditors was caught by them on a boat to France, and threw himself (and the ship's master) over-board.[28] These stories exhibit neither horror nor bereavement, they were neither moralistic nor sympathetic, but, like stories about two-headed calves and other natural oddities, seemed to cater to a widespread appetite for unusual or curious happenings.

In contrast to the rather bland tone of the reporting of actual suicides were the poems about suicide that various contributors sent to the newspapers and magazines. All the instances of these I have found employ poetic techniques designed to raise horror and to instill a proper repugnance for the foul deed. Thus "Belinda," writing to the *Morning Chronicle*, noted that since that paper "made room a few days since for some lines said to be written by a gentleman who put a period to his own existence," she sends along what she describes as "an antidote to the poison" of those lines, an excerpt from Edward Young's *Night Thoughts*. In his poem Young portrayed suicides as "selling their rich reversion . . . to the Prince who sways this nether world" and when they grow sick of their condition, "with wild Demoniac rage" they kill themselves. Young argued that "the deed is madness; but the madness of the heart." Another letter, signed "B," sent to the *Westminster Magazine*, quoted both Pope and Blair to illustrate the iniquity of self-murder; for those who kill themselves, Blair prophesied that "Unheard of tortures/Must be reserved for such." Finally, the *Gentleman's Magazine*, in its review of the poems of Thomas Warton, published his "The Suicide," as that piece, which once read, will make the reader wish for more. The poem begins with an invocation of the life and self-murder of a failed poet, and his lonely untended grave on the moors. Then, lest the message be lost in the sympathetic tearfulness of it all, an angelic voice breaks into the poet's reverie, warning him to "Forbear, fond bard, thy partial praise;/Nor thus for guilt in specious lays/ The wreath of glory twine." In these popular poems, the reader was invited to sympathize perhaps, but quickly to step back, to bewail the doer, but not the deed, to understand that the madness of the heart was culpable and demonic. Though MacDonald and Murphy agree that "none of these poets condoned suicide," they nevertheless hold that their "sentimentalization of death inspired pity for self-slayers and eroded the revulsion that suicide had formerly inspired." I can find little evidence to support their contention.[29]

Through the 1770s and 1780s (and, in some cases beyond) when well-known or powerful people killed themselves, not only were their deaths often presented as due to natural causes, but perhaps because of medical complicity, their bodies often seem not to have come under the notice of the coroners' juries. Two of the most famous of such instances were the deaths of Charles Yorke, Chancellor of England, and of Robert Clive, the great Nabob of India. When, just a few days after accepting the Chancellorship, Yorke killed himself, the first reports in the press merely noted that on Saturday the 20th, at five in the afternoon, the Right Honourable Charles Yorke, Lord High Chancellor, had died at his home, but remarked that "the immediate cause of this gentleman's death is differently reported," citing fever and cold, an overstrong emetic or a "scorbutic eruption" as some of the proffered explanations. Most of the press settled on the undoubtedly true immediate cause of death, that Yorke had died "by the rupture of a vessel inwardly." And, in two of the leading monthly magazines a poetical epitaph appeared almost immediately, perhaps family-sponsored, which concluded with the lines "Here Heaven clos'd the temporary scene; and snatched her Favorite, to celestial Honours."[30] Similarly, four years later, when Robert Clive took his life, the press noted only that "Last Tuesday night died the Right Honorable Lord Clive. . . ." When the press speculated on the cause of his death, the most they could come up with was "a nervous disorder of the stomach." But the causes of this last death, despite the press whitewashing, was clearly known to some of the public, for it evoked a powerful and angry front page letter from "A poor Man with a good Conscience," published in the *Morning Chronicle* just four days later. Comparing these "late circumstances in the world" with the deaths of classical heroes like Cato and Brutus, the writer wondered how it was possible that "we who have a better religion than the Romans, have worse principles and less refined sentiments." Unlike the ancients who died for love of their country, modern men killed themselves "to avoid the pain and ignominy of an enquiry into our conduct, or to decline surviving the loss of an overgrown fortune, extorted from people by barbarous usage and indiscretion."[31] This clear reference to Clive's life and death shows that, for one person at least, the omission of the facts of the nature of Clive's death prevented disapproval neither of the act nor of the man. These two deaths continued to be talked of in a conjoined fashion, even though, ostensibly, no one knew they were suicides. Thus, in the *Town and Country Magazine* of May 1778, there appeared *A Dialogue in the Shades between* Lord C[live] *and the Hon.* Mr. Y[ork], which openly admitted the nature and discussed the causes of their self-inflicted exits. After the two met in the after-world, they concluded that "ambition has been the ruin of us both," though both agreed that "many of the leading men" of the day "envy us our present situation; but want the courage to shew themselves Catos." A much blacker, fuller, and more interesting piece, which we shall consider in more detail later, also made reference to Clive's suicide, albeit it was published fifteen years after the fact. Complaining of the unfairness of coroners' juries in finding only poor people *felo de se*, "J. A." expressed a hope that

> the next Eastern plunderer, debauched lord, or corrupt commoner, who, in his sober senses, makes use of a pistol as a remedy against the *tedium vitae*, or the stings of a guilty conscience, may meet with a jury so uncomplaisantly mindful of their oaths, as peremptorily to doom them to all the penalties of a *felo de se*, which no after-connivance may set aside.

Another correspondent to the *Gentleman's Magazine* wrote in with regard to the life of Clive as published in Kippis's *Biographica Britannica*. Criticizing this biography as an attempt to gloss over Clive's "most tyrannical cruelty" which led, "Academicus" suggested, to his untimely and self-inflicted death, he said: "The judge [of the dead] there [in the after-life] is not long to be flattered by ambition, soothed with pleasure, or bribed by riches, but he rises to take ample vengeance."[32]

This letter reminds us that eighteenth-century readers took the opportunity to write in to the press when they disliked or disagreed with something they had read, heard, or felt. Though the press had a fairly consistently negative attitude toward the topic of suicide in the abstract, when readers discerned what they deemed a "palliation" of the act in a particular suicide account, they wrote angry responses to the journal. Thus when, in November 1784 a loving and gentle obituary of the writer Theodosius Forrest appeared in the *Gentleman's*, a response was swift in coming. Criticizing the mildness of the treatment of Forrest's death, "HOC," quoting the lines from Hamlet cited at the beginning of the previous section, agreed with Shakespeare, but argued that the same severe justice must be shown to all those who killed themselves.[33]

We have looked at the death of Clive, surely the Eastern plunderer referred to by "J. A.," but what of the debauched Lord or corrupt commoner that he also cited? In the self-inflicted death in 1776 of the Honorable John Damer, eldest son of Lord Milton, we have a fine example of the former, and in the suicides of Samuel Bradshaw in 1774 and John Powell in 1783, outstanding examples of the latter.

When the *Morning Post* first announced the death of Damer on the day after his suicide, it reported that he had died at his house in Tilney Street, Mayfair, and gave no further information. This polite untruth about the place and manner of his death was soon set aside and the London press indulged in an orgy of hints and innuendoes, honoring Damer's high-born status, however, either with oblique references to him as "the unfortunate gentleman," "a certain man of fashion" or the "unfortunate Mr. D—."[34] Who could resist the tale of the young aristocrat, heir to £30,000 a year, who spent his last moments in a pub in Covent Garden, drinking with "four women of the town" and a blind musician? All the papers hinted at dissipation: the loss of a sum of money said one, the granting of annuities said another, being of a "turn rather too eccentric to be confined within the limits of any fortune," said a third. The *Morning Post*, as befitted its reputation as London's premier scandal-sheet, gave several reasons, ranging from "the unfortunate temper" of his wife, which "had long been a bar to their domestic happiness" to the "profusion of his table" which "was ill suited to an annual income of five thousand pounds."[35] Yet, at the end of the day, perhaps most significantly, the inquest jury found Damer to have committed the act in a state of lunacy, and therefore neither criminal nor to be punished.

More surprising perhaps were the similar verdicts on the self-murders of Bradshaw and Powell, two important, unpopular, though non-noble government officials. Of Bradshaw the London newspapers merely reported that he had died at his home, "after a few days' illness." But in the next month's issue of the *London Magazine* the secret was given away. In an extraordinary article entitled "The Character of a late Placeman," its author, using the standard dashes instead of spelling out Bradshaw's name, not only negatively assessed his life but also revealed the secret of his death, though he attributed his self-murder to "a dejection of mind, and melancholy." Comparing Cato's crime with Bradshaw's, the writer noted that "that the former was a man, the latter was but a minister's man." Perhaps Grafton, "his" minister, performed a last kindness for his "man" and saved his family from the embarrassment of an inquest jury.[36]

Ten years later, when John Powell, a self-made man like Bradshaw, the cashier at the Pay-office, killed himself after being dismissed from his government employments, and under Parliamentary investigation for peculation, he was less lucky than Bradshaw in evading a coroner's inquest. His death was also correctly and minutely reported by both the daily and the monthly press, and evoked interesting comments from correspondents. While "X.Y.'s" letter to the *Gentleman's Magazine* was very guarded, it is quite possible that he, and others, felt that Fox, Burke, and Rigby had generously exaggerated the extent of Powell's mental derangement and thus "X.Y.'s" comment, that "suicide is too much the fashion of the present day to be considered only as an act of a lunatic!" was a condemnation of the exculpatory verdict of insanity. A similar, delicately worded complaint appeared in the *Gazetteer* of May 30th, 1783: its author suggested that the "increase and fashion of suicide is such that the Legislature should extend the penalties, and confiscate the property of the self-murderer, whether the verdict of the Coroner be or be not Lunacy."[37]

This reticence of the press either to report, except in the briefest comment, the suicides of men of family and position, or to comment on those deaths, like Yorke's, Clive's, and Bradshaw's, which may never have been brought before a coroner's jury,[38] or those like Damer's and Powell's, which did come to such a trial, but were mitigated, was a mark of the sensitivity of the issue, of the general shamefulness about the act that people felt, and the sense that the press tacitly agreed that the hoi polloi had no business in judging the lives or deaths of their betters. Perhaps the press developed a code to signal, without having to say so, that a person had killed himself. In several cases the newspapers described the deaths merely as "sudden," as Walpole had suggested. Of the thirteen suicides mentioned by Horace Walpole, only six appeared in the press as people who took their own lives. Lamenting the detailed though quite sympathetic account that the *World* printed of the suicide of Lord Say and Sele, Walpole, in a letter to Hannah More, bemoaned the degeneracy of the modern press; "They now call it a *duty* to publish all those calamities which decency to wretched relations used in compassion to suppress, I mean self-murder in particular."[39]

Suicide not only appeared obliquely in the press, was the subject of many sermons and pamphlets, and featured in poetry, but it was also debated and discussed at least twenty-one times through the last three decades of the century at nine of London's commercial debating societies. The questions raised dealt with the issue of Cato's death, wondered whether suicide was an act of courage or of cowardice, and asked whether it proceeded most "from a Disappointment in Love, a State of Lunacy, or from the Pride of the human Mind?" Unfortunately we have the votes in only three of the debates, and these are inconclusive and contradictory. Still, this was a topic that people wanted to talk and hear about, especially in 1789, the year in which one debating society declared that there had been "a late alarming number of Suicides" and claimed that "fifty-three suicides were reported in the newspapers within the month" of October alone.[40] Perhaps spurred by this popular enthusiasm, perhaps responding to what was perceived to be a growing incidence of suicide, the press in the late 1780s began fulsomely to report on many of the suicide cases of the day, especially when they involved "public" figures, people who moved in the "great" world, who fell from eminent heights to the depths of despair and death. Such stories had more color and drama, more popular appeal—elements that no commercial venture like the highly competitive daily papers could afford to neglect. These stories often contained some heart-wrenching detail—the last acts of the deceased, the letters left behind, the grief of an agonized widow, the generous tribute of mourning friends. This only served to increase the stories' impact, and, of course, to sell more papers.

While the tone of these stories was not condemnatory but somber, neither was it generally mitigating or exculpatory. At best the press usually explained the fatal act as an instance of general luxuriousness, of the badness "of the times" or just threw up its hands, arguing that the cause was unknown. When the journals and papers discussed the topic of suicide abstractly or generalized from specific instances, their comments were harsher and more one-sided. Thus, a letter in the *Town and Country Magazine* from "Anti-Suicide" contained the bald assertion that "few if any, have been driven to the deed by insurmountable distress." In the twenty-two periodical pieces I have found on the topic which discuss the reasons for suicide from 1772 to 1797, the two most common causes cited were the over-gratification of the passions and desires, and the fear of shame or contempt. Thus an article in the *Lady's Magazine*, by "a young physician" argued that ". . . the gratification of every sensual desire, if carried beyond the bounds of reason, is attended with a proportional degree of subsequent uneasiness or pain" and for this reason assigned, as the first cause of suicide, "[e]xpectation, elevated above the bounds of prudence and reason, disappointed; as in the respective cases of love, honour, riches or any other predominant passion." A letter from "Plato" to the *St. James's Chronicle* agreed; "Despair, indeed, is the natural Cause of these shocking Actions [of self-murder]; but this is commonly Despair brought on by wilful Extravagance and Debauchery."[41] The second motive, fear of contempt, might spring from apprehensions of imprisonment, execution, or merely the loss of honor. Thus a correspondent writing to the *Morning Chronicle* noted that those who killed themselves frequently "steal a death, perhaps in prison, to avoid the scandal of a public execution, to avoid the pain and ignominy of an enquiry into our conduct, or to decline surviving the loss of an overgrown fortune, extorted from people by barbarous usage and indiscretions." A comment in the *Times* agreed:

> The numerous *Suicides* we have in this country, are a melancholy proof of the depravity of the mind, as they in general arise from the fear of encountering the inquisition of justice, from despair at obtaining the object sought for,—or from remorse of conscience at the recollection of some mischief done to a fellow creature.

And at least two military men left notes with the phrase "Death before (or preferable to) dishonour!" and killed themselves.[42]

I have found only four instances in anything published in the press in the later eighteenth century which argued that the suicide in question had been a noble act, or that suicide was the irresistible result of illness, mental or otherwise. Let us look at these examples, and then consider the widely reported, much lamented, but discreetly and clearly condemned death of George Hesse. The first piece, entitled "Thoughts on Suicide" by "Cato," appeared in the *Sentimental Magazine* in 1775. It was an effusive attempt to evoke sympathy for those "whose real life misery renders their continuance in life a tremendous hydra" and expressed a hope that "the God of Immortality" would not doom such suicides to eternal perdition. The second, an essay by James Boswell in *The Hypocondriack*, playing on the same sentimental tone, argued that

> people of humane and liberal minds cannot feel the same indignation against one who has committed Suicide, that we feel against a robber, a murderer, or, in short, one who has daringly counteracted a clear and positive command . . . [for those who kill themselves] have generally their faculties clouded with melancholy, and distracted by misery.

The third, which appeared as a newspaper article, was much of the same sort. Entitled "Suicide, a Fragment," this was a Sterne-like, "man-of-feeling" type of piece, apostrophizing the suicide of James Sutherland, who had been the judge-advocate of Minorca until suspended from that position in August 1780, by its governor. Three years later he won a case against that governor, General Murray, and was awarded a £5000 settlement. By 1791, according to the *Annual Register*, he was "reduced . . . to great distress," and on August 16th of that year he killed himself in front of the carriage carrying the King. When a laudatory account of his life and death appeared in the *Times*, it was filled with long dashes, with exclamations and rhetorical questions à la Sterne. Presenting Sutherland as a rational and conscious suicide, it compared his act to that of Brutus and Cato, and argued that "there are situations in which death is preferable to life—." The piece concluded by noting that Julia (a character hitherto absent in the fragment) had said that she "would rather be the dead Sutherland, than the living man who caused thy misfortunes." This, the author concluded, demonstrates that "her heart, like thine was intersected by some of the finest fibres of nature—and when sensibility touched one of them, the whole vibrated to the centre."[43]

The fourth piece, published almost exactly a year later, was a curious reflection on suicide in both England and Geneva. After a beginning which seemed to blame suicide on the absence of a belief in "the soul's immortality, and a future state," and which castigated "those philosophers . . . who have endeavoured to shake this great and important conviction from the minds of men,

. . . thereby open[ing] a door to suicide, as well as to other crimes," its author confessed that "there is a disease sometimes which affects the body, and afterwards communicates its baneful influence to the mind . . . render[ing] life absolutely insupportable."[44] These four instances, along with the letter to the *London Magazine* which was earlier cited, are the only statements I have found which express neither horror nor blame, or which see the act as either noble or caused by disease. An examination of the various accounts given of the suicide of George Hesse will illustrate the extent and limitations of a medicalized and sympathetic public response to this act.

When Hesse, *bon vivant* and friend of the Prince of Wales, killed himself on June 2, 1788, the newspapers, after a brief hiatus, eagerly covered the story. The *Times* explained the delay in reporting this death by confessing they had "from delicacy suppressed" the news. But two days after the event, the papers were full of it. On the whole, the early accounts were factual and non-judgmental, merely stating the time, place, and manner of death, and Hesse's activities on the evening preceding his fatal decision. They also remarked on the coroner's verdict, which was lunacy. The second reports, a day later, expressed sympathetic pity, noting that "every one who knew him, must pathetically lament—and those who knew him not, sincerely pity" his fate. However, even here, much more space was given to a fiscal reckoning of Hesse's road to advancement, wealth, and prosperous marriage, than to compassion. His father had secured him a place in the office of the paymaster general, and in the years after, he had advanced as government agent to the forces, "so that his official income amounted annually to the sum of fifteen hundred pounds." Added to this was the "liberal fortune" brought to him by his marriage with the daughter of a West-India merchant. Clearly, in terms of the goods of this world, he was a man particularly fortunate; the long catalogue of his wealth and offices made such comment unnecessary. How shocking it must have been then to read that Hesse had killed himself because "his pecuniary affairs, from deep play, had, it appears, sustained a shock of the most momentous nature—and from which he expressed his apprehension, that he could not speedily extricate himself."[45] Other papers, however, did not refrain from making pointed comments, even while discussing Hesse's "very liberal and fine feelings." A paragraph repeated in several papers alluded to what, it was thought, had led to this disastrous situation: "Some connexions too splendid not to be broken, and too high not to dazzle, may have led him astray." Hesse, one observed, "had very early a propensity for gay life" and it was this desire to live with and like the Great that led to his downfall.[46] In its next issue, the *General Evening Post* continued their exposé of Hesse's failings, while simultaneously lamenting the fact that his death had "too prematurely deprived society of one of its most amiable and accomplished ornaments." Noting, however, that this "unhappy gentleman" (as was not unusual; negative comments about important people did not mention them by name) "possessed, in places, estate and interest of money, very near three thousands pounds per year," the paper concluded that "this, without children, surely was enough for all the elegant conveniencies of life." It was a "too strong propensity" for the "pernicious practice of gaming" that led him to lose £50,000 and his own life.[47] *The Star and Evening Advertiser* added yet a further "wrinkle," recounting a perhaps fictitious story of a practical trick that had been played upon him by his high-born friends, which, according to the paper, "contributed to convince him he was rather permitted to enjoy the high intercourse which in the end produced his lamentable fate, than deemed a partner in it." One paper, the *Morning Post*, underlined the moral of this sad fable even more sharply:

> We are afraid, however, from some expressions which dropped from the unhappy man a few days before, that the coldness with which he had been treated by some of those elevated connections, which he seemed particularly to court, was too much for his feelings, as he foresaw, in this high neglect, the rapid desertion of every other society above the level of his own rank.

The *Morning Post* went on to connect his suicide, or, as they described it, "his aweful farewel," with his desire to tread "the delusive and dangerous paths of *greatness*."[48] Finally two poems written to commemorate Hesse exemplify the ambiguities felt by the press, and probably by their readers, about the death of this likeable man. The first, entitled *On the Death of Mr. Hesse,* was all praise: it extolled "The virtues of the *man*, who's now the *saint!*/For merit sure he shar'd in ev'ry part,/Merit most true—the integrity of heart!" The second poem, published in the *Town and Country Magazine*, ended with the lines "Altho' restrain'd by tender ties,/Into Eternity he flies!/A lesson leaving to the gay,/To tread with care life's slip'ry way."[49]

Whatever the truth of these constructions of Hesse's death, their point was clear and made even stronger and more acute when, a day after the event, another "gentleman . . . of some distinction in the county of Middlesex," identified only as A—k—n, killed himself, it was said, because of "some heavy losses which he sustained at Ascot races." Several of London's newspapers printed the same concluding paragraph to this story, which linked suicide not with mental illness but with moral decay:

> The progress of *bankruptcy* and that of *suicide* seem to keep pace with each other—and both are to be ascribed to the same causes, dissipation, extravagance, and speculation. No matter whether the speculation is in

trade, on the course at Newmarket, or in relying upon one's connexions with the great.[50]

Thus sympathy could be mixed with criticism, humane fellow-feeling with condemnation. And though there is no doubt that sentimental portrayals in verse, the novel, and the theater became very popular during the last four decades of the century, there is no reason to think that this taste was carried over and looked for in newspaper stories. For most eighteenth-century newspaper readers, the experience of consulting their daily report was quite unlike that of reading a sentimental novel; the latter was designed to invoke strong feelings, to draw tears, to serve as a holiday retreat into a world of overheated emotions and acts. Though they lacked our developed literary understanding of genre differences, eighteenth-century readers knew that a novel was not a newspaper account, and that "real life" was not to be confused with light reading.[51]

Inquest Verdicts: What Went on in the Minds of Jurors?

Used more and more frequently, it [the *non compos mentis* verdict] was the tangible expression of the secularization of suicide, of the opinion that self-destruction was in itself an act of insanity, an end more to be pitied than to be scorned . . . .

The leading legal authorities of the day protested against the lenient interpretation of psychiatric evidence. . . . The lawyers were worried that juries' disregard for the rules of law would undermine the rule of law.[52]

It was well known at the time, and has been reaffirmed ever since, that, starting in the later seventeenth century, coroners' juries, faced with the bodies of those who had killed themselves, came increasingly to decide that such deaths were the result of lunacy, and therefore not culpable. Of course, some were still found *felo de se*,[53] but the vast increase of mitigatory verdicts requires some explanation. MacDonald and Murphy conclude, "At some point during the mid-eighteenth century the men of middling rank who served as coroners' jurors adopted the medical interpretation of suicide."[54] But it might repay a few moments' consideration to examine eighteenth-century medical opinion on the nature and causes of suicide and lunacy, and to speculate on the circumstances and influence of such changing ideas.

We have already seen the dismissal of supernatural causes in favor of medical insight in an article in the *London Magazine* of 1762, but, in this context, it is worth revisiting this piece and considering the pivotal importance here given to the medical professional. In the second part of the same essay, published in the journal's next issue, its author advised the friends and relations of possible suicides "to remark the first approaches of the disorder; and to apply immediately to some able physician; for the least delay in these cases is particularly dangerous. . . ." The young physician-correspondent to the *Lady's Magazine* maintained, despite his opinion that suicide was frequently caused by over-gratified sensual desires, that suicide was now generally understood as a disease and "ranked amidst the number of those which every regular physician does, or ought, to pay attention to; and as mental complaints are in many instances the objects of our practice, from their intimate connection with the body . . .," and therefore that the services of a doctor were vital. William Rowley, noting that changes in people's physical constitutions could also lead to changes in their mental states, added that "[p]hysicians have frequent opportunities of observing the diminution of human courage and wisdom from long-continued misfortunes, or bodily infirmities. . . . The man is then changed, his blood is changed; and with these his former sentiments."[55] By 1808, a correspondent to the *Gentleman's Magazine* confidently stated that suicide was always the result of lunacy, the conclusion of "all such medical men who have for many years devoted that time and attention to the development of the disease termed Insanity, which it greatly merits. . . ." That doctors, especially "mad-doctors," increasingly subscribed to the notion that suicide was caused by mental derangement, is undoubtedly true; what is less clear is how compelling their views might have been to the men who composed coroners' juries, men familiar with the expanding world of claimed medical expertise, men who may have thought that such assertions of particular insight into the roots of suicidal impulses was part of what has been dubbed the "medicalization" of insanity.[56] For, in the eighteenth century, insanity and all its circumstances became a growth industry, with mad doctors doing much to insist on a need for trained medical expertise and for an expanded role for their professional assistance.

What other bodies of thought might have influenced coroners' juries to arrive at lunacy verdicts? The concern frequently stated through the eighteenth century, which MacDonald and Murphy have so cogently expressed, that the actual workings of inquest juries would undermine the rule of law, was the widely shared view of many moralists, whether lawyers or not. Commenting on such decisions, many contemporaries felt that the refusal of juries to find people *felo de se*, like the refusal of juries to find duellists guilty of murder, undermined the credibility of the English legal system and the confidence of men and women in English justice. The comparison with duelling broke down at this point, however, for while a duellist theoretically could be punished, it was impossible to punish a suicide. Yet juries continued to find lenient verdicts, even as commentators continued to lambast their decisions. Could this very discomfort with mitigation have been responsible, at least in part, for the continuance of the practice that gave rise to it?

The unease with coroner's juries was based on several grounds. Late seventeenth- and early eighteenth-century commentators thought that coroners' juries had misunderstood the true meaning of lunacy, and therefore found verdicts incorrectly. The *Occasional Paper*, for example, believed that where "a Man is capable of Rational Actions in other respects, the Law justly supposes him capable of having us'd his Discretion in this [act] also." A constant and total state of derangement was clearly the only criterion for finding a verdict of *non compos mentis*, according to law. John Jeffery made a similar point, linking the impropriety of mitigatory verdicts for suicides with the assessment of the culpability of duellists. Coroners, he argued "willfully mistake the already named false estimate of things for reason's full decay: otherwise they must, in some degree, upon duellists (nay other culprits) pass the same decree; what yet they never do, and why? but that here no confiscations are made to take place, at least, which is not a little strange, since the crimes appear of equal dye."[57] Such criticism did not end in the mid-century. Thus, in one of the most frequently cited texts of the eighteenth century, Sir William Blackstone explicitly argued against the view "that the very act of suicide is an evidence of insanity." In volume four of his *Commentaries on the Laws of England*, a volume entitled "Of Public Wrongs," he concluded that suicide is properly ranked as "among the highest crimes." Blackstone noted that if one interpreted insanity in a tolerant manner, "as if every man who acts contrary to reason, had no reason at all," then this argument would overthrow all law, "for the same argument would prove every other criminal *non compos.*" And even in 1829, when a new guide to the duties of the coroner and his jury was issued, written by the Lord Chief Justice of the Court of Common Pleas, John Jervis, Blackstone's comments on suicide were included virtually word-for-word.[58]

Even more troubling than what might be innocent mistakes or kindly meant mitigation was the widely shared belief, whether rightly or wrongly held, that the verdicts of coroners' juries could be purchased, that, as a consequence, there was one law for the Great and another for the small. In a funny mock-serious advertisement inserted after the death notices in the *Gentleman's Magazine* of 1755 there is an account of a cheap, painless, and untraceable "medicine" to help "men of pleasure" kill themselves. This cure is offered as an alternative to the usual practice:

> AND WHEREAS such is the prejudice still remaining among the great and little vulgar, that this necessary and heroic act reflects indelible dishonour upon

such men of *wit, honour* and *pleasure*, and their families, and makes the experience of bribing a coroner's jury to perjury absolutely necessary, to prevent a forfeiture of their personal estate, if any such there be . . . the advertiser offers his potion as an alternative, cheaper solution.

In the same year, this charge was seriously and forcefully made in *A Discourse against Self-Murder* by the Anglican clergyman Francis Ayscough. Commenting on the notion that suicide is itself a mark of insanity, he wondered

> . . . what is it that the Jury is called together to enquire into? The Truth is, they are called together to keep up the Formality, and to set aside the Spirit and Intention of the Law; to receive, I am afraid, a stated Fee for a directed Verdict; in plain Words, to be bribed, and to be forsworn.
>
> Thus, indeed, is to charge on them a high Degree of Wickedness. But if it be true, it ought to be spoken, and if it be not so, I would only ask—How comes it to pass, that no Man of Rank and Fortune was ever subjected to the Penalties of this Law . . . .[59]

This charge went beyond the commonly recognized fact that, in this, as in every other facet of eighteenth-century life, social position mattered. Thus the *Connoisseur*, in a popularly reprinted issue, commented on this inequality:

> . . . of hundreds of lunatics by purchase, I never knew this sentence [*felo de se*] executed but on one poor cobler, who hanged himself in his own stall. A penniless poor dog, who has not left enough to defray the funeral charges, may perhaps be excluded the church-yard; but self-murder by a pistol genteely mounted, or the Paris-hilted sword, qualifies the polite owner for a sudden death, and entitles him to a pompous burial and a monument setting forth his virtues in Westminster-Abbey.[60]

But what was merely hinted at by many, that money had actually changed hands, that the coroner and/or his jury were bribed by friends or family to find the correct verdict, i.e., *non compos mentis*, was also unambiguously made. Sometimes this allegation was thundered from the pages of the press, sometimes more coyly and matter-of-factly included in contemporary journal stories. In "She Met Her Match," a moral tale published in the *Town and Country Magazine* in 1773, a Mr. Portland killed himself because of marital infelicity, whereupon "Mrs. Portland, when she had bribed a coroner to bring in a verdict of lunacy, proceeded to the opening of her husband's will." MacDonald and Murphy point out, quite correctly, that such "[b]ribery has left few records, for obvious reasons." However, they also note before dismissing the charge, that "[s]ome critics complained that bribery was widespread." Citing Defoe's opinion "that it was less important than sympathy in securing favourable verdicts," they conclude that they "are inclined to agree with him."[61] A brief reconsideration of this point may be in order.

In *Sleepless Souls*, MacDonald and Murphy tell the story of the one coroner's verdict they found, the report of the inquest on the body of Edward Walsingham, on which someone had made a note stating that the verdict was paid for by his family. I also have found such a case, but have much more evidence than just that rather obscure notation. My source is from the voluminous correspondence of Margaret Georgina, first countess of Spencer. In 1780, in a letter to her oldest friend, Mrs. Howe, Lady Spencer made a curious inquiry. Lady Spencer, an aristocrat and a correspondent to the Bluestocking circle, was a woman of quiet, though deep-felt religious conviction. It is her exemplary moral character, well noted by contemporaries, that makes her request so odd and interesting. Telling her friend of the suicide of Hans Stanley on their estate, Lady Spencer recounts a letter she had received from Stanley's family, asking her to "pay off" the coroner. Here is the nub of Lady Spencer's problem; she expresses no hesitation about the act itself, or about corrupting the legal system, but wonders instead how much money should change hands, and requests that Mrs. Howe ask her acquaintance for such information. If someone as truly Christian and morally upright as the Countess could treat the suborning of a jury as a standard, everyday sort of practice, this, I think, lends weight to those eighteenth-century contemporaries who saw this as a widespread practice.[62] By the late 1780s this practice had become so common as to be denounced in a letter to the *Gazetteer*. Why, asked the writer, do candidates for the job of coroner "spend a thousand pounds to obtain their election? What is their object?" His answer is plain: "[t]hey are inspired by hopes of eventual emoluments."

> A great man may commit suicide; to save the forfeiture of his property it must be brought in Lunacy. The jury (who, God knows, are seldom philosophers) are persuaded that insanity, and self murder are convertible terms.—The deceased's relations are satisfied with the verdict of the jury, and the Coroner with the *price* of it.[63]

Just two months before, the *Times* reported that a coroner's jury had found a certain nobleman's brother *felo de se*, and they hailed the verdict. The *Times* expressed a hope, that though the verdict was "a matter of regret" to the family "that this rigour may operate, as it ought, in prevention of the crime." If, it added three days later, "the burial in a public highway, and the stake, was put in force against a very few suicides of rank, the crime of self-murder would soon be extinguished."[64] This was never reported as happening, however. The weight of such comments, as well as the Spencer example, though not an irrefragable proof of the widespread nature of such corruption, still convinces me that Defoe was, in this instance, uncharacteristically trusting.

The strongest and most coherent newspaper letter on the laws concerning suicide was one which I have already cited, published in the *Gentleman's Magazine* in 1789, and signed only "J. A." Arguing for a repeal of the law of suicide, this correspondent stated his strongest objection to its operation.

> [T]his is one of those few instances in which that equal distribution of justice to all ranks of people, which is the greatest boast of our country, is violated. It is violated too, I fear, in a very heinous manner, namely by *direct perjury* on the part of juries; thus contaminating the very source of all public justice.

Though "J. A." did not directly refer to the bribery of coroners or their juries, he did note "that coroners' juries have often been influenced to bring in false verdicts." Referring to those lines of the second clown quoted at the beginning of an earlier section, "J. A." hoped that "a little serious consideration will convince every one, that partiality in the administration of justice, and the violation of a solemn oath, were evils of no small magnitude." This was neither a conservative nor a traditionalist speaking: "J. A.'s" argument was for an amelioration and improvement of the entire criminal law, beginning with a repeal of this particular aspect of it.[65]

Thus jurymen, moved either by instructions from their coroner, or by ideas picked up from the press about the corruption and venality of other unspecified coroners, might well have been willing to find the great majority of suicides who came before them to have been *non compos mentis*. This may have meant for these jurors, that men and women with no resources to expend, no bribes to tender, no friends to forswear, were deemed no less innocent of crime than those other suicides, equally culpable but richer or better situated.

"to abolish the disgusting ceremony":[66] *How Was Suicide to Be Punished?*

We have looked at a range of opinions about and representations of suicide in a variety of popular venues, and seen much dissatisfaction with the way that suicides were dealt with by the agents of the law. What proposals however, were made for a more effective, more humane, or more egalitarian process in dealing with such cases?

For most of the writers on suicide in the popular press from the 1730s through the 1780s, the answer was unambiguous; a misplaced sympathy with the families of the deceased and the corruption of the law by the families of the Great, had caused a diminution and corruption of the proper treatment of the self-murderer—dissection and display. The classical cases were frequently cited as examples of how suicide might be curtailed: if the virgins of Miletus stopped killing themselves when the corpses of some of their more resolute sisters were dragged through the streets, why would this not work equally well in London? Some suggested that special charnel houses be established to display the remains of suicides, with engraved accounts of their deaths and decorated with "the glorious Ensigns of their Rashness—the Rope, the Knife, the Pistol or the Razor."[67] Shaming rituals continued to be supported as a method for diminishing the number of suicides: rather than burying a suicide "in a crossroad and a stake driven through the body," ventured "Humanitas" in a letter to the *New Monthly Magazine*, "might it not act more *in terrorem* if the body were given to the Royal College of Surgeons for dissection?" Not only would this cause a decline in the incidence of suicide, but, argued "W. T. P." in a letter to the *Gentleman's Magazine*, "it would probably supply the want of the Profession, and stop the trade of the resurrection men." Even correspondents like "Ordovex" who, in 1818 wrote a letter on suicide to the *Times*, commented that while he did not "approve, in an unqualified manner, of the penalties assigned by our law to this crime," he thought it imperative that "some signal and indelible mark of infamy be attached to the memory of that man who has wantonly become the murderer of himself; let his name be raised as a beacon, to warn away others from the same fatal shoal." Though he did not refer to him by name, perhaps "Ordovex's" proposal owes something to the compromise position adopted by Richard Hey, in his *Dissertation on Suicide* of 1785. Hey proposed the abolition of the forfeiture of property as a punishment for all suicides, but, at the same time he advocated that "no regard should be paid to Lunacy, but that, in all cases, alike, some certain Mode of treating the Body of the deceased should be invariably observed, and some certain Marks of Infamy affixed to his Memory."[68] Hey's proposal may have rested upon the view, expressed two decades before, that "[t]his clause of the law [the expropriation of property] indeed, is now seldom put into execution." Arguing that "the untimely death of a cottager or mechanic must occasion more exquisite distress than that of a peer or senator (for very few consider the indigent as proper objects of consolation)," the author of *Reflections on Suicide* concluded, like Hey, that justice demanded an equitable and equal treatment of all suicides.[69]

Others thought persuasion might have some effect, especially if it were serious in tone and religious in content. A correspondent to the *General Advertiser* advocated that every minister should deliver an annual sermon "on the causes and cure, or consequences of temptations, to self-murder" and another, to the *Times*, concurred: "Should not our Divines frequently make this the subject of their pulpit discourses? If they did it would have its good effects." Still others hoped that their published inquiries into the history of ideas about suicide would have some positive influence on its prevention; in this spirit Charles Moore stated his wish that his *Full Inquiry into the Subject of Suicide* would be of use

> to instruct the ignorant, to persuade the wavering, to uphold the weak, to caution the unwary, to guard the avenues through which youth and inexperience must pass, and to confirm and strengthen every previous good inclination to moral and virtuous habits.[70]

Many, however, thought some change necessary in the law, either in how it was enacted or how it was enforced. Most of the discussion resolved itself to one of two positions: some people seemed to think the law as it stood was fine, but that its enforcement was inadequate, and others thought the law itself was too stringent, too barbaric, and needed to be modernized and tamed. In addition, there were those who thought that coroners and coroners' juries needed a clearer idea of what the state of *non compos mentis* involved. If some guidelines could be laid down, juries' verdicts could be more uniform, less liable to outside interference, and thus more equitable.

We have already seen that many contemporaries believed that coroners and their juries were corrupt and could be bribed to return the correct, exculpatory verdict. In addition to this perhaps overly cynical view, there were many who just could not understand how inquests could reach their verdicts. Though the *Morning Chronicle*'s comment on such decisions was a bit too facile and tongue-in-cheek, it betrays the kinds of confusion that many must have felt in reading accounts of suicide verdicts in their daily papers.

> The *proofs of lunacy* required by Coroners' Juries are among the most extraordinary *phenomena* of the law of evidence. Within these six months, the following have been considered as decisive.—Speculating in the funds—believing in Lord MALMESBURY's mission—leaving off a course of physic—paying debts (this was in the case of a *nobleman*)—not being able to obtain a seat in Parliament—having a very bad wife—going to church three times a day— talking Greek in a fruit-shop —and being neglected by Mr. Pitt!

But by the early nineteenth century, public opposition to this condemnatory view of the coroners' juries was also finding public voice. In a letter to the *Gentleman's Magazine* entitled "The Disease termed Insanity little understood," its correspondent took umbrage at "the stigma thrown upon our Juries by the term "fashionable verdict of Lunacy" and denounced such slurs as "very undeserved." Similarly, writing about the suicide of Abraham Goldsmid, the *Examiner* noted that it was "a most difficult task" for any jury to decide "whether the unhappy suicide was in his senses or not. The Jury, therefore, with much propriety and feeling, in all such cases of *doubt* (99 out of 100) bring in a verdict of lunacy. . . ." Furthermore, added a correspondent who signed himself "Medicus Ignotus," not only was it difficult to tell real self-murder from acts of lunacy, but also "the disease of the mind is totally out of the reach of all bodily remedies" and therefore its unhappy sufferer can in no way be considered culpable.[71]

Both those who stressed the difficult but real medical causes of suicide, those who thought inquest juries correct in their verdicts, and those who did not, but wished for a stricter and less expansive understanding of lunacy, desired a change in the law. Thus Richard Hey condemned the leniency of coroners' courts. "Juries," he argued, "in opposition to Law, have shewn a compassionate attention which, in the deceased person, both Law and private Duty had called for in vain." Charles Moore's impressive and much cited *Inquiry* agreed that the mistaken kindness of the juries had a significant and deleterious social impact. "It is self-evident then, that the abettor of suicide," and by this Moore meant inquest juries, "undermines the basis of all civil society, that he defies all threatenings of law and terrors of judicial process, and consequently that the executive authority loses by these means its firmest hold over the decent and regular conduct of its dependents and citizens."[72] In this view, if law was partial, was corrupted or corruptible, whether through humanity or bribery, it ceased to have the authority needed for maintaining a safe and fair society. The clash of these points of view occurred frequently during the Napoleonic and postwar period, and was still raging when, in 1818, Sir Samuel Romilly took his life.

The Deaths of an "incomparable person" and an "unfortunate and unpopular Minister":[73] Romilly's and Londonderry's Suicides in the Press

When Sir Samuel Romilly, Member of Parliament, eminent civil lawyer, crusader for the abolition of the slave trade and a reduction in the severity of the criminal law, killed himself on November 2, 1818, London's newspapers were filled with the story. In the following weeks, the story of Romilly's demise continued to be discussed as the press published not only reports of the inquest, details of the funeral, the contents of his will, and the implications of his death for the political situation, but also poems, editorials, and letters to the editor eulogizing his life and bemoaning his death. Seldom has the demise of a non-royal received so much public attention. Let us examine these posthumous comments on Romilly's life and the manner of his death, before turning to another suicide in public life, which occurred only four years later, that of Robert Stewart, Lord Londonderry.

We have considered that body of thought that argued that all suicides were the result of mental illness, and should thus be treated medically rather than as criminal acts, and have also noted a remaining widespread horror and disgust, a fear and revulsion toward the act and its consequences. Since Samuel Romilly both killed himself, and was enormously loved and respected, in the accounts of his death we can observe early nineteenth-century writers attempting to come to terms both with the man and with his heinous end.

It is instructive to consider press reports of the mourning occasioned by Romilly's death. It was said that "never perhaps was a more sincere tribute of respect and veneration paid to an individual, than what was exhibited on Tuesday morning in the two Courts of Equity." The Lord Chancellor, glancing at the spot where Romilly normally had stood, "could no longer restrain his feelings; the tears rushed down his cheeks; he immediately rose and retired to his room, to give vent to his feelings." But grief spread far wider than the courts; the loss of Romilly, "that incomparable person . . . filled the metropolis with sorrow." It was, judging from press reactions to popular upset, as if a terrible national calamity had occurred. "We have never witnessed a sensation at once so strong and so general as what at this time occupies all minds." But to judge his death merely as a national disaster did not seem enough for some commentators. Thus one writer, noting that "his death is indeed a great national calamity," went on to add that the loss was "not confined to his country, for the range of his mighty and extraordinary mind encompassed every class of his fellow beings. . . ." Rather than his death being presented only as that of an exemplary Englishman and an ardent advocate of improvement, it was described as having "given a shock, wholly without example, to every heart which cherishes a hope for the advancement of its species."[74] By these accounts Romilly appeared as a species-hero.

The qualities most lauded posthumously were threefold. Romilly was mourned for three sorts of excellencies: as an uncorrupted law-maker and politician, as a self-made man of business and endeavor, and as an exemplary family man, a father, husband, and son. Described as a patriot and sage, lauded for "the purity of his intentions" and characterized by his "love of constitutional liberty," in his public capacity Romilly seemed to exemplify a particularly valuable and perhaps rare sort of man. These attributes of the statesman were matched by his devotion to his profession, and his success at it. The press repeatedly insisted that though Romilly's father, a jeweler, had given him a good education, "all the rest had been achieved by himself." He was a model of the rewards of hard work and industry, having "acquired those habits which usually promote health and success in life. . . ." Rising early, he caught "those moments for improvement, which others too often waste in indolence. . . ." Known as a "most indefatigable labourer," he was widely praised for his "knowledge, learning and eloquence."[75] In a phrase redolent of his philosophic mentor, Jeremy Bentham, the *Constitution* summed up his life as "useful."[76]

While rather overheated panegyrists hailed him as "the Citizen of the World" and "the Father of his Country,"[77] it was his private virtues that received most praise. Only a year before, in 1817, Princess Charlotte had died, but the press noted that while the Princess and her stillborn child "were beings out of the sphere of ordinary occupation, Sir Samuel Romilly was one of ourselves. . . ."[78] Unlike the Great, whether of birth or talents, Romilly was seen as an ordinary man, albeit one of extraordinary achievement. The *Monthly Magazine* presented his life as epitomizing the new self-made leaders of the country; in the new nineteenth century, it boasted, "no longer looking up to nobility for true greatness, men were beheld starting daily from the democratic floor, and snatching away the prize of knowledge, learning and eloquence" from the privileged orders.[79]

But if any aspect of his life or career was praised, if any role was considered illustrative of and central to all his other virtues, it was his conduct as the head of his family, "as a son, a father, a husband, and a master." On the one hand it is not surprising that this side of his life received so much attention, for, it was said, he had killed himself because of his grief at the death of his much-loved wife. On the other hand, however, this sentimental exaltation of the domestic life of a married man was surely something relatively recent. When thirty years before, a Mr. Green had hanged himself in his chamber following the death of his wife, the inquest jury sat for seventeen hours before they arrived at the verdict of lunacy. Commenting on the verdict, the *Times* rather facetiously noted that "to be inconsolable for one's wife, and to follow her to the grave—is *madness*." But by the time Romilly committed the same act for the same reason, the tone was graver, more respectful, and much more sympathetic. The *Lady's Magazine*, for example, noting that "in the bosom of his family . . . he was the tender husband—the fond father," presented his familial devotion and his public service as inextricably combined. "This weakness and this wisdom—this combination of all that is delicate and all that is great, shew human nature in a point of view, which commands at one and the same time our utmost love and highest veneration."[80]

For many of Romilly's contemporaries, as for his friend, George Crabbe, the public and the private man, the political and the domestic talents, were of a piece, "the best of guides to my assuming pen,/ The best of fathers, husbands, judges, men." Claiming that Romilly's reputation was "inferior to none, in the annals of modern times," a newspaper writer declared that "beginning with his own family, the circle of his attachment increased until it included friends, relatives, his country, and finally, the whole human species."[81]

Though there were less detailed speculations about the larger causes for Romilly's rash act (most seemed to feel that the recent death of his wife was reason enough) than praise for his character, his public and private conduct, and his critical political importance,[82] we have a number of interesting comments which hint at contemporary understandings of these other motives. Of course, many press reports gave multiple explanations and interpretations for his self-destructive act. An examination of these will not present us with a coherent and comprehensive account of Romilly's suicide but will illustrate contemporaries' efforts to try, with considerable unease and some mystification, to explain and understand, if not to justify, the event.

First, of course, were those sorts of explanations that arose most easily and naturally from the inquest itself. "Sir Samuel Romilly when he committed the act was in a state of mental delirium. He was suffering under a brain fever. And, indeed, the evidence before the Coroner proves that it arose from an instantaneous paroxysm of the brain." The *British Neptune* agreed, commenting that Romilly's death

> was merely the result of disease derangement. . . . Suicide in such a case is merely a symptom of physical disorder, and no more to be connected with the moral condition of the sufferer than any of the bodily ills that flesh is heir to. It has nothing of the imposing energy, or guilt, or imbecility, or mistaken virtue, which strike the attention of the heroes of antiquity, or the victims of passion, profligacy, or criminality in modern times, who have fallen by their own hands.[83]

Shortly after the first publicity surrounding his death, the *Courier* launched an attack on this sort of mitigation of Romilly's action, arguing instead that many had borne what Romilly had suffered, and had not had recourse to suicide, that Romilly's act betrayed if not an irreligious frame of mind then perhaps an insufficiency of character and resolve. Comparing the stoic responses of Princess Charlotte's husband and of Edmund Burke to the death of their loved ones (in the first case, a wife and child, in the second, an only son), the *Courier* remarked: "Surely these and similar examples of religious fortitude under the severe visitations of this life, are those which should obtain our highest sympathy, and greatest admiration. The weakness which bends, which falls, before the storm, may call forth our pity, but no more." The response to the *Courier's* comments was immediate. Not only were they held to be invidious but also incorrect, for, as several papers asked, "must similar results arise in the minds of various men from causes apparently similar? Human reason cannot be measured like objects of sense, nor can the experience of one individual's endurance be considered as evidence of what another can safely encounter. The cases, however, are very far from being similar. . . ."[84] In attempting to answer the calumnies of the *Courier*, the press came to propose a variety of extenuating circumstances by which to explain what in this particular case caused Romilly's act.

One common explanation for Romilly's deed was the years of toil which he had endured, not only in building his career, but in fighting for and defending the causes to which he was committed. *The Country Herald and Weekly Advertiser* argued that "it seems beyond a doubt, that the mental derangement to which Sir Samuel Romilly fell a victim, was brought on in part by the unremitted professional toil which had first weakened his frame. . . ." His many activities "left no time for bodily exercise, mental relaxation, or domestic comfort. . . . He became a devoted servant to the Public, he made more than fair use of his talents; and this probably tended to subdue that vigour which had well known how to advise and to exercise equanimity and resignation in the hour of affliction," commented the *Gentleman's Magazine. The Monthly Magazine* concurred, remarking that it was "easy to trace the causes of the frenzy which destroyed him. Its foundations had been laid in years of inconceivable and distracting labour. . . ." The most prevalent explanation for Romilly's act, however, was his extreme tenderness of feeling, which, it was held, was also the source of his many virtues. His speech against the slave trade, for example was described as exhibiting "the most melting pathos, the most overwhelming eloquence." Similarly it was this very "tenderness of nature which led Sir Samuel Romilly to embrace with love the whole of his fellow creatures, and to exert himself to serve them. . . ." Romilly's final act was described as springing "from an excess of feeling, or rather from a sentiment, which is the most binding one in our social system" and thus rather too much of a good thing than a crime or an evil.[85] "To [Romilly], unfortunately, his virtues have proved holy traitors," commented the *Globe*. "With a heart less susceptible and feelings less acute, Sir Samuel Romilly would be now living. . . ." *The New Times* summed it up most succinctly; Romilly, it said, "fell a victim to the acuteness of his sensibility."[86] Living a life of duty, a life bereft of even the consolations of fancy and imagination, Romilly sought above all to appear unruffled and calm. It was this very laudable stoicism that the *News* felt must have given him the *coup de grace*.

The endeavour to keep his grief in a subdued state, appeared to claim all his attention. . . . This tension of feeling at length produced its natural consequence. It broke down the frail barrier which separates man from the brute which perisheth, and in the momentary bereavement of his faculties, the act of suicide was committed.

We have seen how the press and the public seemed floored by Romilly's death, unable to find adequate words to explain his act or to express their pain. The *British Review* remarked that "every one who heard was struck dumb with the intelligence; or had only the power, for the moment, to utter some ejaculation of astonishment. . . ." But newspapers are filled with words, and despite the shock, the Romilly suicide was a story which fascinated and troubled the reading public; in a word, bad news makes good sales. Everyone, it seemed, wanted to read and discuss this horrifying death. Thus the *Philanthropic Gazette*, describing "the gloom [spread] over the country" by Romilly's demise, commented on what was most newsworthy about it—"the manner of it being still more painful than the event itself."[87]

It was but a short step from this sort of palliation, of blaming an impersonal fatality rather than Romilly himself, to the image of Romilly as warrior, fallen in battle. Though prefacing its remarks with the mandatory disclaimer, i.e., that it "lament[ed] the manner of it [Romilly's death]," the *News* went on to comment that "Yet not more natural is it for a warrior to die on the field of battle, than it was for this most amiable man to fall a sacrifice to the excess of his affections and tenderness." This is as close to an apotheosis for his private virtues that a public man has ever come.[88]

There were those, however, who, like the *Courier*, discerned in Romilly's action an insufficiency of religious attachment, a proof of the necessity for absolute faith and reliance on God in all of life's adversities. The *Independent Whig* saw this lack of faith and overreliance on reason not only as a flaw in Romilly's constitution, but as a symptom of the age. "This instance of the dreadful infirmity of human nature, and the insufficiency of the mind of man, however exalted and cultivated, to sustain himself, in the hour of heavy calamity, is by no means a solitary occurrence, even in modern times." So, despite the exculpatory tone of the press in general, there were some papers who took a harder, more censorious attitude toward Romilly's death, and did so, not surprisingly, on religious grounds.[89] Most of these condemnations focused on the act as betraying a lack of proper Christian submission, an insufficiency of Christian faith. Not only condemning the act itself, but attacking the verdict of the inquest jury as well, *Bell's Weekly Messenger* remarked that it is the express command of our religion . . . to exert all our human powers of body and mind [to fight against adversity] . . . and if we find those powers insufficient, to call for that divine aid . . . human resolution is [usually] found sufficient to restrain other sallies of inordinate passion. And if they break out in despite of such restraint . . . the human legislator does not the less punish them, because they were the acts of a passion, blind, furious and uncontrollable, in the instant of the communication.

Denounced as an act of cowardice, a betrayal of friends and family, Romilly's suicide seemed to some the undeniable proof of his pride and his irreligion. "We are left only to lament that his resignation to the dispensations of Providence was not sufficiently humble, nor his reliance on the support of Him who is our strength and our safety, and who loves while he chastens, sufficiently great to enable him to bear up against so severe a trial," proclaimed the *St. James's Chronicle.*[90]

Other periodicals presented Romilly's act as that of a man whose principles, if not corrupted, at least were unhinged, and even perhaps fatally tainted by the miasma of deism. Many papers were only willing to hint at this, as when the *Philanthropic Gazette*, comparing Romilly's and Whitbread's suicides, commented that "whether we impute their derangement to intense attachment on the one hand, or to disgust of the world's ingratitude on the other, it is sufficiently evident that some principle must be wanting, that is necessary to support the mind under trials and bereavements." Whitbread, like Romilly, an ardent Whig reformer, had killed himself three years before, overwhelmed, it was said, by the difficulties he had encountered in his attempt to rescue the Drury-lane Theater from debt, though the *Gazette* implied that what really impelled both men to their fatal ends was their rationalist irreligion.[91] The *Morning Post* was franker, rhetorically asking its readers "who does not acknowledge and lament the awful inroads made on our moral character as a nation by the diabolical *Modern Philosophy*, which aims at extinguishing every principle from the human heart on which our present and future hopes are founded?" When suicide and sentiment were connected with deism and dangerous foreign radicalism, it is no wonder that to some Romilly's action appeared less than glorious, that his end was not like the soldier on the field of battle, but a death which "dash[ed] every better feeling with horror and agony. Human nature seems humiliated by this catastrophe." Especially worrying was the possibility that Romilly's death might cause others to imitate it, and, when, in fact, within days, such a suicide occurred, some of the papers did attribute this second death to a terrible sort of mimicry.[92] Thus some newspapers, though unwilling to forgo publishing accounts of well-known suicides, insisted that they owed it to their readers and to the nation to present such culpable deeds without sugar-coating or exoneration.

> We intend nothing against the memory of so good a man as the late Sir Samuel Romilly . . . but there is nothing more *contagious* than examples which appeal strongly to the public passions . . . any theatric exhibition, or dramatic and ostentatious dressing-up of such actions to popular effect, are amongst the most culpable efforts of public writers, inasmuch as it is attacking mankind through their best feelings and misleading them into vice by their admiration of eminent virtue.[93]

In discussions of the death of Sir Samuel Romilly we can see three contemporary themes emerging. The first is the lack of agreement about whether Romilly's self-destruction was caused by sickness or sin. Part of a much larger discussion of the causes of suicide and the best means by which those fatal acts could be lessened, the publicity surrounding Romilly's death added a poignancy to the debate hitherto unknown. How shocking some found the public revelations, the newspaper intrusions, into the private affairs and grief of the Romilly family. And yet others saw his death as an awful warning. "How painfully instructive the awful lesson which it reads, upon the instability of this world's greatness, upon the insecurity of man's proudest hopes." Some thought that the case proved the need to do away completely with coroners' juries: "I must own," commented a columnist to the *British Monitor* in a piece about Romilly's demise, "that I have ever considered the institution of a Coroner's jury incompatible with the character and feelings of a civilized nation." Others thought that the problem with coroners' juries was their excessive kindness, their failure to find correct verdicts and, through a mistaken kindness, to promote charity at the expense of justice. Such "a false sense of clemency," if extended, would render the law a dead letter. If this should occur, "Suicide will remain, as it has so long been, the reproach of our nation; and the impunity of the past will ever prove a lamentable encouragement to the future."[94]

Accompanying these discussions about inquest juries and their operations came a disquieting recognition of the social biases of such bodies and of the public itself. One observer, for example, noted that the public's interest in this story had more to do with Romilly's accomplishments than with the nature of his death. "Not a week passes," commented "X.Y.," in a letter to the *Sunday Advertiser*, "without our having a report of three or four instances of the kind; but numerous as these are, they excite very little attention. It is only when a man of celebrated talents, is impelled, by whatever cause, to rid himself of life, that we take alarm, and meditate on the crime." Even more damaging was the point made by another anonymous correspondent who remarked "that not once in a thousand did a Coroner's Jury bring in a verdict of *Felo-de-se* against a rich man, but principally against poor criminals alone. . . ." Charging, yet once more, that the law was tenderer to the rich and famous than to the poor and condemned, that inquest verdicts depended on the class rather than the guilt of the accused, was a very serious and frank accusation. But, as we have already noted, Romilly was generally not described as a man of rank or riches, but was presented as an ideal man of the middle class, self-made, publicly active though emotionally grounded in the familial, hard-working and dedicated to social improvement. Was there, perhaps inevitably, some price to pay for pulling oneself up by one's bootstraps? Romilly's death raised, but did not answer, any of these questions. When aristocrats, dandies, or criminals killed themselves, their acts confirmed rather than challenged common wisdom: vice, self-indulgence, or law-breaking not surprisingly led to despair and death. But the enigma of Romilly's suicide seemed more troubling, for in his case it seemed his virtues which caused his demise, his sentiments which led to his fatal act. Though his death could be read as the inevitable outcome of philosophic radicalism, of Enlightenment self-confidence, the anxiety raised by the event suggests contemporaries saw in it the specter not only of an individual but of a class of men flawed by the very attributes that made them admirable.[95]

When, only a few years after Romilly's death, the most influential member of the King's Ministry, Robert Stewart, the Earl of Castlereagh, died suddenly, it was certainly not surprising that the press covered every aspect of this unexpected event. The *Morning Post* declared that it had "had to record in our time many national losses and inflictions; but never have we had a more painful task to perform than that which the sudden demise of this accomplished Nobleman and highly gifted Minister imposed upon us."[96] The initial reports were brief, noting that it was thought he had died of gout; only the next day did the truth come out. Castlereagh had killed himself and a coroner's inquest was called to find a verdict. Unsurprisingly, as in Romilly's case, they decided that the cause of the suicide was lunacy, and that perhaps should have been that.

But Londonderry, unlike Romilly, was both a much-hated and much-admired political figure, and so press responses naturally reflected this deep divide. While Romilly's life had been described by news-men as having had a triple focus, i.e., that of a statesman, that of a hard-working professional lawyer, and that of a family member, Castlereagh won almost unanimous praise only for his private life. Thus his strongest press supporter, the *Courier*, declared that "in the sweet retreat of private life—in the bosom of his family—in retirement, the Marquis of Londonderry was the most amiable and beloved of men."[97] Servants weeping copious tears for their departed master were a standard item in all reports. Details of Londonderry's kindness to neighbors and dependents were repeatedly discussed. While it was said that Romilly's grief for his dead wife, as well as his engaged and strenuous public life, had led to his death, Londonderry's was attributed solely to the "anxiety and care for the welfare of his country"; he was "a victim to the toils and anxieties of the high duties which he executed in so admirable a manner." While Romilly had been described as falling victim to his uxorious affections, Londonderry, it was said, was rewarded with "a martyr's grave" for his many attentions to Britain's welfare.[98]

The heart of the press debate following Londonderry's death and the assessment of his life, however, hinged on whether his policies had been the correct ones to follow, whether he had acted from principle or from ambition, and whether his death would or could have some positive national outcome. The *Times*, reviewing his political biography, noted that early in his career he had changed his commitments when "he caught a glimpse of the seductions of office and the rewards of ambition." It concluded that a future historian, scanning his career, "will find his name to more treaties and conventions for clipping the boundaries, impairing the rights, or annihilating the existence of independent states, and to fewer for promoting commerce or aiding the struggles of liberty than any other minister for the last century." And the *Times* was one of the more middle-of-the-road papers in appraising his legacy. The *Examiner* facetiously noted: "*Not* to be debauched and profligate, is almost a virtue in a Lord; but beyond those negative qualities we are not inclined to think he went." The *Liverpool Mercury* commented that, in their opinion, even his private virtues were probably spurious, for they did not "believe it [to be] possible, that a career of public turpitude and of private integrity can be compatible, or co-existent . . .," and the *British Freeholder* added that "while we deplore his death as a man, . . . we cannot [but] regard it as a boon, because we hope that by it the present administration have received a death blow . . . ."[99]

Even accounts of his funeral procession stressed the political character of Londonderry's life. The *Morning Chronicle* declared that they did not "hear one sound of public sorrow escape from the vast multitude assembled to witness the last honours which earthly power could pay to the memory of a most unfortunate and unpopular Minister," while the *Courier* said that "Among the respectable classes of spectators [at the funeral] we particularly marked a strong expression of unaffected regret." *Baldwin's London Weekly*, however, noted that "On the arrival of the hearse among them [the crowd] a most discordant yell displayed the animosity which they felt to the deceased nobleman," going on to describe these noisy comments as coming from "the vilest of the populace" and "the Canaille."[100]

Yet in both cases the issue of suicide, or coroners' courts and their processes, and of the relationship between religious belief and "this rash act" was also discussed and contrasted. Papers of varied political views connected the suicide deaths of three notable public men, Whitbread, Romilly, and Londonderry, in less than a decade, and saw in their exits a reminder of the weaknesses of even the strongest men.[101] Whether or not such individuals were religious seemed to have little bearing on their ability to resist "the appetite for self-destruction."[102] Several of the papers criticized the continued functioning of the coroners' inquests in such deaths, which the *Morning Chronicle* character-ized as "barbarous and brutal." The *Liverpool Mercury* also condemned the comments made preemptively by the coroner to the jury; he advised them that if they valued his opinion, Londonderry was clearly insane.

> [N]o man, [he said] could be in his proper senses at the moment he committed so rash an act as self-murder. His opinion was in consonance with every moral sentiment, and of the information which the wisest of men had given to the world. . . . He therefore viewed it as an axiom, and an abstract principle that a man must necessarily be out of his mind at the moment of destroying himself.

This comment, the *Mercury* noted, "went, if correct, to render all inquests in cases of self-destruction unnecessary. The circumstances of the case did not surely demand this sort of appeal to the jury, an appeal which a victim who had moved in a less distinguished rank of life, would probably not have elic-ited." The *Morning Chronicle* agreed, adding that the finding of *felo de se* was "never indeed enforced but in the case of some neglected foreigner . . . or some wretch too poor for any one to care what becomes of him."[103]

At the end of the day, however, whatever the continuing differences between newspaper supporters of Romilly or Londonderry, there seemed to be a growing sense that it was perhaps inappropriate to subject notable public men, if not all men and women, to the processes of a law that, in any case, would only inflict a punitive verdict on the most impoverished and defenseless.

"Decidedly for the repeal":[104] *Newspapers and the* Felo de Se *Act of* 1823

If Sir Samuel Romilly's was the most publicly bemoaned case of suicide in the years following the end of the Napoleonic Wars, he was by no means the only man of his stamp to have killed himself. Shortly after the triumphant news of the victory at Waterloo hit English newspapers, the account of a more tragic event, the suicide of Samuel Whitbread, slowly appeared, though in muted and muffled tones. The *Examiner* alone gave his death premier coverage, under the heading "Deplorable Public Loss."[105] Three years later, when one of the most famous medical men of the day, Sir Richard Croft, accoucheur to the ill-fated Princess Caroline, also took his own life, the *Morning Post* commented that "[i]t has long been remarked, by all Dr. Croft's friends, that he has been sinking ever since the dreadful catastrophe which threw this afflicted nation into deep mourning." Croft had acted as man-midwife to the Princess, and, it was said, his error had caused both her death and that of her male offspring. "Never," concluded the *Post*, "has the deceased held up his head since."[106] A self-made man, who studied with "the celebrated Dr. Hunter" and who later married the daughter of Dr. Denman, "the most celebrated *Accoucheur* Doctor of his time," he succeeded both to his father-in-law's practice, and also to the title of his brother, Sir Herbert Croft.[107] With the death of the Princess and her son, due perhaps to his mismanagement, his good fortune came to an end. In death, however, three months later, his end was shielded, at least in part, from the prying eyes of the press. Though reports of the inquest were published in several papers, only the radical *Examiner* included the following:

> The utmost industry was also used to suppress all knowledge of the manner of Sir Richard's death: . . . an Editor cannot yield to the applications of friends on such events, without incurring the charges of corruption, even where he indulges the kindest emotions of the heart.—Our Reporters were prevented from access to the Inquest; a prohibition which the Coroner was not justified in authorising, since the law of the Coroner was intended undoubtedly to operate as a preventive of the dreadful and abhorrent crime of suicide, a crime which is probably rendered more frequent by the concealment too often arranged, and by the lenity of the verdicts.[108]

The impact of these two deaths, combined with the massive outpourings of thought and sentiment following Romilly's demise and Londonderry's mysterious exit, perhaps was responsible for the appearance of a series of letters and comments on the topics of suicide, insanity, and the law in London's press.[109] Almost two-thirds of the letters were clearly of the opinion that the coroners' courts were not operating properly, that too many rational self-murderers were being found lunatic, and not only that such findings could only be attained by jury perjury, but also that such findings in fact encouraged self-killing. So, for example, "Humanitas," a correspondent to the *New Monthly Magazine*, argued that "were he [the willing or sane suicide] to know that such juries would act up to the meaning of the solemn oath they have taken *in foro conscientiae*, without respect of persons, it might in some instances prevent the horrid catastrophe." With the exception of three letters from "A Coroner" which we will shortly consider, only two other letters appeared which did not support this critical view of inquest findings; the first, which appeared in the *Examiner*, argued that it was merely customary prejudice that blinded people to their natural right to end their lives whenever they chose; the second, a letter that advocated the extension of legal counsel before coroners' juries, contended that their findings were sometimes swayed by external political factors.[110] The most interesting interchange, however, one clearly representative of both sides of the issue, took place between "Homo" and "A Coroner," spurred by the latter's published advice to an inquest jury about the evidence necessary to bring in a *non compos mentis* verdict. In that original peroration, the coroner had advised the jury that "it is proper there should be a leaning to that side of the question, which is most favourable to the memory of the deceased [for insanity was] a disease of the most horrible nature, which can *at once* extinguish the strongest of human passions, that of self-preservation."[111] About two weeks later, "Homo's" first letter appeared, which took as its target this coroner's pronouncements. Attacking the coroner for deliberately misquoting accepted legal authorities, he broadened his critique to include coroners in general:

> I apprehend it to be clear that the whole charge of the Coroner (like other charges of his brethren) assume the very point to be proved, vis. the existence of insanity in the case in question . . . he first argues back from the cause [of death] which he says was grief, and then forward to the verdict, which he suggests should be insanity; whereas his obvious course should have been simply to detail the evidence, and then leave it to the jury to decide whether such evidence did or did not establish the fact of insanity.

The "Coroner's" response was swift—three days after the publication of "Homo's" letter, his reply appeared in the *Times*. Defending his reading of Hale, he introduced the notion of "partial insanity," that is, that a person could "take *rational* measures for an *irrational* object" and challenged "Homo" to come up with a workable, practicable set of guidelines for juries in like circumstances.[112] Instead of doing this, however, "Homo's" second letter reiterated the older view that prior moral decisions, freely made by rational individuals, could have a determining influence on their later susceptibility to suicidal insanity, and therefore their culpability to punishment. When a man in a state of total inebriation committed a crime, "Homo" argued, his guilt was in no way diminished by his claim that his action was done while he was in "an altered state of being." For "Homo," a great many suicides were thus to be attributed to "the pride of reason, the love of this present world, the absence of all Scriptural piety, and the entire want of submission to the righteous will of God." In "Homo's" final letter (after raising the specter of corruption and bribery while maintaining he refused to believe in such vice, "for the honour of human nature"), he savagely mocked the incompetence and contradictory nature of medical evidence and inquest findings. A man who, he said, wrote a will before killing himself, which was subsequently probated and found sound, was then declared a lunatic by a coroner's jury. Most of this last letter was, however, devoted to ideas for the improvement of the law.[113]

Both those, like the "Coroner," who represented an enlightened or a medical point of view, and those like "Homo," whose comments were traditional, religious, and legal, thought that it was important that the law be changed; first so that jurors could not be forced to find lunacy when their consciences and their minds told them that full-blown insanity was not proved, and second, so that jurors, unswayed by the barbarous rites of a *felo de se* burial, would be more rigorous in their determinations, and find lunacy only when it was clearly established by existing criteria. Thus both positions, coming from diametrical poles, agreed on the need for some legal amelioration.

It is surely significant not only that, in the early decades of the nineteenth century, ordinary men and women witnessing the burial of a self-murderer at a crossroads, with a stake driven through his or her heart, expressed shock and horror, but also that the premier newspapers of the day reported those sentiments as worthy of note. So, for example, less than a month after Romilly's death, "[g]reat numbers were collected together at the time the excavation was being made" for the interment of a Spanish officer found *felo de se*. The crowd "expressed great disapprobation of the proceedings, and during the absence of the labourers for a short time they endeavoured to fill up the hole again," only to be stopped by some City constables. Later, "a great concourse of persons, females as well as males, had assembled to witness the disgusting scene" amidst cries of shock and horror at the exposure of the naked corpse. When the body was "thrown headlong into the hole prepared to receive it" the crowd voiced its opinions: "Disgraceful to a civilized country," "Horrible and inhuman exposure." Even after the hole was filled, the City officers ordered guards to remain on the spot "to prevent the body from being removed."[114] Most seemed to agree that this posthumous ritual was repugnant and the public display of violence upon a dead body undesirable. Thus "Ordovex," in a letter to the *Times* entitled "Frequency of Suicide," published just three weeks after the event discussed above, after characterizing suicide as a crime of "the deepest dye," went on to note that he did not "approve, in an unqualified manner, of the penalties assigned by our law to this crime. They are certainly characteristic of a barbarous age, as is the case with others that might easily be enumerated." Instead, he continued, he wished that "the law be amended, and even considerably alleviated; but by all means let the principle be retained . . . ."[115]

Just a few weeks later, in presenting a petition from the City of London to the House of Lords, Lord Holland asked them to "enter into a consideration of the criminal code, with a view to render it more consonant to the general feelings." What he seemed to think particularly upsetting, not only to the City, but to the kingdom as a whole, was the fact that the Law was under attack because of "the continual breach of its enactments, which was the every day practice." Juries, moved by the harsh penalties of the criminal code, were refusing to find guilty persons guilty; without proper enactment, the Law would become a sham, a mockery. Furthermore, Holland noted that when France had substituted lenient for severe criminal penalties, both successful prosecutions and findings increased.[116] And although this attempt to amend the bloody code was unsuccessful, and it was to be several decades before its most savage punishments were eliminated, publicly witnessed judicial violence was clearly under attack.

In 1823, when Romilly's successor in the Parliamentary campaign to reform the penal code, Sir James Mackintosh, argued for the need to consider the amendment of the Law, he cited, along with other notorious improprieties, the barbarous interments of those found *felo de se*. After a brilliant, much applauded speech, the plan to modernize the Law was once again shelved, though just a month later, with no warning and little discussion, a bill was proposed by a junior member, to eliminate the degrading burial of self-murderers, and passed, almost immediately, into law. In a curious sort of way, the passage of this Act can be seen as pleasing both sides of the discussion. The enlightened, secular, or medical point of view could feel that it had scored a victory, having convinced legislators that it was wrong to punish the insane, while the traditional, legal, or religious observers could feel that, finally, with the penalties eased, those guilty of self-murder would be found guilty, and the crime not whitewashed by the lunacy verdict. Even "Homo," who, as we have seen, expended considerable energy in proving the iniquity of suicide, agreed that he was "decidedly for the repeal of this law—not upon the principle of the Coroner, because the law is wrong, but—because such an abuse of law as we constantly witness is indefensible upon every principle of religion and reason."[117] Thus, because it suited both the hard-liners, the legal, traditional, or religious proponents, and their opponents, the enlightened, medical, or secular supporters, the public humiliation and degraded rites surrounding the burial of self-murderers finally ended.

Was this the first, though not final, triumph of humanitarian concern, of secularization or of medical insight into the vagaries of the human psyche? Or rather was it the realization of "Ordovex's" hope, that the punishment of self-murder might be mitigated, but the principle of legal condemnation be still preserved? There are two reasons for thinking it was "Ordovex's" hopes that were fulfilled. First was the willingness of some medical men, men who thought suicide was usually caused by insanity, to propose dissection for those found *felo de se*. Thus "C," who in his letter to the *Times* asserted that the suicide attempt itself was often the first manifestation of insanity, and that all the many cases he had examined of unsuccessful attempts clearly displayed insanity after, though they had displayed none before the attempt, also argued for a change in the law:

> A prohibition of all religious ceremony at the interment of such as are really and on sufficient evidence proved to be self-murderers, or privately delivering the body for dissection, as is done to persons who murder others, is, perhaps, all that a wise legislation should decree.

Public humiliation should be replaced by private disposal, argued Chevalier. A year later, a correspondent to the *Gentleman's Magazine* agreed, suggesting that "every individual who died by his own hand, under whatever circumstances, should be delivered to properly authorized and designated persons for dissection." Finally, less than a year before the passage of the Act allowing private burial for all suicides, whatever the verdict of the jury on their bodies, the *Times*, responding editorially to an earlier letter, noted that:

> we see nothing objectionable in the suggestion of our correspondent: we see no objection to giving the bodies of burglars and highway robbers . . . for the purposes of dissection. Perhaps the *felo de se* might be added to the list: at any rate, the present useless and barbarous custom of running a stake through the body of the suicide might be well replaced by giving the body to the anatomist . . . .[118]

Thus it is clear that while everyone wished for the disappearance of public humiliation of the corpse, the willingness of many to allow for discreet, private dissection, a notoriously unpopular practice, demonstrates the inadequacies of seeing this legal change only as a result of the growth of humane sympathy.

The second ground for thinking that "Ordovex's" desire to preserve the principle while mitigating the punishment of self-murder triumphed, is signalled in the question asked by MacDonald and Murphy about the timing of the repeal of the forfeiture clause. This clause, applying equally to all those found guilty of felonies, was allowed to remain "on the books" for almost half a century after *felo de se* burials were no longer penalized and made into public spectacles. For, in practice, the forfeiture clause remained largely a dead letter through most of the eighteenth century and beyond, and thus perfectly served as a condemnatory principle, but one which, not acted upon, served only as notice that rational suicide was not a condoned option, but that such acts were still held to be destructive to families, to religion, and to society as a whole.[119]

By eliminating public interment, the *Felo de Se Act* also addressed the important legal inequity between the treatment of the suicides of the *ton* and of more ordinary folk. For it is important to remember that both popular and Parliamentary opinion saw in suicide a sin which, while all were liable to it, was a particular pitfall of the fashionable. Sir James Mackintosh, in his address to Parliament, noted that "Suicide was rarely the crime of the poorer classes occupied with their daily labours. It was the effect of wounded shame, the result of false pride, and the fear of some imaginary degradation." And while "G. W.," in a 1822 letter to the *Gentleman's*, argued that suicide was caused by overexcitation of any sort (he included gin-drinking and opium use as stimuli employed by ordinary folk), he too spoke of most inflaming practices as upper-class activities; overindulgence in the pleasures of the table was listed first and foremost as an example of such stimulation and described as "deviations from Nature's laws which have the sanction of Fashion, and the highest classes."[120] Thus, though not perhaps the triumph of medical or secular thought, the 1823 Act can be seen as yet another attempt to apply society's laws and moral injunctions more equally, or at least to give that appearance.

"Lady Worsley dressing in the Bathing House." *The Cuckold's Chronicle* (London: H. Lemon, 1793). Courtesy of the British Library

4

"The Chief Topics of Conversation": Adultery and Divorce in the Bon Ton

Adultery from the Glorious Revolution to the Reign of George III

In his fine book *Fashioning Adultery*, David Turner has very persuasively argued that, though adultery was by no means a new vice in Restoration England, there was a new level of concern, even anxiety, about it.[1] And, in the face of some arguments to the contrary, Turner holds to an older view that, despite Filmer's defeat by Locke, the link between familial stability and political, national stability was still widely upheld. Or, to quote a "Person of Quality," writing in the 1690s, "a *Family* is the *Epitome* of a Kingdom."[2]

It is worth spending a moment unpacking this widespread belief. In which ways were the fates of nations dependent on the health of individual families? Perhaps at the most fundamental level, it was held that the possibility of all sorts of governance and obedience rested on the security and inviolability of property, whether in land, women, or progeny: ". . . the whole band of *civil society*, and of a regular communion betwixt Men in the World, proceeds from the succession of a Lawful Issue, which is the *Broad-seal* of Heaven."[3] Stability of marriage, it was said, would inevitably produce stable government, "as *Marriage* abates the Irregular Lives of Men, so it produces a *sober*, and well-disposed *Posterity*."[4] Adulterers, in contrast, not only ruined family peace, but sowed social and civil discord, "For the Disturbers of Government are usually those who decry Marriage among themselves, and invade it in others."[5] And once the sixth commandment, forbidding adultery, was breached, it was just a matter of time until the seventh, against murder, was also ruptured.[6] A corollary to the powerful analogy between families and governments, often supported by references to the decline and fall of earlier kingdoms and empires, was that adultery would inevitably lead to the military decline and fall of whichever nation accepted its imperatives. "And certainly if this lustful fire be not quenched, or else be timely not restrained, it will soon emasculate the age, consume the strength, and melt down the courage of the nation. . . . If we design to maintain our martial valour, for which we are now renowned thro' the world, we must keep a distance from Venus's tents."[7] In a period of intermittent though frequent warfare and the acquisition of empire, such a threat was taken seriously. This was perhaps significant for the "legislative initiative in 1699 to make adultery a capital offence . . . [which] only narrowly failed to become law."[8]

Another widely held belief about this vice was that some segments of society were more apt to commit adultery than others, that for some it had ceased being viewed as a crime or even as a sin, but was instead treated gently, called "gallantry," and formed a part of the mores of a privileged group in society. Most historians agree that from the Restoration to the mid-eighteenth century many believed that the *beau monde* lived by a code of sexual manners significantly different from the rest of society, and it was this belief that spurred calls for moral reform.[9] At mid-century, Alexander Jephson summarized this attribution by noting that adultery, one of the "reigning and fashionable Vices of the Age," was "favoured and encouraged by the Great and Powerful." Unmindful of their influence, led by their vain and promiscuous passions to indulge in adultery, the upper classes, according to Jephson, were to blame for what he and many of his contemporaries saw as the growth of this grievous fault. "Nothing," he commented, "hath contributed so much to the quick and extensive Propagation of these accursed Vices, as that so many Persons of the greatest Fashion and Distinction . . . have given so much Countenance to them by their own Example."[10] Adultery, commented the *Grub Street Journal* of 1730, was esteemed by "all well-bred persons . . . as a piece of gallantry and not a crime."[11]

What did late seventeenth- and early eighteenth-century contemporaries think could or should be done to end this vicious indulgence, this pernicious breach of God's and man's laws? The suggestions bear a strong resemblance to the proposed punishments for duelling. Some Members of Parliament thought that, from being a misdemeanor, adultery should become "criminalized." This was a suggestion raised many times during the century, though never adopted. Thus, in 1724, Richard Smalbroke, Bishop of St. David's, seemed to bemoan the leniency of British law.

> it is a Duty the more incumbent on the Magistrate, to turn the keenest Edge of the Laws against those that notoriously live in a State of Adultery, both in order to rouze them by the Smart of the Inconveniencies they incur, out of their stupified Condition to a better Sense of things, and to deter others by their Sufferings from so pernicious a Crime. It must be confessed, indeed, that this Part of our Civil Constitution is defective, and that our Laws are not so severe as those of most other Nations, that punish Adultery with Death . . . .[12]

Others argued that a revival of a devout Anglican Christianity would be more effective than punitive legislation, though this too faltered in the practical implementation. Yet another suggestion that was periodically rediscovered though the eighteenth and nineteenth centuries was the public use of shame, either through the practice of ducking adulterers in neighboring ponds, through the attachment of marks of eternal infamy to their persons or dwellings, or through corporal punishment like horsewhipping. "[E]verlasting Reproach, and the Detestation of all the World, are deservedly the Portion" of those guilty of adultery, opined the *Universal Spectator* in 1734. In addition it was sometimes argued that officers of state, whether serving in the nation's government or the military, should be evicted from these occupations if they were found guilty of adultery.

Though all these recourses were suggested, the only major changes that occurred in the way that adultery was treated was the institution, late in the seventeenth century, of full divorce through a private Act of Parliament for the cuckolded husband and the use of a civil suit of trespass or assault against the wife's lover, which soon came to be called "criminal conversation," and which awarded the aggrieved husband a monetary compensation for his loss.[13] It is unclear, despite the pioneering work of both Lawrence Stone and David Turner, how lawyers and parliamentarians first came to invent these devices. What is certain, however, is that by 1680 both were being used and, for a small section of the population, full divorce with the possibility of remarriage became possible. It is ironic, perhaps, that for that section deemed in print most likely to be guilty of the sin in the first place, remarriage became, if not cheap or shameless, certainly negotiable for people of fashion.

If neither the vice nor its condemnation was therefore new, but in the post-Restoration period felt to be more predominant and more dangerous, was anything novel in the way that writers and readers, moralists and theater-goers, understood it or experienced it? David Turner argues that it was the appearance of printed criminal conversation trials in the first half of the eighteenth century that raised the issue in the public's consciousness. "Since prosecutions for criminal conversation were not routine, trials generated huge public interest when they occurred." Furthermore, both he and Lawrence Stone argue that "the lively publicity surrounding these trials," largely in the form of pamphlets produced immediately after, widened and deepened this interest.[14] While many of the most notorious of such cases, in the main involving at least one aristocratic male, did result in the production of a number of pamphlets about the trial, we may wish to reconsider the effect and scope of their influence. Before we examine their coverage and impact, however, let us briefly look at what other sorts of material dealing with adultery were popular before the accession of George III.

By the early eighteenth century, the London stage had become less aggressively libertine, less astringent in its humor or biting in its commentary, than had been the theater of Charles II. Though male adultery continued as a frequently featured and only mildly censured activity on this more moral eighteenth-century stage, female adultery was seldom condoned or left unpunished. This is not surprising, nor are the casual, offhand comments on the connection between adultery, divorce, and the morality of people of fashion in the first half of the century. Thus in David Garrick's trifle of 1741, *The Lying Valet*, the young heroine, in the guise of a man of the mode, instructs a would-be member of the *beau monde* about what can and cannot be done by them. Addressing him, she comments "breaking of Contracts, suing for Divorces, committing Adultery, and such like, are all reckon'd Trifles now-a-days; and smart young Fellows, like you and myself, Gayless, should be never out of Fashion." Similarly, in Garrick's 1749 play, *Lethe*, Aesop informs a Mrs. Tatoo that she doesn't need Lethe's waters to divorce her from her husband; all, he says, she needs to do in order to forget him, is to remember "continually [that] he is your husband. There are several ladies have no other receipt." She then explains to Aesop that, longing to be in fashion, she has been told that this is impossible for a happily married woman, but that if she would "but procure a separate divorcement . . . [she] should be as complete a fine lady as any of 'em." These "throwaway" lines, these casual references to the manners and sexual standards of married people of fashion, show that, at least as "background" noise, eighteenth-century theater-goers were widely exposed to a shared set of assumptions about the married improprieties of their betters.[15]

The theater, however, was not the only medium for airing views about adultery and divorce. A wide variety of other sorts of popular writings, usually though not always religious or moral in character, also treated the same bundle of notions surrounding marriage, female honor, and class privilege. An interesting set of such views was expressed in Mary Wray's discussion of "chastity" in *The Ladies Library* of 1722. First, recalling the failed bill of 1698 that had proposed to make adultery a criminal offense, Wray asked rhetorically why this wholesome piece of legislation had failed to pass; her answer was both ironic and pointed:

> But to our Shame be it spoken, the Crime was too general, the Offenders too great, and not the Nation too merciful; for God forbid, that those who with pleasure see daily poor Criminals carry'd to the Gallows; for little Thefts and Robberies, shou'd be griev'd to see those punish'd with Death, that had robb'd whole Families of their Peace, and Honour, and Estates, by bringing into them Bastardy and Infamy.[16]

According to Wray, then, it was both the widespread nature of the sin and its practice by the Great that doomed this proposed change. More unusual, perhaps, was Wray's verdict in her judgment of the relative sinfulness of men and women in committing adultery. Since men, she argued, have stronger understandings and resolution than women, "in respect of the Person" they were more blameable, though, she admitted, women were more at fault "in respect of the evil Consequences of Adultery," i.e., the introduction of spurious heirs to property not rightly theirs. However, she concluded, "In respect of the crime, and as relating to God, they are equal, intolerable and damnable."[17]

Several writers, both men of religion and others, blamed the decline of religious practice for the growth of this dreadful sin. According to Philogamus,

> The first, and more general Cause of Lewdness, is the want of Religion, and the Decay of Christian Piety. . . . The poisonous Infusion of the most horrid Principles is sucked in, by both Sexes, with the greatest Avidity: The Deformity of Vice is extenuated, and even denied by some; and all intrinsic Virtue, particularly Chastity, is turned to ridicule; and almost *catcall'd* away.[18]

Arguing against the code of "modern gallantry," whose chief activity was adultery, the anonymous author of the *Essay on Modern Gallantry* explained why religious arguments could not be used when discussing the vices of the fashionable:

> [B]ecause most of these pretty Gentlemen, with whom I have to deal in this Controversy, have Stomachs too nice to digest any Arguments drawn from Religion, I shall throw Divinity entirely out of the Question, and address

> myself to them in their favorite Characters, as they profess themselves *Men of Honour, Men of Pleasure and Men of Sense.*

But this essay was not only addressed to men of the mode, did not only warn men of honor that adultery was a grievous offence in a code of secular friendship, sociability, and good manners, but also included a warning to those women who did not belong to the privileged fashionable world:

> You will also do well to consider that Ladies of Rank, Fortune, and Distinction, may do a thousand irregular Things, without Censure, or at least with no other bad Consequence, by the very Circumstance of their being *above the World*; they have the same *Privilege* of being unaccountable for their Conduct, as *Men*, in the same high Station, have of not *paying their Debts*, unless they please. Whereas the World will not make the same Allowances to Women of an inferior Rank, but exacts the severest Account of their Actions, under Pain of Infamy and Reproach.[19]

In making this distinction between women of different ranks, this author was taking one side of a more controversial position. While most commentators agreed about the sanctioned irresponsibility of fashionable men, others, like Timothy Hooker, argued that all women, whatever their class, irrevocably lost their public repute through an act of sexual impropriety:

> [E]very Woman who has once been so unhappy as to offend in point of Chastity, cannot by the most sincere Repentance, by all the merciful Abatements that ought to be made for human Frailty, and a thousand amiable Qualities besides, thrown into the Balance, be ever able to wipe off an indelible Mark of Infamy fixed upon her by all the ill-natur'd Prudes and Coquets about Town.[20]

Rank protected men and perhaps even women of the upper classes from ignominy, most authors agreed, and neither Christian religion nor morality was a significant hindrance to the vicious activities of these fashionable folk. " 'Tis true, Custom and Fashion, and false Notions of Gallantry, have in great measure defaced the Boundaries of Vice and Virtue, Infamy and Honour in the Fashionable World . . .," Hooker complained.[21]

As we have noted, both Stone and Turner have commented on the importance that criminal conversation trial accounts, published as pamphlets, had on stirring interest in, and familiarizing the general public with, the sexual vices of the Great. These, no doubt, were of some importance, though they probably served a reasonably restricted readership because of their price. There were five "great" trials that all produced published accounts in the period before 1760; these were the trials between Abergavenny and Liddel, Morice and Fitzroy, Cibber and Sloper, Biker and Morley, and Knowles and Gambier. Counting the pamphlets that have survived, however, we find that, on average, just over four pamphlets or editions were published for each case. Though this is by no means a negligible number, it is no more than the number published for other sorts of "interesting" cases from the 1690s onwards.[22] These undoubtedly whetted the appetite of the reading public, and perhaps, over time, helped to create the seemingly endless interest in the sexual improprieties of the upper classes, which we will see was so glaring by the late 1760s. However, these early single accounts, and the few collections of cases I have come across for the first half of the century are not only scantier, but have a different "flavor" than later publications of this sort. For one thing, these early pamphlets tended to be shorter in length and unadorned by the colorful, imaginary illustrations that, we shall see, enhanced later pamphlets. Those earliest in the century were also, unsurprisingly, shortest in length; the average for the first three of these cases was a pamphlet of about 30 pages. The pamphlet of the Morice case of 1742 was longer (50 pages) while that of the Knowles trial of 1757 was twice the size of the earlier ones. When compared to the pamphlets covering the criminal conversation cases of the 1770s and 1780s, these earlier works are both fewer and briefer.

Equally "transitional" are the collections of notorious cases published before the 1760s. Morer's *Two Cases the first of adultery and divorce* was more concerned with the punishment for adultery than in giving details of actual cases. In Edmund Curll's *Cases of Divorce for Several Causes* of 1715, for example, only half of that book was devoted to trials that had occurred within the last three decades, and the judge's verdict in the Duchess of Cleveland's case was entirely in Latin, which would hardly have made it attractive or accessible to a broader reading public.[23] The 1732 compendium *The Cases of Polygamy, Concubinage, Adultery, Divorce, etc. by the most eminent hands* contained a diversity of material, but only a passing reference to the case of Lord Roos, whose Parliamentary divorce of 1670 is widely considered as the first non-regal complete divorce. And though the 1739 volume *A Collection of remarkable trials* did include the Cibber and Abergavenny trials, it also included "four original letters" as well as an account of the trial of the infamous Colonel Chartres for rape. Not until the 1761 publication of *Adultery Anatomized: in a select collection of Tryals for Criminal Conversation. Brought from the Infant Ages of Cuckoldom in England to its full growth in the present times* did the reading public have access to a single work dedicated to the sordid details of actual criminal conversation cases.

What of the press, however? What sorts of items concerning divorce, adultery, crim. con. trials, etc. did they present to the wide reading public in the

first six decades of the century? Of course, these topics had been discussed in
a general way by the great pioneering essay-journals of the century. Thus,
Addison in the *Spectator*, comparing the chief quality that made males and
females virtuous, concluded that women's virtue resided in their chastity.[24]
These sorts of general discussions continued in the magazines, covering many
pages in the competing journals in the century's second quarter. A quick run-
through of this material will illustrate the point. In the 1730s, both the
Gentleman's and the *London Magazine* published an essay on marriage and
divorce, and the *London* and the *Grub Street Journal* exposed "certain
Fashionable Vices"; in the 1740s the *Gentleman's* (copying this time from the
Universal Spectator) discussed adultery in the context of what they called
"modern conversation," while in the 1750s, the *Covent Garden Journal* (later,
once again, recopied in the *Gentleman's*), in a mock dictionary entitled "A
Modern Glossary" identified adultery as a central component of "gallantry."[25]
The strongest, if by no means the only, denunciation of adultery, however,
came from the repeated attacks made on it by Henry Fielding's *Covent Garden
Journal*:

> By what means our Laws were induced to consider this atrocious *Vice* as no
> Crime, I shall not attempt to determine. Such however is the Fact: for as to
> the Action for criminal Conversation, tho' some have severely smarted by it,
> yet the Lawyers well know the Difference between criminal and civil
> Proceedings, between that Process which is instituted for Punishment and
> Example, and that which hath merely the Redress of an Injury and Damages
> only in its View.[26]

Like many others, both before and after him, Fielding believed that adultery
should be a matter of criminal, not civil law, that it was an offence against
the stability of the state, and not merely a loss to a private person or family.
These rebukes, however, only obliquely pointed at the Great and, however
plentiful, still were moralistic in tone and general in target.

Given the reticence of the press to report on the suicides and duels of the
beau monde in this period, it is hardly surprising that their adulteries and
divorces only received scant magazine or newspaper coverage. Thus, one of
the earliest of such reports, involving two men of quality, was only a single
sentence long. "At a Trial in the Court of Common Pleas at Westminster,
Dingley Goodere, Esq., Son of Sir Robert Goodere, Bart. Recover'd of Sir
Robert Jason, Bt. 1000l. for criminal Conversation with his Wife." In contrast,
only two months later, when the *Gentleman's Magazine*, which had also
reported on the Goodere trial, published the story of another adultery trial,
this time in "low life," many more details were forthcoming:

A Cause was tried in the Court of Common Pleas at Westminster, between Joseph Green, Plaintiff and Joseph Molineux, Defendant, for criminal Conversation with the Plaintiff's Wife. The Fact was proved; but it appearing that the Plaintiff's House was a reputed Bawdy-House, and that some of the Witnesses had lain with his Wife and two of his Daughters, a Verdict pass'd for the Def.[27]

Similarly, when the Biker *v* Morley case of 1741 was reported, only one of the ten popular magazines or newspapers commented on it. Noting that it was "a remarkable Case" and that the hearing "had lasted twelve hours" the *Daily Gazetteer* merely reported that the jury "brought in a Verdict for the Defendant."[28] By the 1750s, though more accounts of adulteries and court cases appeared in the press, these either were mainly comic or had middling folk as featured protagonists. A good example of the former was the story told in the *Gentleman's Magazine* of a dealer, coming home from a business trip, and finding his wife and her lover in bed. Tying them together in their naked state in front of a roaring fire, he invited the neighbors in to view them, and partake of the "tea, coffee and punch [which he] provided." That same journal contained accounts of crim. con. cases involving Messrs. Teat and Craven, in which the former was non-suited (his wife, it appeared, was bigamous) and that of two eminent merchants, in which the husband received the rather large compensation of £2500.[29] It is not until the 1757 suit between Admiral Knowles, whom we have already met in our previous discussion of duelling, against a Captain in his fleet, James Gambier, for the latter's criminal conversation with his commander's wife, that any significant press reporting of an upper-class adultery occurred.

In 1756, Knowles, then governor of Jamaica, sent his wife and children back to London on a ship commanded by Captain James Gambier. When, a year later, Knowles sued Gambier for adultery with his wife, the press reported the event, though without giving any of the steamier details or reflecting on the individuals or families involved. Both the *Gentleman's* and the *Universal Magazine* matter-of-factly reported that the case had come before the courts, the former using dashes to imply, but not state, the full names of the participants, the latter merely referring to a case "between a late Governor of one of our Islands in the West Indies and his Lady" in their account of the ecclesiastical court procedures.[30] The *Public Advertiser*, which also reported the affair, merely noted "that a certain Person of Distinction, having Reason to be much discontented with the Conduct of his Lady, is very soon to be separated from her." The *London Evening Post* utilized the same euphemism employed by the *Universal*, noting that "a late Governor of one of our Islands

in the West-Indies was Plaintiff, and a Captain of a Man of War Defendant."[31]
Even in this most widely covered case of upper-class adultery of the 1750s,
the tone was restrained, the names suggested but not spelled out, the details
few. In terms of public involvement in the sexual improprieties of the fashionable, though some peepholes had undoubtedly been provided for those interested in upper-class adultery by the availability of pamphlet and press reporting
of these affairs, this publicity would only have whetted the appetite, without
satisfying the hunger, of any prurient moralist or critic of Society.

Adultery, Politics, and the Press

Thus we have seen that, while there were many critics of the sexual
mores and free-and-easy ways of the *bon ton*, of fashionable gallantry, through
the first almost seven decades of the eighteenth century, there was a real
reluctance in the periodical press to attack, or even extensively to report, these
affairs in the particular, or to give any specific details. It was only after a daring
and path-breaking set of anonymous letters written under the name *Junius*
was published, and quickly reprinted, collected, and republished, that the
domestic world of society's leaders was held up as a proper object of discussion, proper, at least initially, in so far as it had some bearing on the political
arrangements and power relations of the day.

When George III ascended to the throne in 1760, a young, virtuous, and
English monarch, there were many panegyrics to his private character and
worth. One of the very few monarchs of Britain who not only abstained from
sexual dalliance, but also made his family life an important symbol of both
his personal morality and his public authority, George nevertheless found it
impossible to rid his court of such behavior, or to select his ministers only
from men of impeccable personal morality. Thus, the incongruity between his
upright private life and the immoralities of members of both his family and
ministries was to be a problem for the first quarter-century of his reign.

Through the second half of the eighteenth century, the view that "the
personal was political," that the morals of statesmen and their public conduct
mirrored each other, became increasingly prevalent. Of course men in public
life had always been chastised for various kinds of corruption, but, until this
period, it was the sins of venality rather than those of immorality, that were
seen as the most frequent, and attacked as the most nationally threatening
vices of the ruling classes. Bribery and fiscal dishonesty, it was said, by
appealing to the desire for private gain, disordered the public realm and
introduced an imbalance of power and a misuse of authority. "Old Corruption"
was the purchase of political support, and had little or nothing to do with the

private, that is to say, domestic arrangements of its adherents and followers. Of course, this sort of venality continued, and continued to be attacked; what was new, however, was the focus on other kinds of personal and political vice.

Though the King's tutor and confidante, the unpopular Earl of Bute, was frequently imputed to be the lover of the Princess Dowager, it was Junius' attack on George's chief minister in the late 1760s that inaugurated a campaign whose purpose was to cleanse political life by publicizing and focusing opinion "out of doors" on the hitherto passed-over questions of private sexual morality.

The main target of Junius' attack was the Duke of Grafton. Grafton, who had married the daughter of Baron Ravensworth in 1756, had, despite his married state, continued to keep a number of mistresses and to lead a separate life from his duchess. When she eloped in 1768, pregnant with a child by her lover, the Earl of Upper Ossory, Grafton launched a criminal conversation suit against him, and petitioned for a complete Parliamentary divorce. Rather than becoming an object of sympathy or even of humor, however, the cuckolded Duke was condemned for his public immorality, especially for taking his mistress, Nancy Parsons, to the Opera, thus flaunting her and their relationship, in a public venue. This furnished Junius with the opportunity he desired:

> Did not the duke of Grafton frequently lead his mistress into public, and even place her at the head of his table, as if he had pulled down an ancient temple of Venus, and could bury all decency and shame under the ruins?[32]

Yet whatever blame was heaped upon Grafton for this public display of his unrepentant immorality, he was also criticized by Junius for breaking with Parsons after his divorce was announced, and shortly thereafter marrying one of Ossory's cousins.

> Is there not a singular mark of shame set upon this man, who has so little delicacy and feeling as to submit to the opprobrium of marrying a near relation of one who had debauched his wife?—In the name of decency, how are these amiable cousins to meet at their uncle's table?—It will be a scene in Oedipus, without the distress.[33]

In this attack Junius claimed, although in a sarcastic and biting manner, that the morals of the upper classes did not concern him, that what he attacked was the publicity of Grafton's offence. A later article in the *Town and Country*, in a satiric account of Grafton's installation as Chancellor of Cambridge University, playing on the fact of the close relation between the two sets of families, noted that there was "Dropt, two courtsies between the present and the late duchess of G—, who appeared very magnificently dressed, in honour of his grace's installation."[34] Grafton's virtuous remarriage, as well as his immoral public display of Parsons, thus inevitably involved public attention.

> The example of the English nobility may, for aught I know, sufficiently justify the duke of Grafton when he indulges his genius in all the fashionable excesses of the age. . . . But if vice itself be excused, there is yet a certain display of it, a certain outrage to decency, and violation of public decorum, which, for the benefit of society, should never be forgiven. It is not that he kept a mistress at home, but that he constantly attended her abroad. It is not the private indulgence, but the public insult, of which I complain.[35]

Yet at the same time, Junius also attacked Grafton's remarriage on grounds that were purely personal.

> His grace, it seems, is now a regular domestic man; and, as an omen of the future delicacy and correctness of his conduct, he marries a first cousin of the man who had fixed that mark and title of infamy upon him which, at the same moment, makes a husband unhappy and ridiculous.[36]

Attempting to make intimations about the public delicacy, the public intelligence, and the public morality of Grafton by referring to his private life, Junius concluded, powerfully if illogically, in his address to the Duke, "Your grace's public conduct, as a minister, is but the counter part of your private history; the same inconsistency, the same contradictions."[37]

This rhetorical strategy, using the public press to target a political actor for his private failings, could also be used in the reverse. Thus "Tullius," beginning an attack on the political character of the Duke, opened his letter to Grafton by arguing that he would not reproach him with his "private conduct in life," but only with his conduct as chief minister.[38] This elaborate refusal to discuss his private life underscored its reprehensible quality, while ostensibly taking the high road of abstaining from domestic slurs and focusing only on public issues.

Junius also tried this contradictory tactic on the conduct of the young king himself. In effect accusing George of using his private moral purity as an exculpatory device to skirt questions of public responsibility, Junius addressed the king, asking:

> And if you are, in reality, that public man, that king, that magistrate, which these questions suppose you to be, is it any answer to your people to say that, among your domestics you are good-humoured, that to one lady you are faithful, that to your children you are indulgent?[39]

In his muddling of the domestic and the political, Junius and his press associates made it possible to go from the private, personal, and secret to the public, political, and open, in either direction, in a single bound.

Though it is difficult to tell the chicken from the egg, the causes from the effects, this period of political turmoil also saw the appearance of a variety of newspapers and magazines which featured both political and sexual scandals. The best known of these were probably the *Town and Country Magazine*[40] (which contained at least ten stories relating to adultery and divorce in its first year of publication), the *Oxford Magazine*, and *Bingley's Journal*; all began in 1769 and all had a significant role in making the adultery of the famous not only widely known but a topic of discussion amongst the hoi polloi. Their success also forced the older magazines like the *Gentleman's Magazine* (or perhaps gave them the courage) to feature this kind of item. Thus, in February 1769, the *Gentleman's* reported, in its *Historical Chronicle* section, that "the cause depending between the D. of G—n and his D—ss, was determined, and a divorce pronounced."[41] The Grafton case got more publicity elsewhere: the *Town and Country* noted, "We hear that the lately divorced lady of a noble d—, who has been since married to a noble lord, has had, on her divorcement, her whole fortune returned to her, which, as she was an only daughter, amounted to above eighty thousand pounds."[42] Many of the magazines published what purported to be the letters which Grafton wrote to Parsons, announcing their break and his impending marriage, and her heartbroken responses.[43] In addition, a tell-all anonymous pamphlet was published before the year's end, with the unambiguous title *Memoirs of the Amours, Intrigues and Adventures of Charles Augustus Fitz-Roy with Miss Parsons*. At the hefty price of 2s6d, it expanded on and gave the details of what the press had been reporting much more cheaply for a wider reading public.[44]

Just as the Grafton cause célèbre was running out of steam, another, much juicier affair engaged the public's notice, and was covered in loving detail by the eager press. This was the adultery case featuring Lady Grosvenor and the Duke of Cumberland, the younger brother of good King George. The extraordinary criminal conversation case and divorce bill that followed kept the public riveted and the press filled for the next several years.[45] The timing and connection between the two cases was not lost on periodical writers. Thus, in a mock letter addressed to Grafton, just one month after the Grosvenor affair was detected and made public, "A Cuckold" urged the Duke, as a way of securing "the interest and countenance of even your professed friends" to pass an Act in Parliament which would allow his friends "to get rid of their wives" more cheaply, by ordering "that all such acts might pass the house *duty free*. . . ." In addition, "Cuckold" recommended that Grafton "[get] another law, or resolution, to abolish all prosecutions and actions for *crim. con.* R[oya]l or otherwise. . . ."[46]

While the private affairs of the Duke and Duchess of Grafton had been discussed by Junius and others as indicative of the corrupt public morality of the ministry, the Grosvenor case, which featured the antics of Cumberland, linked this offence against the married state with the Court and the royal family itself. "An affair that has made much noise in the polite world," announced the *Town and Country*, "is likely to be the first action that was commenced in England against one of the b[loo]d R[oya]l, for criminal conversation; except in the reign of James II, in the case of Clarendon."[47] When the case first came to light in December 1769, it was immediately picked up by the press. Even the high-minded *Gentleman's* printed a paragraph in its *Historical Chronicle* section for that month, noting

> An assignation at the White Hart at St. Albans, between lady G and a certain great D—e, was disconcerted by the forcible intrusion of my lord's gentleman, who about two o'clock in the morning burst the chamber door open, and found the lovers sitting together in close conversation. An affidavit has since been made in the Commons with a view to a divorce, and a suit is likely to commence, in which the ablest lawyers will be employed.[48]

That same month, both the *Town and Country* and the *Oxford* published the story of the Grosvenors' courtship and marriage. Before his marriage Grosvenor had, it was asserted, "by his irregularity brought his health into a very critical state, and his physicians recommended matrimony to him, as the most certain way of living regularly. . . ." Miss Vane, the future Lady Grosvenor, was almost the first woman he met after taking the resolution to marry; he proposed and they were married "within a month from that day."[49] Though neither magazine commented on this account, they certainly molded the story into the familiar tropes of male aristocratic license and female aristocratic greed. A month later, in its 1769 Supplement, the *Gentleman's Magazine* repeated the story, prefacing it with the remark that it would "serve as a caution to youth against entering for life into hasty connections."[50] However, another, competing picture was suggested by a piece that purported to be a letter written, after the affair was discovered, by Lady Grosvenor to her husband. In it, she, in best sentimental rhetoric, threatened suicide if he did not accept her back, signing the missive *Yours, or Eternity's for ever.* In contrast, the *Oxford Magazine* published immediately underneath this letter, a piece entitled *Memoirs of his Royal Highness, William, late Duke of Cumberland, a Friend to Liberty, and an inexorable Enemy to the Scottish*

Rebels.[51] Comparing the silly trifling Duke with his illustrious, public-spirited predecessor was one way, albeit an oblique one, of casting shame on the latter Cumberland's life and actions. We will see this comparison repeated. Though the Earl's conduct was, on the whole, exculpated, and the Countess's reputation was somewhat tarnished by the affair,[52] it was the conduct of Cumberland, and by extension of the upper ranges of the nobility, that were most adversely affected.

Referred to as "the illustrious personage, who descended to play the seducer," Cumberland was found in Lady Grosvenor's room at an inn, in a disguise which had led the inn's servants to believe that he was a lunatic brought to visit "an eminent mad Doctor in the town."[53] When the discovery of the adultery was made, the Earl parted with his wife, and started a prosecution against Cumberland for criminal conversation. The *Town and Country* suggested that the Duke had written Grosvenor, "proposing an accomodation with Lady G—," which the Earl self-righteously refused, not only because of his personal "sense of injuries received" but equally because he thought himself "bound to society to bring the perpetrator to justice."[54] Another note suggested that Lady Grosvenor might have been "framed" by her husband, who, seeking to rid himself of his wife, concerted "a diabolical scheme to get them separated."[55] Only one pamphlet, harshly reviewed in the *Gentleman's Magazine*, attempted a similar whitewashing of Cumberland's actions. While the reviewer agreed with the anonymous pamphleteer "that the Duke of Cumberland is pursued with personal malice rather than zeal for virtue . . . [and] reviled for a passion which is excused in others, although indulged with the same irregularity," he found the implication, that private vice could have public benefits, contemptible and pernicious.[56]

That the trials (there was an ecclesiastical divorce suit, initiated by Grosvenor and begun in March 1770, a criminal conversation case, held before Lord Mansfield at King's Bench on July 5, 1770, and a further counter-suit by the countess at Doctors' Commons, initiated in December of that year) held the public attention is an understatement. Horace Walpole, in a letter to his friend Mann, noted that "We have lived these two months upon the poor Duke of Cumberland, whom the newspapers in so many letters call *the royal idiot.*"[57] What becomes clear from the consideration of these trials is the degree of ridicule of as well as the contempt for the Duke, the role of the press in bringing these issues to light, and the questions that these trials raised about the influence of rank, and its responsibilities.

Three pieces of evidence were crucial in making the trials farcical: the first was the mawkish, ill-written, and misspelled love letters from the Duke to Lady Grosvenor that were read and reread, published, and commented on;

the second was the various disguises adopted by Cumberland in his trysts with the Countess, and finally, third, was the patently false justification that Cumberland, discovered in Lady Grosvenor's bedroom, uttered, that he would take a "bible oath he was not in my lady's room."[58]

In a fine copperplate featured in the September 1770 issue of the *Oxford Magazine*, entitled *A certain great Personage learning to Spell*, the Duke is portrayed at a table learning his ABCs. On the table along with his primer (open to a page which features the word *Boo-by*) is a scroll headed *Specimens of R—l Spelling*. Behind the studious Duke, the devil is holding up a dunce's cap above his head. This picture accompanied a totally misspelt fictitious letter, addressed "*To hiz Royal hynes they Dook of Comburrland*," which promised to make Cumberland as great a scholar as himself.[59] Walpole commented that "The greatest abuse continues to be published against the Duke of Cumberland, and his governors for not having taught him to spell." The *Public Advertiser*, in its brief report of the crim. con. trial, noted that when Cumberland's letters were read out in court, they "raised a universal Laugh, while such as saw them, were astonished at the Method and Manner in which they were written." Finally, in the Wilkite journal *Bingley's*, which we shall consider in more detail shortly, its editor remarked that "Nothing, says Juvenal, is so cutting as an *ill-timed* joke. No sooner did the Duke of Cumberland enter Portsmouth, but some men at the engines asked, if his Royal Highness would take a *spell* at it."[60] That a prince of the blood and an Admiral of the Fleet could thus be teased, even fictitiously, by lowly tars and seamen, illustrates the devastating effects of mockery on aristocratic hauteur and the ridiculous public situation that Cumberland had brought himself into.

Similarly ridiculous and demeaning was Cumberland's use of disguise in his rendezvous with Lady Grosvenor. Wedderburn, Lord Grovenor's lawyer, recounted how the Duke assumed, at different times, the names of 'Squire Morgan, 'Squire Jones, the Farmer, etc.

> that he sometimes appeared as a young 'squire disordered in his senses, and used to be called at the inns the Fool. . . .[61]

An item of dress came to seem symbolic perhaps of both the foolery and the duplicity of Cumberland's disguises: a large rustic black wig that he wore in his Squire role. Thus *Bingley's* reported, most likely tongue firmly in cheek, that Foote,

> the witty [theatrical] manager has lately purchased of a certain chamber maid, the remarkable black bob worn by a Great Personage on a late amour, at no less a sum than two guineas; whence it is conjectured, the adventures of

St. Alban's, by a dramatic *hocus pocus*, may be translated to the theatre in the Haymarket.[62]

The *Oxford Magazine* that very month featured an engraving entitled *A certain personage in the Character of a Fool as he perform'd it at Whitchurch & elsewhere*. Cumberland, wearing a dunce's cap, is kneeling at Lady Grosvenor's feet, looking intently at her half-covered bosom. She remarks "Your H—s enters into the true Spirit of that Character," the Duke responding, "It is not the first time I have play'd the Fool," while his servant, addressing the viewer, comments "He is a very natural Performer, he looks for all the World like a Fool." On the facing page was a poem called *Duke of Cumberland*, but it referred to that earlier Duke who conquered the Scots. Some lines capture the implicit comparison:

> He [William] was wise, and he was brave,
> Hated Fools, and scorn'd a knave;
> He had learning, taste, and wit;
> What he wrote was wisely writ;
> Or he burnt each foolish letter,
> Or he wrote none, which was better;
> Never scribbled, never gabbled,
> Nor with neighbour's spouses dabbled . . . .
> Strictly kept this golden rule—
> *Princes ne'er should play the* FOOL.
> Tell me—lives there such a one?
> O, no—alas! he's dead and gone.[63]

Finally, though this theme was more developed after, than during, the immediate aftermath of the criminal conversation suit, there was Cumberland's blatantly untrue assertion that he "would take his bible oath" that he had not been in Lady Grosvenor's room when the door to it was broken down.[64] "A certain Gentleman," reported an unnamed correspondent in the *Public Advertiser* two weeks after the trial, "instead of his *Bible*, should have offered to take his *Spelling-Book Oath*." And though "Fair Locks" alluded to the "falsity" of this Bible oath in August of 1770, it received a much longer and more condemnatory play in a column written a year later in *Bingley's Journal*. "When a Prince of the blood," claimed the author of *Anecdotes of his R—l H—ess the Duke of C— and the celebrated Lady G—r*, "solemnly declares to those people, with whom by nature he is nearest connected, 'That upon his honour, and by all his hopes of future happiness, he is innocent of the accusations laid to his charge' . . . the unbecoming, the unhandsome circumstances, which attended this part of the Royal Lover, fired the indignation of every impartial man in the Court." The attack continued with the column-writer noting "how odious and despicable a Prince of the Blood must appear in the eyes of every honest man [when he swears to something] he knew to be a most atrocious falsehood."[65]

That the story offered the press an almost endless set of tales about the lives and loves of the great and famous was not merely accidental. Many historians have noted the development of the press at this time, and emphasized how the newspapers and periodicals of the Wilkite era were instrumental not only in creating political ferment, but also in creating new spaces for and encouraging greater participation in public debate. While the initial impulse behind this press expansion was political, commercial possibilities, in this, as in most eighteenth-century things, soon suggested other related interesting areas of discussion, discussions that increasingly turned on the twin subjects of rank and morality. Both of these areas crossed the public/private divide and both appealed simultaneously to principle and prurience, a winning combination. By the time of the Grosvenor divorce, those directly involved knew both the power and the intrusiveness of the press first-hand. Thus in a letter written by Lady Grosvenor's sister to her just before the final exposé of the affair at the inn at St. Albans, she noted that "a story [was] now about town" linking her with the Duke, but, she continued "what is worse, I have enclosed a paragraph that was in the News Papers to day, from which you will learn how scandalously you are talked of; it frightens me to Death."[66]

When the adultery case first came up in King's Bench, lawyers for both the defendant and the plaintiff argued about the role that rank was to play in the proceedings. Laying the damages at the astonishing sum of £100,000, Wedderburn "particularly insisted on the defendant's rank as an aggravation of his crime." Though the Duke's counsel argued that this penalty was "very excessive and immoderate," the opposing lawyers cited several precedents, which, they argued, were necessary to "shew society, that where particular duty and respect is required, an action of criminality becomes doubly so, when these ties are broke through."[67] Thus, argued Wedderburn, the case was not just about the immorality of one particular man and woman, but about the ties that bound, or threatened to dissolve, a society of deference and rank. This theme was reiterated by a "Civilian," writing shortly after the case's conclusion:

> To make loyalty the source of licentiousness and betray the confidence which superior rank might claim from superior virtue, is to pollute the streams that immediately flow from the fountain of honour, with the filth of the foulest drains of demerit and debauchery.[68]

For many the Cumberland-Grosvenor affair was about aristocratic license, about the sullied state of upper-class life and the epidemical effects of upper-class adultery. "By high Example, thus the Marriage State/Is *epidemically* stain'd of late," noted one anonymous poet.[69] In contrast to this privileged life of debauchery and fashionable vice, said another, Britain's middling sorts were still untainted.

> Thank Heav'n amongst those who hold Life's middle Way
> Nor blest with Pow'r, or Splendour's dazzling Ray,
> Such glorious Crimes we very seldom know,
> Our Sentiments for such bright Deeds too low,
> We think our Wives to ease our Troubles giv'n,
> That Nuptial Faith is guaranteed by Heav'n,
> Upon our Consorts Honour build our own,
> And owe our Happiness to that alone.[70]

In fact, noted a letter-writer to *Bingley's Journal*, although ideally the conversation of the upper orders should be more polite and virtuous than that of people beneath them in rank, their chat, like their morals, was depraved and often smacked of the gutter:

> Persons in the middling walks of life, are very often led to consider the conver-sation of people of distinction to be adequate to their rank. . . . However this deception may be serviceable in supporting the system of subordination, nothing is, very often, falser in fact; and if we were to judge sometimes by our *ears*, instead of our *eyes*, we would find a fashionable *tete-a-tete*, approaching more to the meridian of Gutter lane or Billingsgate than the supposed politeness of St. James's.[71]

The ending of this aristocratic romance seemed as tawdry and immoral as the conduct of the entire affair. And the legal issues were not yet settled, for though Lord Grosvenor won his suit at King's Bench, Lady Grosvenor launched a recrimination against him at Doctors Commons, a countersuit which, if proved, disallowed for full divorce if the husband had also been guilty of adultery during the marriage. When the cases finished in December of 1770, not only had the newspapers had a year's worth of stories, of jokes and corre-spondence, but their attention continued for another six months afterwards.

For one thing, though the affair between Cumberland and Lady Grosvenor received nothing but condemnation from the press, its termination was equally condemned. In July 1770, it was said that Cumberland spent all his time with Lady Grosvenor, and that "a great Personage has forbidden a certain Gentleman the Court, unless he desists from visiting a particular Lady";[72] by

August of that year, a poem-epistle was published in several magazines, ostensibly by Lady Grosvenor to the Duke, bemoaning his faithlessness to her. An extraordinary letter, published six months later in the *Town and Country*, discussed this new affair. Supposedly "written by a certain eminent divine," it was a "Letter of Remonstrance" to the Duke of Cumberland, for having taken up with a Mrs. Bayley of Hatton Gardens. Its author alluded to both the impropriety of the new affair and the political consequences of such repeated aristocratic misdeeds. "The illicit commerce which you carried on with lady G— was scarce publickly proved in a court of justice, ere you appeared at a summer watering-place, playing the same shameful part with another married woman," he thundered. "Adultery, Sir," he continued, "notwithstanding the modish doctrine of the times, is a crime of the blackest die, and the most pernicious of any to society. . . ." The consequences of such behavior would be devastating to the public weal.

> If the peace and felicity of families are thus to be broke in upon by rank and power; if virtue and chastity are to be banished from this isle by title and elevated stations, will not the rational part of the nation consider such distinctions as fatal to their welfare, and justly lament the dreadful influence of superior birth and fortune?[73]

It was in response to this *annus horribilus* that Parliament attempted, albeit unsuccessfully, to pass a law making adultery a graver offense.[74] But perhaps even more important than this legislative effort was the continuing and growing trend of newspaper and magazine reportage of the salacious and anti-social sexual activities of the well-born and infamous. Beginning with the publication of Junius' criticism of Grafton for political immorality, which his private immorality mirrored, through the affair of the Duke of Cumberland and Lady Grosvenor, which implicated figures among the very highest rungs of privilege and social hierarchy, the press soon realized the advantages and interest to be gained by this sort of reporting. Losing no opportunity to tie the public and private worlds together, the *Town and Country* published a mock tri-alogue between the Duke of Cumberland, his mistress Mrs. Bayley, and her husband. When her husband complained that "it is impossible any longer to support this infamy in England [seemingly referring to Cumberland's repeated adulteries]—something must be done. . . ." his wife responded "To be sure, my dear, something must be done, and something shall be done—you must be provided for." The duke, giving the matter some thought, replied "I have it. The d[uke] of G[rafton] you know is come into place again; I can do anything with him; his sentiments upon these matters are exactly like mine; I'll open the thing to him this very day, and if there are any vacancy, I'll push it home."[75] That public, political immorality was seamlessly linked to private, personal, domestic vice was a commonplace, illustrated in these three years by the careers of England's prime minister and one of the princes of the blood royal. And so, less than a dozen years after the acquisition of her great Empire, many in England would have agreed with "Theophilus," whose letter to the *Oxford Magazine* prognosticated "approaching ruin." Listing first, as a proof of such national decay, the allegation that "Patriotism has been insulted by a majority in the House of Commons with imprisonment, and the maxims of Lewis XV adopted under George III," he immediately followed this up with his charge that the "primary law of civil society, which establishes the order of the world, and secures the chief end of the two sexes, is treated with a most prophane and unhallowed freedom." Bemoaning the laxity of the law of divorce, which had, he claimed "impiously established the lawfulness of adultery" he waxed Jeremiah-like:

> The bodily prostitutions, both of the great and the vulgar, are shameful beyond example. The herd of the people are converted into brutes, and the modest oeconomy of the sexes is every where banished from society—this is another sure presage of ruin.[76]

But, as we shall note, more, much more was to come, and the coverage of such a disordered national economy was to remain a topic both of grave censure and of lively salacious interest for at least another half-century.

Genres of Adultery

Thus we have seen how, in the late 1760s and early 1770s, building on an earlier wave of general condemnation of adultery, a new type of involvement and publicity occurred, arising from the combination of a contingent and particular set of marital scandals involving ministers and relations of the Crown, and the growth of new political circumstances and challenges by supporters of both Wilkes and Junius. In both the earlier and later discussions of aristocratic mores, we have noted the use of a variety of forms or sites of communication: sermons, magazine and newspaper articles, trial accounts and theatrical content. In this section I would like to extend the range of materials examined to support the contention that in the years after 1770, the topic of aristocratic adultery was "in the air," could be found in all the venues of popular discourse, and engaged not only the passive participation of consumers of sexual scandal, but the active involvement of pamphleteers and letter-writers, parliamentarians and debating society orators, commercial publishers, advertisers and dramatists, satirists and poets.

Elsewhere I have considered in some detail the several attempts to pass legislation that, it was hoped, would decrease the incidence of such fashionable depravity. In that context I contrasted three different strands of the discussion: the arguments for and against these bills in Parliament, the several pamphlets published in support of the proposed legal changes, and the questions and responses of ordinary people discussing adultery and divorce in London's many public debating societies. Let me briefly summarize those findings, at least for the legislation introduced in the 1770s, before considering additional sites and sources.

The first such bill, of 1771, was intended to prohibit the "person [always the wife] against whom the adultery has been proved, from marrying or contracting matrimony with the person with whom he or she shall be proved to have carried on such criminal intercourse; and to declare the issue of such marriage, incapable of inheriting." Though this bill was lost in the House of Commons, it was the model on which the next bill was proposed by the Bishop of Landaff in 1779. He gave as his reason for introducing such a measure, that "the vice of adultery has risen" to a "shameful height," which has brought "great misfortune on some of the first families in the kingdom." It was imperative, he argued, that this vice be controlled, especially as it "was chiefly among persons of high rank that this crime had prevailed. . . ." This bill, like the last, was also lost in the House of Commons.

Three important pamphlets were written as the first bill was being discussed, and three more were written at the same time as the second was proposed. In 1771, the pamphlets stressed the importance of female conjugal faithfulness to both the stability of property and the endurance of the strength and happiness of the state, and attributed the degeneracy of the times to "the Profligacy of our Women."[77] By 1779, the arguments were both further-ranging and more varied. Publishing a pamphlet in support of the 1771 bill a year after its defeat, the cleric Thomas Pollen repeated the older view that the "state is one great family made up of many small ones: if these, by frequent and improper divorces, be dissolved, that must necessarily be weakened." Therefore, he argued, it behooved the Legislature to find some proper punishment for so heinous an offence. "For an ignominious life deserves an ignominious death: and he who has wallowed in another man's bed like a swine, ought for so doing to be hang'd like a dog."[78]

Perhaps the most interesting essay on this topic was the *Letter to My Lords the Bishops, on the occasion of the Present Bill for the Preventing of Adultery* of 1779. In this, its author argued that vices grow from an inordinate liberty given to an innate human propensity, self-love. To balance this important though dangerous impulse, each human was also endowed by Nature

> with *controuls*, both within and without his constitution, to balance these impulses and prevent their *excess*. Out of different governments arise different controuls: in a mixed or free state, the great controul is in *the power of the people;—public trust* cannot be obtained without *popularity;—popularity* can not be obtained without *character;—character* can not be obtained but by a conformity of manners and conduct to *public opinion;—public opinion* is always in favour of *virtue*; and thus *virtue itself* becomes necessary, and *vice*, of course, discountenanced and despised.

So why was it that vice had grown, that virtue seemed in retreat? The author dated this imbalance to a period nineteen years before (i.e., with the accession of George III) when "there was in truth no democratic interest in the state . . . and thus, my Lords, on the sudden inertion of an ancient interest, were all the old controuls taken off, as it were in a day, and at a time, too, when a very great accession of wealth and of empire had created new temptations, requiring more controul than ever. . . ." What was to be done? Increased punishment would not help: "Penalties, my Lords, go, at the most, only to the *support of manners*, not to their *formation*. Manners, my lords, it has been observed, are derived from the constitution of government, not from *law of any kind*." It was the corruption of the "public will" that was responsible, argued this polemicist, and it was the "democratic interest" which must be restored. For otherwise, without this countervailing force, "if the legislators themselves, in their private and public capacities, be the great objects of necessary reform —where is the remedy?"[79]

In addition to these essays and the many discussions that took place in London's debating societies, letters to the editors of various newspapers and magazines provide us with important clues about popular literate thinking about adultery. Of course not every communiqué, nor every "letter to the editor," was, in fact, a real letter. Some were tales or dreams in the guise of epistles. Some were updates on recent adulteries, such as the letter to the *Town and Country* in August of 1769. This note from one "T. L." told of a visit to the Highlands of Scotland, during which its author said he had encountered Lady Sarah Bunbury, who had eloped from her husband with Sir William Gordon, retired to a secluded cottage, and was awaiting a hoped-for divorce from her spouse. Others were satires disguised as letters, as was the mock letter from a Parliamentary candidate to his electors, telling them of his intended reforms, the sixth of which was "To prevent Crim. Con. amongst the nobility, and thereby abolish divorces."[80] However, many of them were, or purported to be, real letters from real people, and to express strong opinions on this topic.

Like many moralists, these letter-writers frequently decried the degeneracy and drift away from marital fidelity of the present period. Some compared the licentiousness of English aristocratic wives with the modesty and chastity of those of Rome, "in the better times of the republic." In the same magazine a dozen years later, "BW" noted that, though divorce was allowed in pagan Rome, "it was 523 years before any one made use of it," yet in a "*nominally Christian*" England, in the five years from 1776, "the number of them were very considerable."[81] Other letters compared the virtuous conduct of British wives in past times with their flightiness in the present era. "If we look back half a century past, a detection of *crim con* was mentioned as a prodigy, and it was reprobated by all the decent part of the sex; the culprit pronounced a monster, and shunned as such," remarked an "Old Observer." Comparing Edinburgh in the year 1783 with its condition twenty years before, "Theophrastus" noted that at the earlier date, "Any instance of conjugal infidelity in a woman would have banished her from society, and her company would have been rejected even by the men," while in the present, "[w]omen, who have been rendered infamous by public divorce, have even been again received into society, notwithstanding the endeavours of our worthy Queen to check such a violation of morality, decency, the laws of the country, and the rights of the virtuous."[82]

Several of the letter-writers had ideas about how such violations could be checked or diminished. These ranged from keeping women "to a stricter discipline," to improving "the education of the fair sex, in order to preserve their morals, and make them hereafter good wives and mothers," to training up daughters "in the ways of piety and modesty," for as "Megaronides" commented, it was not that women of the present day were "now naturally more lascivious than in former ages" but that female sexual misconduct was due "to a real change in the circumstances or education of our women."[83] Others blamed male conduct, not female frivolity, for fostering the "fashionable vice."[84] Still others thought harsher punishment would cause the vice to decrease: suggestions ranged from the loss of the ring finger to exposure in the pillory and imprisonment to a tax on the adulteries of the rich.[85]

Two general points can be made in conclusion. The first is the almost unanimous agreement on the source of this vicious conduct and its significance; that adultery and divorce sprang from the habits and lifestyles of the upper classes was a commonplace. So, for example, "Tullius," in his letter to the King on the Grosvenor adultery case sarcastically noted that if Cumberland had only seduced a wife or daughter of "honest, though poor, parents, no one would have thought it remarkable"; his fault consisted, at least in part, in his having hunted "after *noble game*, [and therefore] the atrociousness of the crime becomes more conspicuous, and he is deservedly esteemed the violator of an injured husband's honour, and the destroyer of the domestic happiness of a whole family." "A Friend to Fidelity in the Marriage Bed," discussing the adultery of a clergyman's wife, noted that "[h]itherto adultery was chiefly confined to women of spirit and fashion." Another, examining "the frequent accounts of the infidelity of married women," in giving examples of the bad marriage practices which inevitably led to such behavior, discussed only the adulteries of anonymous men whom he called Lord A, Lord C and the duke of E. "Flesh and Blood," a correspondent to the *Morning Post*, concluded "That men of quality have a natural tendency to become cuckolds. . . . That women of quality have natural propensities towards granting this honour to their Lords [and] that, comparatively, rich men and men of rank, are more liable to be cuckolded than the middling or poor classes of society." "Civis," in his letter to the *Times*, in discussing "what is called *gallantry*," questioned whether "it [would] ever have entered into the head of any man of middling life, and common understanding, that the seduction of married women . . . was a harmless piece of amusement, and necessary to finish the education of a Gentleman." Though some thought that the infection could be caught by other ranks, most agreed with "Civis" and with "X," a letter-writer to the *Town and Country*, "that in the middle stations of life, there is more real felicity found in wedlock, than in any other."[86] The other point, though less frequently made, was of real importance, and that was the central role of the press in making the wider public aware of such immorality. It is worth quoting in full from one such letter, commenting on the role of the press in disseminating this sort of information.

> [L]et it be remembered, that till lately the newspapers were confined entirely to what might properly be called news, and that private memoirs and anecdotes never crept into them. We were then satisfied in knowing what ships arrived at Deal, the price of stocks, when the mails arrived from Holland, and when a labourer fell from a house and broke his neck. But the case is altered, curiosity is awakened, and we are desirous of knowing who and who are together; when a woman of fashion makes a *faux pas*, and when her husband takes another Dulcinea into keeping.[87]

That publishers realized the commercial value of such sexual scandal becomes very clear if we examine the coverage of one particularly "juicy" adultery case, and consider especially the innovative advertising campaign designed, using the popular press, to entice the reading public into buying the many published accounts, satires, and poems which dealt with the incident. These many publications centered on the adultery of Lady Seymour Worsley, a great heiress and beauty, the attempt of her husband, Sir Richard, to sue her lover Maurice Bissett for criminal conversation, the salacious evidence presented at the trial, and the light all this cast on the lives and amours of the rich and infamous.[88]

About ten days after the trial, at which five of Lady Worsley's other upper-class lovers had testified, the first trial account was published. Lady Worsley had run away with Maurice Bisset at the end of November 1781, sending her husband a note by a previous lover, Lord Deerhurst, that she would never return to him. Even before the case came to court, the press leaked some of its details. It is even possible, if her later actions are any evidence, that Lady Worsley gave the press the story herself, in a move to make sure that her husband, an apparently compliant cuckold, did proceed with the divorce. In any case, early in the new year, both the *Public Advertiser* and the *Whitehall Evening Post* alluded to the new, "blush-coloured Dress which Lady W— has lately appeared in," since, they claimed, her husband had burnt all of her other clothes when he had discovered "her being Naughty." Less than a week after the trial, the *Whitehall Evening Post* asserted that, though only five of her previous lovers had testified to her promiscuity, "no less than twenty-eight were subpoenaed, at her own express command, every one of whom was fully competent to speak decisively on the pliancy of her Ladyship's disposition."[89]

Two days after publication of the trial, an item appeared in the *Public Advertiser*, which to all appearances was a piece of news, but which in reality was a puff for an account of the trial. Claiming that the first edition had sold out within a few hours of release, and "a great number of purchasers were consequently disappointed," the public was notified that two more presses would be employed in producing sufficient copies for all. A day later, a similar item, this time appearing as an advertisement, announced that there were *three* presses at work producing enough pamphlets "to gratify the curiosity of the public." A week later, another ad announced that "At the request of a respectable and learned Personage, a late very singular and interesting Trial is to be advertised in the following, instead of the former manner"; the change was only superficial and attention-grabbing, largely consisting of an omission of the names of the persons involved.[90]

On the same day that the trial proceedings appeared as a pamphlet, another work on the same topic, this time a satirical poem entitled *The Whim!!! or the maid-stone bath, a Kentish poetic, Dedicated to Lady Worsley* was also advertised. Four weeks later, a blurb appeared in the *Whitehall Evening News*, which, again masquerading as a news item, was designed to promote its sale. Remarking that "[n]otwithstanding a late decision, it appears yet a matter of doubt, whether Lady W— seduced the gentlemen, or they seduced her ladyship," the puff claimed that "the matter will be best explained by a perusal of the *Whim, or the Maid-Stone Bath*, which is the product of Genius, assisted by the best information."[91]

A number of other satirical works on the same topic appeared that year, but undoubtedly the one which had the most interesting advertising stratagem was *An Epistle from L[ad]y W[orsle]y to S[ir] R[ichar]d W[orsle]y Bart*, probably published towards the end of April 1782. This was a short satiric poem, in which Lady Worsley freely owned her many indiscretions, said that her giving nature accorded with the bountifulness of Nature itself, and accused Worsley of being unable to give her the satisfaction that all women required. Although, in reality, it was a pretty nondescript piece, neither pornographic nor particularly poetic, its advertising was original and probably quite effective. Three puffing paragraphs appeared in the *Morning Herald* in the week following its publication. The first, from "a correspondent, who professes himself an enemy to immorality," warned the reading public that the pamphlet was "certainly one of the most licentious and immoral productions that has been issued from the press for some time" and thus that "he hopes no one who is not totally lost to every degree of decency, will, after this public notice of its contents, by any means deign to read it." If this were not enough to rouse interest and sales, another "correspondent," just one day later, referring again to the *Epistle*, remarked that its purported author, Lady Worsley, by writing this piece, "leaves us at a loss to know which we are most to detest, the very extraordinary supineness of the husband, or the libidinous and insatiable passions of the wife." The final advertisement for the *Epistle* is perhaps the best. Citing the *"very extensive circulation, amongst all ranks, of the new publication, entitled an Epistle from L—y W—y to S—r R—d"* as evidence for the increasing licentiousness of the age, the puff's author continues, and it is perhaps worth quoting the rest of his "condemnation" in full:

> The uncommon popularity of this pamphlet is infinitely to be dreaded, not only from the abandoned morals and severe scandal it contains, but on account of the singular elegance of the language, which is so truly infatuating, that while it steals on the senses by the beauty of the poetry, it pictures in such irresistible colours, that it cannot fail rooting from the mind every sentiment of virtue and morality. Yet so strange is the depravity of the age, that it is no less extraordinary than true, that a capital bookseller, at the

West end of the town, has actually orders to send 500 copies to a neighbouring kingdom—a number quite sufficient to corrupt the minds of all its inhabitants.[92]

Clearly sexual scandal had become an item well worth advertising. And, as we shall soon see, in the later decades of the century the press had a large stake in its packaging, promotion, and sales.

"No End of Adultery":[93] Scandal, Privacy, and the Press

If the popular coverage of adultery had begun to become more flamboyant and more accessible in the 1760s and 1770s, there was a veritable avalanche of such stories in the following two decades; seven such cases appeared in the press in the 1770s, while twenty-six were reported in the following decade, and seventy in the one following that. And while pamphlet accounts of the cases continued to appear, there is some evidence that as press reporting became more lengthy and regular, fewer pamphlets were produced.[94] The age of a mass readership for adultery cases had arrived.

We have already considered the press coverage and marketing possibilities of the Worsley divorce case. At least six other adultery cases of the 1780s, which occurred before the appointment of Lloyd Kenyon as the Lord Chief Justice of the Court of King's Bench in 1788, were sold as pamphlets, which frequently contained illustrations, appearing shortly after their trials, and also gathered together in two volumes of *The Cuckold's Chronicle* of 1793.[95] Yet while the newspaper and periodical press itself contained many satiric comments, jokes, and smutty asides, as well as an expanding coverage of the many legal venues where such adultery was being tried (the ecclesiastical courts, the trials for damages for criminal conversation, and the debates within the House of Lords and Commons), as early as 1783 the press contended that the public "are made duly sensible [of the increase of divorces] by the publication of the *modest trials*." Others thought the avidity for such details among the reading public displayed a worrying incongruity: "They complain loudly of the Scandal often circulated in Newspapers and Pamphlets, yet they always encourage those that deal most in that Article! The Sale of the Tryal relative to the Conduct of a certain Baronet's Lady, and her Gallant, is a most convincing Proof of the Truth of this Observation!"[96] By the 1790s, however, the newspapers themselves were being taken to task for their increased and increasing coverage of such trials.

> The daily papers are constantly retailing connections of this kind; and thus they become the vehicles of vice from the center to the most distant corners

of the kingdom. . . . . Adultery and elopements constitute a material part of our news, and, being commonly retailed with numerous and minute circumstances, help to inflame the passions, and abate our horror for the crimes. No paragraphs are more greedily read, than those which relate to business of this kind.[97]

When the press explained or justified the inclusion of such material, it usually took the position adopted by that expensive purveyor of upper-class scandal, the *Town and Country Magazine*. The publication made its first appearance in 1769, at a time of seemingly growing public hunger for stories of glamour and illicit sex, and continued in being for the next quarter-century, specializing in monthly exposés of the amours of the world of fashion. In the introductory preface to its fifth volume, its editors argued for their role as moral improvers:

> Arduous as the Task has been, and in some Degree perilous, they [the editors] have the Satisfaction to find that the Judicious and Impartial still read these Histories with Rapture, and think them proper Portraits to discourage Vice and promote Virtue.

Of course, no contemporary would have missed the self-interested reality underlying this noble rhetoric; it was clear that smut sold. And yet others, untainted by such sordid motives, also argued that an intimate connection existed between private morality, of which marital fidelity was the core, and the public good:

> . . . the Ruin of Matrimonial Happiness . . . which alone is a deplorable Infamy in private Life, is, at the same time, a most enormous Evil in its Consequences to the Publick. Conjugal Attachment is a Virtue the more to be prized, as it is usually the Foundation of the most persevering, invincible Courage and Manliness, Qualities that have never forsaken a People that was noted for the other.

For, despite John Barrell's dazzling exposition of the way in which political radicals of the 1790s used a beleaguered notion of privacy to defend their rights to free speech and free debate, to mark off "private" spaces like the home or public table from the "public" spaces of debating societies or street corners, the notion that "the personal was political" was rampant through the whole of the century. Barrell's protagonists, who feared that the eradication of this demarcation would encourage servants and other domestics to inform on private household activity and speech, were out of date, for it was already a reality that many divorce trials featured servants as well as family friends, whose testimony might ensure imprisonment for those found guilty, for sights seen and sounds heard through chinks in the wall, or keyholes. And few expressed any concern, few argued for the need to keep the bedroom, that most private of all spaces, free from such prying ears and eyes.[98]

Lord Kenyon's "Reign of Terror"

In Lawrence Stone's opinion, when Lloyd Kenyon became Lord Chief Justice in 1788, he "promptly inaugurated a reign of terror in King's Bench against adulterers."[99] The section in which he discussed Kenyon's "reign" is entitled "The Moral Panic of the 1790s," a shorthand reference to the enormous anxieties of this first decade of the wars with France. But Kenyon came to the Bench four years before England's engagement with the old enemy, and it may be worth considering his work in this early period, unclouded by the specter of republican revolution and warfare, to see just how fearsome his leadership of the court really was.

The first thing one notices is how many cases of criminal conversation he judged during these early years at King's Bench. There is no question that Kenyon was determined to give such cases the publicity and notoriety he felt they deserved. In many of his addresses to the jury in divorce cases, Kenyon reminded them that they, the jurymen, were "the guardians of the morals of the public" and asked them to give damages "of such a nature, as to give stability and security to domestic life."[100] And while, during these years, the juries, under his admonition, did award some enormous damages (between five and ten thousand pounds), such fines accounted for less than a third of the awards; more than half resulted in fines of between forty shillings and one thousand pounds, with the remaining cases either non-suited, or found for the defendant.[101] Rather than seeing Kenyon as a Robespierre-like figure, I think it more appropriate to view him as a convinced, active, and stern, but by no means tyrannical improver of public morality. This is certainly what the *Times* said of his campaign:

> Lord Kenyon, to his honour, has behaved with peculiar severity against those who have committed the crime of adultery,—and he is intitled to the thanks of every virtuous man and woman in the kingdom for so doing. His conduct on those occasions will no doubt, in time, have a proper effect.[102]

And I think these early cases must have convinced Kenyon just how "far down" the infection of infidelity had spread; only two of the thirty-six men who came before him in these years, either as plaintiffs or defendants, were of the upper class; for the most part they were men of the wide "middling sort." Exposure to adultery among these sorts, men and women, the solid, no-longer-silent, immoral minority, must have both saddened Kenyon and strengthened his resolve to conquer this pernicious vice.

That is not to say that Kenyon did not have his hobby-horses, or that he did not exhibit them in these adultery cases. The cases that usually raised his greatest ire were those where private or domestic connections had led to the illicit act; where the bonds of family, friendship, and obligation had served to introduce the vile seducer, and then given him the opportunity to betray these most sacred and significant bonds by practicing the arts of enticement and deceit. But that was a judicial attitude that predated Kenyon's leadership of the court,[103] though it does explain Kenyon's remarkably long closing remarks to the jury, published in the press, in the Parslow *v* Sykes trial. Here is Thomas Erskine, speaking for the husband, Parslow, and encapsulating the particular offensiveness of this case:

> ... there was no case had happened like that which he was about to state. There was no instance where one brother officer had so grossly abused the friendship and confidence of another; because there was a spirit of noble heroism, which was the foundation of that profession, which made men stand aloof from such unchaste ideas.[104]

Kenyon, in this, as in many things, would certainly have agreed with Erskine, and, like others in his position, he also had total and open contempt for unbridled female sexuality; in one case he remarked of the erring wife, that

> there never was a woman so contaminated in body and mind, and whose profligacy was beyond all example. She had lost all sense of shame, and there was no person within the walls of her house, excepting her children, who had not been witnesses to her prostitution.[105]

In some respects, however, Kenyon went some way beyond both precedence and perhaps even public opinion. Unlike most civil judges, he frequently remarked that if the defendant could not pay with his purse, then he must pay with his person, in effect treating the man found guilty of adultery as though he were a criminal, to be punished by incarceration; "the law says," Kenyon noted, that "the captivity of the person may pay for the deficiency of the purse."[106] Kenyon also took an unequivocal stance on the impropriety of married women appearing at public events by themselves, or being left without a guardian, except in unusual circumstances. Thus in the case of Sheridan *v* Newman, which occurred during his first year as Chief Justice, Kenyon exculpated Mr. Sheridan from blame for having left his wife alone while he served in America: "The plaintiff went out to defend his country at a time when his services were extremely wanted, and no blame is imputed to him for not being her protector." In contrast, eleven years later, in the case of Hennet *v* Darley, Kenyon nonsuited the husband because he "had contributed to his own dishonour" since "he had suffered his wife to go to plays, balls, masquerades, &c. without any person to protect her. A man who did that had no right to come into a Court of Justice to complain that his wife had been debauched."[107] In contrast, at least one husband thought otherwise, and stated his views in a letter to Mr. Baldwin, editor of the *St. James's Chronicle*:

> In my humble opinion, we pay no very great compliment to the ladies, when we suppose that they want to be more closely watched and guarded *after* marriage than before it . . . That which requires so much watching is seldom worth the care and trouble of it; and small, indeed, is our security, if bolts and bars are all we have to depend on.[108]

Juries also were more resistant to the view that husbands who did not keep a watchful eye on their wives should not receive compensation for spousal adultery, especially when not under the watchful eye of Chief Justice Kenyon himself. Thus, for example, when damages were to be decided in the case of Crewe *v* Inglefield, the sheriff's jury (the defendant had let judgment go by default, and a common jury deliberated on the level of fiscal penalty) was addressed by Inglefield's lawyer, who argued that damages should be minimal, since he had only minor responsibility for the criminal act. "The Lady" said Mr. Gibbs, "had been cast in his way, unprotected by the presence of her husband, and unshielded by his love and attention." Furthermore, "Mr. Crewe had suffered his wife to go abroad at one time alone. . . ." Despite this evidence, the jury awarded Crewe a hefty £3,000 in damages.[109]

Finally, Kenyon was unusual among presiding judges of King's Bench in making an argument about the moral obligations of the aristocracy, similar to that frequently found in the press, a part of his charge to the jury. In his address to the jury in the case of Sir Godfrey Webster *v* Lord Holland, he intoned:

> In every community of men, those who move in the higher ranks of life . . . [were those who] owed to the lower classes of society, that of setting a good example. . . . For if the lower orders observed their superiors . . . violating the most sacred obligations to indulge their vicious passions, it was vain to preach to these orders morality in words, while every part of the preacher's own conduct was most immoral.[110]

When assessing Kenyon's judicial accomplishments at the end of the century, a contemporary commented that "he has most effectually vindicated the cause of virtue and morality, in those trials of adultery, which, at different times, have come before him. He has expressed a virtuous indignation in terms at once impressive and appropriate. Neither rank, nor wealth, nor station, are protected from the just animadversion they incur in these loathsome and detestable transactions. . . ." Presiding over more than four dozen criminal conversation cases in the period between the failed attempts to pass a harsher adultery bill in 1779, and the last attempt to pass similar legislation in 1809, Kenyon, acting from the Bench, endeavored "to make the law of the land subservient to the laws of morality and religion."[111]

Severity and Sentiment: Arguing about the "Wages of Sin"

On Saturday, March 14, 1798, a new play starring two of London's premier actors, Sarah Siddons and John Philip Kemble, opened to a packed Drury Lane Theater. The play, "The Stranger," was a translation of one of the German playwright Kotzebue's works, adapted and strengthened, it was unofficially said, by Richard Brinsley Sheridan.[112] "The House overflowed at an early hour, and was the fullest we have seen this season," reported a correspondent to the *Times*. Needless to say, it was a great success. The receipts for the first ten performances alone amounted to almost four thousand pounds. "We have no doubt that this piece . . . will become a very great favorite with the Public," concluded the *Morning Post*. Both the *Times* and the *Post* agreed that, in the latter's words, "The public morals are likely to be highly benefitted by the frequent appearance of *The Stranger*."[113]

What about this play, what in its plot or depiction, made critics think it particularly likely to improve public morals? For the main action of the drama occurred before the story even began, and centered around the adultery and elopement of the Countess Walbeck, as portrayed by Siddons. Overcome by repentance, by the realization that her only true affection was for her husband and children, the Countess retired to the countryside, and, as Mrs. Haller, became the guardian angel of the poor and worthy of the locale. In the meanwhile her heartbroken husband became "The Stranger," and each, unbeknownst to the other, spent their days in anonymous charitable acts, friendless and alone. At the play's denouement, the couple were reunited by their children's love, with Mrs. Haller all the while protesting her unworthiness and undying affection. As the *Morning Chronicle* noted: "It is certainly a bold and in some measure a new attempt, to represent a character like that of Mrs. Haller, notwithstanding the error she has committed, amiable, virtuous and delicate." Equally surprising as the play's popularity, however, was surely the conclusion of these remarks by the anonymous critic:

> We behold a woman, who has been guilty of a crime, but not debased by vice. We are led to pity and forgive error where the heart is uncorrupted, and taught that a single false step does not preclude the return to virtue. We see that she is still worthy to be loved; and we are forced to overcome the prejudice, which condemns the woman, who has been guilty of one frailty, to hopeless exile from honour and esteem.[114]

There is no doubt that many in the audience would have shared this emotion; "The progress of the story interests our sympathy, and its completion gratifies our wishes," remarked the same reviewer. The *Times* reported a quip, reputedly made by Sheridan, about the play's happy ending: "Mr. Sheridan, to whose pen many of the most striking passages in *The Stranger* are attributed, replied to a critic who wished for the sake of the moral, that the piece had ended tragically, 'that he had thought of destroying Mrs. Haller, but he could not do it without killing the audience, too.' "[115] But how was it that the same sort of people who could spend their evening sympathizing with the plight of a confessed adulteress could at the same time so glowingly commend Kenyon's war on this crime, and on its perpetrators? Why was it, that in the discussions in both Houses of Parliament in 1800, everyone seemed to agree that adultery was a profoundly deleterious vice, that the nation's welfare depended on its diminution, and yet were still able to attend the many performances of this drama, allowing their sympathy to overcome these frequently repeated moral stances?

A number of possibilities, of course, occur. The first and most obvious was that it was possible to love the sinner, while abhorring the sin. A second is that in the play sympathy was directed towards a seduced female, while in "real life" crim. con. damages punished the seducer. A third is that what people were willing to enjoy in an evening's performance at the theater may have borne little relation to what conduct they were willing to approve of in the actual doings of their compatriots. Whichever of these, or other options, we chose to explain this seeming paradox, we can see similar, disparate strands of opinion in a host of other settings in this confused and confusing period. It is to the clash of these rhetorical and ideational stances that we must now turn.

Just a month before *The Stranger* first appeared at Drury Lane, a sensational criminal conversation case opened at King's Bench before Lord Kenyon. The plaintiff, Ricketts, was represented by that darling of such cases, Thomas Erskine, and the defendant, Taylor, by George Dallas, an up-and-coming attorney. Part of the reason for this case's notoriety was the familial relations invoked; Ricketts was the nephew of "a man who, in a most critical period, saved the honour of the country, and secured its lasting prosperity," Admiral of the Fleet, Earl St. Vincent. In Kenyon's closing remarks to the jury, the fact of Ricketts's family ties, "related to one whose actions would form a distinguishing feature in that part of the history of this country which recorded the splendid exploits of its naval heroes," would argue for hefty damages. Taylor, Member of Parliament for Wells, on the other hand, was described rather scurrilously, after the trial's conclusion, as the descendant of "the German Commissary" and nephew to a man lately imprisoned in the Fleet gaol.[116]

The evidence for the commission of "the act" rested on the testimony of one Crook, a tailor who lived near the reputed house of assignation, and who kept his eyes peeled on the comings-and-goings, especially of women, to this building. He also "knew" that the house belonged to Taylor's valet, who kept it for him. He swore that he had seen Mrs. Ricketts enter this dwelling three times, stay for a while, and leave in a surreptitious manner later. Mr. Taylor always admitted her, and once was in a dressing gown when she left.

Dallas, Taylor's lawyer, argued that the adultery was unproven, that Crook's testimony only showed that "improper familiarities had taken place between his client and Mrs. Ricketts, but yet it by no means followed she had permitted that last act," i.e., adultery, to occur. Kenyon disagreed with Dallas's assertion that this was "the first time an attempt was made to get a verdict on evidence of this kind" and insisted that "he had no doubt but circumstantial evidence was admissible." The general newspaper readers, who clearly had followed the trial in the press, were not so sure; for two weeks after its conclusion, a debate occurred at the Westminster Forum, with the question for the evening being "In this age of conjugal depravity, ought the singular conduct of Crook the Taylor, as displayed in a recent Crim. Con. Trial, to be shunned as a mean and mercenary exposure of Female Frailty; or imitated, as a virtuous and laudable communication to an injured Husband?" Though we do not, alas, have that evening's vote, the very formation of the question testifies both to the detailed interest ordinary people took in such cases, and to the possible presence of a more sympathetic, sentimental response to the plight of poor Mrs. Ricketts.[117] In addition, a rare critical letter, ostensibly from one of the jurors, appeared in the *Times* less than a week after the case's conclusion. Addressed to Kenyon, it explained that he, as a juror, had voted for large damages because, while doubting the evidence, he had thought "the well-known sagacity, the unimpeached integrity of your Lordship, a safer guide than the imbecility of my own judgment. . . ." Concluding, he explained his letter as a "caution [to] all those, who will in future form the Juries of the Country, to erase from their minds every impression but that which is made by the establishment of evidence, before they pass their verdict."[118] This letter, though very unusual, deserves to be quoted because it is one of the very few indicators we have of some sympathy, albeit after the verdict, for the people found guilty of adultery, or at least some unease about Kenyon's acceptance of circumstantial evidence.

For, as far as we can tell, most expressed opinion was strongly hostile to those engaged in such acts, and many supported those members of the Lords and Commons who wished to criminalize adultery in 1800. Four pamphlets were published supporting this attempt in the years immediately before and after the bill's introduction. All condemned the laxity of the law; one thought that the proposed bill, which would have made adultery a misdemeanor, too lenient: "To punish, as a misdemeanour, a crime which endangers the very existence of society, if an error, is certainly one on the side of lenity." All agreed that "a civil war of lust" was raging in the country, and that the growing tide of adultery cases had "almost converted an action, in which reparation is sought for a private injury, into a trial for a public offence." Two of the pamphlets explicitly paid tribute to Kenyon's labors in trying to come to grips with this problem, one calling him "the Cato of the Age."[119]

After the bill's failure, there were calls for the speedy reintroduction of such a measure. The *Times* expressed a hope that "the very virtuous and able Peer who proposed it, will renew it another session, according to his own first and genuine conceptions, without any compromise with the wishes and opinions of others." Two years later, it noted that "The great majority (as we sincerely believe) of the Public, are anxious for the introduction of an Adultery Bill, although a difference of opinion may prevail with regard to the extent of its prohibitions, or the severity of its penalties." The severity of opinion expressed by the *Times* found articulation elsewhere, for example, "Observator's" letter to the *Gentleman's Magazine*, which suggested corporal punishment as well as the deprivation of certain civil privileges for such offenders. A correspondent to the *Times* also hoped that "Parliament may take the hint, and enact that these convictions [for adultery] shall *disqualify* not only for the Legislature, but the Bar, and the Magistracy."[120]

Acts speak as loudly as words, however, and one can see men other than Kenyon or the supporters of the harsh new Adultery Bill acting severely against adulterers. For one thing, sheriffs' juries, empaneled to award damages when the defendant did not contest the issue, increasingly awarded enormous amounts to the husband; for example, in the case of the crim. con. case between the Marquis of Abercorn and Captain Copley, the jury, after only a short deliberation, awarded Abercorn £10,000 in damages, the same amount that the Duke of Cumberland had been fined thirty years before. While it had been thought that cases in King's Bench, especially under the eye of Kenyon, were awarded maximum penalties, by 1802, according to Erskine, this had all changed:

> Plaintiffs had formerly suffered much inconvenience from the course pursued by adulterers, in suffering judgment by default, and withdrawing the question from the superior Tribunals. This had not been the rule of late, because, in consequence of a Rule of Court, the same gentlemen were called upon to decide upon an inquisition who would have formed the jury upon a trial before the Chief Justice.

By the later 1790s, juries in other courts, not presided over by Kenyon, were also awarding very large damages.[121] If the size of penalties awarded is any measure of the perceived severity of the offence, many people shared Kenyon's views on the need for fiscal punitiveness.

But this was by no means the whole of the picture, nor everyone's judgment; take, for example, the letter that "A Methodist" sent to the *Gentleman's Magazine* in 1801. "There is a manifest and kindly leaning towards the frailties of the fair sex," he commented, but added that "no sentiment of chivalry should compel us to forget what is due to truth." He concluded by noting that he dreaded "that immorality of principle, which excuses every crime to which *beauty* gives occasion, which softens criminality by sentimental names, which argues from the point of an epigram or the stanza of a song." It was this sort of palliation, he noted, that had overthrown France. The connection between adultery, revolution, and France seemed part of a single evil, so that, when a possible peace with France was being discussed in Parliament, the *Gentleman's Magazine* reported on "an observation of Mr. Windham's, that an alliance with France would tend to render adultery fashionable. . . ." And the defense attorney, in his address to the jury in the Taylor *v* Birdwood criminal conversation case, noted that he was not trying to excuse vice or exculpate adultery:

> He did not stand there as an advocate for French vices, which had been employed in corrupting the morality of this nation, and of which the very cause furnished a proof. For it resulted from the same origin—the same French education which this Lady [Mrs. Taylor] had received in that detested land and which had led to the commission of this crime.

Counsel also made another interesting comment in this address. Arguing that he believed adultery to be a crime, "so declared by the promulgated will and law of God," he added (and the *Times* reported the following, all in capital letters, indicating perhaps the gravity or loudness of his voice): "AND NOT EVEN A HOST OF TITLED ADULTERERS SHOULD BE ABLE TO INDUCE HIM TO CONSIDER IT IN ANY OTHER LIGHT."[122] The connection made here was between the moral licentiousness of France, some licentious English legislators, and the failure of the Divorce Bill of 1800. Here the reference was to the argument, made in the House of Lords by the Earl of Carlisle just a week before the outset of the trial, that the bill before the House was written by men of "monkish seclusion" and that "the studies of a recluse did not lead to a knowledge of the world; in order to correct morals, it was necessary to mix with society, to dive into the minds of men, to be acquainted with their actions, and search the motives of their conduct." Not only did Lords Eldon and Auckland take umbrage, but so did Kenyon. In both this case, and in one two months later, at Maidstone, Kenyon strongly joined these slurs with French immorality and English aristocratic profligacy. In June he remarked that "somebody or other" had called judges "legal monks" and that he thought "that a more infamous, a more unqualified assertion, and that a more scandalous conduct never disgraced the pages of Daily Histories"; by August he said

> he had heard and believed he knew a little of the character of the persons who had taken upon them to censure his conduct in the administration of justice; they were persons of the highest rank and elevation in society; but high and elevated as they were, he thought it right to say, that . . . he never wished to have any intercourse or acquaintance with them, moral, religious or social.[123]

That Kenyon reacted so strongly in public is perhaps not surprising; that the press chose to report his remarks in both instances is more revealing, both of their own views, and of what they thought the public wished to read on this contentious issue.

But, as we have seen in "A Methodist's" letter, there was another sentiment which also found expression, one which while condemning the act of adultery, evinced sympathy and a painful sensibility for those caught up in love's untidy and unfortunate trammels. Even Kenyon at least once seemed moved by such an appeal, perhaps because it came wrapped in a critique of the immorality of the upper classes, a favorite topic of his. In 1794, in the case of Howard *v* Bingham, the defendant's attorney, Erskine, argued that no "real" adultery had occurred, because Howard's wife had been coerced to marry the heir to the Norfolk titles and estates by her parents, and that her heart was never really his. Here is Erskine's description of Mrs. Howard on her wedding night: "You must behold her given up to the Plaintiff by the infatuation of parents, and stretched upon this bed as upon a rack, as a legal victim to the shrine of Heraldry; torn from the arms of a beloved and impassioned youth, himself of noble birth, to secure the honors of a higher title." Bingham, he went on to note "has only to defend *himself*, and cannot demand damages from Mr. Howard for depriving him of what was his by a title superior to any law which man has a moral right to make: Mr. Howard was never married: God and Nature forbid the banns of such a marriage. . . ." Most extraordinary, however, was the closing summation that Kenyon made to the jury at the case's conclusion:

> To the defendant, for a great part of the time, I can impute no blame at all; he did that which was difficult for a young man. He seems to have bridled his passions for a considerable time; he retired with his friends, young men, branches of honourable families to the country, to see whether absence might not wean his affections. Unfortunately for both, the absence was not of very long continuance; he returned to town—they saw each other. The half extinguished flame was again lighted up, and the unfortunate consequence followed which you have heard. . . . You will not give large damages which shall press a young man, who, it is clear, at one time of his life had weaned himself from the unfortunate snare the beauty and perfection of this lady had got him into.

The jury decided on damages of £1,000, a small sum considering the status and wealth of both men.[124] Sometimes, occasionally, even with Kenyon, sentimental appeals worked.

More often, however, they did not. Juries usually seemed to unwilling to be swayed by such appeals, even when free of Kenyon's weighty presence. In a case that closely recalled the Bingham defense, the lawyer for Captain Copley argued that an "early attachment" had existed between him and the Marchioness of Abercorn, that he had gone "abroad to avoid being in her company" and that he had done "every thing which depended on man to obliterate his affections for her," only to be swept away by his feeling on his recall to England. Still, the jury returned a verdict of £10,000 damages, an enormous sum for a man who claimed to be worth less than £300 a year. Similarly Sergeant Best defended his client, Fawcet, by "ascribing it [the adultery] to the excess of his passions, heated by his constant intercourse with a lovely and beautiful woman." The jury rewarded the wronged husband £7,000. Even the great Erskine himself, pleading before Lord Ellenborough, failed with an extravagant appeal to the jury. In the Lingham adultery case, he argued that while it was true that the defendant, Hunt, had committed adultery with

Lingham's wife, the fault was rather the husband's: "Such was the nature of man, such was the impetuosity of his passions, that he was not always capable of resisting a temptation. The defendant had been placed in situations from which the prudence of the plaintiff should have withheld him; he was sensible he had committed a wrong, and was distracted at the sense of it— he was a victim of his passion." In this case, following Ellenborough's stinging response to this attempt to exculpate the adulterer, the jury awarded £5,000 to the injured husband.[125]

While lawyers repeatedly instructed juries in such cases that these were civil, not criminal proceedings, that it was not "consonant to the law of England to make a civil action the medium of inflicting criminal punishment," juries often resisted, awarding high and punitive damages.[126] It was well and good to go to the theater, to allow sympathetic effusions of the heart for the penitent adulteress-heroine of *The Stranger*, perhaps to read and thrill to romances of illicit love, but faced with "real" adultery, they usually seemed unwilling to be so moved.

While it may be that moralists wrote to newspapers more than sentimentalists, we have no comparable series of newspaper letters to those of "J. S.," written to the *Times* between May 23 and June 24, 1811. The first supported and reiterated the plea of the "hard-liners" in the Lords for the practice, in every instance, of a standing order "prohibiting the future marriage of the guilty person with the sharer in [her] guilt." The second, written a month later, was a harangue against the practice, usually insisted upon by the lecherous elements in the Commons, of granting the divorced wife a maintenance. Even the French, "J. S." noted, had condemned adulterous women, and by the "298th article of the Napoleonic code, the wife is condemned to imprisonment for a term not exceeding two years." The third letter, which responded to a mistake in the second that another letter-writer had pointed out, went on to condemn such a "most false and pernicious practice of liberality, contrary to the conduct of wise legislators in all other times and countries." Though another series of three letters were written just two years after, in the *Universal Magazine*, arguing the need for an enlarged and simplified divorce law, the great body of expressed opinion seemed, both in thought and practice, to favor severity.[127]

In the thirty years between Kenyon's appointment to the position of Chief Justice in 1788, and the retirement of his successor, Lord Ellenborough, there were interesting continuities and differences, not only between these two men, but among presiding judges of different courts. Kenyon took on many more cases during his tenure than did Ellenborough; furthermore, criminal conversation cases in which he presided appeared at least twice as frequently in the press. Both judges strongly condemned the vice of adultery and both held that it was not merely against the laws of the land, but against the laws of God and morality; there were, however, some interesting differences in approach. Although Ellenborough was clearly very incensed at the behavior of William Smith, the defendant in the crim. con. case of Smith *v* Smith, in his address to the jury he instructed them that "[it] were not to punish the Defendant for a crime, but to give the Plaintiff a compensation, as far as money could make it." Furthermore, he noted, after telling them what the defendant was worth, that "they would not give such a verdict as would utterly ruin the defendant." One can hardly imagine Kenyon making either of these judgments. Another interesting difference was the lengths to which Kenyon and other judges were willing to go in terms of circumstantial evidence. We have already seen the strength of Kenyon's reliance on such evidence in the Ricketts *v* Taylor case; in a case which presented similar evidence, Chief Justice Gibbs of the Court of Common Pleas was more cautious. When Robert King brought a criminal conversation suit against Lord Middleton, Gibbs, in his summation, noted "that there was no proof of any express acts of adultery, but only of visits at untimely hours, from which it would be, perhaps too much to infer adultery."[128] Kenyon, if he could have, would have uttered a loud and angry harrumph from the grave.

"Mild-Mays too often deceive. . . .":[129] *The Roseberry Affair*

Only a month after Lady Roseberry eloped with Sir Henry Mildmay, leaving her husband and four children for her widower brother-in-law with whom she had been conducting an affair, her husband had his suit of criminal conversation before the courts. Because Mildmay had "suffered judgment to go by default" the inquiry into damages came before the Sheriff's court. Even more remarkable than the trial's testimony was its coverage by the press. Every newspaper in London covered it, most at extraordinary length, often filling the bulk of an entire issue with the account.[130] In interesting ways this trial offered the public many of the same features that the Grosvenor-Cumberland case had more than four decades before; the lover arranging meetings in disguise, saving love letters, and being discovered in the bedroom with the guilty wife. However, in addition, this trial also contained the frisson of incest; Lady Roseberry and Mildmay's dead wife were sisters, and, it was hinted, the intimacy between the two arose when Lady Harriet acted as comforter and confidante to Mildmay following the death of his wife in childbirth. In other ways the tone of reports and comments about this trial was significantly different than that earlier case, blacker, less satirical, and more Byronic.

When Lady Mildmay, the sister of the countess of Roseberry, died in 1810, Sir Henry became a regular visitor to the home of his brother-in-law, the Earl of Roseberry. At this point the Roseberrys had been married for two years, and Lady Harriet was only twenty. However, it was not until 1814, four years later, that the affair started. Called to Scotland to the deathbed of his father in March 1814, the Earl on his return noticed "a difference in the conduct of Lady Roseberry to him." Informed of the many morning visits that Mildmay had made to the Countess in his absence, he requested that Mildmay no longer visit, and did not "notice" Mildmay in the street. In addition, Lady Harriet's father spoke to Sir Harry "on the impropriety of breaking in on the comforts of this domestic circle." To no avail. When the Earl removed his family to Scotland, hoping perhaps that time and distance would restore his wife's former affections, Sir Harry followed in disguise, traveling "under the assumed name of Col. DeGrey of the Guards." Settling into a pub near Roseberry's home, he let his beard and whiskers grow, dressed as a sailor, and attended to "some errand or other every evening." When the ladies of the Roseberry family retired from the dining table, Lady Harriet, rather than joining them, began instead to retreat to her bed chamber. One evening, suspicious of this activity, Lord Roseberry's brother caused the door of her room to be breached, and found her with Mildmay, "in disguise and with a pair of loaded pistols before him." After a bit of heated discussion, Mildmay left and the next morning, Lady Roseberry, claiming to be retiring to her father's house, eloped and joined her lover. Within a week they were on their way to France.[131]

At the ensuing trial, the appeals of both lawyers to the jury were presented and published at length. In opening, the Attorney General, Sir William Garrow, speaking for the plaintiff, remarked that "in the whole course of his life, he had never felt any thing, approaching the difficulty, distress, and embarrassment he now experienced . . . the circumstances of this case differing so much from every thing he had ever read, or heard of before, in the extraordinary atrocity by which it was peculiarly distinguished." He indulged the jury and courtroom spectators with excerpts from Mildmay's letters to Lady Roseberry, and remarked that in these "she was addressed in language which a man of the most libidinous character would not have used toward a lady of rank, even if he had succeeded in debauching her person." In contrast, though Brougham, the defendant's lawyer, also made "a speech of great length, eloquence, and feeling," he did not attempt to mitigate the extent of his client's fault but noted instead that "justice should be tempered by moderation" and that Garrow's "artful address" "should not wash away the cool, the dispassionate, the equitable feeling of their hearts."

Though Garrow had presented this case "as the most atrocious that had ever come under consideration," Brougham reminded the jurors that that courtroom had "witnessed many cases which were marked by circumstances far more heinous, and of a deeper and more guilty dye."[132] He then proceeded, in an extraordinarily effective rhetorical move, to note that "his hands were bound by his instructions" which forced him "not to breathe a whisper of reproach against any one branch of the noble families" affected by the adultery, intimating that if his hands were free, he could tell them a great deal to these families' discredit. Finally, Brougham vigorously denied that Mildmay had been ordered out of Lady Harriet's bedchamber, "and that he had gone out . . . disgraced, spiritless, and lost to all those manly feelings by which he had previously been characterized." This slander, he continued, "if it had been proved . . . would have been worse than all that had been imputed to the Hon. Baronet . . . because it would have called in question that which was the dearest to his heart as a man of honour—his courage." This self-identification of Sir Harry's as a man of honor was also made earlier in the trial, when Garrow read out a letter of Mildmay's, in which he explained that he meant to coerce Roseberry into fighting a duel with him, but that he would refrain from firing, and thus shame the cuckolded husband into a reconciliation and renewed invitations to his home and, implicitly, renewed access to Lady Harriet. Other than adverting to the "the agony, the sorrow, the wretchedness, which the conviction of the transgression had excited in the minds of the guilty pair," Brougham ended the defense's case.[133]

This defense became the subject of a lengthy satirical poem published less than a week after the trial, entitled "How to serve a client who cannot be defended/ Or/ The Apotheosis of Courage." In it, the narrator, the defense attorney, after remarking—

> I'm forbidden by my instructions,
> To presume to make deductions,
> From whatever may occur,
> 'Gainst the Plaintiff's character;
> Thus tied down I'll nothing say,

revealed explicitly what Brougham had only suggested:

> He in fault was all along;
> If his wife, or friend he'd started,
> And for ever kept them parted,
> Ere the business far had gone,
> There had never been "Crim. Con."

Like Brougham, however, the poem's narrator insists on Mildmay's repudiation of any slurs of cowardice, or that he had retreated from Lady Roseberry's bedchamber through fear of chastisement:

> Brand his name unnumber'd times
> With all sorts of wrongs and crimes;
> These, if they fall to his share,
> He may well contented bear;
> They from Fortune should not sever,
> Nor yet exile him forever;
> But to say he courage lack'd,
> That with fear he ever back'd;
> That's what cannot be endur'd.[134]

Unlike the earlier trials of Grosvenor or Worsley, this case inspired the immediate publication of only this single satirical piece. What of the other items which were published soon after? A week after the trial, an item appeared that listed "the matchless assemblage of Royal Sevre, Dresden and French porcelaine" which were being sold at auction to pay off some part of Mildmay's damages. Two short poems, both sentimental and playing on the floral appellations of the parties in the case, the Lady Rose(berry), whose family name was Primrose, and the seducer who was personified as a cruel Mild-May, also appeared, which, while condemning the adulterer most strongly, noted of the injured wife: "Thy hour is past—thy little day is run,/Nor can the morrow raise thee with its sun."[135] In addition, the same paper published an unattributed comment on Brougham's defence. Speaking of the couple's anguish for their misdeed, it noted

> The fearful perversion of moral principles, and disregard of every social and sacred duty displayed on this melancholy occasion, will, we trust, operate as a beacon against the indulgence of criminal passions, without the aid of persuasion to enforce the palpable truth, that the fruit of vice is indeed full of bitterness and ashes.[136]

And in a letter which appeared in the *St. James's Chronicle*, a correspondent linked this particular case with broader questions of the appropriate response among men of different ranks to such betrayal, and, by the way, with the upper-class need to avenge lost honor by the duel. Noting the general civility of the Roseberrys towards Mildmay, he contrasted their recourse to the law with the violent and horrific assault by an "Irish peasant" on the man sleeping with his wife, and concluded:

> When we consider what trivial circumstances render it *indispensably necessary*, according to the notions of high life, to seek the life of the offending

party, one cannot but be surprised at the coolness with which are borne affronts and injuries calculated to excite the liveliest indignation in the natural man.[137]

When the Roseberry divorce, and its provisions, came to be argued in Parliament, several of the themes that had already appeared before resurfaced. In the Lords, Ellenborough, sounding surprisingly like his predecessor Kenyon, remarked of Lady Harriet's offence, that it was "a crime than which, under the circumstances, nothing short of the higher felonies could be more atrocious." In the Commons, on the other hand, M. A. Taylor, arguing against the clauses which would harshly penalize Lady Roseberry, said he would vote against them because if they passed, the "unfortunate woman" would not have the peace she needed "for reflection and repentance." And during these deliberations, a letter appeared in the *Times*, which spoke for the importance of such punitive clauses, not so much for their effects on the guilty woman, as for their influence on the public. "Under the notion of liberality we are daily obliterating all those stigmas which create a horror of vice, and which broadly and palpably distinguish it from virtue," noted "X.Y."; furthermore, he remarked that "the greater frequency of this crime in modern days is plainly enough to be traced to the greater indulgence it meets with. It is rendered interesting on the stage, and extenuated in the Senate."[138]

"The Contagion of this Canonized Adultery":[139] *Morality and the Stage in the Early Nineteenth Century*

"X.Y.'s" reference to the sympathetic portrayal of adultery on the stage was surely a comment on the current production of *The Stranger* at Covent Garden. Now, in 1815, almost two decades after its debut, the play's reception by the press, most notably by the *Times*, was vastly different from what it had initially been. Perhaps influenced by the Roseberry case, the condemnation of the play was formidable. Though her performance of Mrs. Haller was praised, the *Times* hoped that in future, the young actress who performed this role would be "attracted by a character of less doubtful morality." For, it noted, though Kotzebue's intent was clearly to portray the power of redemption, adultery should not be so palliated; it was "a crime which ought to be, in all public senses, considered as beyond the chances or lenitives of reform. . . ."[140] Even harsher were its remarks on the play three months later, when Kemble gave it "the sanction of his first appearance" that season as its eponymous protagonist. It was, they said, "a play . . . fitted to do evil" and worse still, to spread its evil among vast numbers. "It is, perhaps, a strongly diminished estimate, that no less than 50,000 of that class of citizenship whose virtue is most essential to the state have been already exposed to the contagion of this canonized adultery," it noted. The metaphor is significant. Earlier moralists had bemoaned the force of example, but while the vices of the Great were sometimes called "contagious" this notion had not been invoked in judgments of theatrical performances. However, in postwar Britain, contagion had replaced imitation, even in the theater, and moral weakness had been replaced by the metaphor of epidemical disease.

Less than a month later, Edmund Kean, a rising star on the English stage, and a challenger to Kemble for male theatrical pre-eminence, appeared in a play by Richard Cumberland, *The Wheel of Fortune*. Though it was based on, or inspired by, *The Stranger*, the *Times* praised Cumberland's play, whose "genius was satisfied in culling from 'the misanthropy and repentance' of Kotzebue" the outline of an interesting fable, and who had the "judgment and morality to throw aside with contempt the false taste and mischievous sentiment of the German." Two decades after Bowdler had lent his name to the "sterilization" of noxious books, the theater was also undergoing a similar Bowdlerization.

And the *Times*, the incipient "Thunderer," was at the forefront of this campaign. But, as we have seen, adultery trials, replete with the publication of sordid actions and scandalous letters, were a staple in its pages, as in the pages of most of the press. "This is a subject," a *Times* editorial confessed, "which occasions us some perplexity." After noting that it "suppress[ed] as much as possible all indelicate and offensive matter" from its published adultery reports, it went on to give three reasons for such continued public notice. First, that publicity given to court cases ensured "pure impartial justice"; second, that the publication of immorality, by naming names and circumstances, was itself a form of punishment or chastisement; and finally that if such cases, involving "persons of some opulence," were omitted, readers might suppose that journalists had been paid to delete such stories. "We may therefore be the more zealous in giving notoriety to trials for adultery, the more our suppression of them might subject us to unjust imputations."[141]

This seemingly nice balance between publicity and prurience, between reporting and advocacy, was nowhere evident in the *Times*'s handling of the Cox *v* Kean adultery trial and its aftermath. On January 17, 1825, Robert Albion Cox, an alderman of London and failed banker, took the great actor Edmund Kean to court, to sue for damages in a criminal conversation case. Not only, and perhaps unsurprisingly, was this trial given remarkable coverage, but, starting the next day, the *Times* launched a campaign to remove Kean from the English stage. "It is of importance" it argued, "that public feeling be not shocked, and public decency be not outraged" by the appearance of "such a creature as this to the gaze of a British audience." Though the managers of Drury Lane, and Kean himself attempted to continue with his announced appearances, two weeks of the *Times*'s incitement and of mayhem at the theater made that impossible.[142] Kean shortly after left the country for a tour of America. Though the public could not stop adulterers from sitting in the Lords or the Commons, the power of the press declared itself as firmly opposed to their appearance before the public, either as the subjects of or the actors in theatrical performances. Adultery did not vanish, but became instead much, much more discreet.

Thomas Rowlandson, "E. O., or the Fashionable Vowels." Courtesy of the Beinecke Rare Book Library, Yale University

5

Deserving "Most the Cognizance of the Magistrate and the Censor": Combating Gaming

The Laws against Gaming are not only severe in their Penalties, but recite in their Preambles such Consequences attending this Vice, as shew that, of all others, it deserves most the Cognizance of the Magistrate and the Censor; since the Offended, as well as the Offenders, are alike cautious of speaking, and the Injured agree with the Criminals in burying all Things in Oblivion.[1]

Gambling is an activity found almost everywhere and among all sorts of people. Both men and women indulge in it, both the great and the small, and its excesses have always been, and will continue to be, denounced and deprecated. In this chapter we will concentrate mainly on the condemnations of the gaming of the Great, and the relation between their gaming habits and the impact of these on the national weal. Omitted will be those sorts of gambling which did not involve cards, dice, or gaming tables; i.e., private bets on agreed-upon outcomes, horse-racing or boxing bets. It is not that these activities do not partake of the gaming spirit, but that they were less part of the everyday sociable life of the men and women of the *bon ton*. What is most striking about the condemnations of sociable gaming is their reiterative quality; whether in the 1730s, the 1760s, or the 1790s, many of the same criticisms were repeated, many of the same calls to action voiced.

"the gaming madness, guilty joy! The fashionable vice of later years"[2]

In chapter 3 we saw suicide referred to as "the fashionable vice"; here we wish to look at that other act, also described in the quote above as "the fashionable vice" and frequently seen as conjoined or leading to suicide, that is, gaming or gambling. The link between the two vices was an eighteenth-century commonplace. The *Connoisseur* of 1755 published a mock Bill of Suicides in which three of the nineteen causes of death were various forms of gaming—on lotteries, at the races, or at gaming tables. In a poetical *Essay on Gaming, in a epistle to a young Nobleman* published just a few years later, the anonymous author argued:

> Gross Food, thick Air, a cold inclement Sky,
> Are not the Cause so many rashly die;
> But Vice, Profuseness, modern Unbelief,
> Despair, high Play, and Pride that spurns Relief.[3]

The newspapers were full of stories of wretches who, unable to pay their gaming debts, did away with themselves. For example, this vignette from the pages of the *Public Advertiser*:

> Last Thursday a young gentleman shot himself at his apartments near Hatton Gardens. A note was found in this pocket giving his reasons for committing the rash action, viz his having been enticed to gaming-tables, where he lost his whole fortune, which was sufficient to have supported him, and was reduced to the last shilling. He concludes the note with wishing that the Magistrates would use their authority to suppress all gaming-houses, as it would be a means of saving many a person from destruction.[4]

There were also contemporary studies which connected these vices, and joined them to the evil of duelling. The best known of these were Richard Hey's *Three Dissertations on the Pernicious Effects of Gaming (1783), on Duelling (1784) and on Suicide (1785)* and Charles Moore's *A full inquiry into the Subject of Suicide to which are added (as being closely connected with the subject) Two Treatises on Duelling and Gambling*. In this later work, Moore, talking of the three subjects of his inquiry, argued that "these are crimes so great in themselves, so intimately connected with each other, and such increasing evils . . . as to require every nerve to be strained in reprobating their practice." A few years after Moore's work appeared, another clergyman, in a sermon against suicide, connected self-murder with gaming, noting that the practice "involves almost every human vice; almost every evil and detestable passion." It was in this same spirit that an allegory, entitled *The Origin* of *Gaming, and her two Children, Duelling and Suicide*, appeared in the *Gentleman's Magazine*. Gaming, according to this tale, was the offspring of the rape of the goddess Fortune by the God of War. In her infancy the child was soothed only by the sound of dice, and in her maturity, by some unknown "man of the sword," she became the mother of twins, duelling and suicide, who resembled both their parents and grandparents in their inclinations and illegitimacy.[5] Finally, this "triple-headed Cerberus" of vice often had another "head" engrafted onto its vicious neck, that of adultery. Thus the *Times* denouncing "the vice of gaming" argued that it led inevitably to "SUICIDE, ADULTERY, BANKRUPTCY and the GALLOWS."[6]

If gaming was seen to be like other vices, that is, in being conjoined in a grand constellation of misdeeds, all springing from the prevalence of fashion, custom, and pride, all deriving from an unheeding and selfish pursuit of passion and pleasure, it was strikingly different in at least one major respect—unlike duelling, its votaries came from all classes and genders, from all walks and occupations of life; unlike suicide, it seemed inextricably intertwined with the sociability of large sections of the population; unlike adultery, it offered its attractions to young and old alike, to the married as well as the single. Thus, for many, its ubiquity made it not only the most prevalent but also the most dangerous of the vices. However, in two important respects, which we will consider in more detail below, gaming shared some basic characteristics with the other vices under review: that one major source of its corruption, like that of the others, seemed to be found in the practices of the Great and that the Law seemed unable to cope either with successfully regulating or with eliminating any of these practices.

In this chapter we will consider the evolution of thinking about gambling by beginning with a consideration and comparison of James Shirley's 1637 play *The Gamester* with Edward Moore's drama *The Gamester* of 1753. We will also examine the way in which discussions of gaming changed in the periodical literature through the first half of the century, paying particular attention to questions of public versus private gaming, and the gender of the archetypical gamester. These themes will be continued with a more detailed scrutiny of the intersection between public political life and private gambling. In addition the question of the stance of the law towards both private and public gaming must be treated, in terms of both legislative action and enforcement.

In 1637, James Shirley published his play *The Gamester*, ostensibly based on a story that Charles I had given him. Its plot was simple and predictable, its main characters were a circle of reckless, fast-living young men, down on their luck, but of "family": Wilding and Hazard, the two main heroes,

Beaumont and Delamore, two others who became involved in a drunken and nearly fatal duel, and a trio of minor male libertines, Acreless, Littlestock, and Sellaway, who were seldom found away from the gaming tables. Along the way, a wealthy "cit" and his pusillanimous nephew are ridiculed, a husband is duped into faithfulness, a ward and the man she loves receive her withheld fortune and marry. The play ends in celebration and partying. In so far as there is any criticism of the characters or their acts, it consists of a rather smug tittering at the follies of those who wish to appear "better than they are," and at the foolishness of a man wishing both to fornicate and to game, who loses at both in consequence. Though this play was quite successful in its day, and continued to be performed through the eighteenth century (though largely in David Garrick's emendation, which condensed and simplified the plot somewhat), the tone of the play is more Stuart and courtly than Hanoverian and popular. As an early twentieth-century commentator on Shirley has noted:

> One closes a volume of Shirley with the same feeling with which the poet's audience of courtly ladies and gentlemen must have left the Cockpit, that of having been pleasantly and worthily entertained, without a rankling thought or startling fact left in the memory to disturb one's ordinary view of life.[7]

When, in the early eighteenth century, Susanna Centlivre wrote her own *Gamester*, the play was interestingly different, though still set in high life. Its hero, Valere, is a compulsive and uncontrolled gambler. His love interest, Angelica, determined to save him from his downward gambling spiral, first gives him a ring which she makes him swear to preserve, then, in the guise of a rakish young gentleman, wins it from him. Not surprisingly, the play ends well, with Valere promising to abstain from all gaming, and the couple wed. A triple wedding also culminated the next play Centlivre wrote about gambling, *The Basset Table*. In this play, the gambler is a female, Lady Reveller, but for her gambling is only one part of an interesting and complex life; she is the proprietor of a high stakes gambling establishment, whose exclusivity is an infallible lure to wealthy citizens who wish to move in fashionable circles. She also uses her position to flirt shamelessly and yet remain free of all restrictions, being a young and very beautiful widow. Only when Sir James Courtly, best friend of the hero, Lord Worthy, pretends, in order to aid Worthy, to attempt a rape, does Reveller realize the desirability of marriage and of the reliability of Worthy, and thus gives up the business of gaming. However, the similarity of setting and moral demonstrate that, in the theater at any rate, gaming in high life, whether male or female, was, until the mid-century, largely comedic. Beautifully clothed and coiffed, the gambling Great preyed on the ambitious citizen, and, to some extent on each other, only to be redeemed by love to a path of more prudential play, rather than total abstention from gaming activity.

The success of George Lillo's *The London Merchant*, first performed in 1731, a new kind of tragedy with its characters and protagonist belonging not to the great of society but to its middling ranks, is often credited with serving as the model for Edward Moore's tragedy *The Gamester* of 1753. This drama, by portraying the terrible perils into which an untrammeled passion for gaming could lead an otherwise honest and honorable man, sought to convince its audiences "that the want of prudence is the want of virtue." The tale of the drama is quickly told; Beverley, married to a virtuous and beautiful wife, is convinced to game by his false friend Stukeley, who not only has contrived to be the secret recipient of Beverley's gaming losses, but also hopes, by his inevitable bankruptcy, to corrupt the virtue of his faithful wife. Thrown into prison for debt after having pawned his wife's jewels and sold his heirship to an elderly uncle's rich estate, Beverley takes poison from self-disgust and disdain for life. Just before his death, however, the villain, Stukeley, is punished, and Beverley dies proclaiming his affection for his spouse and his hopes for divine mercy. Its moral is perhaps too obvious, and the play's popularity can only be explained by the growing enthusiasm for dramatic sentiment, and by the opportunities it afforded to some of the great dramatic actors and actresses of the later eighteenth and early nineteenth century. Its prologue, written by Garrick himself, announced and underlined what was to come:

> Ye slaves of passion, and ye dupes of chance,
> Wake all your pow'rs from this destructive trance!
> Shake all the shackles of this tyrant vice:
> Hear other calls than those of cards and dice:
> Be learn'd in nobler arts, than arts of play,
> And other debts, than those of honour pay:

These prefatory lines indicate that Garrick, if not Moore as well, hoped that the regenerative actions of this play would not only convince ordinary folk to watch their gaming proclivities, but would also awaken the consciences of those denizens of the world of honor, those persons for whom gambling debts were called debts of honor, to reject its trivializing and addictive pleasures for the nobler arts of conversation and governance.[8]

If one considers the performances of these three gamester plays through the eighteenth century, an interesting pattern emerges. While the two comedies (that is Centlivre's *Gamester* and Garrick's version of Shirley's *Gamester*) were performed more often in total than Moore's play, fewer than one-quarter of these comedic performances occurred after 1760, while more than three-quarters of the performances of the tragedy were in the last forty years of the century. Of course this figure is only suggestive, but the difference in late-century popularity between the two sorts of dramas might well indicate a changing attitude toward the central activity with which each of these plays dealt.[9]

"ruined by Gaming":[10] *Attitudes Toward Gaming in Early Eighteenth-Century England*

Looking back at eighteenth-century gaming from the vantage point of the later nineteenth century, Andrew Steinmetz, one of England's first historians of the practice, thought "that the rise of modern gaming in England may be dated from the year 1777 or 1778."[11] In fact, gambling, both public and private, had been an important topic of debate for at least three quarters of a century before the date assigned by Steinmetz. That men, and especially young men, gambled and had always done so, seemed obvious. That aristocratic men lost large sums in this way was not surprising to anyone. And, in 1709 the *Tatler* argued that it was the very virtues of young noblemen that led them to these two undesirable circumstances. The magnanimity, the courage, and the forthrightness of such young men caused them to become the prey to those whom they thought also gentlemen because they "seemed" gentle, i.e., looked well-dressed and acted in a polite and easy manner. Thus the *Connoisseur* described the sharper, the professional gambler who employed various cheats to effect the ruin of the young sprigs of the nobility, as possessed of coolness, politeness, quick and lively parts, and a seeming openness of behavior. Such sharpers seemed almost biologically destined to devour the substance of young and inexperienced men of wealth. Gaming "is now become rather the business than amusement of our persons of quality. . . ." noted the *Connoisseur*. "Thus it happens, that estates are now almost as frequently made over by whist and hazard, as by deeds and settlements. . . ."[12] "How many Young Heirs have fall'n Prey to this rooking Generation of Men?" lamented Josiah Woodward in 1726. The anonymous author of *The Whole Art and Mystery of Gaming* agreed: "The Sons of our Nobility, and the Heirs to large and plentiful Estates, especially those who become too early their own Masters, are the Victims of Sharpers . . . ."[13]

While the gaming of Society was bemoaned in theory, for much of its early modern history the gambling that was considered criminal was largely that in which the lower classes engaged. Gambling, night-walking, and riotous living were all associated, and all perceived to be serious breaches of public order. In addition, such gaming was often joined to other forms of fraud, such as employing false dice or marked cards. By the early eighteenth century a variety of books were available which offered the inexperienced insights into the tricks of the various gambling societies, whose members were often described collectively as "rooks." Cotton's *Compleat Gamester* [1674], Ward's *London Spy* [1703], and Lucas's *Memoirs of the Lives, Intrigues and Comical Adventures of the Most Famous Gamesters and Celebrated Sharpers* [1714] were just three of the better-known examples of this genre.

The descriptions of gaming professionals and their victims employed, from the outset, a language of predatory animality. Gamesters were dubbed "cormorants, sharks, vultures, hawks, foxes, or wolves" as well as "rooks" or "anthropophagi." These flesh-eaters, hunting in packs, dined off "pigeons, geese and sheep," as their victims were called. A gamester was described as "a hawk among pidgeons; a fox among geese, a wolf among sheep."[14] The gambling inns or public houses in which these predators operated were presented, not surprisingly, as scenes of rage and violence: "every night, almost, some one or other, who, either heated with Wine, or made cholerick with the loss of his Money, raises a quarrel, swords are drawn, box and candlesticks thrown at one another's heads." The poet Richard Ames made such a scene of rapine, blasphemy, and malice the motif of his poem:

> Would you my *Muse* of *Hell* the Picture view,
> And what Distracted Looks the *Damned* shew;
> Go to some Gaming-Ordinary where,
> *Shamwell* and *Cheatly* and such Rooks repair,
> To sharp the Citty-*Prigg* or Country-*Heir*.
> . . . The *Pox*, the *Plague*, and all the Ills that fall,
> On wretched Mortals on themselves they call;
> While they by the uncertain chance of *Dice*,
> Loose Mannours, Lands, and Lordships in a Trice.[15]

"Publick *Gaming*," said one correspondent to the *Gentleman's Magazine*, is nothing but "*Publick Theft and Robbery*." And so, to prevent these sorts of violent eruptions and disturbances of the peace, two laws against such houses were passed in 1739 and 1745. Thus, shortly after the passage of the second Act, a meeting was called of all the petty-constables of the City of London and the Liberty of Westminster, to make "a proper Return of all Gaming Houses, Bawdy Houses, Night Cellars, and other Houses of ill Fame . . . in order that they may be prosecuted to the utmost Severity of the Law."[16] It was not that only lower-class men frequented such places, or that men of wealth and position disdained them, but rather that their clientele was socially varied and their "staff" professional, that made them seem especially dangerous. The desire to control or eliminate such places had something to do both with the desire to establish order and control crime and with the wish to protect property in "Mannours, Lands, and Lordships" from being squandered away.

It seems that these laws had some effect, though, as we shall see, not as much as many had hoped for. In June 1742, both the *Gentleman's* and *London Magazine* published a brief account of a remarkable case, tried at King's Bench. Having been the loser at the forbidden game of Hazard seven years before, an unnamed victim prosecuted the successful gambler, and, "after a long trial, . . . the Jury found a Gentleman guilty of the Penalty of 2500l for winning 500l from another Gentleman. . . ." Though the crime had occurred before the passage of the Act, the new environment may have convinced the loser that a prosecution was now possible. However, a decade later, in his capacity as Bow-Street magistrate, Henry Fielding was regularly breaking up similar gaming establishments, and attempting, largely unsuccessfully, to fine the proprietors, and more successfully, to destroy their gaming tables.[17]

As early as the 1740s, gaming houses were occasionally found at a different sort of venue—the homes of two aristocratic ladies, Mordington and Casselis, who claimed that their peerage protected their establishments from legal prosecution, but such upper-class involvement was still, it seems, rather unusual.[18] Just seven years before, after a trip to Paris, the young Horace Walpole had commented in tones of disgust and horror, at the number of gaming houses kept by French people of fashion. "[I]t is no dishonour to keep public gaming houses," he noted; "there are at least an hundred and fifty people of the first quality in Paris who live by it. . . . Even the princesses of the blood are dirty enough to have shares in the banks kept at their houses."[19] In England, the implication seemed to be, such things were rare and never so casually accepted.

After the passage of two mid-century acts to control gaming, an ongoing discussion was waged in pamphlets and the press for the next two decades about the relative destruction occasioned by private versus public gaming. While a few thought that public gambling houses were the source of England's gambling mania, many felt that the real problem was with gambling in private houses. As early as 1736, a correspondent stated that "Play in private houses," which had, he felt, shown a "great Encrease," would "if not timely prevented, . . . end in the Ruin of the young and unwary of both Sexes. . . ." Two decades later, "M. E.," in a letter to the *Gentleman's Magazine*, arguing that gaming was one of those practices that could not be obliterated but only controlled, declared the desirability of an establishment of "public games of chance, under the direction of a groom porter." This regulated and non-fraudulent amusement would allow people to have their "flutter" without being cheated; furthermore he also recommended that games of skill could continue to be played in private homes, but that "none be permitted to win or lose above a certain sum, at one time, under severe penalties." Many thought the distinction between public houses and private homes had become abused, and that all should come under the eye of the law. The polite world, and especially women of the *ton*, wrote the *St. James's Chronicle*, spend much of their days at "routs," gambling parties at private dwellings. But, "instead of a few select Friends" such as they might meet for tea or conversation, they spend their days "with a Croud of Half-acquaintances and Strangers." Routs, this essay argued, were nothing more than "private-publick Gaming Houses." Though its author satirically proposed that "two publick Routs should be instituted, with AUTHORITY to open their doors every night, like the theatres," such a suggestion had been seriously made by Henry Fielding a decade before: "Resolved, that all places of general rendezvous, tho' at a private house, shall be deemed public places, and the masters and mistresses of all such houses shall be considered in the same light as the managers of our public theatres, and shall be equally subject to the jurisdiction of this court." Writing almost a year before Fielding, "Sunderlandensis" went even farther. "*Gaming* for money, or gain of any kind," he argued, "either in publick or private, by great or small, ought to be prohibited under the severest penalties, and a mark of infamy fixed upon it."[20]

By the late 1760s opinion seemed unanimous; "few, if any, men ever lost a considerable sum at play in public; but that private parties . . . are the marts of imposition and villainy." "A Halfcrown Whist Player," writing to the *Town and Country Magazine* agreed, noting that "private parties and card clubs" had become infiltrated by professional gamblers, and, he argued, "there are, at least, one hundred thousand gamesters of both sexes, who live entirely by play." But what was to be done? Few seemed willing to pursue the suggestion that the homes of the Great should be invaded and illegal gaming prosecuted. One of the few who thought this the correct policy, the anonymous author of a 1750 pamphlet identified only as a "County Justice," proposed the passage of a law which stipulated that, among other penalties

> all and every Person or Persons who shall be convicted of any Offence against the Laws and Statutes for preventing of excessive or deceitful Gaming, shall, from the Time of that Conviction, be deemed and adjudged to be incapable of, and disabled from holding or executing any Office, Place, Trust, or Employment, Civil or Military, in the Kingdom of *Great Britain* . . . .

Another, a correspondent to the *Morning Chronicle*, expressed a rather wistful hope that the rise of private theatricals, in which sprigs of the nobility "have lately acted some pieces themselves, for their own and friends amusement" would replace the attraction of the gaming table, while providing "noble and manly relaxation." This hope was destined to be doomed, as many of the young men and women most involved in such performances also found time and inclination for truly heroic gaming stints and monumental gaming loses.[21]

Thus while gaming dens were condemned and the law called on to eliminate them, other sorts of criticisms were being made of a different type of gambling, that which took place in Society, in the world of the great, the leisured, and the beautiful. This body of criticism revolved around four sorts of destructive effects that, it was argued, this activity involved: harm to individuals, to society, and to the economic as well as political life of the nation. Much rested, it was frequently claimed, on the control of such noble play. Upper-class gambling was contrasted to, and seen as the enemy of polite conversation. Furthermore, the publication of Hoyle's guides to "scientific" game-playing raised the question of whether sociable or recreational gaming was being transformed into a more efficient engine for avarice and moneymaking, with the creation of "knowing" scientific gamblers and ignorant dupes. Not only would the purported growth of gaming have serious effects on the property of men of family, it was claimed, but it would do even greater moral damage to their womenfolk. And, with the leaders of society, male and female, enthralled by the lure of the game, the direct and indirect effects of such degeneration would be widespread and potentially fatal.

"national evils of the most enormous magnitude":[22] Gaming and the Nation's Welfare

The gaming of both the town and the *ton*, of high society and ordinary folk, was frequently presented in the journals and pamphlets of early eighteenth-century England as one of the predominant afflictions affecting the public weal. Josiah Woodward called it "the Mother of Many Vices"; an essay in the *Gentleman's Magazine* of 1731 spelled out its effects: it "destroys the Mind, Body and Estate; it contracts the Soul, and narrows the Genius; it gives a Disrelish of more noble and exalted Pleasures, and puts us upon a Thousand mean Things which our Souls abhorr'd." The poet Robert Colvill saw in the popularity of gaming "Th'ignoble scandal of degenerate times, Baneful to public and to private good!"[23] This theme continued to be presented and reworked through the succeeding decades. Thus the anonymous author of *The Essay on Gaming* of 1761 concluded that

Gaming's a Fiend with Harpy Claws and Eyes,
Of Paper Substance, but prodigious Size:
Which like *Eve's* Serpent wears seducing Smiles,
And when it proffers most, the most beguiles:
The sight of Gold its Appetite creates,
And dread Destruction on its Meal awaits . . . .

The *London Magazine*, a decade later, declared that "[t]his vice of gaming, originally descended from the worst of passions, is certainly the most pernicious of any to society." And, in 1784, following the loss of the American colonies, a "Member of Parliament" blamed gaming for the defeat: "To this dreadful vice must every misfortune which has lately fallen on this country be attributed!"[24] What seemed extraordinary about this activity was its addictive quality; it led not only to the derogation of duty, but even to the neglect of other pleasures. This first sort of complaint was traditional, yet oft repeated. Thus, in a general lamentation addressed to gaming, and the avarice which fed it, the *London Magazine* thundered:

> the nation that harbours thee sacrifices her liberty to its pursuits; the statesman, when he becomes thy votary, proves false to his country; and every glowing passion for the publick welfare is chill'd in its embryo by the over-ruling power of self-interest; justice herself is stagger'd by thy enormities, her sword is blunted by thy outrages; when she calls in feeble accents, for assistance, her faithless patrons are deaf to all her entreaties . . . .

A more modern twist was given to this dirge in Samuel Johnson's *Rambler*, which noted "a fatal passion for cards and dice which seems to have overturned not only the ambition of excellence, but the desire of pleasure; to have extinguished the flames of the lover, as well as of the patriot; . . . [and left him] without wishes, but for lucky hands." The situation had become so serious that in 1754 the *Gray's Inn Journal*, discussing gaming, remarked that it was then "the Grand Business of Life, which Mr. Pope, in his usual emphatic Manner, calls the Nation's last great Trade."[25] Forty years later the influence of gaming seemed equally grave, and the cleric Thomas Rennell, arguing against the notion that private vice could be, if not public virtue, then at least publicly neutral, hotly contended that

> I would not be thought to acquiesce in that mischievous distinction, invented by Knaves and current only with Fools; a distinction I mean between PRIVATE and PUBLIC morals, as if any vice or mode of immorality could exist, which doth not by *some channel* convey its poison to the body politick . . . the vice of gaming strikes *immediately* at the vitals of public virtue, public order, and public happiness.

Thus, from the beginning of the eighteenth century and throughout its course, opinion both clerical and popular saw in gaming a dreadful national evil. And many objected to what they dubbed its "fascination" operating in every station and walk of life. Well before the mid-century, critics pointed out the effects that gaming had on the various classes, on the great as well as the small. Though it was the crime of the poor that seemed more threatening to the commonweal than the imprudent vice of the noble, both were lamented. Thus in the 1722 tract *An Account of the Endeavours that have been used to suppress Gaming-Houses*, its author noted: "I am sorry to say it, but I verily believe, that the great Corruptions of late, and the daily Immoralities among People of the first Rank, are entirely owing to extravagant Living, and such Distresses as they have brought themselves into by Gaming *only*. . . ." While the *Whole Art and Mystery of Modern Gaming fully expos'd and detected* commented that current gambling was "the most fatal and epidemical folly and madness, especially among the persons of superior degree, and quality. . . ."[26] observers could still maintain that the truly dangerous gaming, the gaming that might overturn public peace, occurred among the common folk. Everyone knows of Henry Fielding's surprising mitigation of upper-class gambling in his *Essay on Robbers;* speaking in a similar tone, the editors of the *Connoisseur* concurred, and argued that it was the licentiousness of ordinary folk that was truly dangerous. Writing about the baneful influence that such works as Bolingbroke's might have on the common people, they argued that if such notions were to spread "among the vulgar, we shall be knocked down at noon-day in our streets, and nothing will go forward but robberies and murders." However, even here, the vices of the Great were satirized, not ignored or made light of. Unlike the vulgar, "As they [the Great] are placed above extreme indigence and absolute want of bread, their loose notions would have carried them no farther than cheating at cards, or perhaps plundering their country. . . ." This comparison and equation of a particular sort of private and public upper-class immorality had a long and growing significance, perhaps most visibly depicted and argued in the attempt to pass anti-gaming legislation later in the century, which we will subsequently consider. For now, however, let us examine the ways in which, by mid-century and after, such upper-class gaming was thought to hurt the national interest and strength.[27]

Though the notion that the upper orders in a healthy and well-regulated polity should serve as examples of virtue and propriety to the rest of society was something of a time-worn cliché, this view was repeatedly brought to the attention of the Great by those opposed to gambling. Thus the *Essay on Gaming* noted that: "the meanest Sons of Earth,/Embrace the follies of exalted

Birth." A decade later, in a letter to the *Town and Country Magazine*, a correspondent commented that, despite the fact that "our nobility and gentry, both male and female, . . . should be the great examples and encouragers of all virtue and industry," they were badly remiss on the question of gaming. And again, almost twenty years after this complaint, Charles Moore, contrasting the gaming habits of the various classes, commented, "Pernicious as gambling has been discovered to be in the middle ranks of life, yet its consequences are still more dreadful (if possible) in those of superior station; since the influence of their example is so powerful."[28]

A more novel criticism of upper-class gaming was the effect, it was claimed, that it would inevitably have on that small elite who were responsible for governing the nation. Invoking the goddess of gaming, the *London Magazine* concluded that "the statesman, when he becomes thy votary, proves false to his country; and every glowing passion for the publick welfare is chill'd in its embryo by the over-ruling power of self-interest. . . ." Having lost all his possessions by his unchecked infatuation for gaming, the statesman would be forced to beg the Court or Crown, for monetary relief, for "places, Pensions, and Gratuities of every Kind." Trading his independence for a mess of pottage, he would soon find himself a mere pawn, and with the collapse of an independent nobility, the nation's freedoms would, it was feared, soon disappear as well. Addressing the well-born members of the gambling club at White's, Erasmus Mumford warned that "we may expect in a little time to see, by the Progress of this Science [of gaming] only, our liberty as it ought to be, . . . entirely in the Hands, and at the Disposal of the Reigning Monarch, whoever He is. . . ." Equally foreboding was the likelihood that, after having lost their fortunes, well-born members of Parliament would "cringe for places to administrations of any complexion, and thus, after having ruined themselves, contribute to the destruction of the nation at large."[29] And in the collapse of a self-supporting aristocracy, both private and public corruption must follow. "Do we not see noblemen squandering away large estates, and then patching up their broken fortunes by fatal marriages and venal places at court?" asked a correspondent to the *Oxford Magazine*. Some not only thought that gaming led to political venality, but went further, arguing that, in a variety of ways, gaming was deliberately encouraged and fostered to entrap or decoy segments of the nation. They thought that "this destructive fashion of gaming" was the method that "a corrupt administration introduced to engage the people's attention, and prevent them from minding their misconduct, and discerning their bad designs"; others held that "our most crafty Ministers make it a Practice to encourage Gaming in our young Nobility, in order by their Distresses to make them become dependent on the Court. . . ." In either case, however, all agreed that when the political classes became devotees of gaming, "Dupes they commense, and terminate in knaves." Thus the *Oxford Magazine* warned statesmen-gamesters of what "was on the cards" for the nation, if their gaming was not halted. "Ye wicked ministers of night, quit White's, and devote a little time to serious study, to save us from all the horrors of a bloody civil war."[30]

Following the loss of the American colonies, and even more after the outbreak of the French Revolution, the condemnation of venal, gaming politicians became darker and more disapproving. Describing such men as "convicts of a higher order," the *Gazetteer* asked: "what makes so many false patriots?" The answer was simple "—*gaming*." Such men, they claimed, "pretend to adopt the cause of the people until they go into place, then plunder the public to pay their *gaming debts*." Charles Moore argued that the gaming statesman "barters his abilities and his conscience for gold: he procures, by a slavish submission to the nod of power, some rich command or government, in which he may fleece those unfortunate people, over whom he is appointed." "Gambling and modern patriotism are not dissimilar," commented the *Times* in a similar vein. "The benefit of the public is never taken into consideration."[31]

In addition to the actual corrupt practices of gaming politicians, many held up two other moral and psychological national ill effects of such amusements. First was the widely held view that being a gambling addict led to psychological and ratiocinative weakness. Thus the *Monthly Review*, in its 1776 appraisal of *Reflections on Gaming, Annuities and Usurious Contracts*, excerpted the following discussion of the moral and intellectual incapacities of the gaming Parliamentarian: "The science of legislation and the intricacy of political calculation is a very different study from the chances at hazard; the honour that must stand the siege of corruption, and fulfil the sacred trust of the people is not the same principle with the honour of a gamester." Moore reiterated, varied, and elaborated on the theme in a rich rhetoric of condemnation: "[W]hat prevents the improvement of the understanding—what deprives society of the rich fruits of liberal endowments and political abilities—what makes a wreck of virtue, honour, fame, religion—in short, what absorbs all the generous, useful, ornamental, and social faculties of the soul, like the vortex of the gaming-table?" And Thomas Rennell, sounding a dire warning through his use of capitalization, asked "What is it that converts Those designed by Providence to be the GUARDIANS and PROTECTORS, into the BANE and CURSE of their Country? I will answer—the GAMING TABLE."[32]

Furthermore, from the mid-century, fears about England's international power were connected with concerns about the devastating effects of gaming. This theme, which was not unusual in the 1750s, became even more commonplace in the years preceding and following the American war. Along with other vices associated with French luxury, gaming was castigated for allowing Britain's "ever-vigilant and enterprizing enemies to win by stealth what they could not conquer by might." "Shall then *French* Fashions and *French* Modes bring about, what *French* Arms, and even *French* Politicks have so long in vain attempted?" asked Thomas McDonnell in a 1760 sermon. Reprinting an essay that had first appeared in the *Spectator*, the *Matrimonial Preceptor* of 1765 stressed the deleterious military effects of gaming women: "What a race of worthies, what patriots, what heroes must we expect from mothers of this make?" Comparing the degenerate military leaders of her own day with the military leaders of Greece and Rome, Mary Wollstonecraft commented that, in contrast, "our British heroes are oftener sent from the gaming table than from the plow; and their passions have been rather inflamed by hanging with dumb suspense on the turn of a die, than sublimated by panting after the adventurous march of virtue in the historic page."[33]

In addition to its corrupting influence on politics and its dissipating effects on mental and martial acuity, gaming was further seen to have two most significant and destructive repercussions on the nation's well-being, which, while general, had even graver consequences when indulged in by society's leaders. The first of these was that each citizen, and especially each member of the political classes, had a duty to devote at least some of his time and best efforts to the public weal. "Whoever devotes his time to Gaming withdraws from the Publick Good, and is both an Enemy to his Country and himself," said the author of the *Whole Art and Mystery of Modern Gaming*. Another, in a letter to the *St. James's Chronicle* of 1765, made the connection, and the point, even more clearly: "Persons of Fortune . . . from a false Notion of Independency . . . imagine they are at Liberty to do any thing, or nothing; to dispose of themselves or Time; and to fill up their vacant Hours with such Expedients as Folly or Caprice may bring into Vogue. . . . For is not every one, as a Member of Society, accountable for his publick Actions, and the Tenor of his Conduct to Society?"

Thus the suggestion was made, only half satirically, that since "among the many useless members of society, there are none so unprofitable as the fraternity of Gamesters," it would be a gain to the national strength if members of the brotherhood were pressed into the armed forces, were compelled "in handling a musket [rather] than in shuffling a pack of cards, or shaking the dice-box."[34] All members of the polity owed the nation some significant service.

This notion of the duty one owed to one's society and nation was often only part of a larger duty incumbent on all Christians. Whether winning one's personal salvation or assisting in the maintenance and stability of public order, time taken in gaming was time lost from worthier goals. Though half a century apart, both Josiah Woodward and Jonas Hanway agreed on the need to use time and effort frugally and toward proper ends. While Woodward, stressing the individual and eternal, argued that "It is most certain, That no Person, in the short space of this probational Life, can have much Time to spare for Diversion: considering that he has the great Concern of eternal Life to secure. . . ." Hanway's emphasis was on the national and political, "That the service of God is perfect freedom, is as true in a political, as in a *moral* sense; for free government is built on the foundation of religion." Though we some-times speak of eighteenth-century England as a secularized society, where neither God's law nor the Devil's temptations were seen as having major moral influence, most social critics agreed that a polity depended for its continuance, for its prosperity and its proper running, on a bed-rock of a firm Christian practice. Combining the emphases of Woodward and Hanway, Thomas Rennell proclaimed that "Religion as it is the perfection of individuals, so is it the preservation of communities."[35]

For many the most visible indication of the deleterious effects of gaming on Christian practice was the fact that Sunday was, it was said, being devoted not to prayer nor to church attendance, but to cards and dice. Voltaire's notice, though acute, was more ironic and satiric than condemnatory: "No opera, no plays, no concerts in London on Sunday; even cards are so expressly forbidden that only the aristocracy, and those we call well-bred people, play on that day." A decade later, Fielding's *Covent Garden Journal* gave in its dictionary of contemporary usage, under the heading "Sunday" the definition: "The best time for playing at cards." A similar definition was given in the *Town and Country Magazine* of "Boar" as "an old woman who refuses to play cards on Sundays etc." And in the same vein, the foppish aristocrat Lord Aimwell in the satiric *Essay on Gaming*, noting that "Cards on Sundays are my chief Delight," contrasted the pleasure thus afforded with the pains of Sabbath observance: "A Church and Parson would my Soul affright; Of Graves and cold Mortality they smell, Nor can I bear to hear the tolling Bell." Aimwell concluded (in language remarkably similar, though opposite in belief to the letter to the *St. James's Chronicle*) that "I think the Pow'rs above, Who shed o'er Nature their divinest Love, Have left Mankind their Lives and Fortunes free, To be dispos'd of as they best shall see."[36]

As we have seen, while most ranks of people were criticized for gaming, it was the Great who were especially denounced for such activity on the Sabbath, both in print and in practice. Thus we read an odd story of an upper-class woman harassed and kept from her Sunday gaming by the actions of an outraged Christian mob. "Pluto," in a letter to the *Gazetteer* denounced "the scandalous practice of persons of distinction and fortune, in playing at cards on the Lords day, and that in so open and indecent a manner, as not to conceal themselves from the notice of passengers, by neglecting to shut up their windows."[37] Moralists often presented the specter of empty churches, abandoned by the Great, and of Sabbath gaming parties, where other sorts of adoration occurred.

> [They] devote to the pitiful Service of Cards, or Dice, the Evening of that Day, which CHRIST, the LORD of Heaven and Earth, hath, eminently, set apart for his sacred Praise and Worship. . . . The Prince of Darkness is served and attended with all the artificial Blaze of Jewels, Dress, and borrowed Radiance; while he, who brought Life and Immortality to Light, is left forsaken to unfrequented Walls, echoing the languid Prayers of a few, unfashionable, superannuated christians.

And, by the century's end, the tone of such condemnation had become shriller, deeper, and more apocryphal.

> May Almighty God, by his preventing grace, bring it home to the hearts of all those in the higher ranks, who carelessly or contemptuously devote themselves to this practice [of gaming] on the Sabbath, [the account which] is to be given in the hour of death and the day of judgment, that they had been, *"innocent of the blood of all Men!"*[38]

"an unsocial man, an unprofitable man":[39] *Gaming and Sociability*

When, in Henry Fielding's *Amelia*, its heroine announced that she "mortally detest[ed] Cards," she not only affirmed her position as the book's moral center, but also evoked the following comment from one of the novel's less virtuous women. "Detest Cards!" cried Mrs. James. "How can you be so stupid? I would not live a Day without them—Nay, indeed, I do not believe I should be able to exist." This satiric interchange, in which what was at stake was not the national interest, but the nature of normal quotidian sociability, reveals another aspect of the eighteenth-century critique of gaming; that it made men and women, to return to the fragment that started this section, not only unprofitable to the nation, but unsocial.[40]

By the mid-century, according to the *Connoisseur*, fashionable life so much revolved around various forms of gambling that "most of our fashionable diversions are nothing else but different branches of gaming." But why was this sort of amusement especially reprobated, why was this form of passing the time especially censured? We have seen some of the answers already—that gaming was addictive, that it was mind-numbing and unimproving, and that it exerted an alluring counter-pull to religious and spiritual improvement. But in terms of sociability and a life of leisure, what could be said against it? Several ironists in fact commented that it had a positive social role in that, once engrossed in cards, men and women lost their taste for scandalous gossip, and even for illicit amours, thus protecting their various virtues by the indulgence of this absorbing hobby. "Why," asked a "Respecter of Sabbath" in a letter to the *Public Advertiser*, "should an innocent game of cards be more profane than common conversation, which will be taken up perhaps in descanting on Fashions, public places of amusement, or private scandal?" His answer to his own question, and to the conundrum of how a social activity like gaming could be seen as "unsociable," was "that card-playing excludes all possibility, or chance of serious conversation."[41]

For both serious social commentators and newspaper correspondents, the centrality of conversation to a properly ordered sociability could not be over-emphasized. Thus the *Rambler* noted that "it is scarcely possible to pass an hour in honest conversation, without being able, when we rise from it, to please ourselves by having given or received some advantages. . . ." There was nothing like conversation with "the most ingenious and entertaining of his equals" to improve the understanding of a young gentleman, maintained the *Gentleman's Magazine*. It was conversation, said "J. G.," a correspondent to the *Gazetteer*, that "was one of the noblest privileges of reason, and which more properly sets mankind above the brute part of creation."[42] Gaming, however, not only stole time and interest from this far more valuable, far more instructive social activity, but actually diminished the capacity of people to converse. Gaming made conversation impossible, or at best, unlikely. "The universal practice of card playing is particularly pernicious in this respect, that, whilst it keeps people perpetually in company, it excludes conversation," noted the *Universal Magazine*. The *Town and Country* agreed: "It may be true, that in general we are too little qualified for rational conversation; but we shall be less so if we give it up. . . ." Thus, in monopolizing sociability, in diminishing conversational ability and interchange, gaming hurt both the social and national sphere simultaneously. Contrasting the gaming present with the conversational past, the *Lady's Magazine* reminisced:

> People used formerly to meet together for the sake of conversation; but ever since the card table has been in fashion all the pleasures of speech has been suppressed . . . When our visits were intended either to improve our friends or ourselves, several noble hints were thrown out, which might be of service to mankind in general . . . .[43]

Beyond the harmful effect of gaming on the conversational circle, and on solid sociability, gaming was consistently represented as more than just a neutral way of spending time. Instead, it was a form of anti-social sociability, a miniature war of all-against-all. This strand of complaint, unbroken from at least the mid-century, continued to be rearticulated, re-emphasized through the century's end. Unsurprisingly, clerics used this trope in denouncing gaming. Thus in 1760 Thomas McDonnell, attempting to describe the horror of a gaming scene, calling it "so dismal and shocking; and yet so lively and strong," argued that "nothing but an Assembly of Fiends, mutually contending to destroy one another, can, in any Sort, be imagined to equal, much less to exceed it." Thirty-five years later, another cleric commented that "jealousy, rage and revenge exist among gamesters in their worst and most frantic excesses, and end frequently in consequences of the most atrocious violence and outrage. . . ."[44] Much more surprising, perhaps, was the frequency with which this view was expressed in the popular periodical press, both in the form of letters to the editor and in miscellaneous articles in both poetry and prose. Thus in a poem on gaming, which appeared in the *British Magazine* of 1748, we read that when gaming has replaced the pleasures of conversation, "Instead of this delightful grand repast, Noise, discord, animosity, and strife, Deep hatred, rancour foul, and hot revenge, Oft spread their terrors o'er the sporting board. . . ." The *Connoisseur* characterized the gamester as one who "would ruin his own brother, if it might be of any advantage to himself." Friendship was banished, for "friends turn into enemies, and sensible men into madmen; it [gaming] nevertheless is pursued with continual ardour."[45] And the language employed at the gaming table was as debased as the activity itself. Rather than the rational tone of mutual improvement and innocent pleasure that typified the best conversation, at the gaming table "lies, oaths, and the most bitter and opprobrious expressions are vented, which often destroy the most sacred bonds of friendship, and produce in their stead, envy, dissimulation, malice and revenge, with a long train of other diabolic passions." And the man or woman who exhibited the character of the "professed game-ster" would have lost most of his or her human qualities; he "must be devoid of every humane, every generous sentiment: callous to all social sensations, he lives the vulture of mankind, to prey upon innocence and credulity."[46] By 1784, the anonymous Member of Parliament whose *Hints* were designed to diagnose as well as recommend remedies for the evil effects of gambling, wrote that "There is now no society. . . . It is vain to attempt conversation. All is croud and confusion. The social pleasures are entirely banished, and those who have any relish for them, or who are fond of early hours, are necessarily banished." Thus, in a sociable age, gaming acted as an insidious agent of corruption, an engine of disunion and disaffection, emphasizing individual gain over the calls of friendship, or of family. Gamesters were solitaries by choice, alone and self-absorbed in the largest crowds and gatherings. But the object of their devotions not only devoured the gaming addict himself, and anyone who loved or trusted him, but spread its devastation much more widely. Thus a correspondent to the *Town and Country Magazine* argued that "four knaves and the dice-box have been the causes of more quarrels, than ever the king of Prussia and all the monarchs of Europe have been engaged in from the thirst of conquest."[47]

Of course, the most obviously detrimental effect of gaming, both for the gamester and his connections, and for the nation at large, was the loss of estate and of wealth that inevitably ensued when large sums were staked and lost. Both the *Connoisseur* and the *Rambler* considered the activity and its votaries to be "unprofitable" to the nation; Johnson explained his opinion thus: "Gaming is a mode of transferring property without producing any intermediate good. Trade gives employment to numbers, and so produces intermediate good." This commonplace, that the good of the nation could be measured by the numbers of people it employed, seemed an irrefragable condemnation of gaming, though a few facetious commentators tried to make such claims for it. Thus one noted that although card playing seems "a very idle and fruitless occupation" this languid amusement "furnishes work for the cardmakers, who set the paper mills in motion, by which the poor rag-man is supported: not to mention the builders and workers in wood and iron, who are employed in the erection of those mills." "These artizans would," another quipped, "if unemployed in their different vocations, become a burthen to the public, or a pest to society." But the satire depended for its humor on the well-known ridiculousness of the claim, as well as on the fact that the *nom de plume* of one of these satirists was "Matthew Mandeville," who argued, like his forebear Bernard, for the public benefits of private vices.[48]

Contemporaries thought that gaming was more than just unprofitable, but anti-profitable. It hurt the economic interests of both individual and nation simultaneously in three ways: first, by increasing the number of bankruptcies and insolvencies, second by robbing the tradesmen, to whom the Great were indebted, of their just payment, and third, by alienating landed estates from their traditional owners and thus depriving their progeny of their inheritance. In an almost unbroken rant beginning in the late 1730s, the magazines and papers of the day railed against that bankruptcy caused by gaming. The *Gentleman's Magazine* thought that "many of our late Bankruptcies and Insolvencies" resulted from gaming, because it unsettled men's hardworking habits and "naturally introduces Extravagance, Luxury and the Neglect of

Business." It was because of this inattention to business caused by the fascination with gambling, wrote a correspondent to *London Magazine* "that so many shops, once in a most flourishing condition, are now shut up in the very heart of the city, and their owners either bankrupts, or miserable fugitives to foreign countries." And the calamity did not stop with the immiseration of the gamesters themselves, but spread its devastation amongst "the innocent and fair traders, who, by connexions and credit, are involved in the same misfortunes."[49]

However, since gaming was illegal, why did people who lost vast sums voluntarily pay the sums owing? Why did they not just smile and walk away from such debts? There were two answers given to such questions; the first, that pigeons who refused to pay up were intimidated into doing so, since, it was said, many sharpers were also excellent duelists. The second, and more frequently cited reason, though it would only operate on the sentiments of gentlemanly pigeons, was that "a false and most ridiculous notion of Honour hath such an Influence on the Minds of most Gentlemen, that they think it scandalous to put the Laws into Execution, or not to be punctual in the Discharge of all gaming Debts, In Preference to their honest Creditors . . . ."[50]

Thomas McDonnell characterized the spurious honor which paid "debts of honour," i.e., gaming debts, in preference to settling outstanding bills as "the Robbery of our Dependants, our Tradesfolk, and those we deal with for the common Necessaries of Life, not to mention the Ornaments and Luxuries of it." A novel of 1780, entitled *The Relapse*, argued that: "Debts of honour must be repaid. Ridiculous! To pay a set of known villains and to refuse the same justice to the industrious trader! Horrid as this is, it is the maxim of the world." The *Oxford Magazine* painted a still more horrifying and sentimental picture of the fate of the poor tradesman, cheated out of his payment: "By such beings as these the industrious tradesman is immured in the narrow confines of a prison, and perhaps a wife and helpless progeny, brought to beggary through his credulity; while the author of their ruin, move in an exalted sphere, above the reach of punishment, for actions, which in the eye of humanity, are highly criminal."[51]

As distressing as is this picture of the imprisoned and ruined tradesman and his innocent family brought to ruin by others' gaming debts, more distressing still, and even more common was the complaint that gaming severed the primary care that parents had of their families, especially the financial well-being that a father was expected to provide for his wife and children. The *British Magazine* broke into verse to describe this heart-wrenching scene:

A thrifty and penurious dame at home,
A lovely race of harmless heav'nly babes,
Must now perhaps participate his gloom,
And bear with all the miseries of want;
Sad prospect! when a family's support
Is boldly lavish'd by a knave—on knaves.

Women wrote letters to the magazines, asking for guidance for such well-loved, but feckless husbands. And a correspondent to the *Morning Chronicle* attempted to rouse the shame of such men by pointing out that

> To the man of affluence, [such debts led to] inevitable ruin or disgrace; nor are their inoffensive wives, and perhaps deserted children, excluded from the dire misfortune; for how many amiable women are there, who after being fleeced by the sacrilegious hands of fortune hunters, are left to brood over the most fatal misery of nature, and watch the lisping cries of their starving babes!

O Ye Men of Family, and Independence, Where Is Your Feeling?[52]

While all gaming hurt the innocent family of the losing gamester, the most flagrant and egregious of such losses were those that occurred when landed estates were the stakes that were lost. We have seen the poet Ames bemoaning the loss of "Mannours, Lands, and Lordships"; three decades later, the author of the *Whole Art of Gaming* wrote his treatise to warn "young Gentlemen of Fortune" to beware of false friends who, under the guise of play, would win their property and inheritance, reducing themselves "to so low and wretched a state, as to support a set of men in ease and luxury, whose ancestors were beggars." Still later, and in phrases redolent of Ames, Henry Baker also broke into verse in his condemnation of estates lost through gaming. "But Gamesters for whole Patrimonies play:/The Steward brings the Deeds which must convey/The lost Estate:—What more than Madness reigns,/When one short Sitting many hundreds drains. . . ." It is therefore not surprising that the *Gentleman's Magazine*, after the passage of the 1739 Gaming Act, said that they had "wish'd that an express Clause had been inserted in this Act, for the Recovery of all Estates, Lands, or Sums of Money . . . which could be fairly prov'd to have been won by fraudulent Gaming . . . ."[53]

Of course, like the arguments for the salutary effects of card-playing drawn from the increased manufacture of playing cards, satirists applied the same notions to estates lost through excessive gaming. Using the common metaphor of the nation as the body politic, and its wealth as the blood which circulates through it, nourishing and enlivening it, such ironists praised professional sharpers and gamblers as "Friends to Policy, because they make Money circulate, and teach Industry the way to thrive. . . ." This is the same tongue-in-cheek tone taken in Christopher Anstey's enormously popular *The New Bath Guide*. In a letter to his mother, back home in the country, Anstey's Bath tourist explained the virtues of gaming: "And gaming, no doubt, is of infinite use/ That same circulation of cash to produce./What true public spirited people are here,/Who for that very purpose come every year!/All eminent men, who no trade ever knew/But gaming, the only good trade to pursue. . . ." But much more frequently the tone was grimmer and the warnings thunderous. Thus, when "Homo" in a letter to the *Morning Chronicle*, addressed to a Nobleman, warned him against gaming, he insisted that "an habit of gaming must make your richest possessions constantly precarious; that your forests may sink beneath the axe, and your acres be transferred to some more fortunate master. Therefore let me beg you to be guarded against the prevalence of so fashionable a vice." Equally dire were the warnings that the author of *Hints on Gaming* gave to gamesters, but this time the emphasis was on the woes that their progeny and heirs would face: "The father frequently ruins his children; and sons, and even grandsons, long before the succession opens to them, are involved so deeply, that during their future lives their circumstances are rendered narrow; and they have rank, or family honours, without being able to support them."[54]

For women the economic consequences of gaming were even greater. We can perhaps get some sense of the grave outcome awaiting the female gamester by examining the sad tale of Miss Frances Braddock.

"Frail Daughter of Eve":[55] *Criticizing Female Gambling*

On September 22, 1792, a story appeared in the American periodical *The Weekly Museum*, entitled "The Fatal Effects of Gaming, Exemplified in the History of Miss Braddock." The story of Fanny Braddock's short and tragic life, addressed as a warning to other women, was employed to illustrate the truth "that Vice that renders the most beautiful among you disgusting, which debases the most exalted, is GAMING." Braddock, who killed herself in Bath in 1731 because of her gaming debts, and whose story was several times repeated through the century, both in Britain and abroad, offers us an interesting introduction to the fear and concern that the female gambler seemed to evoke.

Braddock's story, at least as told by most of the press accounts, was brief but affecting. Left a fortune at her father's death, and another by her sister's demise a few years later, the young Frances became "a great Admirer of that hazardous Dependance, Gaming." Having, inevitably, lost her last shilling, she hanged herself in her apartment, with her "Golden Girdle." All reports praised her for her "courteous and genteel Behavior, and good sense." And it was not long before other details appeared: an account of her burial at Bath Abbey, and perhaps most poignantly, the verses found written on her window, praising death.[56]

How was the initial coverage of Braddock's death in 1731 different from the coverage of similar male deaths? It is in the answer to this question that we can begin to see how heinous contemporaries found female gaming. Thus, it is important to understand that for most of the first six decades of the eighteenth century, the periodical press exhibits a remarkable reluctance to discuss the misdeeds and wasted lives of specific and named individuals of the upper classes. While the great essay-journals of these decades frequently excoriated male as well as female gambling, calling it the grave of every social and civil affection, neither they nor the news-sheets of the period "named names" or revealed the scandalous lives and exits of the great and not-so-good. No one, for example, wrote of the de facto prime minister Henry Pelham's great gambling losses, while everyone "in society" knew of them. It is perhaps instructive to consider the comments made on the deaths of two upper-class men who killed themselves a generation later, in the 1750s, for the same reasons as Braddock had in the 1730s. Thus when, in 1754, William Bromley, Lord Montfort, a broken gamester, was refused a government pension, he spent New Year's eve playing whist at White's, a great male gambling club, and then shot himself through the head on New Year's Day, after making a foolproof will. The *London Evening Post*, after reporting that he had "died at his house, in Arlington Street," and listing the public positions he had held and who his children were, said no more about either the nature of his death or the reasons for his self-murder. Similarly, when, nine months later, after having lost, according to Horace Walpole, more than £32,000 at one night's play, Sir John Bland shot and killed himself "on the Road between Paris and Calais," the *London Evening Post* merely noted that he had "died suddenly" and that, as he had no heirs, his titles were extinct. In both of these cases, the *beau monde* knew the truth of these lives and deaths, gossiping about the details, but the world at large, the newspaper-reading public, was kept discreetly ignorant.[57]

It must be said, however, that not only this silence protected men, but legal processes as well served to exonerate both men and women of the upper classes who were investigated by coroners' juries, from receiving the same harsh verdicts that men and women of the lower classes occasionally got. Thus, in a mock Bill of Suicide for the month of November (the month in which the English were thought to be most prone to kill themselves) *Gray's Inn Journal* listed the self-inflicted deaths of several men of wealth and family, all of whom were found "lunatic" and thus not culpable of properly understanding the wickedness of their enormity, while the verdict on *"Thomas Hopeless*, formerly a warm Housekeeper in Holborn, but reduced by a Series of Misfortunes to extreme Misery, with a Wife and seven Children" who killed himself, was guilty of *felo de se*, i.e., self-murder. Morally innocent, the wealthy lunatic was buried, as was Miss Braddock, in a place of sanctity and honor. In contrast, the *felo de se* was buried at a crossroads, with a stake through his or her heart. While, in this case, class trumped gender, it was clear that the press was not prepared to hold up the lives and deaths of upper-class male gamblers as exemplary warnings, in the same way that an upper-class female, like poor Frances Braddock, was "available" for such useful moralizing. Let us look more closely then at the female of the species; let us consider the woman of fashion as she was portrayed on stage, in some of the plays of David Garrick.

In his play of 1749, *Lethe*, a character notes that a "fine lady lies in bed all morning, rattles about all day, and sits up all night. She goes everywhere and sees everything, knows everybody and loves nobody, ridicules her friends, coquettes with her lovers, sets 'em together by the ears, tells fibs, makes mischief, buys china, cheats at cards, keeps a pug-dog, and hates the parsons. She laughs much, talks aloud, never blushes, says what she will, does what she will, goes where she will, marries whom she pleases, hates her husband in a month, slips from her gallants, and begins the world again. . . ." Two years before, in *Miss in Her Teens*, Garrick's anti-hero, Fribble, promised the girl he was wooing that if she accepted him, he would provide her with the "life of a woman of quality, for she will have nothing to do but lie in bed, play at cards, and scold the servants." The activity common to both long and short descriptions is playing, or cheating, at cards. In gambling we have the epitome of luxurious expenditure, of waste both of substance and time, driven by the addictive and expansive pursuit of sensation. If both men and women of fashion were criticized for their gambling practices, for their vast gaming expenditures, women were thought to be particularly liable to its allure. As Justine Crump has thoughtfully remarked: "Female gaming seems disproportionately represented in literature and non-fictional texts, suggesting that it was the focus for powerful social anxieties." A few instances of such representation, which stress the continued concern about the gambling habits of genteel women, can serve as useful illustrations of this insight. Thus in 1713, *The Guardian*, defending his title, noted that he "should ill deserve the Name of *Guardian*, did I not caution all my fair Wards against a Practice, which when it runs to Excess, is the most shameful, but one, that the Female World can fall into." Similarly, almost half a century later, a letter to the *London Magazine*, comparing the effects of gaming on men and women, commented:

> It is remarked of men, that they are apt to grow reprobates by gaming, and gradually to desert all principles of honour and humanity. . . . Ought not women, then, to be particularly guarded, against such baits to indecorum, and seductions to turpitude? They should be, in an especial manner, the promoters of delicacy, and the cherishers of innocence; as all their happiness depends on the prevalency of the tender passions; and the brightest ornament they can of course adorn themselves with, is a sanctity of manners.[58]

It was said that women who gamed, lost, at least metaphorically, their human natures. Thus *The Spectator* argued that women who, in the ordinary course of life, were "Gentle, Good-humoured, and the very Pinks of good Breeding" became, as soon as they began to gamble, "immediately Transmigrated into the veriest Wasps in Nature." A "mere carding woman" was characterized by an anonymous letter-writer to the *Public Advertiser* in 1765 as "at best but a *chienne savante*, and too frequently an half-human tiger in petticoats."[59]

What accounts for these fierce denunciations of female gambling? Why were contemporaries so alarmed about the growth of this seemingly innocuous activity among upper-class women? How did eighteenth-century critics explain the prevalence of these habits among such women? To take the last question first, eighteenth-century commentators gave a three-part answer to the question of female vulnerability to such vicious behavior, arguing that in part this was due to their lack of public occupations, in part to their mis-education, and in part to their greater nervous susceptibility. Women were particularly warned to beware "how they suffer this passion [for play] to steal upon them." For, since women had no ordinary paying jobs, they could employ their talents at cards. The author of *A Modest Defence of Gaming* noted that "the Card Assemblies are still open to their Industry; the noblest Scene, wherein the Female Talents can be exerted: neither is any great Fund necessary for this, if we consider the known Prerogatives of the Sex: when they win, they have speedier Payment; when they lose—*they have longer Credit*. And certain it is, whatever Pain it may give us to confess it, the Ladies have the *Powers* of Gaming in greater Perfection than the Men. . . ."[60] In a less satiric vein, another author argued that the source of "the vanity and degeneracy of the present female world upon the *bon ton*" was that women, "instead of being taught housewifry, and other useful female pursuits like their ancestors, Hoyle is put into their hands every morning instead of a Bible; and the polite manoeuvres of fleecing the pool are considered as more valuable acquisitions than needle-work, and the barbarous morality of musty writers." Since fashionable women did not work, they could not be accused of unprofitably wasting time, but nevertheless they were chastised for misusing such hours "without any improvement, or rational delight; . . . all conversation is suspended amongst them, except the frequent repetitions of a few gambling phrases and poignant altercations."[61] Increasingly the vice of gambling in women was attributed to their faulty or misdirected upbringing. "Parents," said one correspondent to the *Town and Country Magazine* of 1787, "are very generally to blame for being so ready to finish this branch of education in their daughters." As a consequence, many women become "accomplished gamester[s]." "There are no bad passions," he concluded, "which cards do not excite in some degree; a reflection which ought never to be forgotten by those whose task it is to rear the female mind." One critic went so far as to urge that all young women be taught geometry as a preservative to their ability to reason clearly and act prudentially. "No young lady should be admitted to a card table, until she had perfected herself under that regulation. . . . [T]he study of geometry," he continued, "will fix the attention of the most volatile female, teach her to think with propriety, compare with caution, and judge with precision."[62]

In addition to the wastefulness of female gambling, it was widely believed that such practices had more destructive consequences ranging from loss of beauty to loss of honor and of life itself. The luxurious practices of female gaming inevitably led to ruin and the grave. That women who gambled would become horrid in appearance was an eighteenth-century cliché. Not only were women's countenances unpleasantly distorted by the fears and disappointments involved in high play, but were the female gamester "only to reflect upon the ill effects of *anxiety* upon *beauty*, and that frequent vigils antedate old age, a woman who has the least regard for her complexion or her features, would forego such a dangerous pastime. . . ." Another commented: "Could a pretty female know that she often forfeits even *temporary* beauty in being bested, she would probably never touch a card again. I have seen one of the finest women in England so agonized at the loss of her last guinea, that could she have seen the distortion of her features, she would have fainted: I therefore recommend to all ladies who play deep, constantly to have a looking-glass before them." And even if the gambling woman felt she had nothing to lose, or was not deterred from gaming by the prospect of ugliness, if she was unmar-ried she risked matrimony itself by the continuance of her luxuriant pastime, for "what man of common sense," it was said, "would wed a female gambler?" "In trade it would be signing his own certificate as a bankrupt; in private life it would be subscribing for his lodging in the King's-Bench. Many married women have lost their husbands at play; but no spinster ever got one by it, though she were ever so successful."[63] More serious, however, than either of these two criticisms, were the well-established views that female gambling led inevitably and inextricably to loss of chastity and/or to suicide. Female gamesters appeared more unnatural, more morally reprehensible because originally purer than men of the same sort. Thus Mrs. Carter remarked: ". . . a male gamester is a most disgraceful and shocking character; but a female gamester seems to be a blot in nature. She must forego all that is good and great belonging to her sex, before she can boldly shake the dice, or offer bets." Richard Hey agreed. In his *Three Dissertations on the Pernicious Effects of Gaming*, he argued that: "to become a Gamester, is to cease to be a Woman in the highest and best sense of the word. . . . The impetuosity of Gaming breaks the bonds of consanguinity, and yet more endearing ties of conjugal union . . . engaged in far other solicitudes, she departs from the truly feminine character; she is worked up to rancorous envy, to masculine revenge, to indecorous violence."[64] The female gambler became unsexed: neither man nor woman, she stood as an emblem of vice. For in losing her money, it was inevitable she would lose her honor, her virtue, and, in a sense, her sex itself. When a woman's money was lost, her chastity, it was frequently said, "must supply the deficiency. Hence the numerous divorces which every day take place, hence the misery of whole families and the ruin of posterity." Thus, in *The Fatal Concession, a Moral Tale*, published in 1771, after the foolish wife of a young gentleman of fortune had lost both her money and her honor through the machinations of an aristocratic cad, Sir James Frolick, her husband challenged and killed her seducer, only to return to find his wife "in her last moments, and in agonies which pierced his soul."[65] The wages of such exorbitant female expenditure were, almost inevitably, adultery and death. Moreover, such tales were not only to be found in novels: an anonymous author, examining "the fatal effects of high gaming," recounted the fate of a clergyman's wife of his acquaintance, who had "lately fallen a victim to this fatal vice." When her husband remonstrated with her on the grave financial difficulties in which she had placed him and her children, the woman, "unable to bear the pangs of conscience which she felt at the horrid prospective . . . attempted to destroy herself; but not having accomplished her design, she still breathes a shocking spectacle of the terrible effects of high gaming." Seldom did a woman escape in time, or with her honor intact, as did the fortunate Letitia Halton, heroine of the tale *The Perplexed Wife*. Despite her great gaming loses to Lord Fleecer, Letitia's husband, Sir James, forgave her, paid her debts, and thus defeated "lord Fleecer's infamous designs." Like all addicts, Letitia realized that she could never gamble moderately, and so, "to prevent the return of a passion which had nearly proved fatal to her, never played cards again."[66]

Miss Frances Braddock, as we have noted, was not so lucky. But her personal tragedy became the stuff of moral lessons, repeated frequently through the century. Her story first appeared in a scandal-mongering book, *Modern Amours*, published just two years after her death. Her suicide, that "execrable Deed," like her reckless gaming, was the effect, it claimed, of "the Wiles of the great Enemy of Mankind," Beelzebub himself. Less than a decade later, Bath's great architect, who also was both Braddock's landlord and employer for the last year of her life, wrote of her end in his *Essay towards a description of Bath*. His account of her life and death revealed that after she had lost most of her wealth, she had served as a respectable decoy to lure other upper-class folk into a local gambling den, though he maintained "her Behavior was such as manifested nothing but Virtue, Regularity and good Nature."[67] The manner of her life and death were also discussed and lamented in Oliver Goldsmith's account of the life of Richard Nash and given even more exposure by the reprinting of parts of that work in the *Gentleman's Magazine*. Twenty-five years later, her story appeared again, both as an article in the *Times*, and in a miscellaneous work called *Pleasing Reflections on life and manners*, in a form that was almost identical to that published in the *Weekly Museum*, though without the opening invocation to the "frail daughter of Eve." This version, however, ended with a brief doggerel verse:

> O CARDS! ye vain diverters of our woe!
> Ye waste of life! ye greatest curse below!
> May beauty never fall again your slave,
> Nor your delusion thus destroy the brave.[68]

A decade later, two more versions of Miss Braddock's life appeared: one largely drawn from Goldsmith's account, the other by Charles Crawford, a sentimentalized "Essay Upon Gaming." Crawford concluded his retelling with the following injunction, which again stressed the use that could be made even of a tragically misspent life: "O ignominious, horrible, and accursed end of beauty, elegance, talents and humanity! It is *painful* to think of this end, yet it is *useful*, that the young and undesigning may be warned." Thus, almost from the day of her demise through the rest of the century, Braddock's life served as salutary dissuasive in the many moralizing accounts warning all the frail daughters of Eve of the delusive dangers of "deep play."[69]

Gaming in the Press: Publicizing and Policing Deep Play in the 1780s[70]

In our survey of attitudes towards gaming we have, to this point, concentrated largely on the literary, periodic, and admonitory, on plays, sermons, and pamphlets. We get differing, though complementary views when we consider its coverage in the newspaper press.

Through the first five decades of the century, though the press included numerous essays and comments critical of gaming, almost all the press accounts of its practices were of the actions of magistrates in shutting down notorious gaming dens. Here is a typical report of one such attack:

> Last Night, about Eleven o'Clock, the Constables of St. Martin's, St. Paul Covent Garden, &c. assisted by a Party of Soldiers, by Virtue of a Search Warrant, went to the New Gaming-House, late the Fountain Tavern in the Strand, where they secured upwards of Thirty Persons, differently employed in unlawful Gaming, and conducted them in great Order, two and two, to Clerkenwell Bridewell; where, it is hoped, they will not only meet with Reward for their Labour, but Labour for their Reward.[71]

By the 1760s and 1770s, the coverage was more varied, and, while still not giving the names of individuals, more personal and pointed. Thus, in 1765, two items appeared which reported on upper-class, male and female, gaming. The first told of an action to be brought against "a Man of Fashion" for having challenged "a Right Hon. Personage, about some misunderstanding which arose at cards." The second, more poignant though still anonymous, involved the "lady of a right honourable personage" who had attempted to kill herself "on account of some losses at play, which she did not choose should come to the ears of her husband."[72] By the 1770s, and the rise of the Wilkite press, accounts of upper-class gaming, and the corruption that such gaming could entail, became more commonplace. The pages of *Bingley's Journal* contained many such stories, giving broad hints as to the identity of the gamester. Thus, for example, in 1771, *Bingley's* reported that "A certain noble Lord, now in the administration of naval affairs, has mortgaged his salary for three years to come to a gentleman, in part of the payment of 50,000l. lost at hazard." Less than a year later, as part of a longer article about upper-class gaming, *Bingley's* noted that "General Scott lost at one sitting, very lately upwards of 10,000l." Other newspapers joined in the attack. In April 1772, the *Middlesex Journal* recounted how, in 1765, "the Rt. Hon. Richard Rigby was so fortunate as to win in one night 60,000l. of Lord Weymouth." When Weymouth, unable to pay this debt of honor in full, tried to amortize the sum, Rigby, wishing a speedier payment, proposed that he would exert "all his interest to procure him [Weymouth] the Viceroyship of Ireland, on condition of paying him the whole sum in three years." Unfortunately for both Rigby and Weymouth, a man with "superior interest," George Townshend, secured the appointment for his own brother. Not content with this, Rigby, at least according to the *Middlesex Journal*, "laboured to sow the seeds of dissent between such members of government as he, or his friends, have any influence over" and so skillful were his machinations, that the *Middlesex* foretold a probable opening in Ireland for Weymouth, and a full repayment for Rigby. A month earlier, the same paper, in commenting on the "astonishment of the public" in reading "accounts of sums daily won and lost by young men of quality at the fashionable gaming houses," cited the losses of "the young Cub" (a popular reference to Charles James Fox) who, by a "few unfortunate casts" of the dice, was "at this time charged with annuities to the full amount of six thousand pounds on this score only."[73] Fox and his friends, though by no means the only young men of fashion who gambled for large stakes, came increasingly, as we shall see, to epitomize the gaming craze that seemed to be sweeping the *haut ton*.

During the 1770s, in a series of letters and articles in the newspapers and the magazines, various writers were beginning to insist that Britain's domestic and international difficulties were exacerbated by, if they did not stem from, the deep play indulged in by several of her young Parliamentarians. Some of these pieces, though mildly scolding, were affable and forgiving, like the illustrated letter to the *Oxford Magazine*, of the "young Cub" having been called from his play to sign legislation in the kitchen of his gaming-club. Increasingly, however, the portrayals became blacker and more censorious: by 1774, when the *London Magazine*'s commentator "Harlequin" visited White's gaming club, he saw two young men playing cards so intently that they "had not been in bed for two nights." Of course, one of these was Charles Volpone (another nickname for Fox), and "Harlequin" related that

> Charles yawned, damned his fortune, slipped into his chair, went home, washed and shifted himself; then in his sulky rattled down to the House of Commons, played with his hat, beat his breast, talked for an hour in favour of the administration, without knowing a word of the matter debated, and then returned again to White's to try his luck at hazard.

And, lest his readers mistake or miss his point, "Harlequin" concluded: "Thus does a modern man of the mode pass his time for the *benefit of himself and family*, and the GREAT GOOD OF HIS COUNTRY."[74] By the later years of the decade, the commentaries grew harsher still; "Every man incumbered with the consequences of his vices or his follies," argued the author of an essay in the *London Magazine*, "Reflections on Gaming," "is a millstone around the neck of his country," on whose shoulders would fall the responsibility for "the destruction of the purest and most durable constitution." How can such perfidious fellows," asked "A Friend to Youth" in a letter to the *Gazetteer*, be promoted "to places of *important trust*, and considerable emolument, in preference to men of unimpeached integrity?" "Every friend to virtue and his country," he concluded, "must shudder at the prospect."[75]

And shudder many did, especially at the news coming from America, from the Caribbean, and from the war with France, Spain, and Holland. By the early 1780s, it seemed increasingly likely that the war would not end well, that, in addition to the imperial and fiscal losses, such an eventuality would only lead to an increase in crime and internal upheaval. And, consequently from 1781 onwards, for the two decades, in two great waves of publicity, the press seemed full of gaming and its deleterious effect on the morals and future of the nation.

The Campaign Against EO

Even before the introduction of the bill formally called The Act to Prevent the Pernicious Practice of Gaming, but commonly known as the EO Table Bill[76] was brought to the House of Commons in June 1782, the press had launched a unprecedented, four-fold attack not only on this one game, but on the whole unregulated, reckless, and socially harmful panoply of gaming practices. EO was an early form of roulette. It was played on a special table, often shaped like an octagon or circle, and punters bet not only against each other, but against the table's proprietor. In some curious way, the EO Table, and its extirpation, became a symbol of what needed to be rehabilitated in the English polity.

The press quickly seized on the popularity of this sort of gambling. Some of the most common of such press items were the reports of the magistrates' doings, and either their negligence or their activities in controlling illegal gaming. Though these sorts of reports were not new, the frequency of their appearance dramatically increased from the early months of 1782. These newspaper comments often stressed the inability of magistrates to properly police gaming shops. "The doors leading to the EO Tables in and about Covent garden are illuminated with additional lamps, and every evening set wide open for the reception of *all comers*—Yet the *proper officers* wisely refrain crossing the threshold of those profane dwellings. Let us hear no more of the *reformed police* of Westminster," remarked the *Morning Herald*. The same paper, however, noting that "a great deal of ill-founded invective has been lavished on the magistrates of the

Westminster police, for not suppressing the various EO tables that are played at within their jurisdiction," argued that, without complaints from the public, no action could be taken.[77] More important, perhaps, and more important to their readers, were the numerous items of magisterial action, of break-ins of gaming houses, and arrests of their denizens. Between April and December of 1782, as many as a dozen such incidents were reported, many simultaneously noted, by most of London's newspapers. But whether reporting police activities, or scolding police inaction, throughout this year the press encouraged and prodded the magistrates and their agents to greater activity. By August 1782, the *Morning Post* confidently asserted that "[t]he interposition of the Justices in the suppression of EO tables, is an act that will gain them the most unbounded applause of the public, and give every reason to hope that the long looked for reform in that body, so necessary to the protection of the subject, and the honour of the city of Westminster, is near at hand."[78]

Throughout the year, as well, the press featured a number of items about gaming and gamesters. The reports of suicides were almost always of young men who had killed themselves because of gaming losses, and the following account was quite typical:

> The young man taken out of the canal in the Park on Sunday morning, proves to be the son of a Mr. Reading, a reputable tradesman of Corke, and is supposed to have put an end to his existence, in consequence of losing a very considerable sum the preceding evening at an EO table.[79]

These acts often led not only to press report; the publicity also generated letters from correspondents, from their grieving parents and their concerned employers. In addition to the accounts of vast sums lost were those, equally disturbing, of large sums won. Perhaps, inevitably, an advertisement appeared, proposing to teach young men "a method to avoid losing" at play, specifically at the EO Tables. The advertiser, addressing his notice to "those gentlemen who have lost money at that too frequented game of E.O.," specified that since he did not wish "to encourage Gaming, he hopes none but persons of property will apply." The *Public Advertiser* reported another, perhaps even more satisfying, solution to gaming losses:

> A Certain Keeper of an EO Table was horsewhipped last Saturday Morning till he implored Mercy on his Knees, by a Gentleman in Westminster, whose Son he had the impudence to arrest for Money he had lent him to Sport with at his own Table. The Gentleman obliged him to kiss the Whip that chastised him.[80]

The press also derived many gaming stories from the sad fate of Dr. Graham's Temple of Health. Dr. James Graham was a Scot who, after extensive travels abroad, returned to London and set up his spectacular Temple of Health and Hymen, which promised both medical and procreative cures for those willing to pay the Temple's incredible fees. Perhaps the most famous element in this opulent theater of promises was the electro-magnetic "Celestial Bed" which promised its users perfectly formed heirs for a fee of 50 guineas a night. By 1782, Graham's "medical" enterprise was in parlous condition, and so one John Wiltshire either rented or bought the Temple of Health and converted it into what the press called "The Temple of Thieves," "The Temple of Hymen," or "The Temple of Destruction." In August 1782, officers of the peace, infiltrating the room, destroyed the EO table with one mighty slash of an axe, "the first intimation that the company received" that their play was ended. In the fray that followed, "Mr. Addington was very severely hurt by a stroke of a bludgeon on his head." Addington recovered, and eventually Wiltshire was found guilty of keeping an EO table and punished.[81]

This story formed the kernel of at least one, perhaps two pantomimes presented in London that summer. The first, called "The Genius of Nonsense," described the arrest of the Goddess of Health at the EO table, and her committal to Bridewell. This quip, the *Morning Chronicle* reported, "produced one of the loudest bursts of laughter and applause ever heard in a theatre." Another pantomine, playing at Sadler's Wells, featured the transformation of Graham's "Celestial Bed" into an EO table, and the entertainment, according to the report, was "executed in a manner as deservedly attracts and merits the applause of the spectators."[82]

In addition to reporting such satires of current gaming concerns, the papers also included a wide variety of satires on gaming practices; a comparison of gaming to the influenza then prevalent; several ironic poems and odes; a "found" letter from Fox to his associates about the purchase of EO Tables; and a "Cross-Reading" in which, by reading across rather than down a newspaper column, some anomalous pairings could be created (in this instance the following: "The Right Hon. the Earl of Effingham's white wand is to go to— Preside at an EO table, to the great disgrace of morality").[83]

When the EO Table Bill came to be voted on early in July 1782, it was "lost" and, though many hoped a new version would be introduced and enacted in the next session, this never materialized. We can never know exactly *why* the bill did not pass or why a new one was not introduced in the next session, but we can find clues about what some contemporaries thought might have happened and indications of what objections others had to it. When a variety of amendments were made to the bill in the House of Lords, the Duke of Chandos objected that he thought this would cause the bill to be lost, as prorogation of the session was imminent. Lord Effingham assured his colleagues of a number of seemingly contradictory things; that the bill could still be passed, that it really was for the best if it were not, since in its unamended form it was badly flawed, and that, in his discussions with London's magistrates, he had been told that they did not need new powers, but just wanted the authority to control EO tables. For whatever reason, the Lords agreed, and when the King prorogued Parliament, the bill was not signed.[84]

Less than a week later, the *Morning Herald* reported a correspondent as saying that "The EO Bill . . . was lost by one of those kind of accidents which seem as if it happened *on purpose!*" The *Herald*, in fact blamed Fox for its loss; once he had lost his post as Secretary of State by the fall of the Rockingham ministry with its leader's death, an event his supporters, it said, had foreseen, "his imps were the loudest against the bill, as they foresaw that their master and themselves would soon have occasion for [such] a resource." And a "found account" of a conversation between Fox and Sheridan made the nature of this resource clear; in it Fox noted that he had ordered a dozen EO tables, which, with himself and his friends as proprietors, would "pick up cash sufficient to support us all the winter." Still others blamed Effingham, satirically suggesting that a "Corps of Sharpers and Pidgeon Pluckers," in addition to presenting him with an inlaid EO table, worth three hundred guineas, had "unanimously agreed to present an Address of Thanks to the Right Honourable the Earl of Effingham" for ensuring the failure of the Bill.[85]

A more potent problem for the success of the bill was that it would have allowed magistrates and constables to enter private dwellings, as opposed to only permitting them to enter taverns or inns where gambling was practiced, to pursue illicit and upper-class gaming. Though this was not a new proposal, having been made, as we have seen, almost thirty years before, it still roused anger and distrust. For, it was clear that it would allow for the punishment of the gaming of the *ton* as well as of the hoi polloi, and that, in a Parliament that contained a large number of extraordinary gamesters, such a piece of legislation was anathema. In its discussion in the Commons, this objection was strongly voiced. Sir P. J. Clerke argued that this was a "bill militating with the liberty of the subject. . . . What a shocking thing would it be, to have private houses disturbed by this new authority at all hours, and to have ladies made liable to be sent to the house of correction, at the will of any magistrate."[86]

In addition to the enhanced powers of entry into both private and public places by constables that the bill proposed and that was objected to by its opponents, an older trope was also frequently invoked; that the men who were to be given these extensive powers were themselves venal and corrupt. As early as July 1769, a long editorial letter in the *Oxford Magazine*, addressed to Sir J[ohn] F[ieldin]g and entitled "Police," argued that, since the "civil magistrate is pensioned by bawds, pimps, whores, vintners and gamblers," it was clear that he would not "enforce the execution of the laws against all transgressors, in all times, and at all places, however highly distinguished by rank or title." Nor, it continued, would he visit those "polite places of private resort for the practice of public vices, and . . . insist that the makers of the laws should be the first on whom they should be obligatory and binding."[87] So too, in the discussions surrounding the EO bill, some argued that it would be "dangerous to extend the authority of Justices of the Peace," for, it was asserted, their existing summary proceedings exhibited only "corruption of heart, and ignorance of head, displayed in the most glaring colours." And the anonymous author of a letter to the Lord Chancellor, published in the *Morning Herald* before the bill's final reading, noting that constables were "a set of fellows, who have no means whatever of livelihood, but those which arise from taking up thieves and other felons, and prosecuting them to conviction, for rewards," prophesied that were the bill to become law, he would not "be surprised if midnight robbers should assume the name of constables, and under the authority of one absurd law, violate all the others." After such banner-waving about the need to preserve inviolate "the sanctuary of private houses" and the venality of London's police, the bill was allowed to fail.[88]

A *"scandalous Devotion to Gambling"*:[89] *Gaming at the Century's End*

Despite the failure of the EO bill to become law, in the two months following its defeat the magistrates of Middlesex and the City were busy shutting down EO houses and prosecuting their keepers. Almost a dozen reports of such crackdowns were published in this period, and the *Morning Chronicle* reported that they were "credibly informed, that the justices throughout every city, town and borough in the kingdom, are determined to exert themselves, and put a stop to the game of EO, especially at the time of races." By the end of August, the *Morning Herald* crowed that "The vigilance of the magistracy has at length obtained a compleat victory over the various keepers of EO tables, those combined foes to every order of civil society," and added four months later that "the almost total extirpation of the pernicious game of EO has gained Sir Sampson Wright the universal esteem of every friend of social virtue and honest industry."[90] Although, when it became clear that a new EO bill was not going to be introduced, the exertions of the magistrates diminished and the reports of EO's reappearance emerged, and within a year or two another game had become the focus of public concern and execration—the game of Faro.[91]

Although there is no reason to think that Faro, like EO, was not played in low houses of resort, the most frequent references made to its site in the press were to private homes, often the homes of the great or fashionable. Unlike the genuine hospitality of "the middling and lower class of people," opined the *Times*, young men were only invited into the homes of "the higher orders" so that they could ruin themselves at Faro, Hazard, or cards. The owners of these houses were well paid for their use, and were often the silent partners of those professional gamblers who actually conducted the games. It was said that "the best place in this country, in regard to an employment of profit under the Crown, is not the Prime Minister's, nor the Duke of Newcastle's nor Lord Mansfield's, though now a sinecure—but the *keeper* of the *Faro tables*, moving about at the different great houses of the nobility." One Mr. M, the *Times* reported, by this employment, earns "clear near 30,000l. a year."[92]

With the rise of this new form of gaming, run by gamblers but in private homes, and as part of an evening's social entertainment, the language of gaming underwent an interesting expansion. When, in his *Dictionary*, Samuel Johnson had defined the activity of gaming, he described it as "to play wantonly and extravagantly for money" and illustrated the character of the gamester by quoting Bacon, "the greater master he is in his art, the worse man he is." Johnson supposed "gambler" to be a cant word which was applied to a "knave whose practice it is to invite the unwary to game and cheat them." By the later 1780s, the *Times*, in an item called "Modern Definitions," described the gamester as one who employed skill and "a very clear head . . . without violating the rules of any game, [to] win the money of hot-headed, inebriated young people of fashion" while the gambler "by the arts of false dice, packing cards, signs and confederates, or by any other means, will, under the title of play, pick the pockets of any one who falls in his way." Another ironic column in the same paper, called "Errata in the Newspapers for the last Three Years," clearly illustrated the way in which contemporaries increasingly viewed social wagering: "For 'play—read 'cheating."[93] From a leisure activity, play increasingly became seen as a corrupt, money-making deception. As shocking as were the large sums reported lost by such activities was the fact that the men and women of the *haut ton* were inviting their friends and acquaintances into their homes to fleece them, that "Faro has become a matter of business, as well as a game of chance, in the polite world, and almost all the houses of fashion are now dealers and chapmen in this lucrative concern."[94] This "vortex" that drew most of the male, and some of the female upper classes seemed so irresistible, that the newspapers started praising aristocrats who did not gamble, as though such restraint was itself a positive virtue.[95]

By the end of June 1787, London's press reported the promulgation of the King's Proclamation against Vice. This edict, while directed at vice of all sorts, took special aim at the profanation of the Sabbath, and forbade "all our loving subjects, of what degree or quality soever, from playing on the Lord's Day at dice, cards or any other game whatsoever, either in public or private houses, or other place or places whatsoever. . . ." Yet, while measures were undertaken to control various kinds of Sunday activities among the middling and plebeian classes, nothing seems to have been directed towards halting fashionable Sabbath gaming.[96] Just a few days after the proclamation's announcement, the *Times* noted that, in response to its regulations, fashionable soirées were now beginning even later on Sunday evenings, and that, at "half after twelve the company then sit down to cards, the time being according to law *Monday* morning. Thus *gaming* on Sunday is *prevented!*" The blatant inequity of regulation was not missed by the press. As one correspondent noted:

> While every pains are taken by the Magistrates to reform the lower class of people, a correspondent wishes that the good effects of the proclamation could be carried a little higher—"Sunday shines no sabbath day" to the great. Routs are formed, and cards played at every nobleman's house on that day, and all the difference between these routs and public houses, is, that the visitors do not pay for their liquor . . . but many pay dearly for their amusement otherwise.

And, in a satirical column entitled "Wants" the following was noted: "Wanted, in the houses of several persons of fashion, a little more respect for religion, and less affection for cards on the Lord's day."[97]

With the growing prominence of Faro and Hazard came renewed attacks on the laxity and corruption of magistrates, new reports of suicides attempted or accomplished because of "debts of honor," and renewed calls for more punitive laws against gambling and gamblers. "Some very strict bill should immediately be brought into Parliament," the *Times* demanded, "making it a felony of death to keep a Faro or Hazard Table." For, added the *Morning Chronicle* "All fashionable pleasures appear now to centre in gaming; people of fashion, in the gratification of their favorite pursuit, display all the ardour of juvenile lovers: 'In Love with ruin, pleased to be undone.' "[98]

Thus the decade following the defeat of the EO Table Bill was decried almost daily by the press as a decade of gaming ruin. Several sarcastically claimed that Thomas Holcroft had stolen the title of his popular play, "The Road to Ruin," from the daily depredations of gambling establishments. That the vice was ancient, all agreed; however the extent, enormity of loss, and new personnel made these practices novel. The first of these innovations, written about so eloquently by Gillian Russell, was the centrality of *tonish* women as hostesses and organizers of such venues. Lamenting their role, the *Times* remarked:

> That women of rank should so notoriously conduct themselves as to revel in all the luxuries of life through open plunder, is a circumstance which would never be credited, were it less public than they themselves make it. What would the ancient honour of our forefathers say to women of title and fortune keeping a FARO TABLE?—and by the indubitable frauds at it, sickening all that is like honest fame and virtue in the metropolis, by the splendours of corruption.[99]

The second novelty, the growing presence of French gaming-house proprietors and gamblers, was also noted and condemned. Describing the Faro Bank in Pall Mall, "on the French firm [which] holds out the temptation of 18,000l.," the *Times* thundered "—that such a gang so notorious in their own country, should be so audacious as to brave the laws and common sense of this, is a proof of the relaxation of our laws in this respect.—John Bull should be let loose among them." Three years later, the *World*'s comment was apocalyptic. "Public professed GAMBLING, made fashionable by great Persons, and current from high authority, taints all the purer sources of life," it noted, and concluded, "It is the last sad sign of a ruined EMPIRE, and a CONSTITUTION tottering to its decay—shall no way be found out, shall no intervening hand of Justice stop this torrent of corruption and debased morals?"[100]

Fighting Gaming in Late Eighteenth-Century London

But, by the early 1790s two new forces, two new "white knights," had appeared to combat the proliferation of vicious play and immorality; the press as a champion of civic virtue and enemy of gambling, and the courts and police as agents of legal rectitude and retribution. Writing to the *Whitehall Evening Post*, a correspondent remarked that he knew "that the Press chastizes many crimes to which the law does not reach." Stung by some criticism of their report that "a certain Lady in St. James's square has ruined herself by FARO!!" the *Times* responded by arguing that since "[s]uch publications . . . will always meet the approbation of the virtuous mind—and ensured of success there, the Press bids defiance to the whole host of gamblers."[101] By the late 1790s, the *Times* stated that since "it is a justice due to the rising generation to guard them" against vices like gaming, it "had taken some pains to expose the Faro-tables, even among the higher ranks of society"; in this effort of moral hygiene its "endeavours ha[d] been *aided* by the magistracy of the country."[102]

Both before and after the establishment of a stipendiary magistracy in London in 1792, the press frequently attacked the supineness and hinted at the corruption of both magistrates and their constables. "Pray why do not the Bow-street Magistrates, attended by their thief-takers, go to all the infamous haunts of gamblers, at the West-end of the town, let their rank be ever so high?" asked the *Times*. Challenged by the justices to "point us out the gambling-houses . . . and we will present them to the Grand Jury," the paper printed the names of six such establishments of "the higher order" and four of the lower.[103] Though they prided themselves on having shamed the magistrates into action, it seems reasonably clear that it was judicial pressure from the high courts, especially from King's Bench, that was responsible for the perceived increase in magisterial activity. Not only had Mr. Justice Ashurst delivered two stinging charges to the Grand Jury, instructing them of their duty to shut down gaming houses in the early 1790s, but after the mid-decade, the many comments and actions that Chief Justice Kenyon launched against the heinous vice of gambling led to a significant rise in the number of stories of increased magisterial vigilance. A good example of this robustness and determination to eliminate gaming "hells," as they were coming to be called, was the application, by the lawyer William Garrow, for a writ of Mandamus "directed to Mr. Addington, the presiding Magistrate at Bow-street, commanding him to proceed to hear certain informations" against proprietors of gaming houses. Kenyon readily agreed to issue the writ, and warned that "every branch of the Magistracy from the highest to the lowest ought to exert themselves to suppress this growing evil." Later the same year, in a case where Garrow accused the London magistrates of inattention to information from those they adjudged "common informers," Kenyon responded, "If the conduct of any Magistrate has been improper—if any witness has been brow-beat or improperly treated, as being an informer, and his evidence considered as inadmissible in a court of justice, . . . I shall hand their names to the Lord Chancellor, who I know, will strike them out of the commission of the peace."[104]

Most of London's papers presented Kenyon as the leader of the fight against deep play; it was "in consequence of the very strong manner in which Lord Kenyon lately recommended prosecutions against the keepers &c of gaming houses, [that] the master of a Hazard table, was yesterday taken before the Magistrates in Marlborough street," noted the *Times*. A few months later, when a well-known gambler and gaming proprietor, a Captain Wheeler, was brought before the magistrates at Bow Street and released as innocent, the *Times* lamented: "Could these people be brought before Lord Kenyon, we have no doubt but that great and moral judge, whose administration of justice has been always distinguished by an unqualified reprobation of vice, would punish them to the utmost extent which the laws would warrant." And both Kenyon and the press repeatedly argued that the law had rather to be overly severe against the offences of the Great in an age of revolutionary upset than to appear to condone or overlook their iniquities. "The higher the station of the person, the higher the offence, and proportionally higher must be the punishment."[105]

Beyond the press's clear and repeated self-descriptions as the outraged voices of "the public," who wished, they asserted, to eliminate or control the spiraling vice of gambling, their coverage of such activity and their assessments of its scope in the last decade of the century were uneven and ambiguous. That such activities, led by England's higher orders, were ruinous to a flourishing state was a commonplace; but what was happening "on the ground"? From late in 1792 the press started suggesting that the great gambling houses were in decline, that gambling among the *ton* at any rate was diminishing. "The profits at Faro are become so considerably reduced, that most of the banks now lose most every evening, after defraying the expenses of the house, which are very considerable," said one account. By September 1794 the decline of press stories of upper-class immorality was attributed to the horrific realities of the Terror; "The Faro Bank Ladies, old Q, Johnny Wilkes, and several other prominent characters, seem to have walked out of the public papers into obscurity. The axe of the guillotine, Robespierre and the French Revolution, have taken the lead of all other diurnal communications."[106] A far greater proportion of newspaper stories, however, were accounts of the actions of the courts and the magistrates against gambling than had appeared earlier in the decade. Still, in the last years of the century, fashionable gaming seemed to have made a comeback as a topic of newspaper tattle. "The gaming tables of our noble dames are thronged with the profligate, the profuse, and the trifling part of creation," the *Morning Post* reported in February 1798; by September of that year the *Times* also noted gambling's resurgence: "Gaming, that hydra of calamities, has again made its appearance with its catalogue of horrors. Notwithstanding the late interference of the police, there are at present, exclusive of subscription tables, no less than eighteen public gambling houses at the west end of the town."[107] But newspaper reportage of gaming and its flamboyant upper-class proprietors was almost at an end; by 1800, if the presence of newspaper reports were any guide, such gambling activities in England hardly existed. The number of such accounts in the *Times* had already started a decline by 1798, and it was not until 1817 that the *Times* once again included as many gaming stories as it had featured almost twenty years before. The average number of such stories for the decade beginning in 1800 was three, the average number in the two preceding years was thirteen.[108]

How are we to understand this precipitous decline? What factors drove the press to so severely reduce such accounts? Some reason may simply be the pressure of the times; with the accession of Napoleon to the head of the French army and state, warfare and foreign affairs were, not surprisingly, the main objects of public interest. Insurrectionary movements in Ireland and an expected invasion from France, as well as the unending wars in India, also took up much newspaper space. However, press reporting of adultery, while sharing some similarities with gaming stories, also showed interesting and different frequencies. In the first two years of the nineteenth century, twice as many adultery stories appeared in the press as had appeared in the previous two years. And while the number of gambling stories in the century's first decade was an average of 3 a year, there were approximately 13 adultery and divorce stories during the same period.[109] So the pressure of more respectable, more significant news events cannot entirely explain the decline of gaming coverage.

Now it may be that stories involving illicit sexuality are more salacious, more "attractive" to newspaper readers than stories of illegal gaming. It may be, in an era of "the world turned upside down" abroad, that newspaper editors thought that only so many stories of corruption in high life were prudent. And while criminal conversation cases and divorces involving fashionable society were matters of public fact, gambling activities of this set were more frequently matters of rumor and innuendo. When, after the family of the newly deceased Earl Cowper sued both the *Times* and the *Morning Herald* for carrying a story about the gambling debts of an unnamed young nobleman, who they claimed was clearly Cowper, a story which, they said, libeled his memory and cast shame on his honor, and won their case against both papers, this may have created an unfavorable climate for the dissemination of other scandalous, *tonish* gaming reports.[110] Still, perhaps this is not the entire picture.

When, after the conclusion of the Napoleonic Wars, the number of gambling stories once again appeared to rise, we are offered another clue to an explanation of the virtual newspaper blackout on gambling accounts among the *ton* for the first fifteen years of the century. From 1816 through 1820, the *Times* published 51 stories about or comments on gambling of one sort or another; of these, 22, or almost forty percent, were negative comments on public lotteries. In addition five accounts dealt with men who, falling into losses at gaming, went on to steal money or bonds to extricate themselves from debt, and six accounts were of the need to repress penny-ante gambling at fairs or roadsides. The tone of these reports is quite different from that of the clichéd comment of the 1790s that "The example [in gaming] should be set by the great, that the little might imitate." Instead, by the second decade of the nineteenth century, the emphasis was almost entirely on the moral condition and the immoral practices of the lower orders. Perhaps this was because some, like the author of the *Microcosm of London* of 1809, in his comments on the history of Brookes's gaming club, noted that "a few years since . . . [the] destructive propensity [for gambling] was carried beyond all the purposes of amusement or pleasure, and that some of our great popular characters have been accused of indulging a most inordinate passion for it; but the taste for play seems, in a considerable degree, to have abated." More likely, however, was the apprehension expressed by a "Hertfordshire Clergyman" in a newspaper letter to Lord Sidmouth. Noting that Sidmouth was an "official guardian of the public morals," he urged him to discharge "your duty to the country."

> That duty, at all times important, is peculiarly so in times like the present, when distress is rapidly demoralizing the lower orders of people, and making them instruments in the hands of turbulent men for subverting that beautiful fabric of social order under which Englishmen have hitherto lived and prospered . . . .

A plebeian gaming loser, said a judge of King's Bench at the beginning of the nineteenth century, was "forgetful or negligent of every true principal of honour and of duty. He was hurried into acts of thefts, forgery, robbery and sometimes murder." This then was the new focus for anxieties about gambling, which explains perhaps the enormous emphasis on such activities in fairs and prisons, or about public lotteries in the years after 1815.[111]

And yet a final thought about the surprising disappearance of stories about fashionable gambling in the newspaper press. When, in 1819, "Orator" Hunt delivered a rousing speech to the Smithfield Reform Meeting, he reflected, in passing, on what he claimed was a widespread press campaign to smear the reform movement with charges of immorality. The press, he argued,

> had made a system of attacking the Prince Regent, in order to keep the people and the Royal Family at variance. Yet of the two the Duke of York was surely a fairer object of animadversion, he having lost in a gambling debt the money given to him to visit an infirm father. This was, he supposed, an example of the morality of the higher orders.[112]

As the vicious immorality of the Great, and the size and scope of their gambling losses, had become part of the political rhetoric of reform, it is perhaps unsurprising that the newspapers chose not to ally themselves too closely or sympathetically with these trouble-making advocates of change in an era of dislocation.

6

Vice in an Age of Respectability

The foibles of the vain and the great are commonly too light to be corrected by serious admonitions from the pulpit, and too evanescent to allow the satirist time to attack them in a volume; but our ephemeral censors, like eagles on the wing, instantly perceive and pursue their quarry, which is seldom able to elude or survive their grasp. A newspaper is indeed a tremendous inquisitorial instrument, and the most abandoned character in high life would tremble at the idea of being publicly exposed through its magnifying medium.[1]

So wrote John Corry in 1801, confidently expressing the not uncommon view that Britain's press had a central role to play in the improvement of the morality of those "in high life." There is no doubt that the Great disliked appearing in its pages, disliked the notoriety given to their vices and faults. The question remains, however: what influence on their conduct did it have? Or was one of its consequences, perhaps unwittingly, to separate and make less admirable the whole sector of society in which such failings were to be found? Did the multitude of reports of such vice in the newspapers, as well as its continuing denunciation in sermons and representation in plays and poetry, convince the "moral" classes that they were not only different from, but perhaps even better than their betters?

"passion for gambling":[2] *Gaming Among the Great After the Napoleonic Wars*

"One of the features of high society after the long war," reminisced Captain Gronow, "was the ubiquity of high gaming." For this reason, he continued, "there are few families of distinction who do not even to the present day retain unpleasant reminiscences of the period." Yet unlike the 1790s, when newspaper accounts of such gaming appeared almost daily, the first decade of the new century saw a marked decline in such press reportage. While accounts of the ruin of young men of the mercantile classes by gaming and subsequent criminality were not uncommon,[3] during this period the press published only a few accounts of similar outcomes for men or women of the upper classes.[4] Yet such comments in other formats continued to be heard and published; thus the Rev. J. L. Chirol, in his *Sermon on Gaming* of 1824 referred unflatteringly to "the *dissolute lives* which those sons of the first families lead, instead of applying themselves, with zeal, to important studies, which would qualify them for filling hereafter, with honour and distinction, the highest posts in the State, . . ." while a pamphlet, *A Letter to Ball Hughes, Esq on Club House and Private Gaming* of the same year, described such an aristocratic gambler as a "noble parasite, a stain on patrician birth."[5] And on the rare occasions when upper-class gaming was given much publicity, as in the case of General Fitzpatrick's refusal to pay his gaming debts to the assignees of Martindale's, a fashionable, though bankrupt establishment, the press comments were withering. though brief. While Fitzpatrick argued that Martindale, unlike the assignees, "is perfectly satisfied with his conduct, which is strictly agreeable to the 'laws of honour,' " the *London Chronicle* responded, "to the gentlemen learned in that refined code we leave the decision of this delicate point."[6] Some newspapers seemed to think that upper-class gambling was no longer a great social problem; thus the *Morning Post* commented that "*Dancing* gains ground, in proportion as *gaming* becomes unpopular. The change is certainly advantageous both to health and morals," while the *Morning Chronicle* noted that "Playing for money at card clubs, assemblies, routs, &c. in the higher circles, is at the request of several ladies of distinction, much suspended for the present."[7] Not all observers were so sanguine. But by and large, during the wars with France, press concerns about the effects of gaming were similar to those expressed by Justice Grose in sentencing a gaming-house keeper. Enticed by such houses, Grose noted, "servants were induced to rob their masters, children their parents and fathers without remorse consigned their families to ruin, and themselves to beggary and infamy."[8] Thus, during the Wars, most papers concentrated, perhaps perforce, on making general statements on the iniquities and dangers of lower-class gaming, fairs and lotteries being two principal sorts of concern.[9]

After the war's end, however, we begin to hear some renewed press murmurings against upper-class gaming, especially on the Sabbath. Thus "Restitutor," writing to the *Gentleman's Magazine*, complained of such Sunday gambling at a Subscription room: "The reproof, Mr. Urban, is at this time peculiarly seasonable, when *the higher orders* of our citizens are associating together to enforce decorum on the Sabbath amongst the *commonality*; and it cries with a loud voice, '*Physicians, heal yourselves.*' " And stories of upper-class men, like that of Lieutenant John Davis, led astray by the lure of gaming establishments ("he moved in the highest circles of society . . . and partook of all those fashionable amusements in which young men of his age and rank but too frequently indulge . . .") who ended up as a forger, became somewhat less unusual.[10]

As worrying, in a rather different way, were the newspaper stories of middle-class men increasingly appearing in gambling hells and imitating their betters in losing vast sums of money. When we look at the press coverage of Crockford's, we shall see this situation noted. For now, however, let us examine the story of one gaming addict, a scion of the middle classes, led to crime. His uncle, a merchant, learning that his nephew had lost most of his monies at a particular gaming den, resolved to investigate its activities. He later reported that he had discovered that "every encouragement was given to merchants' and bankers' clerks and others, who had the command of money not their own."[11] If these cases seem reminiscent of the furor surrounding the Clutterbuck incident of the 1780s, there was, however, a new element at play. Clutterbuck, a young teller at the Bank of England, had in the early 1780s lost both his own patrimony and Bank payments at an infamous gambling house and, before the losses were discovered, had fled to France. His tale, widely reported, featured the attempts of agents of the Bank to secure him, and bring him back to Britain for trial.[12] While in that case the Bank of England, and the law of the land were seen as the appropriate agents against such miscreants, by the 1820s a new force was being called upon. Thus, in a letter to the editor of the *Times*, "W. S." argued that

> If the vice of gaming were confined to the higher ranks of society, the evil would not be of so alarming and destructive a nature; but we behold in the most public streets of the metropolis "Hells" which commence their nefarious system of plunder at 12 o'clock in the day . . . for the convenience of apprentices, tradesmen, merchants' and bankers' clerks . . . Thus the evil is extended, and accessible to all ranks of society; it therefore becomes the interest of the

> mercantile world particularly to consider what measures will be most effectual
> to suppress nuisances of so vicious and demoralizing a character.[13]

"W. S.'s" appeal to the "mercantile world" to address this problem, to bring the weight of its practical understanding to bear on this grievous social issue, underlined a newer appeal to the combined forces of society's "middle" to aid the forces of the law and to help solve such grievous and dangerously immoral activities.

While a fair amount of rather desultory discussion about what could or should be done about large-scale gambling establishments went on in the newspapers during the 1820s, the focus of much concern came to rest on the establishment, initially called "Fishmonger's Hall" after the previous occupation of its owner, William Crockford, but soon renamed, even in the press, as Crockford's Club, the home of fashionable gambling during, according to one historian of the practice, its last "great days."[14] Here is "Expositor" in a letter to the *Times*, discussing its role and character:

> At the head of these infamous establishments [gambling "hells"] is one
> yclept "Fishmonger's Hall," which sacks more plunder than all the others
> put together, though they consist of about a dozen. This place has been fitted
> up at an expense of near 40,000l., and is the most splendid house, interiorly
> and exteriorly in all the neighbourhood. It has been established as a bait for
> the fortunes of the great, many of whom have already been very severe
> sufferers.

"Expositor" concluded that "in a short time" Crockford and his partners' profits from the French Hazard Table they ran, "after all their expenses were covered, [amounted to] upwards of 200,000l." "It is to be hoped," he concluded, "that some notice will be taken of the subject next sessions of Parliament, and that a committee will be appointed to take evidence, in order that a stop may be put to the evil." This, of course, did not happen. And when, at the end of that year, Crockford was charged with his involvement in a gambling house, no witnesses appeared at the trials, and Crockford was acquitted for lack of evidence. The *Times* lamented:

> The manner in which the two cases against Crockford, the late fishmonger,
> went off yesterday will be seen with regret. It was painful, also, to notice the
> names of the persons called on in Court, and who did not appear to their
> subpoenas.[15]

Yet despite this evidence, the *Times* remarked that although the non-appearance of high-ranking and well-regarded witnesses was shocking, that still there [we]re virtuous, and honourable, and pure men in the Peerage of Great Britain, whose characters may serve as a set-off to the frequenters of "hells," and so redeem the whole order from disgrace and obloquy.

Even more worrying, perhaps, was the growing presence of those very men who might have been supposed to be safe from the lure of this sort of vice. Thus the *Times* commented on their presence at Crockford's:

Among the aristocratic members of Crockford's are to be found doctors, surgeons, parsons, wine-merchants, and brewers. Messrs W-, H-, and B-, we regret to say, have become members. The counting house and hazard table do not well accord. It behoves men of business and character to be on their guard, and not allow themselves to be pigeoned by Hell-keepers and their attendants.[16]

Increasingly upper-class vice was seen not only as ruinous to "the fashionable sort" but to be seeping down, perhaps unexpectedly, to those beneath them in standing, but crucial to the prosperity and power of Britain.

By the 1830s a new sort of protest against upper-class gaming began to be reported in the press, occasioned by attacks on working-class immorality by those who claimed that beer and gaming were rampant among this group. Parliamentary spokesmen for the working classes, in response, attacked these habits in the Great. And some of the press led the way.

In May 1830, responding to a pamphlet written by the Bishop of London, Charles Blomfield, which accused the press of pandering to the public appetite for upper-class scandal, the *Times* indignantly replied:

We ask every honourable-minded man whether it would not be much more pandering to the great to conceal their criminal excesses in this respect, as the Bishop would have us do, than to let the offenders know that they cannot practice them in obscurity?[17]

When, a little more than a year latter, a bill was introduced to make it impossible for ordinary people to drink beer on the Sabbath, Daniel O'Connell spoke against it, noting that he did

not approve of this constant interference with the private affairs of the people . . . [and] to subject all their actions to the control of a number of self-elected censors of morals. Many of those *magistri morum* were not, he believed, very remarkable themselves for their moral qualities. None of them attended at Crockford's, or any of those fashionable houses in St. James's street, to lecture on morals. If they did they would be laughed out of countenance. But if a poor man had an extra pint of beer, there was immediately an outcry about morality. . . .[18]

And when a gaming-house client of Charles Phillips came to trial in May 1833, Phillips responded by advising the "parish officers to go to Crockford's, not far distant from the house in question, where they would find lords and other peers of the realm at play."[19] Combined with the publicity given to the extraordinary gambling expenses of the Duke of York,[20] less than a year before, it is small wonder that one newspaper correspondent concluded that "The police appear to be satisfied with the occasional conviction of one or more minor delinquents from the neighbourhood of Leicester-square, but the Leviathans in crime are allowed to continue their nightly course of profligacy and plunder with impunity."[21] Perhaps this widespread publicity may have encouraged or mobilized the calling of the Select Committee on Gaming of 1844 and the subsequent passage of "An Act to amend the Law against Games and Wagers" of 1845, which, according to an early historian of English gambling, meant that "for many years afterwards professional gaming-houses in London were a tradition of the past."[22]

"suicide, Hell's blackest crime":[23] Suicide in the Press After the Felo de Se Act

We have seen how the medical view, that suicide was the effect of derangement, albeit often sudden and temporary, and the legal view, that suicide, unless evidenced by settled and persistent insanity, was the result of wilful self-murder, clashed in the early nineteenth century. Proponents of both views, however, accepted the notion that the penalty for a verdict of self-murder, an ignominious and often brutal burial, both was uncivilized and led juries to mitigate the offence to avoid the punishment. Both hoped, in different ways, that the abolition of this punishment would be salutary; the former that the public would come to see that "the *attempt at self-destruction* is OFTEN THE FIRST distinct overt act of insanity,"[24] the latter that a misplaced sympathy with afflicted family and friends would not now cause jurors to render false verdicts.

There is no question but that many coroners' juries gladly allowed the new leniency to guide them. The verdict of "temporary derangement" became very widespread, for as the press noted of one inquest jury, ". . . the humanity of jurymen generally makes them anxious to lay hold of any circumstances that might justify them in returning a verdict of insanity instead of *felo de se*. . . ."[25] Perhaps it is worth noticing that this account attributed the change in verdicts to "humanity" rather than to a new understanding of mental illness, but it is undeniable that such a strategy was often adopted. Thus many of the nation's newspapers felt the need to inform their readers that "The offence of *felo de se* is still a violation of the law, notwithstanding that part which relates to burial in the highways is repealed. . . ."[26]

The provisions of the new law, of course, also allowed for more, rather than less, discussion of what still constituted "real" *felo de se*, and here the papers reported a very great range of findings, without evidence of any widespread or popularly held agreement. This becomes obvious, for example, in the verdicts given after the suicides of children. Thus, after John Clark, "a boy of nine years of age, . . . hung himself at Hopton, Suffolk, in a saw-pit . . . the jury returned a verdict of *Felo de Se*," hoping, as the account explained, by this verdict to stop a rash of similar local acts, "and in the hope of checking this growing practice in the rising generation."[27] And yet, occasionally, coroners would instruct their juries otherwise. After a lovers' suicide pact gone awry (the woman recovered, the man died), the jury were told that they had only one option in their verdict. They were instructed that since the man was less than twenty-one years of age, and thus a minor, he could not be found *felo de se*. No one questioned this dubious assertion and the jury's verdict was that "the deceased had come to his death by taking arsenic, and he being an infant under the age of 21, was consequently not of the age of discretion."[28]

Other instances of such uncertainty over verdict can be seen in reports of deaths attributed to the effects of alcohol; sometimes these were found *felo de se*, sometimes adjudged to have been the result of temporary derangement.[29] The verdicts in other cases were even more puzzling. The *Examiner* told of the tragic end of Thomas Williams, a poor old man of eighty, who, after being robbed of all his savings, went to the parish for assistance, and was offered the solace of the workhouse. Faced with this option, Williams went home, hanged himself from a beam, and was adjudged *felo de se* by the local inquest jury. The *Examiner* in its coverage headed this item with the tag "Disgusting Verdict."[30] And while the new law was supposed to mitigate severity of punishment, making it possible for the bereaved family and friends to accept what had happened, there were still instances where this did not occur, where those concerned seemed violently and actively upset by the form of burial laid down by "the humane regulations of the new Act of Parliament. . . ." A case in point was the death and burial of Thomas Tomlinson, a young soldier, who, while having an outstanding reputation in his regiment for gallantry in battle, fearing some unnamed disgrace, killed himself and was found *felo de se*. The report of what followed was published soon after in the local newspaper:

> The corpse, in consequence, was seized by the civil power, and lodged in the prison until Monday night, when the remains of this unfortunate young man

were taken about midnight to a short distance from the town, and buried in the lanes usually appropriated to this purpose. The civil officers were attended by a military guard; but neither the presence of the military, nor the silent hour of night, prevented a very loud expression of public indignation on the part of the populace, at what they conceived to be a partial execution of a rigorous law, the recollection of none of them furnishing an instance where it had been enforced except in those cases where the crime of poverty was super-added to that of suicide. The body had scarcely been committed to its ignominious grave, when some of the military, impelled by an attachment to their brother soldier, and encouraged by the populace, jumped into the grave, in the presence of the civil officers, . . . [disinterred the coffin and] carried it to the New Burying Ground at the Parish church, where it was interred with military honours. The corpse has, we understand, since been removed, and since replaced in hallowed ground, where the remains of this unfortunate now rest in peace.[31]

In the face of all this contrariety, one might think that nothing much had changed in the public understanding of the sin of suicide, or the press reporting of inquests and burials of those adjudged *felo de se* after the passage of the suicide Act of 1823, but this would be a not entirely correct inference. While neither those who hoped that the Act would demonstrate the enlightened view that all suicides were caused by insanity, whether temporary or permanent, nor those who, convinced that juries were allowing their sympathy to sway their judgment, hoped that the eradication of the punitive burial rites would lead to severer and more just sentences being passed on all those who rationally chose to kill themselves, were entirely vindicated, both sides achieved some of their goals.

There is no question that the definition of lunacy was broadened, and, after 1823, usually expressed in jury verdicts as "temporary" derangement or insanity. Many were also still "found drowned" or had their deaths attributed to "visitation of God." A new verdict, "found dead," was also occasionally used, as in the case of the man who, "having destroyed himself by firing a pistol-ball into his head at the right ear, but no evidence appears as to who he is, or what induced him to commit the act."[32] The greatest extension of the notion that all suicides were, by the very fact of the act, not culpable, was demonstrated in the verdict returned on the body of Mary Wanstall, a "confidential" servant who was often left in charge, in the family's absence, of the Coleman home near Canterbury. When it became clear that Wanstall had, over a period of time, been selling items of value to local pawnbrokers and changing locks in various rooms to facilitate such thefts, she hanged herself with a towel. Despite the long-held tradition that criminals were always to be adjudged *felo de se*, the verdict in the Wanstall case was that the rash act was due to "Momentary Insanity."[33]

However, those who saw in the Act the first step towards the abolition of the notion of "self-murder" and its replacement by a truer, more humane insight into the physio-medical roots of all such acts, could not have been entirely pleased either. Even if newspaper accounts of coroners' inquests are not to be taken entirely as complete descriptions of contemporary practice, for contemporaries themselves they were the single largest body of information about the nature of verdicts in such cases. And an investigation of the three most recent and significant data-bases of eighteenth- and nineteenth-century British newspapers reveals a surprising paucity of *felo de se* verdicts before, but a growing body of such reports after the passage of the Act. From the earliest mention of a *felo de se* judgment reported in 1733 in the *London Journal* to the end of the Napoleonic Wars, I have only found a total of ten such cases.[34] In contrast, in each decade after the passage of the Act, the number of *felo de se* verdicts reported nationally kept growing, going from 13 in the decade 1815–24, to 28 in the next decade, to 49 in the mid–1830s to 1840s.[35] And it is significant, I think, that in many of these cases, the press published inquest accounts, in which the more punitive decision emanated from a member of the jury. Thus when considering the death of George Wallace, a porter at the Charing Cross Hospital, who killed himself early on the morning of March 25, 1840, the jury foreman explained why "he could not consent to return a verdict of temporary insanity, as the evidence was too slight to warrant such a verdict." He continued:

> From reading the reports of inquests in the public journals, he considered that in many cases verdicts of temporary insanity were returned by juries under false premises—viz, that persons who committed suicide must from that fact alone be necessarily insane. He held no such doctrine, and thinking that in this case, the fact of passing insanity was not sufficiently sustained, he should recommend the verdict of *felo de se*.

The jury concurred.[36] The *Times* added that not only was such honesty necessary for the proper workings of the inquest jury, but that the attempt "to obscure any of these unhappy cases from the public view" in terms of press coverage, was "very objectionable on public grounds, since there is no right more sacred and valuable than that which the law exacts on behalf of the community in the clear and open development of the causes of sudden and unaccountable death."[37]

However, whatever the growing frequency of the press reporting of such verdicts became, one thing remained constant; to quote the *Examiner*, when considering the inquiry into the death of a nobleman (to which we will shortly return), it concluded that "The inquest was conducted, as all inquests are on persons of distinction, without any urgent curiosity as to possible causes, or anxiety for evidence."[38] Take for example the case of Lord Graves and the press coverage of his suicide. On February 9, 1830, many of England's papers featured an item to which the *Times* gave the catchy title of "Melancholy Suicide in High Life," an account of his death and inquest. There were many striking oddities of this affair which immediately appeared. Sometime between 5:30 and 7 PM on Sunday, February 6th, Graves had killed himself, yet by 7:45 the next morning, according to press accounts, a coroner's jury was empaneled by the Westminster coroner, G. H. Gell, though "in consequence of the unusually early hour . . . no reporters were in attendance."[39] After a cursory inquest, "the jury without hesitation returned a verdict" that Graves had killed himself "in a sudden fit of delirium." The *Times* was besides itself and in a stinging editorial denounced the coroner. "We say that his Lordship ought not to be buried on such evidence—the Coroner ought not to have granted his warrant for the purpose." The *Morning Chronicle* denounced the entire proceedings of the inquest, in both specific and general comments, noting that "[f]rom those penalties, which, although recently deprived of their ferocious character, have not been wholly abolished, most suicides belonging to the upper ranks of life escape through the compliance of Juries attributing the fatal act to temporary derangement." Even a paper as conservative and generally pro-ministerial as the *Courier* opined that "the inquiry instituted [wa]s incomplete and unsatisfactory; hastily got up, and inadequately performed."[40]

Of course, all the fuss was not simply about the cover-up of an aristocratic suicide, but had other salacious elements; it was suspected that Lady Graves, separated from her husband, was having an affair with someone in the royal family, and the hush-up of Graves's death was part-and-parcel of a larger and more serious whitewash. Still, despite the *Times*'s later assurance that this was not the case, several letters to the editor harped on the bungled inquest, and raised disquieting questions about its status.[41]

When, eleven months later, William Horace Pitt-Rivers, Lord Rivers, was found drowned in the Serpentine, the inquest on his body was even more hurried than those of most drowning victims. According to the *Times*, "[o]ne Juryman threw out a suggestion that a witness should be called to speak to his lordship's state of mind; but he was replied to by the coroner who said he thought enough had been proved to show that his lordship had fallen in by accident." And when a woman arrived with Rivers's umbrella, which she found by the side of the path, "the Coroner and Jury however did not think it necessary to examine her." Only several days after the inquest concluded did some of the papers comment on its failings, most notably that Rivers was addicted to gambling, and had had severe losses. The *Times* said that on the night he died, he had lost between two and three thousand pounds to his gaming opponent. "These circumstances," it continued, "were not mentioned at the inquest; in fact there seemed to be a great anxiety" to avoid all discussion "of his lordship's circumstances."[42] The *Examiner*'s mutedly ironic comment about the absence of "urgent curiosity" and concern "for evidence" in these investigations of the deaths of the Great seems not only understated, but pointedly acute.

Thus, in many ways the 1823 Act was to prove a disappointment to both sorts of its hopeful supporters. While freed from the possibility of a shameful burial of the self-murderer, juries were much more liable to find mitigating verdicts, especially that of temporary derangement. However, there was one class of people who remained, and were publicly even more visible as likely to be found criminal self-murderers; that is the great body of Britain's working poor. As a correspondent to the *Examiner* in 1831, outraged at the reportage of an inquest and subsequent finding of *felo de se* by the *Plymouth Journal*, noted in closing: "If the law regarding *felo de se* is a law, it ought to be enforced in every case, on rich and poor; but if the poor only are to smart under its application, it would be much better to abolish it altogether." And by 1843, even the *Times* was editorially willing to commit itself to one standard of evidence and punishment in such cases, for rich and poor, for powerful and friendless, and even for prisoners in penitentiaries. Things had certainly changed, but press satisfaction, and public confidence in the application of the law to such cases, seemed, if anything, to have diminished.[43]

"*the two great crimes, peculiar to the civilized state, Adultery and Suicide*":[44] Crim. Con. 1826–45

If, in the years after the passage of the 1823 *Felo de Se* Act, the moral and social problems of determining the causes and punishment of suicides did not disappear, the same sorts of dilemmas arose in considering the proper method of dealing with adultery and divorce. With the failure of the 1809 proposal to introduce stronger measures punishing faithless wives and their gallants, the next four decades were spent in arguing over a proper future course of action. One reason for this was that adultery, like the other vices we have considered, having a multiple nature, was seen simultaneously by most as a sin (against the law of God), a vice (against the public good), and a crime, albeit a peculiar one, dealt with in civil courts, and distantly, with imprisonment, in some cases, as the only possible punishment. It is this last aspect of its nature, which found its embodiment in the criminal conversation procedure, that we must now turn to.

Crim. con. cases served at least three purposes. All agreed that, in so far as pecuniary awards could so serve, one of its ends was as recompense for the damages suffered by husbands for the loss of their wives' "good company." Some others thought that these damages could and should also act as punishments against the sinners, and perhaps as warnings to others tempted to commit such acts. Finally, these cases were thought to have an investigative role in laying the groundwork for full Parliamentary divorce; they acted as a kind of "pre-trial" hearing for such latter final events. Still others, however, believed that the entire process was badly flawed, that the proceedings needed to be simplified, made more accessible to a wider range of applicants, though some of these "modernizers" also wished, while removing crim. con from the civil domain, to criminalize and more severely punish adulterous couples.

Despite these differences, or because of them, the public interest in adultery, in crim. con. trials and divorce proceedings, did not wane, but arguably grew in these years. The courts were often crowded; when Sir Jacob Astley faced his wife's lover, Captain Garth, in the Court of Common Pleas in February 1827, the *Morning Chronicle* reported that "the Court was crowded to excess, at a very early hour this morning . . ."; three years later at the Oxford Assizes, as the case of Clayton *v* Franklyn was coming on, "the Court was thronged during the whole of the afternoon, and there were a great many gentlemen of the county seated on the benches on the right hand of the learned judge." At the trial in 1831 of Miss Love, actress-wife of Captain Calcraft, *Bell's London Life*, after noting that "The court was much crowded to hear the trial" added that "great disappointment was felt at there being nothing more racy in the details." And at the Bligh *v* Wellesley case, the *Times* said that "the gallery was crowded with several women, who listened to all the disgusting details of the trial with the most unblushing intrepidity and assurance."[45] This public relish was not new, but it was more commented on, and more worried about. For, as we have already seen, the line between private vice and public good, between the state of marriage and the fate of society, had always been linked in most accounts of the baneful effects of adultery on the common weal. And, like other vices we have considered, adultery was seen not only as a sin and a vice, but also as a crime. In the criminal conversation procedure, the mixed nature of this combination was particularly noticeable and troubling. For now, along with the courts, along with trial reports in the older newspapers and magazines, along with the presentation of adultery on the stage, came a host of new magazines like the *Crim. Con. Gazette*, the

Satirist, and the *Age*, which dedicated themselves to the public display of private vice, of prurience and perhaps blackmail mixed with moral outrage and reforming zeal.

Despite the failure of the four earlier attempts to "criminalize" adultery, most early nineteenth-century observers did not believe that marriages had become more stable, that fewer adulteries were occurring, or that fewer aristocratic divorces were being allowed. Thus, for example, in 1830, various press reports, citing the Earl of Malmesbury's comments on the Ellenborough divorce bill, noted that "[t]he number of [such] Bills passed in the Lords within the last five years exceeds the number passed in the preceding five, in the proportion of three-and-a-half to one; the total of such bills from 1820 to 1825 amounted to no more than six, while the bills passed since 1825 are no less than *twenty-one!*"[46] However, while it seemed clear that only the "higher classes" could afford full divorce, "because the remedy was so expensive that the middling and lower orders were deprived of it," it was nevertheless the case that through the 1840s, the middling and lower classes appeared in greater numbers in crim. con. actions, actions reported fully, usually in detail, by the press. As Lawrence Stone has pointed out, the percentage of men of title who were involved in criminal conversation cases fell from 16% in the two decades before 1830 to only 4% in the decades after, while the number of such cases only fell from 86 to 79 in those years, or about 10%. Along with this decline, or, to put it another way, the growing appearance of non-elite men in such cases, Stone noted that in the decade 1800 to 1809, in nineteen such suits (or in about 37% of all such cases), the plaintiff was awarded £2000 or more; by the 1840s, the number of such awards had diminished to twelve (or about 34% of all such cases). Much more dramatic, however, was the fact that in the earlier period, while 65% of those awarded £2000 or more were given at least £5000 in damages, and 29% of these awards were for sums of £10,000 or more, in the latter period only 34% of crim. con. awards were for £5000 or more and only 1 (or 9%) was for the sum of £10,000 or more.[47] Pecuniary rewards for marital infidelity were clearly declining. The newspaper accounts were similar in their reports. What Stone does not emphasize, however, were the changes in the small sums given. In the first decade of the century, 20% of the total awards reported by the press were £200 or less (8/41); by the 1830s, 40% (23/58) of the sums were of this amount. Not only were fewer titled men involved in such actions, but, even when they were, large sums were awarded in fewer cases. In the first decade of the century, there were 13 awards of £3000 or more (31%), by the 1830s only four (about 7%), and by the end of the 1840s it was still at about 7% (3/42). Between 1800 and 1809 four awards of £10,000 or more were given, in contrast to the 1840s, when only one plaintiff was granted £8,000 damages, while another two received £3,000. While aristocratic cases still were reported (defendants E. Harborough in 1831, Melbourne 1836, Lord F. Beauclerk 1839, Hon F. G. Molyneux 1841, Lord Cardigan 1843, Sir Charles Elton 1847, and plaintiffs Carden 1831, Lord Langford, 1836, and Lord W. Paget 1843), most other plaintiffs and defendants in such suits in the 1830s and 1840s were men of the middle classes. However, one of the most interesting non-middling cases featured a Mr. Coultas who sued his employer, the Rev. Mr. Bowes, for criminal conversation with his wife, also a servant in the Bowes household. Mr. O'Malley, Coultas's attorney, began his address to the special jury by describing Coultas "as a poor man seeking for justice and compensation at the hands of the jury, from a rich man—a man by birth, rank, and education, one of their own." The jury found for the plaintiff in the sum of £250. However, when a year earlier, a Mr. Absalon, described as one "in humble circumstances," brought a case against the eldest son of Sir G. H. Bunbury for adultery with his wife, his own attorneys refused to continue the case when evidence was presented that Absalon had attempted to extort money from Bunbury, and, unsuccessful, had only brought the suit in consequence. The judge, Mr. Baron Platt, commended the lawyers, commenting, "The bar of England, though open to the grievances of the poor, should never lend itself to facilitate the attempts of profligacy and vice."[48]

There seemed an increasing uneasiness about the whole crim. con. process. In what sense could money assuage the pain of such loss and betrayal, of "the most cruel injury that can be inflicted" by one man on another?[49] Thus, in the case of Eldrid *v* Cross, in which the defendant had conceded a defense, thus admitting guilt, in the opening statement of Eldrid's attorney to the sheriff's jury to decide on damages, he noted that

> the action was one which the plaintiff felt himself compelled bring against the defendant, not so much with a view of the immediate consequences of that day, as to the ulterior steps which their decision must originate, and to a certain extent affect.

He concluded that Eldrid had been "compelled to appear before them" by "the present state of the law to seek pecuniary damages for one of the deepest injuries that could be inflicted upon a man possessing a sensitive and honourable mind. . . ." The jury assessed the damages at £500. In another such case, Lord Langford *v* Barrett, however, though virtually the same language was used about "ulterior steps," the jury decided on the sum of 1 shilling in damages. *Bell's Life in London*, in commenting on the case and the verdict, noted,

> No doubt the main object of this experiment was the desire of Lord Langford
> to obtain a divorce—happily in this respect his Lordship will be disappointed.
> It is a maxim in our consistorial courts that folks seeking such remedies must
> appear with 'clean hands' and it is needless to say that all the soap and water
> in his Majesty's dominions would not reduce his Lordship's digits to that
> condition.[50]

But more serious perhaps, more troubling, than the natural human propensity for greed and gain, was the way in which plaintiffs and defendants in such cases were "compromising" the event by coming to out-of-court settlements before the issues could be aired before the jury. Thus in one such case, Tucker *v* Gooch, the plaintiff's lawyer asked the court "for a few minutes, as from a consultation with the parties he had every reason to believe they would agree to a verdict being returned for £50 [the original sum asked for was £1,000] without having to lay the whole of the facts connected with the unfortunate transaction before the jury and the world." Similarly, in an uncontested case, the parties settled the damages privately between themselves, and "the writ was withdrawn by the plaintiff's solicitors." This was done, the press reported, "in order to avoid the exposure of the circumstances which gave rise to the action, and which are said to be of a peculiar character. . . ."[51]

Furthermore "[t]he careless way in which juries find verdicts for damages in *crim. con.* actions" was a complaint of both the *Examiner* and Lord Brougham. The magazine reported Brougham's speech in the Lords, in which he complained that

> A jury give a verdict, and award damages, without having heard one word
> or knowing one atom of the circumstances of the case, because counsel think
> proper to say when they get before a jury, that as the only object of the action
> is to obtain a verdict with a view to a divorce, he and his learned friend on
> the other side, with the hope of sparing the feelings of the connections of the
> parties, have consented to a verdict for a certain amount of damages.

This, Brougham (and the *Examiner*) concluded, was both "very bad and very improper."[52]

For either the crim. con. process had some justifiable legal function, i.e., to investigate all the facts of the situation and to publicize the punishment of adulterers, or it was merely for pecuniary gain or to facilitate divorce without public scrutiny. It was the absence of this investigation, the absence of such a stage in the divorce process which was one of the most serious challenges in the Ellenborough divorce case, held before the bar of the House of Commons without having gone through the crim. con process. And despite Lawrence Stone's view that the crim. con. action was rapidly falling out of favor in the second quarter of the century, some Parliamentarians at least saw its value. Joseph Hume, for one, commenting on the need for such previous knowledge, remarked:

> It was, therefore, always desirable that some investigation before a competent tribunal should precede the consideration of these matters, before they are brought into that house [Commons], which was of all other places, the least constituted for prosecuting their inquiry.[53]

Others, both within Parliament and without, agreed, finding the procedure in the Ellenborough case only a notable and glaring example of the partiality of the law, and of the advantage that the rich and powerful had over the more lowly in appealing for consideration. This was one of the cases that Dr. Phillimore gave in his address to the House, for a need for a new divorce process more accessible to all, and especially to "all the middle orders of the country, small gentry and farmers."[54] And while it is quite true, as Lawrence Stone has asserted, that after the Ellenborough action, "the titular aristocracy virtually dropped out altogether" of suits for Parliamentary divorces, the language often used in the many letters and comments at the time in the press, which decried the privileges and vices of fashionable life and fashionable custom, still acknowledged the existence of a *beau monde*, a world with its own different moral code. The *Morning Chronicle* argued that the Ellenborough case proved "that there are two codes of morality in sexual matters in this country—one for common life and another for fashionable life."[55] Using the language of fashion, or of rich and poor, was, however, not a way of smudging or mis-recognizing the chasm created by blatantly partial legislation like that employed in this divorce; rather, in an age of euphemistic reference, those terms conveyed the message without raising any particular hackles. It is clear to whom the *Morning Chronicle* was referring, when it noted that "[the] principle, then, of setting aside the law in the case of divorces, and in all other cases where the rule is equally clear, ought to be reprobated as arbitrary and partial—as tending to destroy in the people all reverence for the law, and to persuade them, that while it is binding only on the poor, it is held in no regard by the rich."[56]

Whatever the future of divorce was to be, many seemed clear on the difficulties posed by the need to assess pecuniary damages arising from criminal conversation suits. Thus in one article, entitled merely "Crim. Con." the following suggestion was made:

> We think parliament would gain great glory by a measure erasing crim. con. from the catalogue of expensive luxuries, no longer suffering it to be a privilege of the rich, but adding to the number of felonious offences; making it a crime

against the social state, and not a private debt of hard cash between man and man . . . Prison diet and the tread-mill would, we think, make the sport [of adultery] very ungentlemanly.[57]

These proposals, however, reiterated in somewhat new and perhaps even stronger language the unsuccessful attempts to create a new divorce law, and thus, while evincing the desire for more punitive measures, were unlikely to be adopted. But, spurred perhaps by the growing number of crim. con. cases withdrawn at the last moment, or compromised without the facts becoming publicly known, the press responded by noting such instances. So, in the Wallis *v* Francis case, the *Examiner* wrote that "in order to avoid the exposure of the circumstances which gave rise to the action, and which are said to be of a peculiar character, the affair has been settled, and the writ was withdrawn by the plaintiff's solicitors." Combining a perhaps crass desire to sell papers with a sometimes radical commitment to publicize the crimes of the great and powerful, newspapers of all stripes let it be known that if information was kept from them, that fact would be passed on to its readers. For example, after reporting the Cazelet crim. con. trial, which, it was said, had "excited great interest," the *Morning Chronicle* noted that its reporter had requested certain letters involved in the case, but that "the Solicitor for the plaintiff would not give our reporter copies. "In fact," they concluded, "every thing was done, that could be done, to prevent the publication of the case."[58] Similarly, *Bell's Life in London*, prefacing its denunciation of the conduct of Lord and Lady Langford, as revealed in the case of Langford *v* Barrett, noted that "We have elsewhere expressed our disapprobation of a journal thrusting upon the notice of its readers the private vices of noble Lords and their Ladies. . . . —at the same time admitting that, when these persons rendered themselves amenable to public observation, the severest strictures were justifiable." Having reviewed the tawdry details of fashionable married life, *Bell's* concluded by thundering:

> Comment is unnecessary in such a case; but when our aristocracy set such examples of *virtue* and *honour*, and exhibit themselves with such unblushing effrontery in our courts of justice, with what grace can our Magistrates sentence sinners in the humbler classes for offences immeasurably less disgusting to the silent system and the treadmill?[59]

The most strident denunciation, however, of the "Crimes of the Aristocracy" came in a letter to the editor of the *Satirist*, a journal that called itself "the Censor of the Times." Beginning his peroration with a compliment to the editor, "You have done more to improve the morals of succeeding ages than any other man that ever lived, by drawing the public attention to the vices and immoralities of the aristocracy," the anonymous author continued by exhorting the magazine to publish a "list of all the[ir] crimes and offences" and stressed "adultery, fornication and the like." Where the law was powerless, suggested "TOEB," the censure of the public, especially of the middle class, might have more impact than either penal or financial punishments.[60] Thus, though the titled great no longer made up a significant part of those seeking divorce or crim. con. damages, in the eyes of some of the press, at least, the aristocratic world of fashion was still the seed-bed of sexual impropriety and easy vice.

"the world begins to grow weary of the littleness of great men":[61] Duelling in Post–Napoleonic War Britain

After the long war's conclusion, it seemed reasonable that the number of duels would decline. Given a boost by the number of men at arms, imbibing, often for the first time, the rhetoric of military masculinity and honor, duelling likely reached a new high during these war years. But with peace and victory, many hoped, it was natural to expect that duelling would decline and it may well have done so.[62]

In 1822 three pamphlets appeared which announced and articulated the nature of this long-hoped-for but not yet achieved change. The first, written by Stephen Leach, after the duel between the Dukes of Bedford and Buckingham, was entitled *The Folly and Wickedness of Duelling*; the second, the work of a Scottish minister, the Rev. Peter Chalmers, was first presented as a sermon before being published as *Two Discourses on the Sin, Danger and Remedy of Duelling*; and the third, *The Duellist, or a Cursory View of the Rise, Progress and Practice of Duelling*, was anonymous. These three works argued that social changes had made duelling "old-fashioned," held out hope that the end of duelling was well within sight, and suggested new legal and extra-legal measures that might hasten its demise. Leach characterized "this Age" as one where "thought soars above the prejudices of superstition and bigotry, [and where] freedom has wrestled the rod of authority from the hands of the rude mighty . . ."; Chalmers commended "the enlightened and religious character of the times," while the *Duellist*'s author exulted in "the progress of civilization and society" where "[e]verything gross or reprehensible in the feudal system has died away, or has been exploded by general consent" except, of course, "this inhuman practice [of duelling], which even the force of laws cannot supercede."[63]

All three also recommended measures that might be taken to eliminate this barbarous custom. Leach argued that the judicious use of fines, imprisonment, and private whippings "would be fully effectual to cool this vulgar high life blood, and cause it to flow with a regular pulse"; Chalmers proposed "a forfeiture of property"; while the *Duellist* spoke approvingly of Addison's suggestion that "if every man who fought a duel were to stand in the pillory, it would quickly lessen the number of those imaginary men of honour, and put an end to so absurd a practice." But in some sense the most interesting, and "modern" of these observations came from the clergyman, Chalmers. Seeing in "the tide of public opinion" a powerful, progressive tool for the amelioration of vice, he reflected on its success in having overcome two earlier grievous vices, swearing and excessive drinking.

> If then, the mere force of public opinion, founded too, not so much on religious principle, as upon the maxims of fashionable decorum, can be so successful in repressing the vices alluded to, what might be expected from it, if made to bear upon the particular sin under consideration;—a sin which involves in it present results, personal, domestic and social, much more painful and injurious?[64]

But in the struggles for Catholic Emancipation, in the bitter antipathies of the various groups involved, a remarkable duel occurred which had only one real antecedent; the meeting between Pitt and Tierney in 1798. The cause of the duel between Wellington and his opponent, the Earl of Winchilsea, was clear. In the fracas surrounding the passage of Catholic Emancipation, Winchilsea, a Tory Ultra, in a letter he published in the *Standard*, had intimated that Wellington, by employing the ruse of supporting the godly and very protestant King's College, not only had an "insidious design for the infringe-ment of" all English liberties, but was also plotting the "introduction of Popery into every department of the State." After the item appeared in the press, Wellington sent Winchilsea a number of letters asking for a retraction and apology, and, when the Earl refused, the Duke demanded "that satisfaction for your conduct which a gentleman has a right to require, and which a gentleman never refuses to give."[65] Again, as in an earlier duel, when the two men met, on the morning of March 29, 1829, no injury was sustained, Wellington firing one shot, and missing, Winchilsea firing in the air.

What did the press say about this duel? Most of the papers used the occa-sion to reflect on the larger questions involved in such actions: should public men fight, and if they did, was it their private or their public honor that was at stake? Was there any precedent for such duelling, or was it, as one paper claimed, "until revived by his grace, [a] happily obsolete practice"?[66] Clearly, despite the papers, the practice was not obsolete; many men still duelled and would continue to do so for another two decades. But few of the papers criticized Wellington, or Pitt, or any of the other eminent political men of the previous century, for, by their example, giving a legitimacy and perhaps even a spur to the practice. While the condemnation remained, that connection was not made; when men like Wellington and his duelling predecessors were criticized, they were blamed for the particularities of their engagement, not for the general principles involved. However, as we shall soon see, Wellington's duel was not forgotten, nor forgiven, as subsequent duelling accounts in the press would show.

We have already seen a growth in the publicity, if not in the actual numbers, of respectable men, even men of proven courage like General Coote,[67] who rather than accept challenges, took their challengers to court. Alternately, one of the participants, or a friend or family member of a potential duellist, could arrange to have police officers present, to arrest the combatants, and these arrests also were increasingly published by the press. If we compare the press accounts of challenges brought to court plus the accounts of duels stopped, with the duels reported in the press, an interesting pattern seems to emerge. While almost twice as many completed duels were reported in the newspapers as having taken place compared to the number of incomplete (i.e., challenge brought to court or stopped by police officers) duels in 1800, by the 1830s the numbers were reversed, showing both an increase in aborted duels, and a decline in reported completed ones. Though perhaps only one of many things occurring during these decades, the numbers suggest a correlation, a change in perception and practice.[68]

The two duels that I would like to conclude with were, in their details, not particularly uncommon, their participants not particularly grand, and their legal outcomes not entirely surprising. What distinguished them somewhat was that in both, one of the duellists was killed. In the first, which took place very early one morning on January 8, 1830, two men, Oliver Clayton, an Irish writer, and Lieutenant Richard Lambrecht, late of the Ceylon Regiment, accompanied by their two seconds, fought a duel in Battersea fields, in which the former was shot and died about twelve hours later. After the incident, "a mutual expression of forgiveness took place." There was never a question of foul play, though it was still so dark that a passing laborer, not seeing the conflict, narrowly avoided being shot himself.[69] For almost four months afterwards the papers were abuzz with the story, and we shall shortly return to a consideration of this coverage.

The publicity surrounding the second duel, which took place on July 1, 1843 between Lt. Col. David Fawcett and Lt. James Munro, lasted much longer. For one thing, both men were military men as well as being brothers-in-law. For another, of the five men involved in the duel, the principals, their seconds, and a regimental doctor, two of them (the doctor and Fawcett's second) came to trial reasonably soon; Munro and his second, Grant, fled, and though Grant returned for his trial early in 1844, Munro did not return from abroad until 1847. Everyone but Munro was found not guilty, and his trial ended with the jury returning "a verdict of *Guilty*, but strongly recommended the prisoner to mercy."[70] However, well before that day, the press made their opinions of this particular duel, with its relationship to earlier ones and to the future of duelling, extensively known.

In the first instance, the press commentary began shortly after Lambrecht's surrendering himself to the law. At that point, the magistrate, a Mr. Chambers, to whom he was then brought, was said to have commented that "the prisoner [should] prepare himself for the worst, declaring in his opinion that the law would be carried to the fullest extent." This comment enraged both the *Morning Chronicle* and the *Examiner*. The first wondered whether

> if the Duke of Wellington had shot the Earl of Winchilsea, or the Earl of Winchilsea his Grace, at Battersea Fields, Mr. Chambers would, in addressing the survivor, have carefully abstained from the slightest allusion to the possibility even of any necessity for having recourse to such a personage as the one who "carries the law to the fullest extent."

And, after reproducing the whole of this editorial in its own pages, the *Examiner* added, "It is not *tactics*, but sycophancy, to respect the offences of power; and the virtue which reserves its rage for the weak only is near of kin to a vice."[71] But far and away the most biting critique of Chambers's statement came from the *North Wales Chronicle*. It noted that had the law against duelling "been carried into effect uniformly in all cases of the kind which have occurred within the last forty years, and had the law been sanctioned by the private opinion and personal conduct of those whose duty it was in a special manner to give it their countenance and support" this duel would not have taken place. Asking "what has been the state of opinion on this subject even amongst the highest classes," the *Chronicle* went on to remind its readers of the duel between the Duke of York and Col. Lennox, that between Pitt and Tierney, that fought by Castlereagh and Canning, and finally the meeting between Wellington and Winchilsea. The editor concluded this very long fulmination thus:

> We trust the time is not far distant when the higher classes will perceive, and possess the moral courage to fulfil their duty as Christians, and as the leading members of a civilized state, by adopting some method . . . for the extirpation of this blood-thirsty folly.[72]

When Lambrecht's trial, and that of the seconds, came on, on April 3, 1830, the presiding judge, in his summation, most likely referring to these many press comments, noted:

> It has been said that other persons had conducted themselves in a similar way, and not been visited with punishment . . . but although other persons in high condition might, by their example, have sanctioned the practice . . . still the law was the same, and the highest person in the land might be subject to a similar prosecution to that which had now been instituted against the prisoners at the bar.

He then told the jury that if Clayton had died by the shot of Lambrecht, whatever the circumstances, "they must find, or at least ought to find, a verdict of guilty." Lambrecht and both seconds were, as though to spite the judge, found not guilty after a long and difficult jury consultation.[73]

Less than a week after the second duel, in a letter written to the *Times*, "One Who Has Three Brothers in the Army" appealed to the "Commander-in-Chief" of the Army, asking him, because of the "late sad and most disgraceful affair of honour," to mark "his disapprobation of duelling in the army by dismissing every individual implicated from the service." Two days later, another letter, written in response, asked:

> How can the Commander-in-Chief adopt the suggestion? He must, for consistency's sake, tolerate duelling; must continue to it the countenance which, a few years ago, he, the Duke of Wellington! thought fit to give to the wretched practice by his duel with the Earl of Winchilsea.[74]

Less than two months later, after the trial and acquittal of Lt. Cuddy, the second to Lt. Col. Fawcett in the duel that resulted in the latter's death, further comments in the press began to appear. Thus *Bell's Life in London* declared that the law governing duelling was rendered "totally inoperative" by the support the practice received from "the usages and feelings of society." It concluded by recommending to those desiring to "put down the barbarous absurdity," to "make duelling, so far as they are concerned, unfashionable, and they will go far to attain their purpose. It [duelling] exists upon opinions. Opinion can destroy it."[75]

Probably the most daring attack on Wellington and the tradition of fashionable duelling came in *Punch* shortly after. Complete with a cartoon of a skeleton holding a pair of duelling pistols, the piece was entitled "Present to the Duke of Wellington." It claimed to be the account of a present made to Wellington by "the officers of the British Army" for allowing Munro and his second, Grant, to continue receiving their Army pay, neither of whom had then "surrendered to take their trial" but who were, by indulgence, it was intimated, "upon Her Majesty's Army List, although either absent without leave, or specially allowed permission to stay away." And the presentation of the pistols concluded with this purported speech of a senior Army colonel:

> My Lord Duke . . . we live in an age of revolutionary ignorance; an age in which the ruthless, low-minded vulgar, are too often prone to confound the hallowed distinctions of society, and thereby to test, what I trust we may ever live to call 'the satisfaction of a gentleman,' . . . by the unjust and ridiculous standard of civil society.[76]

Although, in 1829, the press refrained from such comments when Wellington and Winchilsea met, by the 1840s they were widespread and pointed.[77] And, by the 1840s, the attack on this privileged vice was no longer confined to individuals, but expressed in larger, more radical terms. "It is a vain attempt." opined *Freeman's Journal*, "to cover from the public eye a moral leprosy which festers in aristocratic places." The *Examiner* added:

> If being concerned in a duel . . . were to render a man ever ineligible to serve the Crown in any way, or to sit in Parliament, or to acquire or retain any honour or title, the aristocratic classes would be deterred . . . and whenever duelling falls into disuse amongst the upper orders, there will soon be an end of it with the classes that ape their manners and vices.[78]

By 1847, at least one paper concluded that "In fact dueling may be held to have ceased." "Some better method of settling differences between people of high blood and higher pretensions and affections, will speedily be established, now that improvement has become absolutely necessary," added another. What accounted for such a change? "[T]he great alteration which has been effected by means of the press, in public opinion, within the last few years, with regard to duelling" was the answer given.[79] And, in the end, the public character of aristocratic vice and the preferential treatment that people of quality were accorded for these types of behavior, changed. Though upper-class vice had by no means disappeared, it maintained a more discreet presence in an age which valued public decency, respectability, and propriety.[80]

Conclusion:
An End to Aristocratic Vice?

[i]t is the most powerful moral machine in the world, and exercises a greater influence over the manners and opinions of society than the united eloquence of the bar, the senate and the pulpit.[1]

Deeply entrenched practices do not change overnight. By the mid-nineteenth century, however, some customary forms of behavior had changed; one, duelling, had even disappeared from Britain completely. But the other forms of vice considered in this book had also changed. The 1857 Matrimonial Causes Act fundamentally altered the nature of divorce, making adultery one, but not the only, ground for complete divorce, and allowed innocent women the right to remarry. The treatment of suicide had also changed, and by mid-century all who took their lives were allowed a dignified burial, even if not in daylight hours, and within sanctified ground. Gambling had gone "indoors," and become private, occurring most frequently in private homes or gentlemen's clubs. Society, both great and small, seemed more settled and more moral, and for many, that seeming was a great step forward.

These changes, or at least their appearance, had not been the result of any single, even if complex event. Neither the French Revolution nor the accession of the young Victoria to the throne did more than add impetus to the groundswell which began a very long time before, and was manifest in a variety of sources. Duelling, after all, had been criticized by Francis Bacon as far back as 1614; suicide had been the subject of plays and poetry for almost as long; adultery was bemoaned by clerics even while becoming the subject of a new genre of pamphlets. Gaming too, and its offspring gambling, had been the subject of plays, of pamphlet attacks, and of legislation for several centuries. What then had finally "done the trick," had converted Britain's social elite from being the exemplar of such vice to becoming more sedate and decorous, more worthy of respect and leadership?

Of course there is never a single answer to any historical question, but this book has tried to demonstrate that the increasing frequency of newspaper coverage, that is, of publicity, through the eighteenth century, resulted in the transmutation of what might have been considered private matters into public concerns: the rencounter between two gentlemen, the breakup of marriage through adultery, the act of self-murder, and the loss of personal fortune at the gaming tables, became the subjects of popular discussion. As these issues became public, ordinary newspaper readers would have become aware of the magnitude and frequency of these acts, a dimension that they would never have encountered in their day-to-day lives. This awareness, over time, would have given those acts a greater significance, created more demand both for the cessation of what could be stopped or, in the absence of that, fairer and more equitable legal treatment for all affected.

Along with, and validated by the growing knowledge of the immorality of the fashionable world, came a proud assertion of the virtues of the middling orders. Two comments, one from the press, the other from a late eighteenth-century sermon, illustrate this trend. The first, from the *Times*, noted that "Among the middling and lower class of people some real hospitality yet exists–but in the higher order nothing but vanity or avarice . . ."; the second, even more damning, was part of Samuel Parr's *Discourse on the late Fast*, which castigated England's upper classes:

> In the higher stations of life, we see rank without dignity, money without wealth, and voluptuousness almost without enjoyment. Our indignation, indeed, is somewhat stayed in its course, by the virtues which yet keep their ground among the middle orders of men. . . .[2]

Along with increased publicity given to the vices of the world of the Great was the direct articulation of the growing notion that the divide between personal and public character was artificial and misleading, and furthermore that the public had a right to know about the *faux pas*, the irregularities, of their rulers and betters. "Experience's" letter to the *Public Advertiser* stated this position unequivocally:

I have ever been of opinion that a fair moral character was necessary toward forming a good minister of state, as it is highly improbable that those who are vicious in their private lives, should be virtuous in their public. And that there is no doubt that the people have as just a right and as much reason to enquire into and be informed of the private virtues and vices of those, who are entrusted with the care of their liberties and properties, as any gentleman hath, to require a character of a steward, who is to manage his estates; that we know by history and we feel by daily experience, how much private passions influence public actions.[3]

Despite the very significant coverage of these vices by the eighteenth-century press, most press historians have only looked at its relation to politics and political change. This may not be the only, or perhaps even the best way of considering press influence, especially when a great many of its readers were politically disenfranchised. Instead the great advantage of concentrating on moral issues is that, on the surface at least, there could be no disagreement. Anyone who rebuked adulterers could not be accused of being "a mere partisan," and one could not accuse someone opposed to duelling of trying to overthrow established religion or its social system. All opponents to "vice" of any sort could make claims of an unimpeachable moral sanctity, of a concern for the common weal, and for the concept of equality before the Law. And it was these sorts of claims that the press encouraged.

Another great advantage of the press over other venues which also complained about the corruption of the age was its perceived ubiquity. Bemoaning "the follies and absurdities which are crept in amongst us, and are far more numerous than at any time for ages past," "P," in a letter to the *General Evening Post* argued that it was newspapers that both revealed the problems and suggested solutions to the many inconveniencies of the times. "It may be said," he continued, "who reads newspapers? To which I answer, many more people than will own they do. They are read by the learned and unlearned, the wise and otherwise. . . ."[4] As early as the late 1780s, the press had already claimed credit for improving the morals of the nation:

The follies, vices, and consequent miseries of multitudes, displayed in a newspaper, are so many admonitions and warnings, so many beacons, continually burning, to turn others from the rocks on which *they* have been shipwrecked. What more powerful dissuasive from suspicion, jealousy and anger, than the story of one friend murdered by another in a duel! What caution likely to be more effectual against gambling and profligacy, than the mournful relation of an execution, or the fate of despairing suicide. . . . "Talk they of morals"? There is no need of Hutcheson, Smith or Paley. Only take a newspaper and consider it well, read it and it will instruct thee. . . .

But it was not the morals of the great body of the people that many thought most needed improvement. "It has been justly remarked–that the middle and inferior ranks of society are much enlightened," noted "Observator," a correspondent to the *Times*, though he continued, "the superior [ranks] are much corrupted and depraved." And we have already seen Corry's argument that such "inquisitorial instrument[s]" as active press coverage would powerfully affect the sensibilities and perhaps even the behavior of the "most abandoned character[s] in high life."[5] While the long-fought skirmishes against a set of vices may have led to a change in the manners, if not in the morals, of the *ton*, they must also have promoted a sense of moral superiority and self-confidence in the middling orders, for whom, as E. P. Thompson noted, "the Press, itself [was] a kind of middle-class presence in advance of other articulated expression."[6]

While not all the vices considered here had been eradicated, by the second half of the nineteenth century fashionable misdeeds could no longer be reported as mere lapses, aristocratic roués became the stuff of penny-romances and music hall sketches, gambling was more often confined to private spaces and less frequently hit the pages of the press than a hundred or more years earlier. While the skirmishing had not ceased, an odd class without any natural parameters of its own, defined largely by who and what it was not, had come into being.[7] And the cultural skirmishes considered by this book were certainly responsible for a significant part of that self-consciousness, of that significant self-creation.

Notes

PA   *Public Advertiser*
St. J   *St. James's Chronicle*
T&C   *Town and Country Magazine*
White   *Whitehall Evening Post*

Introduction

1. *Observator* December 31, 1709–January 4, 1710; Philogamus, *Present state of matrimony: or the real causes of conjugal infidelity* (London, J. Buckland, 1739), p. 32.

2. *GEP* November 12, 1751, letter from *A Countryman; Conn* January 30, 1755 #53: "There are many customs among the Great, which are also practiced by the lower sort of people."

3. *St. J* May 19, 1761, "A Sketch of the ruling manners of the Age, from a Discourse on Luxury," by Thomas Cole; *Public Register or Freeman's Journal* March 7–9, 1771.

4. Margaret R. Hunt, *The Middling Sort: Commerce, Gender and the Family in England 1680–1780* (Berkeley, University of California Press, 1996), p. 3; Paul Langford, *A Polite and Commercial People: England, 1727–1783* (Oxford, Oxford University Press, 1998), p. 61; Daniel Defoe, *The Life and Strange Adventures of Robinson Crusoe*, 3rd edition (London, printed for W. Taylor, 1719), p. 3; *Diary or Woodfall's Register* October 4, 1790.

5. Amanda Goodrich, in *Debating England's Aristocracy in the 1790s* (Rochester, N.Y., Boydell Press, 2005), pp. 15–22, discusses the usage of the term "aristocracy" in political discourse late in the eighteenth century while Paul Langford, in a section labeled simply 'Aristocratic Vice' (*A Polite and Commercial People*, pp. 582–87), sees this as an important feature of the 1770s. Using the same general, catch-all definition of this group, I am endeavouring to consider a longer, less specific historical period.

6. In her moral tale of 1799, *The Two Wealthy Farmers* (London, F. and C. Rivington), p. 18, Hannah More's Farmer Worthy, describing the dangers of reading frivolous novels, says such novels make the "crying sins" of "ADULTERY, GAMING, DUELS and SELF-MURDER" seem commonplace, rather than crimes deserving hanging.

7. Thomas Erskine, *Reflections on Gaming, Annuities and Usurious Contracts* (London, T. Davies, 1786), p. 3.

8. Henry Fielding, *Amelia*, ed. Martin Battesin (Oxford, Clarendon Press, 1983), p. 375; Henry Fielding, *The Covent Garden Journal* [1752], edited by Bertrand Golgar (Middletown, Conn., Wesleyan University Press, 1988) #68, October 14, 1752, p. 359.

9. Anthony Holbrook, *Christian Essays upon the Immorality of Uncleanness and Duelling* (London, John Wyat, 1727); *LC* January 12, 1790.

10. *PA* May 17, 1765; *Gaz* August 11, 1783.

11. *A Discourse Upon Self-Murder* (London, J. Fox, 1754), p. 15; *Times* November 21, 1786.

12. See Patricia Howell Michaelson, "Women in the Reading Circle," *Eighteenth-Century Life* 13 (1990), pp. 59–69.

13. T. C. W. Blanning, in *The Culture of Power and the Power of Culture: Old Regime Europe 1660–1789* (Oxford, Oxford University Press, 2002), p. 4, uses the most capacious

definition of culture, which he says, was "classically defined by Sir Edwin Tylor as 'that complex whole which includes knowledge, belief, art, morals, law, custom and any other capabilities and habits acquired by man as a member of society.'" This is too large an understanding for my purposes. For Geertz on the web of meaning, see *The Interpretation of Cultures* (New York, Basic Books, 1973), "Thick Description," pp. 3–30. A discussion of *habitus* can be found in Pierre Bourdieu's *Distinction*, trans. Richard Nice (London, Routledge & Kegan Paul, 1984), "The Habitus and the Space of Life," pp. 9–225.

14. David Hume, "On the first Principles of Government" in *Essays and Treatises on Several Subjects* (London, A. Millar, 1758), p. 20.

15. GM January 1752, p. 30. It seems to me that, by omitting the word "public" from discussions of "opinion," one is leaving open and undefined a term which was made, in large part, by appeals to it. By embracing such deliberate vagueness, we avoid problems of locating and specifying who was, or was not, a member of such a group, or who had such an opinion.

16. The *OED Online* gives 1374 as the date of the first use of "skirmish" in the singular.

17. These critics resemble the diverse groups of eighteenth-century newspaper readers, discussed by Bob Harris, *Politics and the Rise of the Press* (London, Routledge, 1996).

18. For debating societies see D. T. Andrew, *London Debating Societies 1776–1799* (London, London Record Society, 1994) and Mary Thale, "London Debating Societies in the 1790s" in the *Historical Journal* (1989), "Women in London Debating Societies in 1780" in *Gender and Society* (1995), and "Deists, Papists and Methodists at London Debating Societies, 1749–1799" in *History*, 86:283 (2001).

19. One of the earliest and most powerful accounts of the centrality of the press to all sorts of political and cultural change, John Brewer's *Party Ideology and Popular Politics at the Accession of George III* (Cambridge, Cambridge University Press, 1976, pp. 139–62) led to a significant change of focus in our understanding of the technologies of social and political power in this period. John Cannon has noted that, in the eighteenth century, "The rise in the number and importance of the middling classes of society—clerks, merchants, teachers, doctors, attorneys, shopkeepers—manifested itself in a great increase in the publication of journals, books and newspapers" (*Parliamentary Reform 1640–1832* [Cambridge, Cambridge University Press, 1972, 1994], p. 48). Kathleen Wilson points out that "printed artifacts" were "one of the first mass cultural commodities" (*The Sense of the People: Politics, Culture and Imperialism, 1715–1785* [Cambridge University Press, 1998] p. 31). For more on letters to the editor or printer, see Robert L. Haig, *The Gazetteer 1735–1797: a study in the eighteenth-century English newspaper* (Carbondale, Southern Illinois Press, 1960), pp. 70–75.

20. Lucyle Werkmeister, *The London Daily Press 1772–1792* (Lincoln, University of Nebraska Press, 1963), pp. 7, 90.

21. Only a few of the most recent or influential works are here cited: *Duelling*: V. J. Kiernan, *The Duel in European History* (Oxford, Oxford University Press, 1988); James Kelly, *"That Damn'd Thing Called Honour"* (Cork, Cork University Press, 1995); Markku Peltonen, *The Duel in Early Modern England: Civility, Politeness and Honour* (Cambridge, Cambridge University Press, 2003); Stephen Banks, "Very little law in the case: Contests of Honour and the Subversion of the English Criminal Courts, 1780–1845" (2008) 19(3) *King's Law Journal* 575–94; "Dangerous Friends: The Second

and the Later English Duel" (2009) 32 (1) *Journal for Eighteenth Century Studies* 87–106; "Killing with Courtesy: The English Duelist, 1785–1845" (2008) 47 *Journal of British Studies* 528–58; Robert B. Shoemaker, "The taming of the duel: masculinity, honour and ritual violence in London, 1660–1800" *Historical Journal* (2002) 45/3 pp. 525–45; idem, "Male Honour and the Decline of Public Violence in Eighteenth-Century London," *Social History* (2001) vol. 26, pp. 190–208; Jeremy Horder, "The Duel and the English Law of Homicide," *Oxford Journal of Legal Studies* 1992, 12(3), pp. 419–32. *Adultery:* Lawrence Stone, *Road to Divorce* (Oxford, Oxford University Press, 1990), and *Broken Lives* (Oxford, Oxford University Press, 1993); David Turner, *Fashioning Adultery* (Cambridge, Cambridge University Press, 2002); Sarah Lloyd, "Amour in the Shrubbery," *Eighteenth Century Studies* (2006) 39.4, 421–42; Gillian Russell, "The Theatre of Crim. Con.: Thomas Erskine, Adultery, and Radical Politics in the 1790s" in *Unrespectable Radicals? Popular Politics in the Age of Reform,* ed. Michael T. Davis and Paul A. Pickering (Farnham, UK, Ashgate, 2007), pp. 57–70; Randolph Trumbach, *Sex and the Gender Revolution* (Chicago, University of Chicago Press, 1998); Karen Harvey, *Reading Sex in the Eighteenth Century: Bodies and Gender in English Erotic Culture* (Cambridge: Cambridge University Press, 2004); Cindy McCreery, "Breaking all the Rules: The Worsley Affair in Late-Eighteenth-Century Britain," in *Orthodoxy and Heresy in Eighteenth-Century Society: Essays from the DeBartolo Conference,* ed. Regina Hewitt and Pat Rogers (Lewisburg and London: Bucknell University Press, 2002) and "Keeping Up with the Bon Ton: the *Tête-a-Tête* Series in the *Town and Country Magazine,*" in H. Barker and E. Chalus, *Gender in Eighteenth-Century England* (London, Addison Wesley Longman, 1997); Marilyn Morris, "Marital Litigation and English Tabloid Journalism: Crim. Con. in *The Bon Ton* (1791–1796)," in the *British Journal for Eighteenth Century Studies,* 2005, vol. 28, pp. 33–54. *Suicide:* Michael MacDonald, "The Medicalization of Suicide in England: Laymen, Physicians, and Cultural Change, 1500–1870," in *Framing Disease: Studies in Cultural History,* ed. Charles Rosenberg and Janet Golden (New Brunswick, N.J., Rutgers University Press, 1992), pp. 85–103; Michael MacDonald, "Suicide and the Rise of the Popular Press in England," *Representations* 22 (1988) pp. 36–55; with Terence Murphy, *Sleepless Souls* (Oxford, Clarendon Press, 1990); Georges Minois, *History of Suicide: Voluntary Death in Western Culture,* transl. Lydia Cochrane (Baltimore, Johns Hopkins University Press, 1999); R. A. Houston, *Suicide, lordship, and community in Britain, 1500–1830* (Oxford, Oxford University Press, 2010). *Gambling:* Nicholas Tosney, "Gaming in England, c. 1540–1760" (unpublished PhD thesis, University of York, UK, 2008); Justine Crump, "The Study of Gaming in Eighteenth Century English Novels" (unpublished PhD thesis, University of Oxford, 1997), Janet Mullin, "We had Carding," *Journal of Social History,* vol. 42, #4, (2009) pp. 989–1008.

22. In this I agree with William J. Bouwsma, who argues that, unlike social history in which "gross discontinuities" and rapid change seem possible analytic modes, they are "generally implausible in cultural history, in which change is very slow." *A Usable Past: Essays in European Cultural History* (Berkeley, University of California Press, 1990) p. 5.

23. Ivor Asquith noted that "Most newspaper proprietors were aware that, if they were to maintain their papers as profitable, or even viable concerns, they had to cater for the tastes of the general reader who was not only interested in politics. Such a committed

Foxite journalist as James Perry described miscellany, or non-political features, as "the soul of a newspaper . . ." Furthermore, "some contemporaries took the view that if a newspaper was of poor quality, it was as much the fault of the public as of the proprietors; it was felt that proprietors had little alternative but to respond to the public's taste" ("The Structure, ownership and control of the press, 1780–1855," in George Boyce, ed., *Newspaper History from the 17th century to the present day* (London, Constable, 1978) pp. 107, 114.

24. Commenting on the symbolic centrality of law to Britons in this period, John Brewer noted that "The essential difference between Britain and other nations was that her constitution was a government of laws . . ." in which, at least in theory, "All those who held power . . . were deemed subject to the law." (Brewer, *Party Ideology*, p. 244).

25. E. P. Thompson, *The Making of the English Working Class* (Harmondsworth, Penguin Books, 1968), p. 8; William Allen (ed.), *The Philanthropist*, 1801, v, p. 187.

Chapter 1. Contesting Cultural Authority

1. The first part of this chapter title is taken from the title of a study by Frank M. Turner, *Contesting Cultural Authority* (Cambridge, Cambridge University Press, 1993) which examines the Victorian period; Julian Pitt-Rivers, *International Encyclopedia of the Social Sciences*, "Honor," p. 510.

2. George Stanhope, *A Paraphrase and Commentary upon the Epistles and Gospels*, vol. 2, p. 94, quoted in the *Oxford English Dictionary*. See *Leviathan* [1651] (New York, Macmillan & Co, 1962), p. 51, for Thomas Hobbes's earlier definition of aristocratic magnanimity as "a contempt for little helps and hindrances," For more on this long history, see Anna Bryson, *From Courtesy to Civility* (Oxford, Clarendon, 1998).

3. See, for a similar usage, Amanda Goodrich, *Debating England's Aristocracy in the 1790s* (London, Boydell Press, 2005), and Paul Langford, *A Polite and Commercial People*, p. 582.

4. Antoine Courtin, *The Rules of Civility or the Maxims of Genteel Behaviour*, with *A Short Treatise on the Point of Honour* (London, Robert Clavell and Jonathan Robinson, 1703), pp. 3–8, 225–72. This work had gone into its twelfth English edition by 1703. For more on Courtin's earlier reception, see Bryson, *From Courtesy to Civility*, pp. 81–100, 131–40.

5. George Berkeley, *The Works of George Berkeley, Bishop of Cloyne*, ed. A. A. Luce and T. E. Jessop, 9 vols. (London, T. Nelson, 1948–1957), "*Alciphron or The Minute Philosopher*" [1732] 3: 112.

6. Edward, Lord Herbert of Cherbury, *The Life of Edward, First Lord Herbert of Cherbury* (London, Oxford University Press, 1976), p. 49; John Mackqueen, *Two Essays: the first on courage, the other on honour* (London, John Morphew, 1711), p. 2.

7. Herbert of Cherbury, *Life*, p. 43; *LM* March 1735, p. 145.

8. *A Hint on Duelling, in a letter to a friend* (London, M. Sheepey, 1752), p. 3; *LM* October 1732, p. 361.

9. John Mackqueen, *An Essay on Courage* p. 13; *The Tatler*, ed. Donald F. Bond (Clarendon Press, Oxford, 1987) 4: July 22–25, 1710, p. 79; see Bernard Mandeville,

Fable of the Bees, ed. F. B. Kaye (Oxford, Clarendon Press, 1924, p. 58) for his discussion of the "Rapture we enjoy in other's esteem [which] overpays us for the conquest of strongest passions." For more on Mandeville's thought and importance, see Thomas A. Horne, *The Social Thought of Bernard Mandeville* (New York, Columbia University Press, 1978), M. M. Goldsmith, *Private Vices, Public Benefits: Bernard Mandeville's Social and Political Thought* (Cambridge, Cambridge University Press, 1985), and J. Martin Stafford, ed., *Private Vices, Publick Benefits? The Contemporary Reception of Bernard Mandeville* (Solihull, Ismeron, 1997).

10. Robert Heath, "To one who was so impatient," in *Clarasella; together with Poems Occasional* (London, Humph. Moseley, 1650), pp. 6–7; 'self-preserving,' *OED*, quoting Ezekiel Hopkins, bishop of Raphoe and Derry, "A Sermon" [on Peter ii 13, 14] preached at Christ's Church, Dublin, 1669.

11. John Prince, *Self-Murder Asserted to be a Very Heinous Crime* (London, B. Bragge, 1709), p. 9. Susannah Centlivre in *The Perjur'd Husband* (London, Bennett Banbury, 1700, p. 15) noted that "if I should betray/You, I bring my self into jeopardy, and of all Pleasures/Self-Preservation/Is the dearest." Anne Finch, most unusually, thought this the philosophy only of freethinkers; see *Free-Thinkers, a poem* (London, 1711).

12. Officer [Defoe, Daniel], *An Apology for the Army* (London, J. Carson, 1715), pp. 8–9.

13. [Bernard Mandeville], *An Enquiry into the Origins of Honour and the Usefulness of Christianity in War* [1732], 2nd. ed. with a new introduction by M. M. Goldsmith (London, Frank Cass, 1971), p. iv; Officer, *Apology*, p. 13.

14. Mandeville, *Origins of Honour*, p. 62; John Oldmixon, *A Defence of Mr. Maccartney* (London, A. Baldwin, 1712), p. 8.

15. Courtin, *Civility*, p. 251; Mackqueen, *Essay on Courage*, p. 1: "Among all the noble Qualities which adorn Mankind, there is none more Excellent in it self, more Illustrious in the Eyes of others, or more Beneficial to the World, than Courage or Valour."

16. Mandeville, *Origins of Honour*, p. 60; see also Thomas Hobbes, *English Works*, ed. Sir William Molesworth, 9 vols. (London, Bohn, 1839–45) 2:160.

17. Daniel Defoe, *The Review* VII, March 6, 1711, p. 590; see also Mandeville, *Origins of Honour*, p. 45. For other articulations of this notion of courage as the centerpiece of male virtue, see Addison in *The Spectator*, edited with an introduction and notes by Donald F. Bond, 3 vols. (Oxford, Clarendon, 1965) #99, June 23, 1711, 1: 416, and *The Man* #14, April 2, 1755, p. 3.

18. Archibald Campbell, *An Enquiry into the Original of Moral Virtue* (Edinburgh, Gavin Hamilton, 1733), p. 179; Henry Baker, "The Universe, A Philosophical Poem, Intended to restrain the Pride of Man," 2nd edition (London, J. Worrall, 1746), p. 6.

19. E. W., *Poems Written on Several Occasions, to which are added three essays* (London, J. Baker, 1711), p. 117, 120.

20. Courtin, *Civility*, p. 236–37; Hobbes, *Leviathan*, p. 200.

21. *GM*, January 1736, vol. 6, pp. 11–12.

22. Anthony Holbrook, *Christian Essays upon the Immorality of Uncleanness and Duelling delivered in two Sermons preached at St. Paul's* (London, John Wyat, 1727, p. 36). In his sermons Holbrook contrasted his own sense of honor as "an honest

Concern for the just Dignity of Human Nature" with that other sort, which was only self-regarding and self-serving. [Edward Ward] *Adam and Eve Stript of their Furbelows: or the Fashionable Virtues and Vices of Both Sexes, Exposed* (London, J. Woodward, 1714), pp. 201–5.

23. Francis Hutcheson, *An Inquiry into the Original of Our Ideas of Beauty and Virtue* (London, J. Darby, A. Bettesworth, 1726), p. 221; Thomas Hobbes, *The Elements of Law* [1650], ed. Ferdinand Tonnies (London, Simpkin, Marshall, 1889), pp. 34–35.

24. Mackqueen, *Essay on Honour*, p. 7. "True courage," argued Mackqueen, "is not the Exercise of an imperious, insolent Power, and going on in domineering, hectoring Language . . ."

25. Captain Abraham Clerke, *A Home-Thrust at Duelling intended as an answer to a late Pamphlet intitled A Hint on Duelling* (London, S. Bladon, 1753), pp. 14–15; Thomas Comber, *A Discourse upon Duels* (London, R. Wilkin, B. Tooke, 1720) p. 17.

26. *LM* September 1732, "Of Courage," p. 278. The essay was also reprinted in the *GM*, September 1732, p. 943. Few would have agreed with Mandeville that the flaws were as integral to the code as its virtues. In discussing the inevitability of duelling, for example, Mandeville argued that "to say, that those who are guilty of it go by false Rules, or mistake the Notions of Honour, is ridiculous; for either there is no Honour at all, or it teaches Men to resent Injuries and accept Challenges" (Mandeville, *Origin of Honour*, p. 219).

27. Timothy Hooker [John Hildrop], *An Essay on Honour* (London, R. Minors, 1741), p. 4, 15–16. *GM* September 1731, p. 375.

28. *GM* May 1737, p. 284; Mackqueen, *Essay on Honour*, p. 11.

29. Courtin, *Civility*, p. 230; *A Timely Advice, or Treatise of Play and Gaming* (London, Th. Harper, 1640), pref. Arguing paradoxically that honor and virtue were two entirely different things, Mandeville applauded the former's efficacy while derogating the latter: "The Invention of Honour has been far more beneficial to the Civil Society than that of Virtue, and much better answer'd the End for which they were invented (Mandeville, *Origin of Honour*, pp. 42–43.)

30. Hooker, *Essay on Honour*, p. 15; Holbrook, *Christian Essays*, pp. 33–34.

31. Duke of Wharton as cited in the *GM* September 1731, p. 383. It seems unlikely that Wharton in fact made this observation. He was a founder of the Hellfire Club, and his entry in the *Dictionary of National Biography* characterized his life as one of "reckless behavior" and "profligacy." Hooker also employs the comparison of a sick and healthy body: "But whatever Similitude there may seem to be betwixt *Pride* and *Honour, Ambition* and *true Greatness of Mind*, they are as far asunder as the Swelling of a Dropsy, from a full and robust Habit of Body." *Essay on Honour*, p. 44; for restatements of this thought, see [Theophilus Lobb], *Sacred Declarations or a Letter to the Inhabitants of London* (London, J. Buckland, 1753) p. 5; [François Vincent Troussaint], *Manners*, translated from the French (London, J. Payne & J. Boquet, 1749), p. 2.

32. Mandeville, *Origins of Honour*, p. 15, 40. Comber, *Discourse upon Duels*, p. 6, and *A Circumstantial and Authentic Account of a Late unhappy Affair* (London, J. Burd, 1765), p. 8; both agreed that modern honor was a "gothic" or Germanic invention.

33. Mandeville, *Origins of Honour*, p. 14; Berkeley, *Alciphron*, 3:112.

34. *An Essay on Modern Gallantry* (London, M. Cooper, 1750), p. 4; *A Timely Advice*, p. 34. The author of this pamphlet, citing St. Augustine, described the gamester as an idolater. "The Gamester therefore may be said to worship the Dice or Cards for his gods, seeing he loveth them more than God. . . ."

35. Well-wisher, *Honours Preservation Without Blood* (London, 1680), p. 25.

36. Mandeville, *Origins of Honour*, p. 2; see Courtin, *Civility*, "A Duel attacks directly the Sovereign Authority and is therefore High Treason," p. 272, and Hobbes, *Leviathan*, pp. 117, 120 for the notion that those who follow the dictates of honor deny the power of their sovereign.

37. *GM* May 1737, p. 284; Person of Quality, *Marriage Promoted* (London, Richard Baldwin, 1690), p. 46. Hooker, *Essay on Honour*, p. 21, also believed that for their own good and the nation's, irreligious immoral men "ought to be laid under proper restraints."

38. Jeremy Collier, "Upon Duelling" in *Essays upon several Moral Subjects* [1692] (London, R. Sare, H. Hindmarsh, 1698), p. 124; Comber, *Discourse Upon Duels*, p. 37.

39. Thus, in Mandeville's dialogue *The Origins of Honour*, when the interlocutor, Horatio, asks his companion, Cleo, how many of the gentlemen of his acquaintance would refuse a duel from Christian principles, and Cleo replies, "A great many, I hope," Horatio retorts: "You can hardly forbear laughing, I see, when you say it" (pp. 79–80).

40. *Timely Advice*, pref.; Well-Wisher, *Honours Preservation*, p. 18.

41. *GM* May 1737, p 286; John Brown, *On the Pursuit of False Pleasures and the Mischiefs of Immoderate Gaming* (Bath, James Leake, 1750), p. 12.

42. Joseph Trapp, *Royal Sin, or Adultery Rebuk'd in a Great King, a sermon delivered at St. Martin's* (London, J. Higgonson, 1738), p. 14.

43. Erasmus Mumford, *A Letter to the Club at Whites* (London, W. Owen, 1750), p. 7.

44. Alexander Jephson, *The henious sins of* ADULTERY *and* FORNICATION, p. 17.

45. Brown, *On the Pursuit of False Pleasures*, p. 14.

46. *An Address to the Great* (London, R. Baldwin, 1756), p. 9; Mandeville, *Origins of Honour*, p. 177; Thus the *Man*, a short-lived essay-periodical of the mid 1750s, argued that "It is of the highest consequence rightly to instruct the people in the nature of virtue, and fit them for society. The best and shortest way of instructing them is by the example of their superiors; whom they as naturally follow, as soldiers follow their leader, when they have a high opinion of his honesty and abilities" (May 7, 1755, p. 5).

47. *Reflexions on Gaming* (London, J. Barnes, 1750), p. 44; William Webster, *A Casuistical Essay on Anger and Forgiveness* (London, W. Owen, 1750), p. 75.

48. *GM* 1731, p. 428; Hooker, *Essay on Honour*, p. 14; see also *LM* July 1732, "Praise of Cowardice," pp. 175–76.

49. *LM* July 1732, pp. 186–87, September 1735, pp. 491–92.

50. Hooker, *Essay on Honour*, p. 18; Webster, *Casuistical Essay*, pp. 14–15.

51. The *Man* January 15, 1755, p. 2; *GM* February 1756, "The Advantages of Ancestry demonstrated," pp. 81–2.

52. Berkeley, *Alciphron*, 2nd Dialogue, 3:69; the *Man* November 19, 1755, p. 5.

53. Mackqueen, *Essay on Courage*, p. 9; *Modest Defense of Gaming* (London, R. & J. Dodsley, 1754), p. 23.

54. Toussaint, *Manners*, p. 1; *GM* May 1737, "The Character of a Man of Honour in the BEAU MONDE," pp. 284–85.

55. John Cockburn, *A Discourse of Self Murder* (London, 1716), p. 6; *Self-Murther and Duelling the Effects of Cowardice and Atheism* (London, R. Wilkin, 1728), p. 43. Not only were the two vices combined and discussed as one in the later work, but Cockburn himself produced *A History and Examination of Duels* just four years after his essay on suicide (London, G. Strahan, 1720).

56. *Timely Advice*, pp. 59, 62; the *Devil* March 1, 1755, p. 40.

57. Comber made the connection between duelling and suicide clear: " 'Tis true, in this case the Dueller falls by another's hand; but he ought to be accounted a Self-murtherer for all that; because he voluntarily and deliberately exposed himself to that Sword by which he fell." *Discourse upon Duels*, p. 13.

58. The *Man*, February 9, 1755, p. 3; *The Whole Art and Mystery of Modern Gaming* (London, J. Roberts, 1726), p. iv. The *LM* of 1735 concluded that "At present, Honour is a Man, a Cheat in Gaming, false to his Friend, a Betrayer of the Liberties of his Country, is maintain'd by—a lucrative Office" (p. 426. Note that the first vice mentioned, the root perhaps of all the rest, is gaming.

59. *The Connoisseur* (London, R. Baldwin, 1755–56), 2 vols., #50, January 9, 1755, 1:296; Jephson, *The heinous sins*, pp. 8–9; Oldmixon, *Defense*, p. 3.

60. Steele, *Spectator*, #75, May 26, 1711, pp. 323–25. Another definition of a gentleman can be found in the *Guardian* (2 vols., 1756) I, 20 April 1713, 146, "by a fine gentleman I mean a man completely qualified as well for the service and good as for the ornament and delight of society."

61. John Wesley, *The Works of the Rev. John Wesley*, 10 vols. (Philadelphia, D& S Neall, 1826–7), *The Journal*, November 1738, 3: 113.

62. *Spectator* #99, June 23, 1711, p. 416; the *Man* #14, April 2, 1755, p. 3.

63. Mandeville, *Origins of Honour*, p. 54; Keith Thomas, "The Double Standard," *Journal of the History of Ideas* 20 (2) (1959), pp. 195–216.

64. Hooker, *Essay on Honour*, p. 2; *Essay on Modern Gallantry*, p. 50.

65. Mandeville, *Origins of Honour*, pref. iii; see also Well-Wisher, *Honour's Preservation*, p. 4.

66. Chishull, *Against Duelling*, p. 5; Holbrook, *Christian Essays*, p. 38.

67. Clerke, *Home Thrust at Duelling*, p. 20. Anthony Fletcher points out that the earliest citation for the word 'masculinity' was in 1748. He notes that "It is not so much that masculinity was entirely different from manhood or manly behaviour, rather perhaps that the word attempted to express a more rounded concept of the complete man." *Gender, Sex, and Subordination in England, 1500–1800* (New Haven, Yale University Press, 1995), pp. 322–23; *The Gentleman instructed in the Conduct of a Virtuous and Happy Life*, 2 vols. (London, R. Ware, 1755), 1:24; the *Man*, March 12, 1755, #11, p. 3.

68. Mandeville, *Origins of Honour*, p. 210; Prince, *Self-Murder Asserted*, pp. 25–26.

69. Chishull, *Against Duelling*, p. 12; *GM* December 1731, p. 523.

70. Joshua Kyte, *Sermon*, "True Religion the only Foundation of true Courage" (London, B. Barker, 1758), pp. 5, 14. Kyte concluded that while many thought "Irreligion and Infidelity, drunkenness and Profaness, with all the appendages of riot and profligacy" necessary to the fighting man, he believed them to have no part of "the polite ingredients for the Military Character."

71. John Locke, quoted in Philip Carter, *Men and the Emergence of Polite Society 1660–1800* (Harlow, England, Longman, 2001), p. 55; Jonathan Swift, quoted ibid., pp. 68–69.

72. Fletcher notes "the gradual substitution from around the 1730s, of the world 'politeness' for the word 'breeding.' The new term indicates a much stronger focus than previously on external manners alone" (p. 336). See also Lawrence Klein, *Shaftesbury and the Culture of Politeness* (Cambridge, Cambridge University Press, 1994) for an in-depth articulation of the tenets of politeness. Carter, *Men and the Emergence*, has an interesting discussion on women's refining role, pp. 68–70.

73. *Essay on Gallantry*, p. 45. See also *Thoughts on Gallantry, Love and Marriage* (London, R. and J. Dodsley, 1754), p. 18.

74. Addison, *Spectator*, June 23, 1711, in *The Papers of Joseph Addison*, 4 vols. (Edinburgh, William Creech, 1790) 2:90; Berkeley, *Alciphron*, 3:70. In this dialogue, Berkeley tells the story of Lady Telesilla, who "made no figure in the world" until her husband introduced her to the ways of the *beau monde*. Thereupon she became a gambler, an extravagant spender, and in exchange for his instruction, gave her husband "an heir to his estate, [he] having never had a child before."

75. *CGJ* #66, October 28, 1752, pp. 350–51; Jephson, *The heinous sins*, p. 7.

76. For the culture of politeness see Lawrence E. Klein, *Shaftesbury and the Culture of Politeness*; "Politeness and the Interpretation of the British Eighteenth Century," *The Historical Journal*, Volume 45, Number 4 (2002), pp. 869–98; "The Polite Town: Shifting Possibilities of Urbanness, 1660–1715," in Tim Hitchcock and Heather Shore, eds., *The Streets of London* (London, Rivers Oram Press, 2003); and Philip Carter, *Men and the Emergence*.

77. The first part of this heading is quoted from the *Edinburgh Review* by Alexander Andrews, *The History of British Journalism* (London, Richard Bentley, 1859), p. 7; the second part is the title of a letter from "Theseus" to the editor of the *MC* (August 23, 1786), bemoaning the inclusion of great gobs of morality among the news.

78. George Crabbe, *The Poetical Works of the Rev. George Crabbe* (London, John Murray, 1838), vol. 2, p. 128. There were those who agreed with him, some, like "Carus" who wrote to the *Daily Courant* (November 14, 1732), arguing that newspapers were not the appropriate fora to discuss matters of high politics.

79. Edward Bearcroft, representing the plaintiff in the Howard *v* Bingham divorce cause, cited in the *Times*, March 6, 1794.

80. Andrews, *History of British Journalism*, pp. 99, 101.

81. Carter, *Men and the Emergence*, p. 25.

82. In terms of dates at which periodicals began, the 1730s saw the birth of 2 dailies, 1 tri-weekly, 4 weeklies, and 2 monthlies; between 1750 and 1770, 6 dailies, 2 tri-weeklies, and 7 monthlies were published. The seven monthlies mentioned were the *Gentleman's Magazine* (begun 1731), the *London Magazine* (1732), Samuel Johnson's *Rambler* (1750), the *Universal Magazine*, the *Annual Register*, the *Oxford Magazine* and *the Town and Country Magazine*.

83. For this book I have consulted more than 150 newspapers and magazines from the 1680s through the 1840s; about half of these cover the period 1760–1800. Robert

Louis Haig, *The Gazetteer, 1735–1797* (Carbondale, Southern Illinois University Press, 1960), p. 4. See also John Brewer, *Party Ideology*.

84. Haig, *Gazetteer*, p. 70, 71.

85. Bob Clarke, *From Grub Street to Fleet Street* (Aldershot, Ashgate Publishing, 2004), p. 86.

86. For recent histories of the roles of the coffeehouse see Markman Ellis, *The Coffee House: A Cultural History* (London, Weidenfeld & Nicholson, 2004), and Brian Cowan, *The Social Life of Coffee* (New Haven, Yale University Press, 2005). Ayton Ellis, in *The Penny Universities: A History of the Coffee-Houses* (London, Secker & Warburg, 1956) especially stresses their role as centers of discussion.

87. Haig, *Gazetteer*, p. 59.

88. *Connoisseur* #45, December 5, 1754, p. 268.

89. Victoria Glendinning, *Trollope* (London, Hutchinson, 1992), p. 399.

Chapter 2. *"That Wild Decision of the Private Sword"*

1. *A Full and Exact Relation of the Duel fought in Hyde park on Saturday November 15, 1712, between His Grace James, Duke of Hamilton, and the R.H. Charles Lord Mohun, in a letter to a member of Parliament* (London, E. Curll, 1713), p. 15.

2. Victor Stater, *High Life, Low Morals: The Duel that Shook Stuart Society* (London, John Murray, 1999).

3. The quotation that serves as title to this chapter comes from Chishull, *Against Duelling*, p. 5.

4. Anthony Holbrook, "The Obliquity of the Sin of Duelling," in *Christian Essays upon the Immorality of Uncleanness and Duelling delivered in two Sermons preached at St. Paul's* (London, John Wyat, 1727), pp. 33–34.

5. See for example a letter against duelling in the *LEP* April 25, 1765, in which its author discussed "the most effectual way to suppress this *devilish* custom"; ten years later the author of *Duelling, a poem* (London, T. Davies, 1775) argued that Satan was the father of both murder and duelling. Even in the late 1820s, following the Wellington/Winchilsea duel which will be discussed in chapter 6, the *Age* commented that the Duke should not have fought, no matter what the charges against him, but "seduced by Satan, he fell into a fleshly snare, and called for pistols . . ." [March 29, 1829].

6. Henry Fielding, *Amelia* [1754], ed. Martin C. Battesin (Oxford, Clarendon Press, 1983), p. 503.

7. For the growth of politeness and civility, see Markku Peltonen, "Politeness and Whiggism, 1688–1732," *Historical Journal* (2005) 2:391–414; John Brewer, "The Most Polite Age and the Most Vicious," in *The Consumption of Culture 1600–1800*, ed. Ann Bermingham and John Brewer (London, Routledge, 1995), pp. 341–61.

8. *The Spectator* #84, June 6, 1711, p. 359; four numbers of the *Spectator* mentioned duelling in its first year alone: #1, March 1, 1711; #2, March 2, 1711; #84, June 6, 1711; #99, June 23, 1711.

9. *White*, April 19, 1750; The *Duellist, or a cursory view of the rise, progress and practice of Duelling* (London, 1822), quoting *Spectator* #97, June 21, 1711; Carter, *Men and the Emergence of Polite Society*, p. 25.

10. Henry Fielding, *The History of Tom Jones, a foundling,* 6 vols. (London, A. Millar, 1749), 3:116–17.

11. See Susannah Centlivre, *The Beau's Duel* (London, D. Brown & N. Cox, 1702), p. 29; William Popple, *The Double Deceit* (London, T. Woodward & J. Wallace, 1736), and for yet another play, see John Kelly, *The Married Philosopher* (London, T. Worral, 1732), p. 70.

12. Samuel Richardson, *The History of Sir Charles Grandison* (London, S. Richardson, 1753–54); Richardson, *Clarissa or the History of a Young Lady,* 8 vols. (London, S. Richardson, 1751), 7: Letters LII–LIV; Eliza Haywood, *The History of Miss Betsy Thoughtless* [1751], ed. Christine Blouch (Broadview Literary Texts, Peterborough, Ont., 1998) and *The History of Jemmy and Jenny Jessamy* (London, T. Gardner, 1753); for Fielding, *Tom Jones.*

13. *Tatler,* #39, July 9, 1709, pp. 281–87.

14. For the Mohun-Hamilton duel, see *The Examiner,* November 13, 1712, Stater, *High Life, Low Morals,* and H. T. Dickinson, "The Mohun-Hamilton duel: Personal feud or Whig plot?" *Durham University Journal* (1965), pp. 159–65; for the Deering-Thornhill duel, see *An Account of the Life and Character of Sir Cholmley Deering, Bart* (London, J. Read, 1711), [Richard Steele] *The Spectator* #84, June 6, 1711, and Richard Thornhill, *The Life and Noble Character of Richard Thornhill* (London, 1711); for the Clarke-Innes duel, *GM* March 1750, p. 137, *Old England* May 12, 1750, *White* April 19, 1750; for Dalton-Paul, *GM* 1751, p. 234; and for the Byron-Chaworth duel, see *AR* 1765, pp. 208–12, *GM* 1765, pp. 196–97, 227–29. Only in the Pultney-Harvey duel do we read of the presence of seconds.

15. For the Andrews-Lee duel, see the *Universal Spectator* August 9, 1735; the duel between the Irish friends, ibid., January 22, 1737; the philosophical duel, which occurred in June 1721, was recounted as part of a letter to the *Universal Spectator* December 25, 1742.

16. For the Grey-Lempster duel see *GM* April 1752, p. 90.

17. See, for example, the *Protestant [Domestick] Intelligence* March 2, 1680; the *Daily Post* April 6, 1723; and the *Evening Post* September 29, 1724.

18. *Woman of Honour* (London, T. Lowndes and W. Nicholl, 1768), ii:131. See also *The Tatler* # 26, June 9, 1709, pp. 202–3: "I expect Hush-Money to be regularly sent for every Folly or Vice any one commits in this Town; and hope, I may pretend to deserve it better than a Chamber- Maid, or Valet de Chambre: They only whisper it to the little Set of their Companions: but I can tell it to all Men living, or who are to live."

19. *The Yale Edition of Horace Walpole's Correspondence,* ed. W. S. Lewis, 48 vols. (New Haven, Yale University Press, 1937–1983), To Mann, 14th May 1765, 22:293.

20. See *The Trial of Captain Edward Clarke for the Murder of Captain Thomas Innes in a duel in Hyde park, March 12, 1749* (London, M. Cooper, 1750). For more on this, see Nicholas Rogers, *Mayhem: Post-War Crime and Violence in Britain, 1748–1753* (New Haven, Yale University Press, 2012). My thanks to Dr. Rogers for clarifying this for me.

21. *Old England* #320, May 12, 1750; see also *White* April 19, 1750 and *GM* May 1750, pp. 219–20.

22. See for another instance of these sentiments, a poem written after this duel, *False Honour, or the Folly of Duelling* (London, A. Type, 1750), p. 9. For a fine analysis of

the difficulties faced by Army officers, see Arthur N. Gilbert, "Law and Honour among Eighteenth-Century British Army Officers," *Historical Journal* 19 (1976), 75–87.

23. See, for example *GM* November 17, 1762, p. 550, and May 23, 1763, p. 256. For Wilkes's own first duel with the Scots Lord Talbot, see John Sainsbury, " 'Cool Courage Should Always Mark Me': John Wilkes and Duelling," *Journal of the Canadian Historical Association*, 1997, pp. 19–33.

24. *LEP* April 25, 1765. The letter appeared on the paper's front page.

25. For these, see "S.Y.'s" letter in the *Gaz* March 4, 1765; the letter from "Bob Short" in the *LEP* April 13 and "Candidus's" reply ibid., April 18, 1765.

26. *LEP* April 25, 1765.

27. "WA," *PA* May 27, 1765; ibid., July 20, 1765, signed "Philanthropos"; ibid., August 2, 1765.

28. *GM*, vol. 35, May 1765, p. 229; *AR* 1765, Appendix to the Chronicle, p. 211.

29. *Tatler* #93, November 12, 1709, p. 83.

30. These phrases taken from a letter, "Thoughts on the unwritten Laws of Honour," published in the *GM* May 1769, pp. 240–41.

31. For Wilkes, see *PA* November 18, 1763, "An Epigram"; for Pitt, *MC* May 31, 1798.

32. *Fog's Weekly Journal*, January 30, 1731 did report the duel, naming names and giving details. See also M. Dorothy George, *Catalogue of Political and Personal Satires* (London, 1978), #2580, "A Parliamentary Debate in Pipes's Ground," p. 460.

33. *GM* October 1762; *PA* October 7, 1762; *LEP* October 5, 1762.

34. In my survey of the Burney collection of seventeenth- and eighteenth-century newspapers, I have found 7 duels in the eighty years between 1680 and 1759 attributed to political differences; in the decade 1760–1769, 16 duels attributed to such differences.

35. *LEP* November 15, 1763; *PA* November 18, 1763.

36. Letter signed "Timidus" in *LEP* November 19, 1763; see also ibid., November 24, 1763. This last letter, as well as that signed "Democritus" ibid., November 29, 1763, and one ibid., December 3, 1763, mentions Martin's failure to return Wilkes's letter as well as his target practice. The letter that appeared in the *PA* on November 30, 1763, and the *LEP* November 27, 1763, sounds as though it came from Wilkes himself.

37. The conversation between the wit and his friend is recounted in the *Gaz* December 24, 1770; *The Lady's Magazine* December 1770, p. 236 for their account of the duel. The *Gaz* (December 22, 1770) also reported that after the duel, Johnstone commented to Germaine that "I must declare that I now look upon the reflections (of cowardice) thrown out against your Lordship to be unjust, although at the time I spoke, I thought them well founded, and supported by the general opinion of mankind." *Walpole's Correspondence*, 18 December 1770, 23:256. Germaine's name at the time of Minden was Sackville; he changed it to Germaine upon inheriting the estate of Lady Betty Germaine.

38. *Gaz* December 26, 1770, see also *Bingley's* December 29, 1770.

39. The Fox-Adam duel was reported in the *MC* November 30, December 2, 3, 1779; the *LC* November 27, December 2, 1779; the *Gaz* November 30, December 1, 2, 1779; *Lloyd* December 1, 1779 and the *PA* December 2, 1779; the *GM* November 1779, p. 610 and the *AR* 1779, pp. 235–35; the poem to Fox appeared in the *Gaz* December 7, 1779. The Shelburne-Fullerton duel received coverage in the *MC* March 23, 24, 25, 27, 1780; the *Gaz* March 22, 23, 24, 1780; the *LC* March 23, 1780 and the *GM* March 1780, p. 151, 152.

40. Two pro-Fox letters, one signed "TW" and the other "WX," appeared in the *MC* December 7, and December 13, 1779. A third signed "JB," violently anti-Foxite, also appeared in the *MC* on December 15, 1779; I have italicized the words in the quote from this letter. "Right"'s letter also in that paper on January 5, 1780.

41. The three letters on the Shelburne-Fullerton affair: the first, signed "Heath Cropper," appeared in the *Gaz* March 29, 1780; the second, in the *LC*, March 24, 1780; and the third, signed "A little further" also in the *Gaz* April 1, 1780. For the comment on the impropriety of duels for parliamentarians, see the *T& C* letter to the *Observer*, signed "Anti-Duellist," October 1784, p. 532.

42. For the debates on duelling in the 1770s, see *MC* October 4, 30, 1773, *August 25, 1777, October 27, 1777, December 29, 1777, July 20, *27, 1778; *Gaz* October 17, *24, 1777, December 22, 1778. The four debates for which we have votes are indicated with *s.

43. The four debates on duelling after the Shelburne/Fullerton encounter can be found in the *LC* March* 24, April *3,* 10, 1780 and the *Gaz* April 1, 1780. The debates which specifically refer to this duel are indicated with *s.

44. *AR* vol. 23, 1780, pp. 150–52.

45. Ibid., p. 151.

46. William Wilberforce, *A Practical View of the Prevailing Religious System of Professed Christians* (London, T. Cadell jr. and W. Davies, 1797), p. 224.

47. *Times* March 2, 1792. These comments were made after a member was challenged for his Parliamentary remarks by a republican Irishman.

48. The *Observer* June 3, 1798; for other expressions of this, see the *Evening Mail* May 25, 1798, the *St. J* May 26, 1798.

49. See, for example, the *MH* May 29, 31, 1798; the *MC* May 30, 1798.

50. The *LP* May 28, 1798; the *MC* May 30, 1798; the *MH* June 2, 1798.

51. The only newspaper I have found that made these sorts of negative comments was the *Weekly Register* (May 30, 1798) "We have repeatedly lamented that a practice so lamentable to civilization, and so criminal in the eyes of God, should be permitted in this country; but that it should receive the sanction of persons so high in office as Mr. Pitt, and that the Sabbath should be appropriate to this horrid practice, can never be sufficiently regretted."

52. For Hodgson's remarks, see the *MC* June 1, 1798; "The Ballad of Putney-Heath" in the *MH* June 4, 1798 and the *LP* June 1, 1798; the *MH* May 31, 1798. The *St. J* of May 29, 1798 argued that there was "no cure for this sort" of offence "but by fire and sword."

53. The *Sun* May 29, 1798, *MC* May 31, 1798.

54. The *Evening Post* June 4, 1798 and the *GEP* June 5, 1798; the *MC* June 4, 1798.

55. Thomas Perceval, *Moral and Literary Dissertations* (Warrington, W. Eyres, 1789), "True and False Honour," p. 28.

56. Of the 311 duels I have notice of for the 1780s, more than half (169) involved at least one member of the armed forces and in a little less than a quarter (76) of the cases, both duellists were military or naval men. Of course, this is very impressionistic, since press descriptions of all duellists are vague and often inaccurate.

57. "XY" in *LEP* September 28/October 1, 1781.

58. The *LP* April 21, 1783; the *MH* April 26, 1783. See the press commendation of such action following the Macartney-Stuart duel in the *Times* June 13, 1786.

59. For similar cases, see *MH* February 2, 1785; *Times* December 21, 1787; ibid., August 4, 1788; ibid., September 21, 1791; *GM* supplement 1805, pp. 1223–24.

60. *MH* April 26, 1783; *GM* 1783, p. 302.

61. The *GM* 1783, p. 443; the *GEP* May 1, 1783; the *LP* May 2, 1783; the *MC* May 2, 1783.

62. The *MC* April 26, 1783; the *GM* 1783, p. 485.

63. The *LP* April 25, 1783; the story about Adolphus appeared in both the *GEP* May 1, 1783 and the *LP* May 5, 1783.

64. The *LP* May 7, 1783.

65. This column, called "Clotted Cream" and signed "Lac Mihi" was an ongoing series. For the one inspired by the Riddell/Cunningham duel see the *MC* April 26, 1783. The essay in the *LP* of May 14, 1783 appeared under the heading "The Companion"; Number CXXVII and was called "Duelling." This last quote appeared in the *Gaz* May 6, 1783.

66. See Andrew, *London Debating Societies 1776–99*, #909, p. 155. Eleven debates on duelling took place in London during the 1770s and sixteen occurred there in the 1780s.

67. This duel was reported in the *MH*, the *MP*, the *MC* September 5, 1783 and the *GM* September 1783, p. 801; the coroner's inquest following it in the *MC* September 9, 1783. The exculpatory note is in the *MP* September 11, 1783. For another bloody duel, the second that the two combatants had engaged in, fought about the American campaign, see the *St. J* August 3, 1784; the *White* August 3, 1784, the *MC* August 3, 1784, the *PA* August 3, 1784, and *FFBJ* August 6, 1784; the *LC* August 7, 1784 and the *Gaz* August 6, 1784 with the *GM* reporting the meeting in its August 1784 issue, p. 634.

68. Thus in the April 27, 1765 issue of the *LEP*, that paper reported that "It is said that duelling will be made a capital offence, without distinction of persons, with regard to the aggressor." Pharamond's edict proposed in the *MC* September 16, 1783 and in the *MP* September 17, 1763; for legislative changes, see the *MH* September 12, 1783 and for the Bishop of London's bill, ibid., September 15, 1783. A month latter, the *MH* reported that 'We are well assured that the practice of duelling has become an object of Royal consideration, and that the Secretary of State will have orders to deliver a message to Parliament respecting it' (October 24, 1783). Needless to say, there is no evidence for this in the public record.

69. The five letters on this duel appeared in the *MC* September 8, 1783 signed "Humanitas," September 9, 1783 signed "A Constant Reader," September 13, and 24, 1783 signed "Scrutator" (the quoted sections are from the second Scrutator letter) and the *MP* September 10, 1783.

70. The *AR* October 17, 1783, p. 219; see also *Gaz* October 21, 29, 1783.

71. An example of the acceptance of duelling as the best of a set of bad alternatives can be seen in the comment of the *Times* of February 8, 1785, if duelling were to be strongly punished by the law, "something little short of Italian assassination may succeed to the generosity and manliness of the English duel."

72. The first phrase, "established etiquette," was used by Lieutenant Samuel Stanton, author of *The Principles of Duelling with Rules to be Observed in every particular respecting it* (London, T. Hookham, 1790), pp. 6–7, to describe the necessity that the gentleman are under for giving and accepting challenges to fight, while the second, used by Rev. Peter Chalmers in *Two Discourses on the sin, danger and remedy of duelling*

(Edinburgh, Thomsons, Brothers, 1822), p. 165, argued that with a such a change men would no longer engage in such rencounters.

73. Jonathan Swift, quoted in the *AR* 1762, p. 166; *A Hint on Duelling*, p. 5.

74. The duel near Kensington was reported in *Lloyd* (June 19, 1775), the *Mdsx* and *St.J* (June 20, 1775), the *MP* (June 21, 1775), and the *CM* (June 24, 1775); the duel at Hyde Park reported in *Lloyd* (September 30, 1795), the *Courier and Evening Gazette* (October 2, 1795), and the *Telegraph* (October 5, 1795).

75. The *MP* January 11, 1775; the *Times* July 29, 1786.

76. The *Times* November 11, 1786; *MP* November 3, 1786.

77. For others wishing only satirical or ridiculous duelling items to appear, see both the *LP* June 7, 1782 and the *PA* November 9, 1786. For the mock duel between Jerry Puff, hairdresser, and Jack Grimface, chimneysweep, the *Times* November 4, 1786. Two years later, a similar mock duel appeared in the *Times* (January 18, 1788), recounting the battle between "Monsieur Stew-frog, head cook to Lord Bayham . . . [and] Roast Beef, head cook to Lord Howe." An impression of the increased coverage can be seen in the rising number of duels and related items in the press; in the 1760s I have found 677 accounts in 20 magazines and papers, and in the 1770s, 1758 accounts in 33 similar works.

78. The *Times*, June 25, 1789.

79. *Thoughts on Duelling* (Cambridge, J. Archdeacon, 1773), pp. 3–5; the *MP* October 23, 1777; William Jackson, *30 Letters on various subjects*, 2 vols. (London, T. Cadell, 1784) 1:12–13; *Gaz* December 22, 1784.

80. The original account of Johnston's trial can be found in the *Times*, April 29, 1788, and the two items arguing for the incapacity of legal means to address slurs to gentlemanly honor, in the *Times*, May 1 and May 2, 1788.

81. *T&C* January 1779, letter to "the Man of Pleasure," pp. 27–29; *A Short Treatise upon the Propriety and Necessity of Duelling* (Bath, 1779), pp. 21–22.

82. The *AR* 1780, pp. 150–52, gives an account of debate in the House of Commons, in which "a gentleman in high office" commented that duelling "would teach gentlemen to confine themselves within proper limits"; the *Gaz* November 5, 1783, who argued that duelling "prevails most in those polite nations where the sense of honour is most refined"; the *MH* November 1, 1783, "The *spirit* of duelling is a *purifier*, and may rid the world of many plagues"; two letters to the *Times* February 7, and February 21, 1785; a letter to the *GM* June 1788, p. 485.

83. Stanton, *The Principles of Duelling*, pp. 29, 35, 4. See also Stephen Payne Adye, *A Treatise on Courts Martial* (London, J. Murray, 1778), p. 32.

84. William Eden, *Principles of Penal Law* (London, B. White, 1771), pp. 223–26; Old Officer, *Cautions and Advices to Officers of the Army* (Edinburgh, Aeneas Mackay, 1777), pp. 149–50; "Scrutator" in the *MC* September 13, 1783; the *Gaz* October 31, 1783.

85. "Tiresias," letter to the *Times*, August 18, 1789; Thomas Jones, *A Sermon upon Dueling* (Cambridge, J. Archdeacon, 1792.), p. 5; the *Times* September 4, 1786. For the connection between duelling and barbarity see also the *MC* September 5, 1780, the *Times* September 1, 1787 and August 18, 1789; for duelling and politeness, comments in the *MP* September 30, 1784, *An Essay on Duelling, written with a view to discountenance this barbarous and disgraceful practice* (London, J.

Debrett, 1792), pp. 29–30, and Edward Barry, *Theological, Philosophical and Moral Essays*, 2nd ed. (London, J. Connor [1797?]), p. 94. "Tiresias," letter to the *Times*, August 18, 1789; Jones, *A Sermon upon Dueling*, p. 5; *Times*, September 4, 1786.

86. The *LP* May 2, 1783; *Thoughts on Duelling*, p. 7.

87. For a later example of the notion that potential duellists should become brave soldiers, see "Tiresias," *Times*, August 18, 1789, who noted that such acts would allow intrepidity to "receive the praises of their bravery without a blush." For the role of such bravery directed against pre-revolutionary France, see Jonas Hanway, *Virtue in Humble Life*, 2 vols. (London, J. Dodsley, 1774), 1:218; Elizabeth Bonhote, *The Parental Monitor*, 4 vols. (London, Wm. Lane, 1796), 4:213.

88. *Times* October 29, 1785 and April 3, 1786, *MH* November 2, 1786; *Times* September 4, 1786.

89. M. J. Sedaine, *The Duel*, trans. William O'Brien (London, T. Davies, 1772), p. 6. See also the Prologue to William Kenrick, *The Duellist* (London, T. Evans, 1773), "Nay, arrant cowards, forc'd into a fray,/Now fight, because they fear to run away." William Cowper noted of duelling "That men engage in it compelled by force,/And fear not courage is its proper source" ("Conversation" in *Poems* (London, J. Johnson, 1782), pp. 220–22.

90. *Duelling, a poem* (London, T. Davies, 1775), p. 18; Samuel Hayes, *Duelling, a poem* (Cambridge, J. Archdeacon, 1775), p. 9. Hayes called the father of duelling Moloch, not Satan, but I take these just to be different names for the same malignant spirit; Gentleman of that City, *Modern Honour or the Barber Duellist, A comic opera in two acts* (London, J. Williams, 1775), p. 27, see also H. H. Brackenridge, "Answer to a Challenge," in *Gazette Publications* (Carlisle, Printed by Alexander & Phillips, 1806), p. 20, "Besides; the thing is now degraded/ The lowest classes have invaded/The duel province."

91. Miles Peter Andrews, *The Reparation* (London, Printed for T. and W. Lowndes [etc.], 1784), pp. 70–72; John Burgoyne, *The Heiress* (Dublin, John Exshaw, 1786), pp. 67–70.

92. *Times* March 13, 1792. This is a reference to the action of the Earl of Coventry in complaining of a young challenger to the House of Lords.

93. For the Coventry-Cooksey contretemps and laudatory comments, *Times* March 13, 1792; for more on the issue, see the *Times* March 17 and 27, 1792. The *AR* of February 1769, p. 72, carried the only account I have been able to find of the Meredith challenge; for a letter hostile to Coventry see "A Clergyman," the *Gaz* May 6, 1769 and Haig, *Gazetteer*, p. 76; for a positive, laudatory letter see "A Freeman of Liverpool" in the *Mdsx* May 9, 1769.

94. Antony E. Simpson has argued that "few misdemeanor arrests or prosecutions occurred in this period" though he mentions in passing, that four potential duellists were charged £600, "a huge amount," to keep the peace. We have seen that legal recourse, whether through magistrates' arrests or cases at King's Bench, grew at the end of the eighteenth century, and that much larger sums than £600 were required as bail. For our story, however, one element that is importantly neglected by Simpson in his fine study is the role of the press in publicizing such options ("Dandelions on the Field of Honour: Dueling, the Middle Classes, and the Law in Nineteenth-Century England," in *Criminal Justice History*, 1988, pp. 99–155).

95. From 1730 through 1759 I have found 6 reports of men taking challengers to court; see the *British Journal* November 14, 1730, the *Echo* February 10, 1730, the *British Journal, or the Traveller* February 20, 1731, the *DA* October 12, 1743, the *LEP* April 26, 1744 and *Old England* May 25, 1751. The case of a man challenged going to the magistrates was reported in the *MP* on November 17, 1778. For a typical case of a duel stopped by the magistrates because "notice had been given" see the *LC* March 3, 1764. For another discussion of these challenges see Stephen Banks, *A Polite Exchange of Bullets* (Woodbridge, Boydell & Brewer, 2010), pp. 154–66.

96. See, for example, the Shaw/Delaval case, reported in the *Times* February 11, 1799; the Cavendish/Bembric case, ibid., February 1, 1800; the Payne/Beevor case, ibid., February 3, 1800, and the Stodthard/Prentice case, ibid., January 26, 1802.

97. Seventeen of the 103 reported King's Bench cases received at least two notices; a very small number, however, were more fully covered—three, four, six, and even seven accounts (the last in the case of the notorious Lord Camelford) occasionally occurred.

98. The earliest of these complaints to the magistrates can be found in the *World*, March 17, 1786; the *Times* July 22, 1786 and March 19, 1787.

99. It was reported that the Duke of Norfolk and Sir John Honeywood were on the brink of a duel, until reconciled by their friends (*Times* April 4, 1791); that the impending duel between the Earl of Belfast and Lord Henry Fitzgerald was stopped by the intervention of the Earl's uncle (*Times* April 14, 1791). For the Scottish courts, see *Times* March 24, 1790 and July 15, 1805; and for the apology of a drunk officer to John Rolle, MP and Colonel of a militia unit, which terminated the conflict, see the *Times* September 10, 1791.

100. The initial notice, under the Law Reports, King's Bench heading, appeared in the *Times*, February 1, 1800; "Anti-Duellist's" letter was published on February 12, 1800. Interestingly enough, though Cavendish refused to fight Bembric, he was a second (to Earl Fitzwilliam) in an interrupted duel five years earlier; see *Times* June 30, 1795.

101. See, for example, the court case brought by the Solicitor General, Sir John Scott, against Robert Mackreth, MP, for issuing a challenge, *Times* February 26, 1793, or Christopher Saville, M.P.'s suit against G. Johnstone M.P., *Times* January 25, 1802. The Earl of Darnley brought his former friend and relation, the Honourable Robert Bligh, to court a number of times for sending challenges or attempting to provoke a duel; for some of these see *Times* April 24, 1801 and August 15, 1805. There was also a suit in King's Bench in which a Mr. Robert Knight charged his brother-in-law, the son of Lord Dormer, with sending him a letter which attempted to provoke a duel, *Times* November 27, 29, 1805.

102. See *Times* June 30, 1795.

103. For Craven's appearance before the magistrates, see *Times* August 15, 1799; for St. Vincent and Orde, *Times* October 5 and October 8, 1799.

104. *Times* March 29, 1798.

105. For the Opera scuffle, see *Times* April 2, 1796; for the Newbon-Gibbons almost-duel, ibid., August 11, 1798.

106. *Times* February 3, 1800.

107. Ibid., September 30, 1796.

108. For the report of seconds being charged £200 see the *Times* August 12. 1806; those charged £500 each were reported in the *Observer* August 3, 1800.

109. *Times* May 4, 1785.

110. See ibid., February 20, 1799.

111. Ibid., June 2, 1794.

112. Ibid., February 5, 1798.

113. Ibid., November 20, 1798.

114. Ibid., February 11, 1799.

115. This fourth case can be found ibid., February 20, 1799. Kenyon's self-characterization came in a case reported ibid., November 11, 1796.

116. On Erskine overpowered, see ibid., November 25, 1799, and Erskine on the other side, ibid., February 7, 1799.

117. Ibid., February 11, 1799.

118. Ibid., June 11, 1801; January 26, 1802.

119. Ibid., November 22, 1796, and the ruling on January 27, 1797; for the gallant naval Captain, ibid., November 23, 1799.

120. Part of the address of Captain Macnamara to the jury, at his trial in 1803, for the murder of Colonel Montgomery in a duel; see Lorenzo Sabine, *Notes on Duels and Duelling* (Boston, Crosby, Nichols, 1855), pp. 247–49.

121. Lord Ellenborough made this remark at a case brought to King's Bench, in which both the challenger and challenged were merchants; see *Times* November 27, 1812.

122. For Lauderdale/Arnold duel, see ibid., July 2, 1792; for Norfolk/Malden duel, ibid., April 30, 1796, and for the Irish duel between A. Montgomery of Conway, Esq. and Sir Samuel Hayes of Drumboe, Bart., ibid., October 19, 1797.

123. *Times* March 2, 1792. For the Lauderdale/Richmond quarrel, see ibid., June 5 and June 6, 1792.

124. The *Times*, the *Courier*, and the *MC* reported the incident, but made no condemnatory comment about the duel itself. A very trenchant satirical poem, *The Battle of the Blocks*, was published shortly afterwards, a few lines of which deserve to be cited: "If this be honour, what is sense of shame?/If this be virtue, who shall murd'rers blame?" (London, Maxwell & Wilson, 1809, p. 14).

125. In his article, "Dandelions on the Field of Honour" Antony Simpson includes a chart of reports of duels which he has assembled from contemporary accounts. He has included in this chart all "duels reported in Britain, or involving Britons overseas." Thus, for the years under consideration, he has found a greater number than I have. Probably the difference comes about in the scope of my search (I have eliminated all duels of Britons abroad) and the sources I've used to find such accounts (a reading of the eighteenth-century press combined with the utilization of the digitalized version of the *Times* of London).

126. For the Macnamara-Montgomery duel, see *Times* April 7, 1803, and for a "copy-cat" duel, resembling this first, and fought for the same motive, *Times* September 23, 1803. For the duel because of the billiard quarrel, see *Times* May 25, 1797. Lord Falkland, a Captain in the Royal Navy, called a Mr. Powell by "the familiar appellation of *Pogey*" and a duel followed, *Times* March 2, 1809. The duel about the girl occurred in Portsmouth, and was reported ibid., October 14, 1812.

127. As early as 1790, the press reported military trials in which officers challenged their superiors, and in which, in all cases, the challengers were found guilty, and faced a variety of punishments. Lieutenant Edwards challenged his Captain and was broke by a naval court, *Times* March 10, 1790; a naval tribunal found two men guilty for having challenged a Lieutenant Ferguson, ibid., December 30, 1791; a court-martial was held in Dublin against two Army Captains for having delivered a challenge, and being the challenger of the Earl of Bellamont, ibid., July 29, 1796; three young military men taken to Bow Street for challenging their Captain, ibid., October 3, 1797.

128. For the case of Major Armstrong, heavily punished for having challenged his superior officer, General Coote, to a duel, see ibid., June 21, 1800, and June 11, 1801. The King's letter can be read ibid., July 8, 1800.

129. Rowland Ingram, *Reflections on Duelling* (London, J. Hatchard, 1804), pp. 98–99; Samuel Romilly, *Times* February 26, 1805; [John Taylor Allen] *Duelling, an Essay* (Oxford, S. Collingwood, 1807), pp. 19–20.

130. Rev. William Butler Odell, *Essay on Duelling, in which the subject is Morally and Historically Considered; and the practice deduced from the Earliest Times* (Cork, Odell and Laurent, 1814), p. 27.

131. Thus in 1823, George Buchan, in his *Remarks on Duelling; comprising observations on the arguments in defense of that practice* (Edinburgh, Waugh and Innes), argued that "It is an interesting thing, what greatly distinguishes the age in which we live, to see many officers, both naval and military, who now dare to be singular on such points [challenges to duel], and who now live under impressions little known a few years ago. This number is every year on the increase . . ." To newspaper readers, the incidence of reports of duels in the press might have seemed to suggest a similar decline, though the rate of this varied with the paper read:

Number of duels reported

	1790–99	1800–09	1810–19
Morning Chronicle	71*	107	79
Morning Post	125*	161	125
Times	137	99	38

* 1790 missing
Compiled from the British Newspapers 1600–1900 database, and the Times Digital Archive.

Chapter 3. *Against "Nature, Religion and Good Manners"*

1. *T&C* December 1773, "Essay on Suicide," p. 455.

2. The chapter title is taken from Thomas Knaggs, *A Sermon against Self-murder* (London, H. Hills, 1708), p. 2.

3. E. Arwaker, *Aesop: Truth in Fiction*, 4 vols. (London, J. Churchill 1708), "Fable XVII; The Fox and Sick Hen"; John Locke, *Two Treatises on Government*, ed. P. Laslett (New York, Mentor, 1963), p. 413.

4. *Populousness with Economy* 1757, pp. 21–22; David Mallet, *Mustapha* (London, A. Millar 1739), p. 134; John Herries, *An Address to the Public on the frequent and enormous crime of suicide*, 2nd. ed. (London, John Fielding, 1781), p. 3; advertisement for "Warren's only True Milk of Roses for the Skin," in the *Gaz* January 28, 1778.

5. *The Occasional Paper: Number X.* "Concerning self-murder. with some reflexion upon the verdicts often brought in of non compos mentis, in a letter to a friend" (London, M. Wotton, 1698), p. 35; John Jeffery, *Felo de Se: or a Warning against the most Horrid and Unnatural Sin of Self-Murder in a Sermon* (Norwich, A & J Churchill, 1702), pp. 13–14; *Self-murther and duelling*, p. 3. The Rev. Matthew H. Cooke, in his *The Newest and Most Complete Whole Duty of Man* (London, [1733?]), followed his essay on the evil of suicide (pp. 118–21) with one on the evils of duelling (pp. 121–23); similarly Caleb Fleming's *A dissertation upon the unnatural crime of Self-Murder, occasioned by the many late instances of suicide in this city* (London, Edward and Charles Dilly, 1773, p. 21), followed his discussion of suicide with a similar analysis of duelling. For a later comment on the conjunction, see "A Poor Man's" letter to the *Gaz* April 4, 1775.

6. Michael MacDonald & Terence R. Murphy, *Sleepless Souls* (Oxford, Clarendon Press, 1990), p. 184.

7. *Occasional Paper*, p. 10.

8. 'The Tragedy of Hamlet, Prince of Denmark" in *Shakespeare's Tragedies* (London, J. M. Dent, 1925), Act V, Sc. 1, p. 559.

9. *Occasional Paper*, p. 34; *Self-murther and duelling*, p. 6.

10. John Henley, *Cato condemned, or the case and history of self-murder argu'd and displayed at large, on the principles of reason, justice, law, religion, fortitude, love of ourselves and our country, and example; occasioned by a gentleman of Gray's inn stabbing himself in the year 1730, A theological lecture, delivered at the Oratory* (London, J. Marshall, 1730), pp. 6–7; Jeffery, *Felo de Se*, p. 9; the *London Journal* August 15, 1724, letter signed "Theophilus."

11. *London Journal* August 15, 1724, letter signed "Theophilus"; *Occasional Paper*, p. 2; Zachary Pearce, *A Sermon on Self-murder* [1736], 3rd edition (London John Rivington, 1773), p. 5.

12. Knaggs, *Sermon*, p. 6; Henley, *Cato condemn'd*, p. 4. See also Zachary Pearce, *Sermon on Self-murder*, p. 13, and *Occasional Paper*, p. 10.

13. See MacDonald and Murphy, *Sleepless Souls*, pp. 306–7. At times, it appears that they wish to have their cake and eat it; after arguing that polite society rejected supernatural appeals (and one would certainly think that university-educated clergymen might fit into this category) they note (p. 164) that "Even [clergy]men like Francis Ayscough and John Cockburn, who conjured with the name and shape of Satan, relied heavily on philosophical arguments in their sermons." Are Ayscough and Cockburn here being blamed for invoking the Devil, or for employing philosophical arguments? At other times they show more wariness about what sorts of people continued to believe in the instigation of Satan, (see p. 211).

14. *LM* March 1762, p. 145; *Occasional Paper*, p. 33. Samuel Johnson agreed, arguing that human desires and impulses "though very powerful, are not resistless; nature may be regulated, and desires governed." *The Rambler* #151, August 27, 1751.

15. *Occasional Paper*, p. 4.

16. The occasional comment on the weather does appear, such as in the article "Of Self-Murder" copied from the *Universal Spectator* and reprinted in the *LM* August 1732, p. 251. The much-copied letter on "Suicide and Self-Murder," which first appeared in the *Weekly Register* of April 29, 1732, was reprinted in both the *LM* of April 1732, p. 32, and the *GM* of the same month and year, pp. 714–15; *Occasional Poems* (London, 1726), p. 22. Addison's hero was Cato the younger, who killed himself; *Self-Murther and Duelling*, p. 7.

17. *The Universal Spectator*, April 13, 1734, p. 1; in 1736, a correspondent wrote to the *Prompter* (in an article later reprinted in the *GM* January 1736, p. 13, which is cited here) asking if his motives to suicide were not as admirable and justifiable as Cato's. While Cato's suicide had some admirers and many mitigators in the eighteenth century, it also had some fierce condemnations; see for example *Paradise regained, or the battle of Adam and the Fox* (London, J. Bew, 1780), p. 13; Richard Hey, *Three Dissertations on the Pernicious Effects of Gaming (1783), on Duelling (1784) and on Suicide (1785)* (Cambridge, J. Smith, 1812), pp. 3–4, William Combe, *The Suicide* from *The English Dance of Death*, 2 vols. (London, J. Diggens, 1815), 2: 11.

18. Knaggs, *A Sermon*, p. 14; *GM* 1756, p. 18; MacDonald and Murphy, *Sleepless Souls*, p. 202.

19. For a clear exposition of the philosophic deist view of suicide in this period, see MacDonald and Murphy, *Sleepless Souls*, pp. 150–64. *LM* July 1737, p. 375; Jeffery, *Felo de Se*, p. 17; *GM* April 1762, the lead article of that month, entitled "A Letter to a Friend, on Suicide and Madness," p. 151; thanks for this reference to Randall McGowen.

20. This account of the deaths of the Smiths is taken from the report in the *LM* April 1732, pp. 37–38. Their deaths were also reported at considerable length in the *GM* of that month, pp. 722–23. This latter report is eerily detailed, noting the cleanliness of the Smiths' clothes, the rope with which they hanged themselves, as well as the fact that Mrs. Smith was seven months pregnant. Both magazines also reprinted a letter on self-murder, first published in the *Weekly Register*, which the *GM* claimed (p. 714), was occasioned by "a late tragical catastrophe" and then cited the Smith suicides. See also MacDonald and Murphy, *Sleepless Souls*, pp. 157–58, 204–5.

21. Voltaire, *The Works of Voltaire*, 25 vols. (London, J. Newbery, 1761), 10: 31–32. Richard Hey, *Dissertation on Suicide*, p. 20. For another reference to this case, in an essay published just after the Budgell suicide, see *LM* May 1737, "On English Suicide," from *Fog's Journal*, pp. 289–90. See also MacDonald and Murphy, *Sleepless Souls*, pp. 319–21. Although the count of articles is unscientific and impressionistic, of the four vices covered in this book, accounts and discussions of suicide in the 1730s are a larger proportion of the total number of such items than similar discussions for the other vices in that decade.

22. Barbara Gates, *Victorian Suicide: Mad Crimes and Sad Histories* (Princeton, Princeton University Press, 1988) pp. 82–83; *GM* 1737, pp. 315–16; *LM* 1737, p. 274, see also the reference to the Budgell death, *GM* July 1737, p. 375. For Johnson, see George Birkbeck Hill, ed., *Boswell's Life of Johnson*, 6 vols. (Oxford, Clarendon, 1887), 2:228–29. The suicide of Fanny Braddock, the third suicide much discussed in the eighteenth-century press, will be considered in chapter five.

23. MacDonald and Murphy, *Sleepless Souls*, p. 301. Though this chapter is, in many ways, a contrary interpretation of the impact of suicide on popular opinion in

eighteenth-century Britain, I would like to express my appreciation for the magisterial quality of their book, and for the assistance it has afforded me in thinking about this difficult subject.

24. Ibid. MacDonald and Murphy argue that "the style and tone of newspaper stories about suicides promoted an increasingly secular and sympathetic attitude to self-killing." I find few grounds for such a conclusion.

25. All cases cited come from *Fog's Weekly Journal* of 1731; the Hunter and Clarke stories are found in the January 2, 1731 edition, the Shelton death in that of April 10, 1731. For a death which cites discontent of mind, see the report of the death of Evan Lewis in the March 20, 1731 edition.

26. *LEP* July 4, 1765. *Lloyd* July 5, 1765, noted that, in their column listing deaths, "His Grace the Duke of Bolton, Mq. of Winchester and premier Marquis of England, at his house in Grosvenor Square." Horace Walpole to Mann, *Correspondence*, vol. 22, p. 312. For Scarborough, see *LM* 1740, p. 101, *GM* 1740, p. 37. The *London Daily Post* January 1, 1740 and the *LEP* January 29, 1740 reported his death as due to "an apoplecktick fit." A review of a pamphlet "A Dialogue in the Elysian fields, between two Dukes," in the July 1765 edition of the *GM*, p. 341, which only includes initials, hints that B – n (or Bolton) killed himself because he was refused an army posting. For Walpole's comment on the use of "sudden" to indicate a suicide, see *Correspondence*, vol. 24, Letter to Mann 28 November 1779, p. 536.

27. *GM* September 1760, pp. 399–400, 404.

28. *Lloyd* June 28, 1765; I have not been able to locate this case elsewhere; *GM* September 10, 1765, p. 440; this story was also covered in the *LM* September 1765, p. 485; *GM* September 17, 1765, p. 441; *GM* October 30, 1765, p. 535; *LM* December 1765, p. 643. The rather mundane story was about the suicide of a Mr. Howard, a "schoolmaster and clerk of parish of Cambridgeshire" who, after killing a Mr. Webb who was attempting to seize his possessions for debt, cut his own throat. See *LM* November 1765, p. 596.

29. "Belinda's" letter to the *MC* December 15, 1775; "AB's" letter to the *Westminster Magazine* October 1775, pp. 524–25; review of Warton's poems in the *GM* 1777, vol. 47, pp. 70–71; for their view of Blair, Warton, and the influence of "the graveyard poets" see MacDonald and Murphy, *Sleepless Souls*, p. 193.

30. See *Gaz* January 22, 1770; *GM* 1770, p. 47. See also, for reiterations, *PA* January 22, 1770, *Mdsx* January 20, 1770, *LM* 1770, p. 53. The epitaph appeared in the *GM* p. 60 and the *LM* p. 61 of January 1770.

31. *MC* November 24, 25, 1774; *LC* November 24, 1774; *GM* 1774, p. 542; *LM* 1774, p. 562; the letter in *MC* November 28, 1774.

32. *T&C* May 1778, "A Dialogue in the Shades," pp. 243–44; *GM* 1789, pp. 1080–81, "Reflections on the Laws concerning Suicide" by "J. A." The rebuke to Kippis came in a letter by "Academicus," published in the *GM* 1785, p. 260.

33. Forrest's obituary appeared in the *GM* November 1784, pp. 877–78, "HOC's" critical response in the same journal, December 1784, pp. 963–64.

34. *Gaz* August 17, 19, 20, 1776; *MP* August 19, 20, 1776. The *GM* (vol. 46, August 1776, p. 383) referred to him as the Hon. C, son to Lord C.

35. Both the *GM* August 1776, p. 383 and the *Gaz* August 19, 1776 noted his fiscal worth and the *Gaz* also reported the company that Damer kept just before the fatal shot;

the debt was reported by the *Gaz* and the *MP* August 20, 1776, as were comments on the annuities he had granted. The *GM* had described him as "eccentric" and the explanations in the *MP* came on consecutively on August 19 and 20, 1776. MacDonald and Murphy also discuss Damer's suicide, but in a different context, see *Sleepless Souls*, p. 280.

36. The briefest notices of his death are found in the *LC* November 5, 1774; the *LM* 1774, p. 592, the *PA* November 8, 1774 and the *MP* November 9, 1774. "The Character of a Placeman" with a very complete description of Bradshaw's career, appeared in the December 1774 issue of the *LM*, pp. 591–92.

37. For Powell's death, see *MH* May 28, 1783, *GM* 1783, p. 454, p. 539, "X.Y.," "Anecdotes of the late Mr. Powell" and pp. 612–13, for evidence from the Coroner's jury. "X.Y." suggested that the testimony about Powell's mental incapacity may have been tainted by noting that Fox "found [Powell] a very useful friend," that Powell had helped Burke "in the accomplishment of a reform in the *little* abuses of his office." Again, MacDonald and Murphy add interesting features of these cases, but with very different emphases; see *Sleepless Souls*, p. 281.

38. Since there were no formal or legal requirements for medical certificates stating the cause of death, or any registration of deaths in England until the passage of the 1836 Births and Deaths Registration Act, it seems quite possible that several instances of suicide were concealed by the families of notable men and women. For more on this, see J. D. J. Havard, *The Detection of Secret Homicide* (London, Macmillan, 1980), p. 39.

39. The deaths of these thirteen men (Thomas Bradshaw, Robert Clive, John Crowley, John Damer, William Fitzherbert, J. G. Goodenough, Sir George Hay, Hesse, Sir William Keyt, William Bromley, Lord Montfort, Perry, Hans Stanley) stretch from the earliest, Sir William Keyt in 1741 to the last, Lord Saye and Sele in 1788. Keyt's death, by self-immolation, Damer's by pistol, Hesse's, in 1788, Powell's, and Saye and Sele's were the only ones that the papers described as self-inflicted. There is an account in the *Gaz* January 6, 1772, which may be that of William Fitzherbert; the victim is referred to only as "a certain Member of Parliament." For Saye and Sele's suicide, see the *World* July 4, 1788 and for Walpole's letter, see *Correspondence*, vol. 31, p. 267.

40. See Andrew, *London Debating Societies*, especially November 4, 1789, pp. 266–67.

41. *Lady's Magazine* June 1773, pp. 298–299; letter from "Plato" in the *St. J* January 8, 1780. For more see *T&C* June 1783, "On Suicide," p. 321 and *Evening Chronicle* June 3, 1788.

42. Letter in *MC* November 1774; *Times* August 12, 1790; *MH* February 25, 1785 and *Public Advertiser* March 4, 1785 for Captain Battersby.

43. See the *Sentimental Magazine* September 1775, pp. 390–92. James Boswell, *The Hypocondriack*, December 1781, p. 262. For a balanced and unemotional account of Sutherland's life and death, see the *AR* 1791, pp. 34–35; the fragment appeared in the *Times* August 22, 1791. This sort of emotionalism was clearly a very potent and widely sought experience. After the suicide of Eleanor Johnson, a servant girl of seventeen, for the love of a black man named Thomas Cato (a perhaps inauspicious name as things turned out), not only did the *Times* print the account of her life, death, and inquest in some detail, but copied the entire tear-streaked letter she wrote to Cato, September 25, 1789. This death also occasioned a debate at the Coachmaker's Hall Debating Society on the question "Does suicide proceed mainly from a disappointment in love, a state

of lunacy, or from the pride of the human mind?" *Times* November 12, 1789. See also MacDonald and Murphy, *Sleepless Souls*, pp. 195–96.

44. *T&C* August 1792, "Reflections on the Prevalence of Suicide in England and Geneva," pp. 351–52.

45. The earliest reports in the *Times*, the *MC*, the *MP*, and the *PA* of June 4, 1788 are identical, except for the brief notice in the *Times* explaining their earlier suppression of the story. The second reports, which the *Times* entitled *Farther Particulars of the late Mr. HESSE*, were also identical and appeared in the *Times*, the *MP*, and the *PA* on June 5, 1788. This case is discussed in MacDonald and Murphy's *Sleepless Souls*, (pp. 189–90) but seen quite differently. They instead report that the "papers were elegiac" and that the *Times* "reporter recounted his life and death without a critical word." I think, even in the *Times*, though most explicitly in some of the other papers, criticism could be, and was read by contemporaries, in the detailed descriptions of Hesse's property and prosperity, blown away by a propensity for "deep play."

46. Both the *English Chronicle* of June 3, 1788 and the *General Evening Post* of June 5, 1788 contain the comment about Hesse's "connexions too splendid." Hesse's desire to partake of the gay life with the Great is also found in the *English Chronicle* of June 3, 1788 and the *PA* June 5, 1788.

47. *GEP* June 5, 1788. See also the sentimentalized account of Hesse's widow in the next edition of this paper, June 7, 1788.

48. *MP* June 6, 1788, June 7, 1788. The story about the practical trick appeared in the *Star and Evening Advertiser* June 6, 1788.

49. *On the Death of Mr. Hesse* in the *PA* June 9, 1788; EPITAPH *on Mr. Hesse* by Edw. Beavan in the *T&C* July 1788, pp. 334–35.

50. The paragraph linking bankruptcy and suicide appeared in *The Star and Evening Advertiser of June 6, 1788, in* the *English Chronicle* of June 3–5, 1788, and its first sentence in the *Times* June 6, 1788. Interestingly the *Times* continued without mentioning the two suicides alluded to by the other papers, but used the occasion to suggest the need for a general moral reform.

51. In this I once again disagree with MacDonald and Murphy's assessment, *Sleepless Souls*, pp. 176–77. Though they claim that "the zenith of sentimental suicide in England … was the massive effusion of emotion that followed the death of the poet Thomas Chatterton" (p. 191) they offer no examples of others who, under the influence of that emotion, either killed themselves or showed increased sympathy to other suicides. For an earlier, sentimentalized and heroic verse whose subject is a female suicide, see *The Fair Suicide: being an epistle from a Young Lady to the Person who was the cause of her death* (London, Richard Wellington, 1733). For a detailed, though specific, instance of genre discrimination among eighteenth-century readers, see D. Andrew and R. McGowen, *The Perreaus and Mrs. Rudd: Forgery and Betrayal in Eighteenth Century London* (Berkeley, University of California Press, 2001), pp. 200–205.

52. MacDonald and Murphy, *Sleepless Souls*, pp. 140–41.

53. In a brief survey of suicides found *felo de se*, as reported in the *Times* between 1786 and 1818, 52 men and women were stated to have been found *felo de se* (38 men and 14 women). Of these, 24 men and 5 women, or more than half of the sample, killed themselves either in jail or after having committed an unlawful act.

54. MacDonald and Murphy, *Sleepless Souls*, p. 114.

55. *LM*, vol. 39, April 1762, "Reflections on Suicide," p. 182; *Lady's Magazine*, May 1773, p. 262; William Rowley, *A Treatise on Female . . . Diseases* (London, 1788), p. 341.

56. *GM* October 1808, p. 880. This is the gist of Andrew Scull's *The Most Solitary of Afflictions: Madness and Society in Britain, 1700–1900* (New Haven, Yale University Press, 1993); he notes that "what concerns me is the process by which. . . the medical profession acquired a monopoly over the treatment of the mad" (p. 9, footnote 22). See also Ian Burney, *Bodies of Evidence* (Baltimore, Johns Hopkins University Press, 2000), pp. 10–11.

57. *Occasional Paper*, p. 34; Jeffery, *Felo de Se*, p. 12.

58. For the centrality of legal discourse in this period, see David Lieberman, *The Province of Legislation Determined: Legal Theory in Eighteenth-Century Britain* (Cambridge, Cambridge University Press, 1989), pp. 1–28. William Blackstone, *Commentaries on the Laws of England*, 4 vols. (Oxford, Clarendon Press, 1769), 4:189; John Jervis, *A Practical Treatise on the Office and Duties of Coroners*, 1829, quoted in Sylvia M. Bernard, *Viewing the Breathless Corpse* (Leeds, Words@Woodmere, 2001), p. 32.

59. See MacDonald and Murphy, *Sleepless Souls*, pp. 124–29, for a general discussion of this. According to Charles Moore, *A full inquiry into the Subject of Suicide to which are added (as being closely connected with the subject) Two Treatises on Duelling and Gambling* (London, J. F. & C. Rivington, 1790), 1:383 footnote, this piece was written by Samuel Johnson. It appeared in the *Gentleman's Magazine* 1755, p. 43; Francis Ayscough, *A Discourse Against Self-Murder, a sermon* (London, H. Shute Cox, 1755), p. 14.

60. The *Connoisseur* quoted in Moore, *A full inquiry*, p. 323 footnote.

61. *T&C* January 1773, p. 22; MacDonald and Murphy, *Sleepless Souls*, pp. 128–29.

62. Lady Spencer, Althorp papers, July 4, 1780, British Library Manuscript Room.

63. *Gaz* January 20, 1787, letter signed "W. A." MacDonald and Murphy quote a passage from an early eighteenth-century writer, John Adams, who blamed the coroner for over-lenient verdicts; they comment (p. 113) that "The coroner's views did not, however, invariably prevail." Frequently, however, they did.

64. The man was probably the Honorable Captain Phipps, brother of the earl of Mulgrave. I have been unable to find any record of this coroner's inquest, nor have MacDonald and Murphy cited it in their account. The comments in the *Times* come from November 14 and November 17, 1786. See also a follow-up story in ibid., November 21, 1786. I have found no other paper which carried the story of the *felo de se* verdict. According to Havard, "as late as 1843 instances were given of parish constables accepting bribes from relatives of the deceased who wished to avoid the annoyance of an inquest." *Detection of Secret Homicide*, p. 141.

65. "J. A.," *Reflections on the Laws concerning Suicide*, *GM* 1789, pp. 1080–81.

66. This is the description, in the *Bury & Norwich Post* (June 4, 1823) of the aim of Lennard's proposed Bill.

67. This quote, from a letter signed "Plato" to the *St. J* January 8, 1780, was the latest of a several comments on suicide, all "copied" from the *Conn* January 6, 1755, and also found in the *LM* of the same month and year, pp. 21–23. An article in the *GM* of November 1741, proposed the treatment that had worked so well on the young women

of Miletus. The *Occasionalist* #12, 1768, p. 71, suggested exhibiting the skeleton in the local town hall while a note in the *General Advertiser* of October 12, 1786, thought that suicides should hang in chains, head downward, "at the four corners of the City."

68. *New Monthly Magazine* December 1816, "On the Means of Preventing Suicide," p. 408; *GM* December 1821, p. 482; the *Times* December 31, 1818; Richard Hey, *Dissertation on Suicide* in *Three Dissertations*, pp. 85–86.

69. *LM* April 1762, "Reflections on Suicide," p. 181.

70. *General Advertiser* October 12, 1786; *Times* August 12, 1790; Moore, *A full inquiry*, introduction, p. 2.

71. *MC* August 25, 1797; the *Examiner*, 1810, p. 635; ibid., letter from "Medicus Ignotus," p. 750.

72. Hey, *Dissertation on Suicide*, p. 25; Moore, *A full inquiry*, 1:4.

73. Romilly was so described in the *Bell's Weekly Messenger* November 8, 1818, p. 353, and Londonderry in the *MC* August 22, 1822. Robert Stewart, Baron Londonderry, Viscount Castlereagh and Earl of Londonderry is usually referred to as either Londonderry or Castlereagh, and both titles are used interchangeably here.

74. *Bell's Weekly Messenger* November 8, 1818, pp. 358, 353; *British Review and Critical Journal* February 1819, p. 1; *Monthly Repository* November 1818, p. 725; *MP* November 5, 1818; *Bell's Weekly Messenger* November 8, 1818, p. 357; *Sunday Advertiser* November 8, 1818; *Imperial Weekly Gazette* November 7, 1818; *Monthly Repository* November 1818, p. 721.

75. *Belle Assemblée* November 1818, p. 227. See also *British Luminary and Weekly Intelligence* November 7, 1818, p. 41, and *Evening Star* November 3, 1818; *Country Herald and Weekly Advertiser* November 7, 1818; *Lady's Magazine* December 1818, p. 549, and *MP* November 5, 1818, p. 82; *British Press* November 3, 1818; *Weekly Dispatch* November 8, 1818, p. 356. *Monthly Magazine* December 1818, p. 421. See also *British Luminary* November 7, 1818, p. 45; *European Magazine* November 1818, p. 422.

76. *Constitution* November 8, 1818.

77. *British Luminary* November 7, 1818, p. 45; *British Press* November 5, 1818; *Constitution* November 15, 1818; *Monthly Magazine* December 1818, p. 421.

78. *Constitution* November 15, 1818.

79. *Monthly Magazine* December 1818, p. 421.

80. *Monthly Magazine* December 1818, p. 426; *Times* June 5, 1790; *Lady's Magazine* December 1818, p. 549; see also John Barrell, *Imagining the King's Death: Figurative Treason, Fantasies of Regicide, 1793–1796* (New York, Oxford University Press, 2000), esp. ch. 1, and Carter, *Men and the Emergence*, esp. ch. 3.

81. *British Review* February 1819, p. 9; George Crabbe, "Miscellaneous Verses Previously Printed: On the Death of Sir Samuel Romilly"; see also Bernard Barton, "Stanzas on the Death of Sir Samuel Romilly" from *Poems* (London, 1825), *British Press* November 5, 1818, *Monthly Magazine* December 1818, p. 426.

82. Although this paper spent little time on this aspect of his death, there were a number of comments on it. See for example, the *Champion and Sunday Review* November 8, 1818, p. 705; *The British Press*, November 3, 7, 1818.

83. *Constitution* November 8, 1818, *The British Neptune* November 9, 1818, p. 249.

84. *Courier* November 4, 1818; the *British Press* November 7, 1818, was only one of the papers in which these sentences were found.

85. *Country Herald and Weekly Advertiser* November 7, 1818; *GM* November 1818, p. 466; *The Monthly Magazine* 1818, p. 721; *Lady's Magazine* December 1818, p. 549; *Bell's Weekly Messenger* November 8, 1818, p. 358; *British Luminary* November 7, 1818, p. 42 and see also *Lady's Magazine* December 1818, p. 550.

86. *Globe* November 4, 1818; *New Times* November 3, 1818. A classic contemporary statement of the view that deep feelings were the source of both public virtue and private misery was published as part of the explanation of Romilly's act: "The affections of the heart borrow their sensibility from the refinements of the soul, which, like treacherous servants, often point the sharpest weapons against those breasts which have most cherished and indulged them. The innumerable accidents and infirmities . . . deeply wound those hearts . . . while they hardly ruffle vulgar minds . . . Yet these fine feelings, however painful to the *possessor*, are the parents of all that virtue, compassion and benevolence, which humanize the heart and are the best bonds of society." *MP* November 5, 1818. For other press comments of a similar sort, see the *Constitution* November 8, 1818, and the *Examiner* November 9, 1818, p. 705. Even the *Courier*, which had started all of this, admitted the danger of hyperactive sensibility; see *Courier* November 3, 1818.

87. *News* November 8, 1818; *British Review* February 1819, p. 15; *Morning Advertiser* November 3, 1818; *Philanthropic Gazette* November 4, 1818, p. 368.

88. *News* November 8, 1818.

89. *Independent Whig* November 15, 1818. Although several of the papers reported the public's sorrow about Romilly's death, or lauded his accomplishments and also criticized and censured his self-inflicted end, only one that I have found, the *British Neptune*, printed both sympathetic and critical paragraphs about the act. Most papers took one side of the controversy or the other.

90. *Bell's Weekly Messenger* November 8, 1818, p. 354; *St. J* November 3–5, 1818.

91. *Philanthropic Gazette* November 4, 1818, p. 368. For Whitbread's life and death, see Roger Fulford, *Samuel Whitbread 1764–1815: A Study in Opposition* (London, Macmillan, 1967), esp. ch. 26.

92. *MP* November 1818. In fact, it was said that a Mr. Elliot, having breakfast, was brought the newspaper on the day after Romilly's death. "When, after reading the melancholy fate of Sir Samuel Romilly, he suddenly put a period to his own existence by cutting his throat with a razor." The *Traveller* November 4, 1818.

93. *British Neptune* November 9, 1818, p. 249; *Sunday Advertiser* November 8, 1818; *MP* November 5, 1818; *Independent Whig* November 15, 1818; *Bell's Weekly Messenger* November 8, 1818, p. 354.

94. The *Courier*, discussing the death of Romilly, noted that "The character of a public man, when its lineaments have been fixed by the hand of death, becomes as it were a part of public history . . ." November 6, 1818, ibid., November 3, 1818; the *British Monitor* November 8, 1818, p. 656, "Varieties"; the *Times* December 31, 1818, letter to the editor, signed "Ordovex."

95. "X.Y." to the *Sunday Advertiser*, November 1818. Roy Porter comments that England's medical men had already diagnosed such a malady: "The Enlightenment thus formulated not just progress but its verso; the idea of diseases of civilization, afflicting

meritocrats of feeling," in *The Creation of the Modern World* (New York, W. W. Norton, 2000), p. 282. See also John Mullan, *Sentiment and Sociability: The Language of Feeling in the Eighteenth Century* (Oxford, Oxford University Press, 1988).

96. *MP* August 13, 1822.

97. *Courier* August 13, 1822.

98. *MP* August 14, 1822; *Courier* August 13, 1822, and August 22, 1822; see also the *Ipswich Journal* and *Jackson's Oxford Journal* August 17, 1822. See Robert Franklin, "The Death of Lord Londonderry," *The Historian*, 96, 2007. Londonderry was another name for Castlereagh.

99. *Times* August 13, 1822; *Examiner* August 18, 1822; *Liverpool Mercury* August 16, 1822; *British Freeholder* August 17, 1822.

100. *MC* August 22, 1822; *Courier* August 20, 1822; *Baldwin's London Weekly* August 24, 1822.

101. The *Examiner*, August 18, 1822, the *British Press*, August 14, 1822, and the *British Mercury*, August 19, 1822, discussed the deaths of these three men together.

102. The *Examiner*, commenting on Londonderry's religious views, noted that "The best thing we can say of him is, that he never canted about *Religion*; and accordingly the hirelings, in the midst of all other eulogies, say nothing about his piety" (August 18, 1822). However, the next issue of the *Courier* contained an anonymous letter asserting Londonderry's religious faith (August 21, 1822).

103. *MC* August 14, 1822; the *Liverpool Mercury* August 16, 1822, *Times* August 14, 1822 for Coroner's remarks to the jury; *MC* August 14, 1822. Interestingly, the paragraph from Adam Smith's *Theory of Moral Sentiments*, quoted in this *MC* piece, which advocates sympathy and commiseration for suicides, only appeared in the sixth edition of that work, published in 1790, the year of his death.

104. *Times*, April 7, 1819, letter "On Suicide" from "Homo."

105. For newspaper notices of Whitbread's death see the *Examiner* July 9, 1815, July 30, 1815; *News* July 9, 1815; the *Public Ledger* July 7, 8, 9, 1815; the *MC* July 7, 10, 1815; the *Courier* July 6, 10, 1815; the *Champion* July 10, 16, 1815; the *Public Cause* July 12, 15, 1815. Comments about Whitbread's strengths and failings resemble those made three years later about Romilly. In his *Memoirs*, for example, Romilly himself noted that "the only faults he [Whitbread] had proceeded from an excess of his virtues" (cited in D. R. Fisher, "Samuel Whitbread," *New Oxford Dictionary of National Biography*). In their report of his death, the *Times* argued that Whitbread had, in some degree, "fallen a victim to his sense of duty; for the state of his health had long been such, that his physicians had frequently advised him to remit something of his exertions in public affairs" (July 7, 1815).

106. *MP* February 14, 1818.

107. Ibid., February 16, 1818, "Memoir of Sir Richard Croft."

108. *Examiner* February 1818, p. 109. For other newspaper comments on Croft's death, see the *AR* March 1818, p. 109; the *MP* February 14, 16, 19, 1818; the *Times* July 14, 16, 1818.

109. From 1816 to the end of 1818, three letters on these topics appeared in various press reports. From the last days of 1818 through 1822, fifteen items, eleven of which were letters, appeared in similar venues.

110. Letter from "Humanitas" to the *New Monthly Magazine*. The letter in the *Examiner*, September 1818, p. 671, signed "Atticus" was first sent to the *MC*, which refused to publish it. The second letter, signed "Milesius," appeared in the *Times*, September 23, 1819, and used the example of the inquest called on the suicide of Lord Ffrench to argue that it was Ffrench's Irish politics, not his demise, which led to an attempt to find him guilty of *felo de se*, an attempt foiled by the presence of an attorney to "speak for" him.

111. Emphasis is mine. This coroner's statement appeared word-for-word in several newspapers; see, for example, the *Courier* January 20, 1819, the *Examiner* January 25, 1819, p. 64, the *Times* January 20, 1819.

112. *Times* February 8, 1819 for "Homo's" first letter; the "Coroner's" response in *Times*, February 11, 1819.

113. See *Times*, April 7, 1819. where Letter III from "Homo" appeared just above another note from "A Coroner." In this last missive, the coroner seemed to agree that insanity was a very difficult condition to diagnose, but that, given the vindictive legal consequences of finding a verdict of *felo de se*, the only just verdict was lunacy.

114. *Times*, December 7, 1818.

115. The early nineteenth century witnessed a general condemnation of judicial violence, publicly performed. Thus, for example, the pillory was severely restricted in 1816 (see J. M. Beattie, *Crime and the Courts* [Princeton, Princeton University Press, 1986], pp. 613–16) and almost yearly attempts were made to temper the ferocity of the Criminal Code. The dishonoring interment of *felo de ses* was frequently presented as yet another example of the bloodthirstiness of the code. "Ordovex's" letter to the *Times* appeared on December 31, 1818.

116. *Times* January 28, 1819.

117. Ibid., April 7, 1819, Letter III "On Suicide" from "Homo."

118. *Times* June 24, 1820, Letter from "C." C was Thomas Chevalier, whose letter was reprinted in the *Pamphleteer*, vol. 23, 1823. Letter to the *GM* December 1821 from "W.T.P," p. 482. The *Times* was responding to a letter from J. Barker on December 14, 1822.

119. See MacDonald and Murphy, *Sleepless Souls*, for a discussion of the decline of forfeiture, pp. 78–86, 114–21, 346–53. J. M. Beattie, in conversation, has assured me that the forfeiture clause was almost never used against those found guilty of felonies from the early eighteenth century onwards.

120. *GM* 1822, Supplement, letter from "G. W.," "On the alarming increase of suicide" p. 580.

Chapter 4. *"The Chief Topics of Conversation"*

1. The quotation from which the chapter title is taken appeared in the *T&C* December 1783, p. 645: "The infidelities of the fair sex have, for some time, been the chief topics of conversation in the polite world . . ."

2. David Turner, *Fashioning Adultery* (Cambridge UK, University of Cambridge, 2002), pp. 1–2. A Person of Quality, *Marriage Promoted* (London, Richard Baldwin, 1690), p. 46, reproduced in *Adultery and the Decline of Marriage: Three Tracts* (New York, Garland Publishing, 1984).

3. A Person of Quality, *Marriage Promoted*, p. 9.

4. Ibid., p. 41.

5. Ibid., p. 44.

6. [Josiah Woodward] *A Rebuke to the sin of uncleanliness* (London, Joseph Downing, 1720), p. 10.

7. Castamore, *Conjugium Languens: or the Natural, civil and religious mischiefs arising from conjugal infidelity and impunity* (London, 1720), p. 221, in *The Cases of Polygamy, Concubinage, Adultery, Divorce, etc. by the most eminent hands* (London, T. Payne 1732).

8. David Turner, 'Representations of Adultery in England c 1660–c 1740: A Study in Changing Perceptions of Marital Infidelity,' Oxford D.Phil, 1998, p. 5.

9. See David Hayton, "Moral Reform and Country Politics in the late Seventeenth Century House of Commons" *Past and Present* #128, August 1990, pp. 48–91.

10. Jephson, *The heinous sins of* ADULTERY *and* FORNICATION, pp. iv, 17.

11. *Grub Street Journal* April 9, 1730.

12. Richard Smalbroke, *A Sermon to the Societies for the Reformation of Manners*, "Reformation Necessary to Prevent our Ruine" (London, Joseph Downing, 1728), pp. 20–21.

13. *Universal Spectator* February 23, 1734.

14. Turner, *Fashioning Adultery*, p. 173; Stone, *Road to Divorce*, pp. 248–51.

15. David Garrick, *The Lying Varlet* (Dublin, J. Rhames, 1741), p. 30; *Lethe* (London, Paul Valliant, 1749), pp. 370–71.

16. [Mary Wray], *The Ladies Library*, 3rd ed. (London, Jacob Tonson, 1722), p. 107.

17. Ibid., pp. 108.

18. Philogamus, *Present state of matrimony: or the real causes of conjugal infidelity* (London, J. Buckland, 1739), p. 15. See also Woodward, *A Rebuke*, p. 10.

19. *An Essay on Modern Gallantry*, pp. 4, 50.

20. Timothy Hooker, *Essay on Honour*, p. 2.

21. Ibid., p. 39.

22. Based on material in the *Eighteenth Century Short Title Catalogue*. This counts each addition as one pamphlet. Abergavenny, 3 pamphlets with 1 to 3 editions; Cibber, 4 pamphlets with one in 6 editions; Biker, 3 pamphlets with 1 in 2 editions; Morice, 1 pamphlet; Knowles 1 pamphlet with 5 editions.

23. *Cases of Divorce for Several Causes* (London, E. Curll, 1715). The three cases mentioned were that of the Duchess of Cleveland, Sir George Downing's non-consummation case, and the Dormer adultery trial. The judge's verdict in Latin was six pages long.

24. Addison, *Spectator* #99, June 23, 1711, p. 416.

25. GM 1732, p. 756; *LM* 1732, p. 83; *LM* June 1734, p. 318 copied from the *Grub Street Journal*; GM March 1742, pp. 153–54 copied from the *Universal Spectator*; *CGJ* # 4 reprinted in *GM* January 1752, p. 30.

26. *CGJ* #68, p. 359.

27. *GM* May 1732, p. 772, for the Goodere case and July 1732, p. 873, for Green's.

28. The Biker case was one of five considered to have had lots of publicity by Stone or Turner. Papers consulted were the *Daily Post*, the *London Daily Post*, the *LM*, the *GM*, the *LEP*, the *Champion*, the *Country Journal or the Craftsman*, *Commonsense* and of course the *Daily Gazetteer*.

29. For the dealer's tale see *GM* March 1751, vol. xxi, p. 136; for the Teat/Craven case *GM* June 24, 1755, p. 282.

30. *GM*, 1757, p. 286, *Universal Magazine*, June 1757, p. 291.

31. *PA*, June 18, 1757, *LEP* June 11, 1757. For more on this case, see *Proceedings in the Trial of Captain Gambier for Crim Con with Admiral Knowle's Lady, June 11, 1757* (London, H. Owen, 1757).

32. Junius, *[Letters]* (London, T. Bensley, 1797), vol. 1, 18 March 1769, p. 88.

33. Ibid., pp. 89–90.

34. *T&C* July 1771, p. 352.

35. Junius, *[Letters]*, pp. 93–94.

36. Ibid.

37. Ibid., [Letters], p. 82.

38. "Tullius" in the *Oxford Magazine* July 1769, p. 20.

39. Junius, *[Letters]*, p. xxviii.

40. See Cindy McCreery, *The Satirical Gaze: Prints of Women in Late Eighteenth-Century England* (Oxford, Oxford University Press, 2004).

41. *GM* February 1769, p. 107. See also *Oxford Magazine* February 1769, p. 77.

42. *T&C* April 1769, pp. 204–5.

43. See, for example, the *Letters of Palinurus and Annabella* in the *T&C* April 1769, pp. 181–82, and *GM* April 1769, *Letters to and from a discarded Mistress*, pp. 196–97.

44. *Memoirs of the Amours, Intrigues and Adventures of Charles Augustus Fitz-Roy with Miss Parsons* (London, J. Meares, 1769). The *Amours* was used as a source by the author of the DNB biography of Grafton.

45. Civilian, *Free Thoughts on Seduction, Adultery and Divorce, with Reflections on the Gallantry of Princes* (London, J. Bell, 1771), p. 8: "The Duke of Cumberland's late amour with lady Grosvenor; a topick that has universally agitated the tongues and pens of the scribblers and tatlers of the present age."

46. *Oxford Magazine* January 1770, p. 24.

47. *T&C* January 1770, p. 53.

48. *GM* December 1769, p. 607.

49. *T&C* December 1769, p. 632, *Oxford Magazine* 1769 Supplement, p. 276.

50. *GM* 1769 Supplement, p. 622.

51. *Oxford Magazine* December 1769, p. 227.

52. Except in a novel, published shortly after the trials, called *Harriet, or the Innocent Adultress* (London, R. Baldwin, 1779), 2nd ed. Here Lady Grosvenor was presented as "an injured beauty thus neglected [by her husband]," who merely "follows his example" in indulging in extramarital amours (pp. x, xii).

53. *GM* 1769 Supplement, p. 621; *Oxford Magazine* 1770, pp. 19–20.

54. *T&C* February 1770, p. 110.

55. This was done by analogy with the Clavering case; for this see *GM* March 1770, p. 123.

56. I have not been able to locate a copy of this pamphlet. It was reviewed by "X" in the *GM* September 1770, p. 431.

57. Horace Walpole, *Correspondence*, vol. 23, To Mann, 31 August 1770, p. 230.

58. *GM* 1770, p. 317.

59. *Oxford Magazine* September 1770, p. 88.

60. *PA* July 7, 1770; *Bingley's* August 4, 1770. See also a satiric letter and poem from "Fair Locks" on Cumberland's adventures in the *Ladies Magazine* August 1770, p. 31. The beginning of a poem ostensibly written by him to Lady Grosvenor, included in this letter, ran:

To my dear angel now at land,
Her love at sea doth write;
But first would have her understand,
I never could indite.
Tho' Dr. Charles, great pains he took,
Yet I ne'er learnt my Spelling book.

Another satiric note was found in a "letter" from Leonora, member of the Female Coterie, who noted that they had "Ordered that a new ROYAL SPELLING-BOOK be printed at the expence of the society, for the use of polite lovers, who propose carrying on an amorous correspondence" (*T&C* August 1770, p. 408). Also, in the *PA*, a fictitious advertisement: "WANTED, For the Parties abovementioned [i.e., the Duchess of Grosvenor and the Duke of Cumberland], two Spelling-Books and an English Grammar" (July 20, 1770).

61. *GM* 1770, p. 314.

62. *Bingley's* August 18, 1770. Some humorously opined that these disguises were adopted because Cumberland was practicing for a stage career: see *PA* July 27, 1770, "Intelligence Extraordinary." "Fair Locks," in the *Ladies Magazine* August 1770, p. 31, poked fun at this wig by "praising" Cumberland for the "difficulties he did for our sex," and paid special attention to his having "turned those pretty red locks of hair of his into a black wig."

63. *Oxford Magazine* August 1770, p. 75; the poem, signed "A True Mourner," p. 74.

64. See *GM* 1770, p. 316; *Oxford Magazine* July 1770, p. 17.

65. *PA* July 21, 1770; *Bingley's* August 10, 1771.

66. *GM* 1770, p. 319.

67. *Oxford Magazine* July 1770, p. 17. The *Oxford* reported the case in much more detail than did the *Gentleman's*; see *GM* 1770, vol. 40, pp. 314–19, and a long review of the published proceedings, ibid., pp. 471–74.

68. Civilian, *Free Thoughts on Adultery and Divorce*, p. 7.

69. *Adultery a-la-Mode* (London, R. Thomas, n.d.), p. 5.

70. *The Adulterer, A Poem* (London, W. Bingley, 1769), p. 13.

71. Letter written by "Q in the Corner" to *Bingley's* September 15, 1770. "Q" is referring to an overheard conversation between Cumberland and O'Kelley about various aristocratic misdeeds.

72. *PA* July 31, 1770; see also *T&C* July 1770, p. 391: "It is a certain fact, that since a late trial, the two lovers are almost daily, and the whole day, together in her Ladyship's house at Barnes."

73. *T&C* February 1771, p. 251.

74. Donna T. Andrew, "'Adultery-A-La-Mode': Privilege, the Law and Attitudes to Adultery 1770–1809," *History* (82) 1997, pp. 5–24.

75. *T&C* August 1771, pp. 418–19.

76. Letter from "Theophilus," "Symptoms of public ruin, not imaginary" in the *Oxford Magazine* June 1771, p. 199.

77. See Andrew, "Adultery a la Mode." The three pamphlets of 1771 were *Thoughts on the Times, but Chiefly on the Profligacy of Our Women; Reflections on Celibacy and Marriage*; and *Reflections on the too Prevailing Spirit of Dissipation*.

78. Thomas Pollen, *The fatal consequences of adultery, to monarchies as well as to private families, with a defence of the bill passed in the House of Lords in the year 1771* (London, T. Lowndes, 1772), pp. 230, 112. This pamphlet was cited in a letter to the editor of the *MC* on March 17, 1777.

79. [Maurice Morgann] *A Letter to My Lords the Bishops, on the occasion of the Present Bill for the Preventing of Adultery* (London, J. Dodsley, 1779), pp. 21–23, 42, 45.

80. "T.L." in the *T&C* August 1769, p. 434. For a story "dressed" as a letter, see ibid., March 1769, pp. 128–29; for a "dream" in the same guise, see ibid., January 1772, pp. 28–29; the candidate's promises in *T&C* October 1774, p. 519. For other letters retailing the latest adultery, see "Alpin McAlpin" to the *T&C* October 1771, pp. 547–48, on the Sutherland adultery; "A Bye-Stander" to ibid., May 1773, pp. 246–47 for the Craven adultery; or the two letters in defense of Lady Grosvenor signed "Cato," in the *MP* September 25, September 26, 1775.

81. Letter from "Hinton" in the *GM* vol. 42, August 1772, pp. 370–71; "BWB" to the *GM* 1784, pp. 743–44.

82. "An Old Observer" to the *T&C* November 1783, pp. 577–78; "Theophrastus" in the *GM* March 1784, i, pp. 171–72.

83. "Hinton" to the *GM* August 1772, p. 370; "A Well-Wisher to the Fair Sex" in *T&C* December 1776, p. 656; "A Parent" in *Gaz* December 31, 1777; "Megaronides," "*To the Lord Bishop of Landaff*" in the *MP* August 2, 1779.

84. See, for example, the essay entitled "Thoughts on the Fashionable Vice," signed "Senex" which appeared in the *LM* of June 1780, pp. 252–55. Others who blamed men for the high incidence of adultery were "An Advocate of the Ladies" in the *T&C* August 1777, pp. 407–8; "Conjux" in the *MP* January 6, 1779; "An Occasional Correspondent" in the *T&C* December 1783, pp. 645–46; and "A contented Caro Sposo" in *T&C* March 1785, pp. 155–56.

85. "Eleanora" in the *MP* January 13, 1779; "A friend to conjugal felicity" in the *MH* July 8, 1783; letter to the *MP* Sept 6, 1784. "Eleanora" may have been Mrs. Thrale, who noted the same idea in her journal: "was a Woman to have her Ring Finger cut off; her Lover would hesitate a little in marrying her I'll warrant him. . . ." *Thraliana*, Katherine C. Balderston, ed. (Oxford, Clarendon Press, 1942), April 17, 1779, p. 379.

86. Letters in the *T&C* May 1776, pp. 654–55; ibid., August 1777, pp. 407–8; *MP* December 11, 1784; "Civis" in the *Times*, March 26, 1786; *T&C* March 1786, p. 172. When the Coachmakers Hall debating society discussed the question of "in which rank of life does conjugal felicity most generally reside?" the audience voted for the middling "by a considerable majority"; *General Advertiser* November 25, 1785.

87. "An Advocate of the Ladies" in the *T&C* August 1777, p. 407.

88. For other accounts of this case, see Peter Wagner, "The Pornographer in the Courtroom," in Paul-Gabriel Boucé, ed., *Sexuality in Eighteenth Century Britain* (Totowa, N.J.: Manchester University Press, 1982), pp. 120–40; Cindy McCreery, 'Breaking all the Rules: the Worsley Affair in Late Eighteenth-Century Britain,' in Pat Rogers and Regina Hewitt, eds, *Orthodoxy and Heresy in the Long Eighteenth Century: 1660–1830* (Lewisburg, Pa., Bucknell University Press, 2002).

89. First notices of Lady Worsley's elopement came in the *PA* January 25, 1782 and the *White* January 26, 1782; the evidence about the many other lovers is found in the *White* February 26, 1782. See also the recent, popular account of this case, Hallie Rubenhold, *The Lady in Red* (New York, St. Martin's Press, 2008).

90. The first notice, on March 4, 1782, which advertised two presses, appeared in the *PA*, the second, which announced three presses, in the *MC* March 5, 1782, followed by another, ibid., which announced the change in the title, on March 12, 1782.

91. The original advertisement for *The Whim* appeared in the *MC* March 2, 1782; the latter puff in the *White* March 30, 1782.

92. All three advertisements for the *Epistle* appeared in the *MH*, which was edited at this time by that past master at scandal, the reverend Henry Bate. They appeared on May 1, 2, 6, 1782. For more on Bate, see W. H. Hindle, *The Morning Post 1772–1937* (London, G. Routledge & Sons, 1937).

93. Erskine's opening remark, "that there was going to be no end of adultery" was made at the criminal conversation trial of Andorff v. Langlands, *Times* July 20, 1791. This connection persisted, and persists: see, for example, Gail Savage, "Erotic Stories and Public Decency: Newspaper Reporting of Divorce Proceedings in England," *Historical Journal* 41, 2 (1998): 511–28.

94. While I have found at least pamphlets for thirteen cases which occurred in the 1780s, I have been able to find only seven for the 1790s.

95. The pamphlets were *The Trial of Lady Maria Bayntun* (London, E. Rich, 1781), *The Trial of Lady Anne Foley* (London, G. Lister, 1785), *The Trial of Mrs. Elizabeth Leslie Christie* (London, G. Lister, 1783), *The trial of Mrs. Harriet Errington* (London, R. Randall, 1785), *The trial between William Fawkener and the Hon John Townshend for Criminal Conversation* (London, M. Smith, 1786) and *The Trial of the Hon. Mrs. Catherine Newton* (London, G. Lister, 1782). Five of these six pamphlets contained illustrations, and four of them were published in at least two editions or versions. Included in *The Cuckold's Chronicle* (London, H. Lemoin, 1793) were the Arabin/Sutton case, the Christie/Baker case, the Errington case, the Fawkener/ Townshend case and the Foley/ Peterborough case.

96. *MH* April 3, 1783; *St. J* March 23, 1782.

97. *The Evils of Adultery and Prostitution with an inquiry into the causes of their present alarming increase* (London, T. Vernon, 1792), pp. 48–49.

98. Introduction to volume 5, 1775 of the *T&C;* [John Andrews] *Reflections on the too prevailing Spirit of* DISSIPATION AND GALLANTRY *shewing its dreadful Consequences to Publick Freedom* (London, E. and C. Dilly, 1771), p. 57. Punishment for crim. con. could well result in lifelong imprisonment, for the damages were sometimes many thousands

of pounds. This brief summary does not do justice to John Barrell's marvelous book, *The Spirit of Despotism: Invasions of Privacy in the 1790s* (Oxford, Oxford University Press, 2006).

99. Lawrence Stone, *The Road to Divorce: England 1530–1987*, p. 273; see also Katherine Binhammer, "The Sex Panic of the 1790s," *Journal of the History of Sexuality* January 1996, pp. 409–34.

100. In his first four years as Chief Justice, Kenyon is reported as having begun 20 and completed 19 cases of criminal conversation; by comparison, the press reported Ellenborough, his successor, as having sat on 17 such cases during his whole seventeen-year occupancy of that position. In his fourteen years as Chief Justice at King's Bench, Kenyon presided at fifty-eight reported cases of criminal conversation, and in only one year (1792) did he preside over only one case. For Kenyon's addresses to the jury see Moorsom *v* Clarke (*Times* July 16, 1791) and Cadogan *v* Cooper case (*Times* June 13, 1794). In his argument opposing Thomas Erskine's writ to have the Boddington *v* Boddington case tried before King's Bench, Mr. Law noted that "no particular advantage could be gained to the Public by the greater publicity of that trial" [referring here to one held at King's Bench] and that this case would be better argued in "a more Private forum," i.e., the Sheriff's court (*Times* July 6, 1797).

101. Of the eighteen cases decided in these four years, only two, Parslow *v.* Sykes and Martin *v.* Petrie, were awarded £10,000. Three cases resulted in non-suits or findings for the defendant, four plaintiffs were awarded 40 shillings or under, three husbands received between £200 and £500, three men between £500 and £1,000, and three were awarded between £2,000 and £3,500.

102. *Times* December 31, 1791.

103. James Oldham notes that this goes back to Mansfield, though he does say he does not quite know why Mansfield felt it to be so; see *English Common Law in the Age of Mansfield* (Chapel Hill, N.C., University of North Carolina Press, 2004), p. 340.

104. *Times* December 10, 1789. The coverage of this trial took almost a complete page of that day's paper.

105. Lovering *v* Sadler, see *Times* July 20, 1791. I have argued elsewhere that public opinion, as exhibited in the debates at London debating societies, was more sympathetic to erring women than were judges like Kenyon; see "Adultery-à-la-Mode."

106. *Adultery, The Trial of Mr. William Atkinson, Linen draper of Cheapside for Criminal Conversation with Mrs. Connor, wife of Mr. Connor, late of the Mitre, at Barnet . . . before Lord Kenyon* (London, Couch & Lakin, 1789), pp. 38–39.

107. Kenyon's comments to the jury were published in the *T&C* November 1788, pp. 489–90, with the comment that they included "an account of the exemplary charge given by Lord Kenyon . . ." For Kenyon's summing-up and verdict in the Hennet *v* Darley case, see the *Times* June 14, 1799. The most famous example of this view was articulated by the defense attorney Thomas Erskine, in a case before Lord Kenyon, in which the husband was described as a mariner who had hooked a whale: "As long as the line is fast to the fish, the fish is yours . . . but the moment she is a loose fish, any body may strike her." Martin *v* Petrie in the *Times* December 26, 1791.

108. Letter signed "Anticornu" reprinted in *The Spirit of the Public Journals for 1797* (London, R. Phillips for M. Richardson, 1798), pp. 245–46.

109. *Times* June 26, 1799.

110. *Times* February 22, 1797. In arguing about the propriety of allowing full divorce in the Williams divorce case, the Lord Chancellor, addressing the House of Lords, commented that though he himself disapproved of divorce, "If however such was to be the law of this country, why not make it general, and let every man be acquainted with it? Why was it not properly framed into a law, and a court appointed for that purpose, where the public at large might have recourse to it, and not confined to a few individuals, who should apply to that House for a decision, which no court or law in this kingdom had power to make?" (*MH* February 28, 1783).

111. "Lord Kenyon" in *Public Characters of 1799–1800* (London, P. Alard, 1799), p. 565; for Kenyon's comments in the Howard *v* Bingham case, *The Trial of the Hon. Richard Bingham for Crim Con with Lady Elizabeth Howard* (London, J. Ridgway, 1794), p. 73. See also Mrs. Carter's comments on Lord Kenyon's campaign in *Letters from Mrs. Elizabeth Carter to Mrs. Montague between the years 1755 and 1800* . . . ed. Rev. Montagu Pennington, 3 vols. (London, F.C. and J. Rivington, 1817), 3: 351–52, June 1797.

112. In a recent piece in *Notes and Queries* (52:4, 2005, p. 452) David O'Shaughnessy, (in "Kotzebue and Thompson's The Stranger: a new source for Godwin's St Leon"), quoting L. F. Thompson, *Kotzebue: A Survey of his Progress in France, and England* (Paris, 1928), p. 55, notes: "At the close of the eighteenth century August von Kotzebue was 'a household name from John o'Groats to Land's End, and there were approximately 170 editions of Kotzebue's works . . . equal in number to the aggregate of the editions of all other German writers translated at that time' available in England."

113. The play came from a translation by Bernard Thompson, although Sheridan was widely credited with adapted and improving it for English tastes; see *Times* March 26, 1798; *MP* March 26, 1798. For the moral improvements to be wrought by the piece, *MP* March 27, 1798, and *Times* March 26, 1798: ". . . above all, there is that which we but rarely meet with in our modern dramas, novelty of virtuous principle and edifying morality, judiciously diffused throughout the serious scenes."

114. *MC* March 26, 1798.

115. The word "sympathy," used ibid., by the *MC* reviewer to describe the emotion elicited in viewing the play, is a concept central to the "cult" of sensibility, which will be discussed in greater detail below. Sheridan's quip in the *Times* March 30, 1798.

116. The report of the trial in the *Times* (February 20, 1798) (which noted that the trial took four hours) took up virtually all of page 3, in other words, one-quarter of the entire issue, or, if one eliminated advertisements, one-half of the newsworthy stories for that day. The account of the trial in the *MP* (February 21, 1798) was equally lengthy. Remarks on Taylor's family appeared in the *MP* February 23, 1798.

117. The account quoted here is from the *MP* February 21, 1798. For the debate at the Westminster Forum, see Andrew, *London Debating Societies*, #2138, p. 374. Like Mrs. Haller, Mrs. Ricketts was married at a very young age (the former at sixteen, the latter at fifteen), both were in their early twenties when the affairs began, and both had children by their husbands (Mrs. Haller two, Mrs. Ricketts three).

118. *Times* March 26, 1798, Letter to the Right Hon. Lord Kenyon, signed "A Juror."

119. These were "A Friend to Social Order," *Thoughts on Marriage, and Criminal Conversation, respectfully addressed and inscribed to the Right Honourable Lord Kenyon* (London, F. and C. Rivington, 1799); *Thoughts on the Propriety of Preventing Marriages Founded on Adultery* (London, J. Richardson, 1800); Adam Sibbit, *Thoughts on the Frequency of Divorces in Modern Times* (London, T. Cadell jr. and W. Davies, 1800); and *A Letter to the Hon. Spencer Perceval . . . of Adultery* (London, F. & C. Rivington, 1801). The comment on the lenity of misdemeanor for adultery is from the last, p. 16; the "civil war of lust" comes from the first, p. vi; the conversion of private injury into public concern comes from *Thoughts on the Propriety*, p. 4, and Kenyon as Cato (probably Cato the Elder, the Censor of Rome) from *Thoughts on the Frequency of Divorces*, p. 44.

120. "Observator" in the *GM* December 1805, pp. 1104–5; *Times* July 20, 1802.

121. Thomas Erskine, in his comments to the jury, in Foote *v* Jones. Erskine represented the plaintiff, and secured a hefty £5000 award for his client. In Dublin, the Earl of Westmeath was awarded £10,000 in damages from his wife's lover (*Times* February 29, 1796); Boddington *v* Boddington resulted in a fine of £10,000 against the lover (ibid., July 3, 1797); Lord Boringdon was awarded £10,000 by a Sheriff's jury (ibid., July 20, 1808).

122. "Methodist" to the *Gentleman's Magazine* May 1801, pp. 398–99; Windham's comment ibid., *Parliamentary Proceedings* ii, p. 1132; the Taylor *v* Birdwood crim. con. trial in the *Times* June 2, 1800. This connection between French morals and revolution was frequently made in English adultery cases. For example Erskine, arguing for punitive damages in the Cadogan/Cooper case: asked the jury for a verdict "of such a nature, as to give stability and security to domestic life. This is the foundation of all that is noble among men. And at the present moment, when the country is rejoicing in the success of our arms . . . every man who hears me, will admit, that all that valour . . . arise from the habits of virtuous life, and from the different relations of a family. . . . This is the foundation of all that is good, of all that is great, and of all that distinguishes the most illustrious nations, from nations that are the most barbarous" (*Times* August 22, 1794). Discussing the conditions under which divorce would be agreed upon, the Bishop of Rochester noted, in the House of Lords, that "the morals of the women depended upon the sanctity of marriage, when he considered the Jacobinical system adopted in a neighbouring country, which made it necessary to take some strong measures to resist its influence on the morals of this, he was sure . . . that the House would not be inclined to sacrifice much to a little sentimental feeling" (*MP* March 29, 1798).

123. For Carlisle's remarks, see *Parliamentary Debates* 40 Geo. III, pp. 279–80, May 23, 1800; Kenyon's charge to the Taylor *v* Birdwood jury in the *Times* June 2, 1800, and Kenyon's remarks in August, while at the Maidstone Assizes, see ibid., August 12, 1800. Even before the Adultery Bill came before Parliament, it was well known that both Kenyon and Erskine favoured a criminalization of the law regarding adultery. In the case of Campbell *v* Addison, Erskine, representing the plaintiff, had hinted 'that perhaps this offence ought to become the subject of the *criminal* justice of the country, since *civil damages* had hitherto been found inadequate to its suppression.' Kenyon agreed, but said it was a matter for the legislature. *MC* February 25, 1799.

124. See the *Times* March 6, 1794, and *The Trial of the Hon Richard Bingham for Crim Con with Lady Elizabeth Howard* (London, J. Ridgway, 1794).

125. The damages in the Abercorn *v* Copley case, in which the defendant had 'suffered judgment to go by default' occurred in the Sheriff's Court and was reported in the *MP* December 21, 1798; the Markham *v* Fawcett case was similarly undefended and the fine determined by the Sheriff of Middlesex's special jury; see the *Times* May 5, 1802 and for Lingham *v* Hunt, at King's Bench, ibid., December 25, 1802. A similar sentimental appeal, stressing his honour as a soldier, was used by the attorney of Sir Arthur Paget in mitigation of damages for his adultery with Lady Boringdon; it was spectacularly unsuccessful with the fine adjudged being £10,000 (*Times* July 20, 1808).

126. This plea was made in Markham *v* Fawcett case, *Times* May 5, 1802; it was also made in the Elgin *v* Ferguson case, where the jury awarded £10,000 damages (ibid., December 23, 1807) and in the Boringdon *v* Paget case (ibid., July 20, 1808).

127. "J. S." sent three letters to the Editor of the *Times*, May 23, 1811, June 21 and 24, 1811. "Benedict's" letters were published by the *Universal Magazine* as their lead articles in three subsequent issues, October 1813, pp. 265–67, November 1813, pp. 353–55, and December 1813, pp. 441–43. Two letters to the *MP* (December 21, 29, 1814), signed "A Clergyman of the Church of England," another sent to the *New Monthly Magazine* (June 1, 1815), signed "Spectator," and an editorial comment in the *Times* (July 23, 1817) all stressed the need for harsher punishments for adultery.

128. As we shall see, Lord Ellenborough's stance on the evils of adultery made itself very clear in his comments on the Roseberry divorce proceedings. There he noted that "It was absolutely necessary to the interests of sound morality, to the peace and happiness of social life, and to the purity of private families, that such offences should be marked out as something against nature" (*Times* June 2, 1815). For Ellenborough's comments on the proper penalties in the Smith *v* Smith case, see ibid., July 8, 1803. However, for another view of Ellenborough on divorce, see Ben Wilson, *Decency and Disorder* (London, Faber & Faber, 2007), pp. 370–71. Gibbs's charge to the jury at the end of the very long trial between Robert Knight and Lord Middleton appeared in the *MC* December 6, 1814.

129. *MP* December 26, 1814, poem, "On a recent event."

130. The *Courier*, the *Evening Star*, the *MP*, the *News*, the *St. J*, and the *Times* all carried extensive reports on the event, the *Post* noting that "A great portion of our Paper of this day is occupied with the report of the *Crim. Con* case of the Earl of Roseberry versus Sir Henry Mildmay . . ." (December 12, 1814).

131. The press reports are remarkably similar, though not identical. For these quotes I have used the account published in the *Evening Star* December 12, 1814. In the *Courier* account of December 12, 1814, Mildmay's piratical appearance, on being found in Lady Harriet's bedroom, was thus described by Mr. Primrose, Lord Roseberry's brother: "Sir H. Mildmay was dressed in a large blue jacket and trowsers and a red waistcoat, which was covered with a profusion of small pearl buttons. His beard was much grown, and his appearance altogether so disguised that [he] was obliged to look twice before he recognised him"(December 12, 1814).

132. Garrow's opening comments in the *Times* December 12, 1814; all remaining quotes from the *Courier*, December 12, 1814.

133. For the proposed duel with Roseberry, see *St. J* December 103, 1814; for the agony of the guilty pair, the *MP* December 13, 1814.

134. This almost column-long poem appeared in the *MP* December 15, 1814.

135. For details of the contents of Mildmay's house that were going to be bid upon, see ibid., December 17, 1814. For the poem, "The Rose. Lines on the elopement of Lady R. by Mr. Wedderburn Webster" ibid., December 13, 1814, and "On a recent Event" by "AWGB," ibid., December 26, 1814.

136. Ibid., December 13, 1814.

137. "Homo" in the *St. J* December 13, 1814.

138. Ellenborough on the gravity of Lady Roseberry's offence in the *Times* June 2, 1815; Taylor in the Commons, ibid., June 15, 1815; "X.Y." ibid., June 19, 1815.

139. *Times* April 17, 1815.

140. Ibid., February 6, 1815. We have seen that in 1741, Timothy Hooker argued that female repentance for adultery was impossible, not because of the heinousness of the sin, but because prudes and gossips would not allow it to be forgotten. By 1815, the sin itself had become seen, at least by the writer for the *Times*, as unforgivable.

141. Ibid., July 23, 1817.

142. Ibid., January 17, 1817. See also ibid., January 18, January 20, January 21, January 25, January 27, January 28, January 29, and February 3, 1825. An advertisement from *The English Gentleman* also appeared in the *Times* of January 25, 1825, which described a pull-out flyer, which could be read by adults, but removed from the eyes of children, with all the details of the Cox/Kean trial.

Chapter 5. Deserving "Most the Cognizance of the Magistrate and the Censor"

1. Both the title of this chapter and source for the quote are from an essay "The Mischiefs of Gaming" in the *LM* June 1736, p. 313. This chapter uses the words "gaming" and "gambling" interchangeably; most eighteenth-century commentators thought all gamblers to be dishonest, and sometimes used the word "gamester" to also mean a person who cheated at cards, dice, or other games.

2. (Robert) Colvill, *Britain, a poem in three books* (Edinburgh, Wal. Ruddiman jr. & Co., 1747), p. 65.

3. *Conn* #50, January 9, 1755, p. 118, also quoted in Moore, 1:388 footnote; *An Essay on Gaming*, pp. 4–5.

4. *PA* January 9, 1782; see also the story in *Lloyd* May 21, 1779, of a clerk to a city merchant, who slit his throat "having lost a sum of money at gaming he was intrusted to receive."

5. Charles Moore, *A full inquiry*, p. 2; George Gregory, *A Sermon on Suicide* [1785] (London, J. Nichols, 1797), 3rd ed., p. 20; *GM* 1787 *Origin of Gaming*, p. 216. According to Andrew Steinmetz, in *The Gaming Table: Its Votaries and Victims* [1870] (Montclair, N.J., Patterson Smith Reprint Series, 1969), vol. 1, pp. 1–3, this allegory originally came from the *Harleian Miscellany*.

6. Moore described his subject using this metaphor in *A full inquiry*, p. 285; *Times* June 9, 1788. For a moral tale that combined all the vices, duelling, gaming, suicide, and an adultery of sorts, see "The Tender Point" in the *T&C* 1769, pp. 579–81.

7. Hanson T. Parlin, *A Study in Shirley's Comedies of London Life*, reprint from the *Bulletin of the University of Texas*, No. 371, November 15, 1914, p. 8.

8. Edward Moore, *The Gamester* (1753), introduced by Charles H. Peake (Los Angeles), Augustan Reprint Society, 1948), publication #14. These lines were also quoted on the frontispiece of an essay by a Member of Parliament, *Hints for a reform, particularly in the gambling clubs* (London, R. Baldwin, 1784).

9. Centlivre's "Gamester" was performed 86 times in the eighteenth century, though only 3 times after 1749; Garrick's "Gamester," performed 38 times during that period, received its greatest number of performances (23) in the 1770s. In contrast, Moore's "Gamester" received virtually the same number of performances through the 1770s, 1780s, and 1790s, and totalled 112 performances for its 48-year run. For this, see William van Lennup, ed., *Index to the London Stage 1660–1800* (Carbondale, Southern Illinois University Press, 1979).

10. After Topham Beauclerk mentioned a new gaming-club, whose "members played to a desperate extent" to Samuel Johnson, Johnson responded: "Depend upon it, Sir, this is mere talk. *Who* is ruined by gaming?" Boswell noted that Johnson loved "to display his ingenuity in argument; and therefore would sometimes in conversation maintain opinions which he was sensible were wrong." George Birkbeck Hill, ed., *Boswell's Life of Johnson*, 6 vols. (Oxford, Clarendon, 1887) 3:23.

11. Steinmetz, *The Gaming Table*, 1:112.

12. *Tatler*, 1709, p. 129; *Conn* #15, 1754, pp. 33–34, 114.

13. [Josiah Woodward], *Disswasive from Gaming* (London, Joseph Downing, 1726), p. 10; *Whole Art and Mystery of Modern Gaming fully exposed and detected* (London, J. Roberts, 1726), p. 110.

14. The term "rook" was probably the most commonly used to describe the successful gamester; see for example, its use in Soame Jennings, *The Modern Fine Gentleman* (London, M. Cooper, 1746), p. 3. The terms "cormorant" and "shark" can be found in the *St. J* December 31, 1762, "vulture" in the *T&C* 1770, p. 686. Gamblers and their victims were described as "hawks," "foxes" and "wolves," "pigeons," "geese" or "sheep" in a front page letter in *Gaz* August 18, 1777, signed "A Friend to Youth." See also the description of gamblers as "harpies" in the *Westminster Magazine* 1775, p. 314.

15. Cotton, *Compleat Gamester*, quoted in John Ashton, *The History of Gambling in England* [1888] (reprinted by Burt Franklin, New York, 1968), p. 17. Richard Ames, *Sylvia's Revenge, or A Satyr against Man* (London, Joseph Streater, 1688).

16. "Henry Hint" in the *GM* June 1736, p. 313; the *Daily Gazetteer* February 4, 1745.

17. See *GM* June 1742, p. 329, and *LM* 1742, p. 307. For a few accounts of Fielding's efforts against public gaming establishments, see Ashton, *History of Gambling*, p. 62, and *GM* December 1755, p. 516. The organization of gambling in midcentury London was sophisticated and thorough; for this see the *GM* 1731, p. 25.

18. The Grand Jury for the County of Middlesex, in its presentment, did specifically refer to the gaming houses of Lady Mordington and Lady Casselis, asking for their closure. The editor of the *GM* in which the presentment was reprinted, added however that they had not yet been shut; see *GM* vol. xiv, May 1744, pp. 278–79.

19. For Mordington and Casselis, see *The Journals of the House of Lords* 29 April 1745. Horace Walpole, *Correspondence*, v. 13, to Richard West, 21 April 1739, pp. 164–65.

20. One of the few essays I have been able to find which strongly suggests that public, not private gaming, should be of more concern to the nation is *Reflexions on Gaming* (London, 1750), pp. 47–48; "Of Private Gaming" in the *LM* September 1736, p. 484; "M.E." in the *GM* February 1760, p. 90; the same opinion was expressed in the *Times* January 24, 1788; *St. J* January 9, 1762; *CGJ* #5, January 18, 1752, p. 45; "Sunderlandensis" to the *GM* April 1751, p. 165.

21. Letter from "Anti-Gambler" in the *T&C* December 1769, pp. 652–53; "A Halfcrown Whist Player" ibid., February 1773, p. 70; Country Justice of the Peace, *Serious Thoughts in Regard to the Publick Disorders* (London, 1750), p. 11; letter to the *MC* February 9, 1773.

22. *St. J* October 5, 1780, front page letter.

23. [Josiah Woodward] *Disswasive from Gaming*, p. 4; *GM* 1731, p. 441; Colvill, *Britain*, p. 66.

24. *Essay on Gaming*, p. 19; *LM* 1770, p. 19; Member of Parliament, *Hints for a reform*, pp. 10–11.

25. *LM* 1749, p. 587; the *Rambler* #15, May 1750, p. 69; *Gray's Inn Journal*, 2 vols. (London, printed by W. Faden, 1756), #100, September 14, 1754, 2: 307.

26. Thomas Rennell, "The Consequences of the Vice of Gaming, preached 1793" in *Discourses on Various Subjects* (London, F. and C. Rivington, 1801), p. 31; *An Account of the Endeavours that have been used to suppress Gaming-Houses* (London 1722), p. 28; *Whole Art and Mystery of Modern Gaming fully expos'd and detected* (London, J. Roberts, 1726) p. iv.

27. Henry Fielding, *An Enquiry into the Late Increase of Robbers* in *An Enquiry into the Causes of the Late Increase of Robbers and Related Writings*, ed. Malvin R. Zirker (Oxford, Clarendon Press, 1988), pp. 92–98. It should be noted, however, that when Fielding spoke "popularly" in the *CGJ*, or novelistically, in *Amelia*, he took a much tougher approach to the gaming of the fashionable classes; *Conn*, #9, March 28, 1754, 1:69. For a fine overview of the contemporary condemnation of gaming, see Phyllis Deutsch, "Moral Trespass in Georgian London: Gaming, Gender and Electoral Politics in the Age of George III," *Historical Journal* 39 (1996), 637–56.

28. *Essay on Gaming, in an Epistle to a Young Nobleman* (London, 1761), p. 25; *T&C* 1771, "Reflections on Gaming," p. 89; Moore, *Full Inquiry*, p. 371.

29. *LM*, 1749, p. 587; Erasmus Mumford, *A Letter to the Club*, pp. 37–39; *LM* 1778, p. 266.

30. *Oxford Magazine* 1770, p. 139; *LM* 1758, p. 224; *PA* May 11, 1775; *GEP* May 5, 1775; *Oxford Magazine* 1770, p. 140.

31. *Gaz* August 11, 1783; Moore, *Full Inquiry*, pp. 378–79; *Times* January 14, 1792.

32. *Monthly Review* 1776, p. 170; Moore, *Full Inquiry*, p. 384; Rennell, *Consequences of Gaming*, p. 32.

33. *GM* 1751, p. 165; Thomas McDonnell, *The Eighth Commandment considered in its full extent, and particularly as applicable to the present reigning spirit of gameing: a sermon* (Dublin, George Faulkner, 1760), pp. 26–27; *Matrimonial Preceptor* (London, T. Hope, 1759), #30, pp. 123–25; Mary Wollstonecraft, *Vindication of the Rights of Women* in *The Vindication of the Rights of Men and the Vindication of the Rights of Women*, ed. Sylvana Tomaselli (Cambridge, Cambridge University Press, 1995), p. 233.

34. *Whole Art*, intro.; letter to the *St. J* January 29, 1765, signed "Libertas"; *Conn* March 6, 1754, 2:181, reprinted in the *GM* 1755, p. 111. For more on this common notion, see McDonnell, *Eighth Commandment*, p. 21; *T&C* 1771, p. 89.

35. [Woodward] *Disswasive from Gaming*, pp. 2–3; Jonas Hanway, *Observations on the Causes of the Dissoluteness Which Reigns Among the Lower Classes of the People* (London, J. & F. Rivington, 1772), p. 86; Rennell, *Consequences of Gaming*, p. 39. For England as an increasingly secular nation, see MacDonald and Murphy, *Sleepless Souls*, C. John Sommerville, *The Secularization of Early Modern Britain* (New York, Oxford University Press, 1992), Callum G. Brown, *The Death of Christian Britain* (London, Routledge, 2001), and Alan D. Gilbert, *The Making of Post Christian Britain* (London, Longmans, 1980).

36. Voltaire, *Philosophical Letters* (1733), p. 26; *CGJ* January 14, 1752, p. 38; *T&C* 1787, p. 80; *Essay on Gaming*, p. 2.

37. *GM* 1761, pp. 152–53; "Pluto" in the *Gaz* January 1, 1770. In an item in the *Times* of February 20, 1792, sarcastically entitled "The Mirror of Fashion" its author notes that "the history of the Four Kings [is] substituted for the Vespers of the Gospel; and those who ought to be the visitors of the Church–the Inhabitants of Gaming Houses."

38. McDonnell, *Eighth Commandment*, p. 26; Rennell, *Consequences of Gaming*, p. 42. Compare the tone of Rennell's condemnation with a similarly critical comment made thirty years before by a letter-writer to the *PA* (April 20, 1765) who signed his note "Respecter of Sabbath": "The practice I mean to censure is that of *card-playing* on the Sabbath. A practice for which no excuse whatever can be brought, as it is directly contrary to the laws of the community; neither can the innocence of the thing itself be pleaded in mitigation of the offense."

39. For Samuel Johnson on gamblers, see George Birkbeck Hill, ed., *Boswell's Life of Johnson*, 6 vols. (Oxford, Clarendon, 1887), 2:176.

40. Fielding, *Amelia*, p. 384; Johnson in Birkbeck Hill, *Boswell's Life of Johnson* 2: 176.

41. *Conn* #30, August 22, 1754, p. 179; "Respecter of Sabbath" in the *PA* April 20, 1765.

42. *Rambler* #80, quoted in *Boswell's Life of Johnson* 2:176; *GM* 1761, p. 389; "JB" in the *Gaz* January 15, 1765.

43. *Universal Magazine* 1775, p. 230; *T&C* 1775, p. 658; *Ladies Magazine* 1770, p. 114.

44. McDonnell, *Eighth Commandment*, p. 25; Rennell, *Consequences of Gaming*, pp. 12–13.

45. *British Magazine* 1748, p. 549; *Conn* 1755, p. 83; letter to the *PA* April 27, 1765. Another letter, to the *St.J* January 29, 1765 noted that "Parties now sit down to a Table full of the spirit of Gaming . . . and much Inquietude, sometimes Quarrels, distinguish Persons of the best Sense and superior Rank."

46. *T&C* 1771, p. 89; ibid., 1770, p. 686. For an article describing the heartlessness of a female gamester, see *LM* 1766, p. 417; for a letter from "A Broken Gambler" who was evicted from his gambling ring when he refuses to strip his best friend, see the *T&C* 1776, p. 308.

47. Member of Parliament, *Hints for a reform*, p. 14; *T&C* 1773, p. 480.

48. *Conn* #58, March 6, 1754, p. 181; *Rambler* quoted in *Boswell's Life*, 2: 176. Both satirical accounts are from the *T&C*, the first from April 1782, p. 173, and the second, signed "Matthew Mandeville," from January 1778, pp. 31–32.

49. *GM* 1739, p. 364; letter to the *LM* 1770, p. 20; *T&C* 1770, p. 685. See also McDonnell, *Eighth Commandment*, p. 21, and *The Occasionalist* #14, 1768, p. 81.

50. *LM* 1738, p. 446; see also *An Account of the Endeavours*, pp. 4–5.

51. McDonnell, *Eighth Commandment*, p. 21; *The Relapse* 2 vols. (London, T. Lowndes, 1780) 1:168; *Oxford Magazine* 1770, p. 253.

52. *British Magazine* 1748, p. 549; a wife's letter to the *LM* 1755, p. 327; letter to the *MC* December 17, 1774.

53. *Whole Art of Gaming*, pp. 3, 11; Henry Baker, "Gaming," in *Medulla Poetarum Romanorum* 2 vols. (London, 1737) 2:416; *GM* 1739, p. 364.

54. *A Modest Defence of Gaming* (London, R. and J. Dodsley, 1754), p. 8; Christopher Anstey, *The New Bath Guide*, Letter VIII, in the *Poetical Works* (London, T. Cadell & W. Davies, 1808), p. 42; letter to the *MC* from "Homo" September 10, 1774; Member of Parliament, *Hints for a reform*, p. 17.

55. Mr. Addison, *A Collection of interesting Anecdotes* (London, 1793), p. 139.

56. The contemporary accounts of her death are virtually identical in both the *LEP* September 11, 1731 and *Fog's* September 18, 1731. By the end of the month, the *GM* posted a longer notice of Braddock's life and death (and the details of her window poetry), not in the obituary page as might be expected, but as an item in a series called "Surprising Discoveries of Murderers" (*GM* #9, vol. 1, p. 397).

57. For Montfort's suicide see *LEP* December 31, 1755, for Bland's, ibid., September 11, 1755. The *GM* noted of Montfort that he had died "suddenly." *GM* January 1755, p. 42. Horace Walpole wrote many of his friends about this pair of suicides, as well as making reference to Braddock's death in a letter to Mann (*Correspondence*, vol. 20, 492, August 21, 1755); he wrote about the two men to Montagu (vol. 9, pp. 172–73, September 20, 1755), Conway (ibid., vol. 37, p. 405, September 23, 1755), Bentley (ibid., vol. 35, pp. 201–2, January 9, 1755), and Mann (ibid., vol. 20, January 9, 1755, p. 461). Charles Selwyn also wrote to Henry Fox about the Bland death; see ibid., vol. 9, p. 172, footnote 3.

58. Justine Crump, "A Study of Gaming in Eighteenth Century English Novels" (Unpublished PhD thesis, Oxford University, 1997), p. 6; *The Guardian*, #120, July 29, 1713, edited by John C. Stephens, (University Press of Kentucky, Lexington, 1982), p. 402; *LM* 1761, p. 206.

59. *The Spectator*, #140, August 10, 1711, 2: 54; *PA* August 10, 1771. Much of this last letter came from an article in the *GM* of August 1735 (v. 5, pp. 480–81) which, in turn, reprinted this piece from *The Prompter* #35, July 29, 1735.

60. *T&C* supplement 1770, p. 686; *A Modest Defence of Gaming*, p. 16.

61. *T&C* June 1771, p. 294, ibid., February 1771, p. 89.

62. *T&C* September 1787, p. 43; *GEP* September 14, 1775.

63. *T&C* supplement 1770, p. 686; ibid., November 1775, p. 57.

64. Mrs. Elizabeth Carter, June 1778, in *Letters from Mrs. Elizabeth Carter to Mrs. Montague* June 1778, 3:73–75; Richard Hey, *Three Dissertations*, p. 48.

65. *T&C*, supplement 1770, p. 686; ibid., February 1771, pp. 73–77.

66. *T&C* February 1771, p. 90; ibid., February 1774, pp. 81–84.

67. [Lydia Grainger] *Modern Amours* (London, 1733), p. 26; John Wood, *An Essay towards a description of Bath* [1742] 2nd ed., (London, James Bettenhem, 1749), p. 448.

68. Oliver Goldsmith, *Account of the Life of Richard Nash* [1762] in the *GM*, October 1762, p. 491, and November 1762, p. 539. The *Times* November 17, 1785 and *Pleasing reflections on life and manners with essays, characters, & poems, moral & entertaining, principally selected from fugitive publications* (London, 1787), p. 84. In a letter which appeared in the *European Magazine* of December 1797, not only was the Braddock story retold, but its anonymous author included the verse mentioned above as having been composed by a gentleman reading the lines she had etched into her window with the only change being that Dice rather than Cards were mentioned as the fatal snares.

69. Another retelling of the Braddock story appeared in *A Collection of interesting anecdotes*, pp. 139–40. Charles Crawford, "An Essay Upon Gaming," *European Magazine*, August 1797, p. 92.

70. The phrase "deep play," often mistakenly thought to have been invented by Jeremy Bentham, was widely used in the eighteenth century to refer to limitless, irrational gaming, and was seen as the result of a profoundly immoral addiction. For Bentham's correct use of the term, see footnote 1, page 106 of his *Theory of Legislation* (London, K. Paul Trench, Trubner & Co., 1931).

71. *White* February 2, 1748; for other, similar accounts, see *Fog's* January 23 and February 27, 1731, the *GM* January 1731, p. 25 and December 18, 1755, p. 569. My thanks to John Dussinger for sharing with the many readers of the 18th Century Interdisciplinary Discussion group the interesting and unusual notice in the *Daily Journal*, September 25, 1722, of the arrest of the participants of a "Female Gaming-House."

72. *PA* March 12, 1765; *Lloyd* September 6, 1765.

73. *Bingley's Journal* October 19, 1771, March 28, 1772; *Mdsx J* April 16, 1772. It is likely that an oblique communique in the *Public Ledger*, June 15, 1761, which reported the gaming of "two great personages" and the resulting loss to one "of the whole of his fortune to within 300l a year" was a veiled reference to the Rigby/Weymouth debt; *Mdsx* March 12, 1772 for Fox.

74. *Oxford Magazine* January 1772, p. 132; *LM* February 1774, p. 55.

75. *LM* August 1777, p. 421; Letter from "A Friend to Youth" addressed "To the Nobility and Gentry who frequent Bath," *Gaz* August 18, 1777. For similar comments, see *GEP* May 4, 1775, "An Epigram: addressed to all Gamblers in High and Low Life" and a letter from "Anti-Aleator" to the *PA* May 11, 1775.

76. For more see David Gadd, *Georgian Summer* (Bath, Adam & Dart, 1971), p. 80.

77. *MH* April 17, 1782, ibid., March 6, 1782. While the *Herald* contained many such evaluations, other papers also included them. Thus, for example, negative assessments of the work of the magistrates can be found in the *PA* February 1, 1782 and the *MC* July 9, 1782. The *Gaz* of November 6, 1782 praised their efforts.

78. It is not always possible to tell, from the newspaper accounts, whether they are reporting the same incident or different ones. For April 1782, for example, we get reports of magistrates, aldermen, and constables breaking up gaming establishments in the *St. J* April 9, 1782, the *White* April 9, 1782, and the *Gaz* April 16, 1782. For activity in July, see the *MP* July 31, 1782, *PA* July 31, 1782, *White* July 27, 1782, *MH* July 31, 1782, and *Gaz* July 31, 1782; *MP* August 6, 1782.

79. *MH* June 19, 1782, *White* June 18, 1782. For letters to the editor from family and friends, see "A Distressed Parent" in the *MC* June 18, 1782; "A Tale of Woe" ibid., July 22, 1782 and *White* July 20, 1782; from "A Father" in the *MC* August 8, 1782 and *PA* August 9, 1782. The Bank of England was very concerned about the gambling of its clerks, often with the Bank's notes. For the most fully recorded story of such a clerk, see *MC* August 21, 1782 and *MH* March 7, 1783.

80. For a typical report of gaming losses, of a "pigeon plucked," see the *PA* March 9, 1782; for the £50,000 reputedly won in the previous year by Charles James Fox and his friends at their Faro Bank, see the *MH* May 5, 1782; and for the unnamed Lord who was said to have won £15,000 in one night's gaming at the EO Tables, see ibid., June 12, 1782 and the *PA* June 11, 1782.

81. For Dr. Graham and the Temple of Health, see Roy Porter, "Dr. James Graham," *Oxford Dictionary of National Biography*. It has not been possible to determine whether or not Graham himself participated in the Temple's subsequent transformation into a gambling house. Its various descriptions are all found in the *MH*: see June 12, June 13 and June 19, 1782. The report of the destruction of the table and the proprietors' appearance before Sampson Wright in Bow Street appeared in the *Gaz* August 7, 9, 1782. Addington's injury was reported in *FFBJ* August 10, 1782 and the conviction of Wiltshire in the *Gaz* December 14, 1782.

82. For notice of the "Genius of Nonsense" see the *White* June 20, 1782, the *PA* August 6, 1782 and the *MP* August 7, 1782. This was probably George Colman's "Genius of Nonsense," performed at the Haymarket in 1780, with topical lines added. For the "Nymph of the Grotto" see the *MC* August 8, 26, 1782 and the *MH* August 12, 1782. I have been able to find no more information on this event. When Byng introduced the EO Table Bill to Parliament, he commented on the ubiquity of these devices, and jocularly supposed that "shortly the electrical bed itself would be turned into an EO Table." *LC* June 4, 1782.

83. The irony of gaming as influenza appeared in the *MH* July 12, 1782; at least six poems concerning gaming appeared in 1782, an example of one is from "To the People, an Ode," by Pasquin, jr., printed in ibid., June 21, 1782; the "found letter" appeared in the *T&C* July 1782, pp. 343–44, and the "Cross-Readings" in the *MH* July 25, 1782. Effingham, thought to be one of those responsible for the loss of the EO Table Bill, had a white staff as an insignia of his office in the Royal Household.

84. For this, see the *LC* July 9, 1782, the *LP* July 10, 1792, and the *Gaz* July 11, 1782.

85. Both the correspondent's comment and the subsequent insinuation that Fox was behind the failure of the Bill are found in the *MH* July 15, 1782; the fictitious dialogue between Fox and Sheridan was published in the *T&C* July 1782, pp. 342–43; Effingham's part in its failure, and the proprietors' thanks appeared in the *MC* July 12, 1782.

86. *LP* June 26, 1782.

87. *Oxford Magazine* July 1769, p. 5. See also letter from "Philanthropos" in the *MC* September 23, 1773, which noted that it was ridiculous to talk of legal enforcement of the laws against gaming when everyone knew such activity flourished in the houses of their parliamentary representatives.

88. *LP* June 28, 1782; letter in *MH* July 1, 1782. See also the front page article in the *White* of June 29, 1782, "On EO Tables," reprinted from the *European Magazine*. This piece, while stressing the grave threat of gaming, concludes by warning against the threat of "a gang of constables" intruding at will into the family life of London's citizens. The *MC* of July 8, 1782, however, argued that the justices, if granted this enlarged authority, would act with "all proper caution, circumspection, and with conformity to the laws of the land."

89. This tag comes from a front page letter in the *PA* July 27, 1782; the full sentence reads: "[W]e are now unhappily distinguished for Want of Principle, and Profligacy of Manners; an universal Passion for Dissipation of every Kind, an Indifference to our public Concerns, and a scandalous Devotion to Gambling, marks our national Character. . . ."

90. *MC* July 15, 1782; *MH* August 31, 1782, and January 1, 1783.

91. For the decline of magisterial activity against EO houses, see the *MH* May 14, 1783; a letter to Sampson Wright from "AB" ibid., August 6, 1783, and another complaint ibid., August 11, 1783. However, in 1785 the *Herald* remarked that "The suppression of EO in this metropolis proved of such an infinite service to the public, that we hope the magistrates will immediately interfere and stop the increase of *Faro tables*, which have made a rapid progress within these last few weeks, and are no less destructive of the morals, fortunes, and, we might say, honesty of the unfortunate youths, who frequent them" (June 25, 1785).

92. *Times* December 25, 1789; see also *Sketches of Modern Life*, 2 vols. (London, W. Miller, 1799), 1:100.

93. Samuel Johnson, *Dictionary of the English Language*, 2nd ed, 2 vols. (London, W. Strahan, 1755–56), vol. 1; *Times* November 8, 1786, February 16, 1786.

94. The *Times* (March 5, 1787) reported that Lord Duncannon had lost £5,000 (and not £50,000 as other papers had claimed) at play in one evening. A month before (February 1, 1787), the same paper noted that "The house lately established in St. James's street, for the purpose of carrying on a Faro Bank, has already proved materially injurious to some of our young noblemen."

95. The *Times* praised Lord Belgrave for being unlike others of his generation, "whilst the greater part of our rising nobility have been anxious to excell at the gaming table, his object has been to make himself acquainted with the constitution of his country" (January 30, 1789); it noted of the Duke of Clarence that he had "an aversion to horse racing, and all kinds of gambling" (August 13, 1789); in its eulogy of the late Earl of Huntingdon, that "gaming and its concomitant vices he not only disapproved, but detested" (October 7, 1789); and facetiously commented that one of the chief imperfections of the Marquis of Abercorn is that he is "is too economical to dissipate his estates at the gaming table . . ." (October 13, 1790).

96. The King's Proclamation as reported in the *Times* June 29, 1787. For actions against Sabbath activities see M. J. D. Roberts, *Making English Morals* (Cambridge, Cambridge University Press, 2004), chapter 2, and Vic Gattrell, *City of Laughter* (New York, Walter and Co., 2006), chapter 15, and especially the Cruikshank cartoon, "The Enraged Politician or the Sunday reformer," which "shows Belgrave [the introducer of the Bill to prevent Sabbath-breaking among the poor] getting furious at the bawling news-sellers outside his window while he ignore the din made by a fashionable rout in the grand house opposite" (p. 476).

97. *Times* July 2, 1787; ibid., September 15, 1787; ibid., April 4, 1791. See also the moralistic tale of Sunday card-playing among the better sort ibid., January 21, 1791.

98. One example of the voluminous attack on the magistrates is found in the *Times* March 5, 1790; for the suicide of a "a young gentleman of the west of England, who would have inherited at his father's death, a very considerable family estate," ibid., February 2, 1790; for the new law, see ibid., December 29, 1790, and for the ascendancy of gaming *MC* January 10, 1792.

99. Comment about Holcroft's drama and gambling-houses to be found in the *MP* January 4, 1790, in the *Times* of February 23, 1792, and February 6, 1793. For gambling and aristocratic females, see Gillian Russell, "Faro's Daughters: Female Gamesters, Politics and the Discourse of Finance in 1790s Britain," *Eighteenth Century Studies* 33 #4 (Summer 2000): 481–504; *Times* January 31, 1792.

100. *Times* December 29, 1789; for later attacks on French gambling houses in London, see *MP* November 25, 1794, *Times* November 3, 1796, and *MP* March 20, 1797. For the *World's* cry of despair see February 8, 1792.

101. Letter to the *White* August 24, 1790; *Times* December 27, 1791.

102. *Times* January 8, 1798 (emphasis is mine); see also ibid., March 20, 1797, and July 3, 1797.

103. Ibid., December 31, 1791, February 4, 1792.

104. For Judge Ashurst's two charges to the Grand Jury see the *Times* November 16, 1790, the *Evening Mail*, February 1, 1792, and the *Times* February 3, 1792. While only 7 reports of magisterial activity against gaming houses appeared in the *Times* for the first six years of the 1790s, 30 such reports appeared in that paper from 1796 to 1799. In fact, in the last four years of the century, public reports from both King's Bench and the magistrates' and quarter-sessions courts increased four-fold. For Garrow's move for a rule to show cause in issuing a writ against Addington and Kenyon's response, see the *Times* April 22, 1796. For Kenyon's threat to act against magistrates, in the case of The King v. Miller, see *MC* December 1, 1796.

105. For Kenyon as the force compelling magisterial action against gaming, see the *Times* May 2, 1796; in comparing the severity with which Kenyon would have acted to the lenity taken by Ford of Bow Street, who blandly commented that "Captain Wheeler, or any other private gentleman, did not act illegally by having such a table as found in his house for the amusement of his family and friends," see ibid., July 28, 1796; for the need for stiff punishment of the Great in a period of democratic turmoil, see the *MC* June 28, 1796, and for Kenyon's remarks on the same issue, see the case of Atkinson *v.* Holbrook, reported in the *Times* November 17, 1797.

106. The *Times* February 16, 1793; ibid., September 18, 1794. Although the number of stories about gaming had been diminishing from 1792, they virtually disappeared in 1794 and 1795.

107. *MP* February 5, 1798; see also ibid., January 30, 1798; *Times* September 13, 1798.

108. For the fate of the gambling ladies, see Russell, "Faro's Daughters," pp. 489–96. *The Times Digital Index* lists 36 gambling and gaming stories in 1796, 47 in 1797, 16 in 1798, and 25 in 1799. These, however, while useful, are only "gross" figures, including stories about overseas gaming, and gambling used as a euphemism, rather than as an activity. In terms of real stories published in that paper, the number of

actual gambling accounts in 1798 was 14, the same number that appeared in the *Times* in 1817.

109. In 1798, the *Times* reported 19 stories about adultery and divorce, in 1799, 16, but the numbers rose to 29 in 1800 and 51 in 1801. While the *Times* published 100 adultery stories for the first decade of the nineteenth century, it only reported 30 gambling stories for the same period.

110. The *Times* was the first to report the story of an unnamed young nobleman who had lost £70,000 at play on February 4, 1799; the *MH* repeated the story a day later, as did the *White* on February 2, 1799. On February 11th, the *Herald* added salacious details, only to note, three days later, that Cowper's death (and only after this occurred, did any of the papers refer to him by name) "commenced with a severe cold, which his Lordship caught while doing duty with the Hertfordshire Regiment of Militia, of which he was a Captain." Despite this attempt to mitigate the situation, on April 18, 1799, two suits were introduced to the Court of King's Bench against both the *Herald* and the *Times* (criminal informations sought and reported in the *Sun*, February 14, 1799, and *MH* April 18, 1799, the King *v* Bell and the King *v* Brown). The case against the *Times* was decided in an extraordinarily lengthy trial report (more than 2800 words long) on July 3, 1799 (see the *Times* for that date).

111. *Times* April 2, 1795. While this item dealt with gaming on Sundays, we have seen more generally that through the eighteenth century the example of the Great was always held up as an important contributory to the gaming of the rest. This comes from volume 2 of the reprint of *Microcosm of London, or London in Minature* [1809], 3 vols. (London, Methuen & Co., 1904), 2: 95. The clergyman's letter to Sidmouth appeared in the *Times* November 15, 1816, and it was Judge Grose, in his observations on King *v* Moore, reported in the *Times*, February 11, 1800, who made the connection between gaming and other crimes.

112. *Times* July 22, 1819.

Chapter 6. Vice in an Age of Respectability

1. [John Corry] *A satirical view of London at the commencement of the nineteenth century* (London, G. Kearsley, 1801), p. 231.

2. *Reminiscences and Recollections of Captain Gronow 1810–1860*, 2 vols. (London, John C. Nimmo, 1892), 1:131.

3. See, for example, the account of "The young man apprehended a few days ago by Carpmeal and Miller, with a large amount of forged bills of exchange, and 2000l in Bank notes, supposed to have been obtained by discounting these bills at the Bank, [who] is of a respectable family and connections. He is lately returned from the West Indies, and it is believed the gaming table has been his ruin," in the *MP* March 4, 1800. See also the comment in the *Oracle* February 28, 1800.

4. One interesting exception was the court case between a Mr. Whaley and Sir Thomas Southcott, which came before King's Bench, and was widely reported; see, for example, *White* November 6, 1800. The Whaley/Southcott case, according to the account in the *MC* of February 17, 1801, "has made a very great noise in the gay world . . ." For other accounts see the *LP* November 7, 1800 and the *Times* February 7, 1801.

5. J. L. Chirol, *A Sermon on Gaming* (London, C. & J. Rivington, 1824), p. 21; in his *Sermon on the Vice of Gaming* (London, C. & J. Rivington) of 1825, Rev. Benjamin Sanford warned his audience that, among its many other evils, in gamesters, "the heart soon becomes callous . . . [to] every sentiment of honour" (p. 15); *A Letter to Ball Hughes, Esq on Club House and Private Gaming* (London, J. Evans, 1824), p. 5.

6. *LC* March 6, 1800; for more on this case, see the *St. J* March 4, 1800, and the *MP* March 6, 1800.

7. *MP* March 5, 1800; *MC* November 5, 1800.

8. See *GEP* February 11, 1800.

9. See for example *Times* October 4, 1810 for the EO table at the Croyden Fair.

10. "Restitutor" in the *GM* 1818, pt. ii, p. 586; for Davis's story see the *Times* April 10, 1820.

11. For the unnamed merchant seeking to understand his nephew's losses, see the *Times* May 23, 1820; Similarly, in case of King *v* Lee, the tradesman who had lost all his property at Lee's house "had not confined himself to the loss of his own money; but had actually been induced by his appetite for play to pawn the goods with which other persons had intrusted him." *Times* July 4, 1820.

12. For more on the Clutterbuck case, see D. T. Andrew, " 'How frail are *Lovers vows*, and *Dicers oaths*': Gaming, Governing and Moral Panic in Britain, 1781–1782" in *Moral Panics, the Media and the Law in Early Modern England* (London, Palgrave Macmillan, 2009), pp. 176–94.

13. *Times* December 25, 1822.

14. See, for example, the letter to the editor, signed "BB," in the *Times* November 24, 1821; another letter which argued that gambling houses could not be put down by actions of the government or the law, but that "the cause of their extinction is likely to be the progress of good sense, just taste, and right feeling in the community . . ." in the *Times* October 21, 1821; for more points of view see the *Times* December 23, 1822, February 13, 1823, July 24, 1824, July 28, 1824, August 31, 1824. For a look at Crockford's and its history see Henry Blyth, *Hell and Hazard or, William Crockford versus the Gentlemen of England* (London, Weidenfeld, 1969).

15. "Expositor" in the *Times*, July 23, 1824. Between this letter and 1827, "Expositor" wrote another four letters about gaming-houses to the *Times* (August 17, 1824, October 14, 1824, December 10, 1824 and July 25, 1826). Captain Gronow also spent several pages of his *Reminiscences* dwelling on the luxury of the apartments, and the size of the gaming profits, of Crockford's, 2:81–6. Editorial in the *Times* December 16, 1824.

16. *Times* November 29, 1827.

17. Ibid., May 10, 1830. Blomfield's missive, *A Letter on the Present Neglect of the Lord's Day*, was also criticized by *John Bull*, and defended by *A Letter to the Editor of the Times* and Christianus, *A letter to the Editor of the Times* (London, Rivington's, 1830).

18. *Times* August 25, 1831.

19. Reported in the *Times*, May 10, 1833.

20. The *Times* (October 3, 1832) noted that most of the £45,000 per annum income that the Duke received was "swallowed up by regular payments of interest and annuities upon gambling and other bonds . . ."

21. The *Times* September 26, 1843.

22. Ashton, *The History of Gambling*, p. 149. For more on postwar gambling see Mark Clapson, *A Bit of a Flutter* (Manchester, Manchester University Press, 1992), chap. 2.

23. Thomas Dibdin, *Pilgrim's Progress* (London, Harding & King, 1834), p. 109.

24. Thomas Chevalier, *Remarks on Suicide* [1824], p. 367.

25. *Derby Mercury* September 26, 1827.

26. The *Ipswich Journal* July 26, 1823, *Jackson's Oxford Journal* July 26, 1823, the *Examiner* July 27, 1823, the *Derby Mercury* July 30, 1823, and the *Aberdeen Journal* August 6, 1823.

27. *Hampshire Telegraph* September 28, 1829. See also the account of the inquisition on the body of Rebecca Mabbett, a seventeen-year-old girl, in the *Examiner* October 22, 1826, or the notice of the boy of ten who drowned himself, and was found *felo de se* in the *MC* March 27, 1842.

28. The *Examiner* June 7, 1840.

29. See for example, the verdict in the case of a servant girl who killed herself, and was found to have taken "mercury in the morning, in a state of temporary derangement, from the effects of the liquor she had taken the night before," in the *Hull Packet* August 3, 1833.

30. *Examiner* September 9, 1838.

31. *Leeds Mercury* November 25, 1809, *Aberdeen Journal* January 10, 1810.

32. *Times* March 1, 1831.

33. Ibid., June 16, 1831.

34. The three data bases employed were the Times Digital Archive, the 17th and 18th Century Burney collection, and the 19th century British Library newspaper collection. Those found *felo de se*, who died while committing a criminal act, or in any sort of prison or holding institution were systematically eliminated from the count. For the period before 1800, I used the first two of these collections, and for the period after, the second two.

35. These numbers come from the national 19th century British Library collection, though the Times numbers (3 in 1815–24; 5 in 1825–34 and 7 in 1835–44), while smaller, go in exactly the same direction.

36. *Times* March 18, 1840. The *Champion* of April 26, 1840 reported a similar comment coming at an inquest, this time from a member of the jury: "A juror said, that whatever might be the opinion of his fellow jury men, he for one would not consent to return any other verdict but *felo de se*. These matters were treated too lightly by juries in general."

37. *Times* October 24, 1826.

38. *Examiner* January 30, 1831.

39. In his response to press outrage, Gell, in a letter sent to the *Times* (February 11, 1830) remarked that he set the inquest to begin at 9:45 AM, and that it "was held in a public room, open to all persons . . ."

40. *Times* February 9, 1830, *MC* February 10, 1830, and *Courier* quoted in the *Caledonian Mercury*, February 13, 1830.

41. See, for example, the two letters in the *Times* of February 12, 1830.

42. *Times* January 31, 1831; *MC* January 27, 1831. Other papers which mentioned the umbrella were the above-mentioned *Times*, the *Hull Packet* of February 1, the *Derby Mercury* of February 2, 1831 and *Freeman's* of February 4.

43. "Indicator" in the *Examiner* July 17, 1831; *Times* December 25, 1843.

44. John Galt's introduction to his play "The Apostle, or Atlantis Destroyed" in *The New British Theatre*, 4 vols. (London, Henry Cobourn, 1814–15), 4:346.

45. Astley *v* Garth in the *MC* February 20, 1827; the Clayton *v* Franklyn case in the *Times* of July 26, 1830; Calcraft *v* Harborough in *Bell's Life*, February 13, 1831, and the Bligh *v* Wellesley trial ibid., July 13, 1827.

46. *Ipswich Journal* March 17, 1830; *MC* March 18, 1830, *Examiner* March 21, 1830, *Bristol Mercury* March 23, 1830, and the *Times* March 18, 1830.

47. Lawrence Stone, *The Road to Divorce*, pp. 430–31; tables 9.1, 9.3 and 9.4.

48. *Hull Packet* March 20, 1846; see also *Bell's Life*, April 1, 1832 for the plaintiff, a Mr. Corner, suing his attorney from debtor's prison for crim. con., and collecting £500 in damages. In another case reported in the *Times* of August 25, 1847, Gould *v* Elton, the plaintiff's lawyer, in his opening speech to the jury, noted that "the plaintiff, who was a man in humble circumstances, and who brought this action to recover compensation from the defendant, a gentleman of station and fortune . . ." For Platt's comments see the *Hull Packet* February 21, 1845.

49. Traveller, *The Art of Duelling* (London, Joseph Thomas, 1836), p. 2.

50. Eldrid *v* Cross in the *MC* December 2, 1839. Langford *v* Barrett in *Times* February 9, 1836. Langford could not have been pleased, however, at the damages of 1 shilling awarded by the jury; *Bell's Life* February 15, 1836.

51. Tucker *v* Gooch in *Times* January 5, 1842; Wallis *v* Francis in the *Examiner* March 12, 1842. The plaintiff in this last case originally asked for £10,000 damages. Similarly in the case of Worrall *v* Atkins (*Times* April 6, 1833), the plaintiff agreed to accept £200 and costs to terminate the trial, or the case of Ward *v* Sinkler, reported in the *Era* December 13, 1840, in which the plaintiff settled for the sum of 20 shillings, explaining he too had "ulterior goals."

52. *Examiner* June 5, 1847.

53. *Times* April 7, 1830. Stone comments that "it was said this was one of the first cases for decades in which there had been neither a prior crim. con. action nor an explanation why not." *Road to Divorce*, p. 324 footnote 68.

54. Phillimore on "The Law of Divorce" in the House of Commons, reported in the *MC* June 4, 1830. Stone argues that "contemporaries were well aware" that from being a preserve of the aristocracy, divorce had become accessible to wealthy people of other classes [*Road to Divorce*, p. 327]. However, popular discourse, both within and outside of Parliament used different language to describe those with and without access to such remedies.

55. *MC* April 7, 1830; see also the *Examiner* April 4, 1830.

56. This notion of the strategic use of the language of fashion, or of rich and poor, rather than the language of class, owes something to both E. P. Thompson's *Making* and Gareth Stedman Jones's *The Language of Class. MC* April 7, 1830. See also two letters to the editor on this issue, one signed "Homo" to the *Times* May 15, 1830; the other signed "Civis," ibid., June 5, 1830.

57. *Bristol Mercury* August 22, 1840; this piece is attributed to an unspecified "London paper" which I have been unable to identify. "Homo" cited above, went even farther, and recommended solitary imprisonment as an appropriate punishment for those convicted of adultery.

58. The *Examiner* March 12, 1842, p. 171. The *MC* November 7, 1828, for the Cazelet cause; the fact that the adulterer was both a clergyman and a cousin of the husband gave this case a special piquancy.

59. *Bell's Life* February 14, 1836, "Crim Con in High Life."

60. *The Satirist; or, the Censor of the Times*, "TOEB," letter to the editor, May 14, 1843, p. 159.

61. Stephen Leach, *The Folly and Wickedness of Duelling* (London, 1822), p. v.

62. A very rough count of duels reported in the press gives us the figure of fifteen duels fought in the five years between 1805 and 1809 and six in the same length of time between 1816 and 1820.

63. Leach, *The Folly*, vi; Rev. Peter Chalmers, *Two Discourses on the sin, danger and remedy of duelling* (Edinburgh, Thomsons Brothers, 1822), pp. 10–12; *The Duellist, or a cursory view of the rise, progress and practice of Duelling* (1822), pp. 95, 112. For an analysis of the first of these duels, see James N. McCord Jr., "Politics and Honor in Early Nineteenth-Century England: The Dukes' Duel," *Huntington Library Quarterly* 62 (1999), pp. 88–114.

64. Leach, *The Folly*, p. 15; Chalmers *Discourses*, pp. 138–39; *The Duellist*, p. 105; Chalmers, *Discourses*, pp. 194–95.

65. Winchilsea's letter and Wellington's challenge quoted in Elizabeth Longford, *Wellington*, 2 vols. (London, Weidenfeld & Nicholson, 1969), vol. 2, "Pillar of State," pp. 186, 187.

66. The *Standard* March 23, 1829; the *New Times* March 30, 1829. For more on this duel, see Kathryn Beresford, "The 'hero of a thousand battles betrays us!' The duke as hero and villain during the emancipation crisis and after," *Wellington Studies* IV (2008), pp. 274–98.

67. The Coote *v* Armstrong case was reported in the *Times* June 21, 1800; the *MC* May 18, 1801, and the *Times* June 6 and 11, 1801. The King's letter applauding Coote's correct action appeared in the *Times* July 8, 1801.

68. These figures are based on the *Times Digital Archive* and *British Newspaper 1600–1900* database for the years 1800, 1810, 1820, and 1830:

Duelling in the Press

	Stopped Duels or Challenges	Completed
1800	10	22
1810	9	20
1820	13	16
1830	11	6

69. See *MC* January 11, 1830 and the *Times* of the same day for the first reports of this affair; the *Bristol Mercury* carried the story the next day.

70. The *Daily News* August 19, 1847.

71. The original comment of Chambers, published in the *MC* January 14, 1830, was widely reprinted; it appeared in the *North Wales Chronicle* on January 14, 1830, which said its report was copied from the *Observer*. *Freeman's Journal*, an Irish newspaper,

published the story on January 15, 1830, saying that its report was from the *Globe*, and the *Liverpool Mercury* ran the story also on the 15th. The editorial on this comment in the *MC* appeared on January 19, 1830, and the *Examiner's* reprint and further criticism on January 24, 1830.

72. This remarkable editorial was published in the *North Wales Chronicle* on January 21, 1830. For an equally savage commentary, see the letter to the *Age* of January 17, 1830, entitled "The Force of Example," and signed by "FRIEND OF POOR CLAYTON, Who is convinced that he fell a sacrifice to a too-rigid adherence to the Wellington-Principles of Duelling."

73. The trial was fully reported in the *Times* April 3, 1830. The jury wished, it seems, to find a verdict of manslaughter, but Bayley, when asked said that "if they found the prisoner guilty of any crime, it must be murder . . ." and so, again after a long discussion, the jury came back with a Not Guilty verdict. See the *Examiner* April 13, 1830.

74. "One Who Has . . ." in the *Times* July 5, 1843; "J.B." in response in the *Times* July 7, 1843.

75. *Bell's Life* September 3, 1843.

76. *Punch*, October 24, 1843, p. 162.

77. Thus the *Ipswich Chronicle* (March 9, 1844) criticized unnamed Cabinet Ministers and the Attorney General, Smith, of either fighting duels or challenging others to fight. *Freemans* (March 14, 1844) pointed their finger at Sir Henry Hardinge, a minister of state as did the *Era* in March 17, 1844 and again, following Munro's conviction, in August 22, 1847.

78. *Freeman's Journal* March 14, 1844; the *Examiner* August 21, 1847.

79. The *Caledonian Mercury* of August 23, 1847, thought duelling had ceased, and the *Preston Guardian* of August 21, 1847, felt that new methods of conflict resolution among the Great would now be found. It was the same editorial which contained the self-congratulatory view of the press's role in shaping public opinion. Different historians give different dates for "last duels" fought in Britain; if 1843 is not the very end of the line, perhaps 1847 is not far off.

80. See Antony Taylor, *Lords of Misrule* (Basingstoke, Palgrave Macmillan, 2004) for the argument that such vicious behavior spurred active dislike of the upper classes till the early twentieth century.

Conclusion

1. *The Periodical Press of Great Britain and Ireland: or an Inquiry into the State of the Public Journals, Chiefly as Regards their Moral and Political Influence* (London, Hurst, Robinson & Co., 1824), 1. See more generally Aled Jones, *Powers of the Press: Newspapers, Power and the Public in Nineteenth Century England* (Aldershot: Scolar Press, 1996).

2. *Times* December 25, 1789, Samuel Parr, *A Discourse on the late Fast* (London, J. Dodsley and H. Payne, 1781), p. 28. See James Kelly, "The Decline of Duelling and the Emergence of the Middle Class in Ireland," in Fintan Lane, ed., *Politics, Society and the Middle Class in Modern Ireland* (Basingstoke, Palgrave Macmillan, 2010), p. 97: "The

rapid expansion of the public sphere in the second half of the eighteenth century, epitomized by the surge in print, is crucial to the growth of a middle-class voice."

3. "Experience" in the *PA* June 13, 1765. See also "Tranquilius" to the *Gaz* September 16, 1765, "Salus Populi Suprema Lex" to *Bingley's Journal* June 9, 1770. William Pitt junior was complimented by one of "those who, perhaps rightly, think private and public Virtue to be inseparable" for his attributes of moderation and economy in the *PA* July 31, 1782. See also John Brewer, "This, that and the other: Public, social and private in the seventeenth and eighteenth centuries," in Dario Castiglione and Lesley Sharpe, eds., *Shifting the Boundaries: Transformation of the Languages of Public and Private in the Eighteenth Century* (Exeter, University of Exeter Press, 1995), pp. 1–21.

4. "P" in the *GEP* March 30, 1773.

5. *Olla Podrida* September 8, 1787. "Observator" to the *Times* October 11, 1785; Corry, *A satirical view of London*, p. 231.

6. E. P. Thompson, "Eighteenth Century English Society: Class Struggle without Class," *Social History* (May 1978), p. 144. Bob Harris has also pointed out the reciprocal relationship between this group of people and the rise of the press in his fine book *Politics and the Rise of the Press* (p. 28): "it is from the growing middling ranks, both in urban and rural areas, that the biggest impetus behind the rise of the newspaper in the eighteenth century appears to have come."

7. Although this book has argued for the moral condemnation of the mores of the world of fashion as central to the creation of a middling self-consciousness, two other, different, and provocative accounts of this development can be found in Dror Wahrman, *Imagining the Middle Class* (Cambridge, Cambridge University Press, 1995) and *The Making of the Modern Self* (New Haven, Yale University Press, 2006). See also Peter Earle, *The Making of the English Middle Class* (London, Methuen, 1989).

Selected Bibliography

Primary Sources

An Account of the Endeavours that have been used to suppress Gaming-Houses (London, 1722).

An Account of the Life and Character of Sir Cholmley Deering, Bart (London, J. Read, 1711).

Addison, Joseph, *The Papers of Joseph Addison*, 4 vols. (Edinburgh, William Creech, 1790).

Addison, Mr. *A Collection of interesting Anecdotes* (London, 1793).

An Address to the Great (London, R. Baldwin, 1756).

The Adulterer, A Poem (London, W. Bingley, 1769).

Adultery a-la-Mode (London, R. Thomas, n.d.).

Adultery and the Decline of Marriage: Three Tracts (New York, Garland Publishing, 1984).

Adultery, The Trial of Mr. William Atkinson, Linen draper of Cheapside for Criminal Conversation with Mrs. Connor, wife of Mr. Connor, late of the Mitre, at Barnet . . . before Lord Kenyon (London, Couch & Lakin, 1789).

Adye, Stephen Payne, *A Treatise on Courts Martial* (London, J. Murray, 1778).

[Allen, John Taylor] *Duelling, an Essay* (Oxford, S. Collingwood, 1807).

Allen, William, ed., *The Philanthropist* (London, 1811–19)

[Andrews, John] *Reflections on the too prevailing Spirit of DISSIPATION AND GALLANTRY shewing its dreadful Consequences to Publick Freedom* (London, E. and C. Dilly, 1771).

Andrews, Miles Peter, *The Reparation* (London, Printed for T. and W. Lowndes [etc.], 1784).

Anstey, Christopher, *The New Bath Guide*, Letter VIII, in the *Poetical Works* (London, T. Cadell & W. Davies, 1808).

Arwaker, E., *Aesop: Truth in Fiction*, 4 vols. (London, J. Churchill, 1708).

Ayscough, Francis, *A Discourse Against Self-Murder, a sermon* (London, H. Shute Cox, 1755).

Baker, Henry, "Gaming," in *Medulla Poetarum Romanorum* (London, 1737).

Barry, Edward, *Theological, Philosophical and Moral Essays*, 2nd ed. (London, J. Connor, [1797?]).

Barton, Bernard, "Stanzas on the Death of Sir Samuel Romilly," from *Poems* (London, 1825).

Berkeley, George, *The Works of George Berkeley, Bishop of Cloyne*, ed. A. A. Luce and T. E. Jessop, 9 vols. (London, T. Nelson, 1948–57).

Blackstone, William, *Commentaries on the Laws of England*, 4 vols. (Oxford, Clarendon Press, 1769).

Blomfield, C. J., *A Letter on the Present Neglect of the Lord's Day* (London, B. Fellowes, 1830).

Bonhote, Elizabeth, *The Parental Monitor*, 4 vols. (London, Wm. Lane, 1796).

Brown, John, *On the Pursuit of False Pleasures and the Mischiefs of Immoderate Gaming* (Bath, James Leake, 1750).

Buchan, George, *Remarks on Duelling; comprising observations on the arguments in defense of that practice* (Edinburgh, Waugh and Innes, 1823).

Burgoyne, John, *The Heiress* (Dublin, John Exshaw, 1786).

Campbell, Archibald, *An Enquiry into the Original of Moral Virtue* (Edinburgh, Gavin Hamilton, 1733).

Cases of Divorce for Several Causes (London, E. Curll, 1715).

The Cases of Polygamy, Concubinage, Adultery, Divorce, etc. by the most eminent hands (London, T. Payne, 1732).

Centlivre, Susannah, *The Beau's Duel* (London, D. Brown & N. Cox, 1702).

———, *The Perjur'd Husband* (London, Bennett Banbury, 1700).

Chalmers, Thomas, *Two Discourses on the sin, danger and remedy of duelling* (Edinburgh, Thomsons Brothers, 1822).

Chevalier, Thomas, *Remarks on Suicide* in *The Pamphleteer*, vol. 23.

Chirol, J. L., *A Sermon on Gaming* (London, C. & J. Rivington, 1824).

Chishull, Edmund, *Against Duelling, a Sermon Preached before the Queen* (London, J. Round, 1712).

A Circumstantial and Authentic Account of a Late unhappy Affair (London, J. Burd, 1765).

Clerke, Captain Abraham, *A Home-Thrust at Duelling intended as an answer to a late Pamphlet intitled A Hint on Duelling* (London, S. Bladon, 1753).

Cockburn, John, *A Discourse of Self Murder* (London, 1716).

Collier, Jeremy, "Upon Duelling," in *Essays upon several Moral Subjects* [1692], (London, R. Sare, H. Hindmarsh, 1698).

Colvill, Robert, *Britain, a poem in three books* (Edinburgh, Wal. Ruddiman jr. & Co., 1747).

Combe, William, *The Suicide* from *The English Dance of Death* 2 vols. (London, J. Diggens, 1815).

Comber, Thomas, *A Discourse upon Duels* (London, R. Wilkin, B. Tooke, 1720).

[Corry, John] *A satirical view of London at the commencement of the nineteenth century* (London, G. Kearsley, 1801).

Courtin, Anton, *The Rules of Civility or the Maxims of Genteel Behaviour*, with *A Short Treatise on the Point of Honour* (London, Robert Clavell and Jonathan Robinson, 1703).

Crabbe, George, *The Poetical Works of the Rev. George Crabbe* (London, John Murray, 1838).

[Defoe, Daniel] *An Apology for the Army* (London, J. Carson, 1715).

Dibdin, Thomas, *Pilgrim's Progress* (London, Harding & King, 1834).

A Discourse Upon Self-Murder (London, J. Fox, 1754).

Duelling, a poem (London, T. Davies, 1775).

The Duellist, or a cursory view of the rise, progress and practice of Duelling (London, 1822).

Eden, William, *Principles of Penal Law* (London, B. White, 1771).

Erskine, Thomas, *Reflections on Gaming, Annuities and Usurious Contracts* (London, T. Davies, 1786).

An Essay on Duelling, written with a view to discountenance this barbarous and disgraceful practice (London, J. Debrett, 1792).

An Essay on Gaming, in an Epistle to a Young Nobleman (London, 1761).

An Essay on Modern Gallantry (London, M. Cooper, [1750]).

The Evils of Adultery and Prostitution with an inquiry into the causes of their present alarming increase (London, T. Vernon, 1792).

E. W., *Poems Written on Several Occasions, to which are added three essays* (London, J. Baker, 1711).

False Honour, or the Folly of Duelling (London, A. Type, 1750).

Fielding, Henry, *Amelia*, ed. Martin Battesin (Oxford, Clarendon Press, 1983).

——, *The Covent Garden Journal* [1752], edited by Bertrand Golgar (Middletown, Conn., Wesleyan University Press, 1988).

——, *An Enquiry into the Late Increase of Robbers* in *An Enquiry into the Causes of the Late Increase of Robbers* [1751] *and Related Writings*, ed. Malvin R. Zirker (Oxford, Clarendon Press, 1988).

——, *The History of Tom Jones, a foundling*, 6 vols. (London, A. Millar, 1749).

A Full and Exact Relation of the Duel fought in Hyde park on Saturday november 15, 1712, between His Grace James, Duke of Hamilton, and the R.H. Charles Lord Mohun, in a letter to a member of Parliament (London, E. Curll, 1713).

Galt, John, 'The Apostle, or Atlantis Destroyed,' in *The New British Theatre*, 4 vols. (London, Henry Cobourn, 1814–15).

Garrick, David, *Lethe* (London, Paul Valliant, 1749).

——, *The Lying Varlet* (Dublin, J. Rhames, 1741).

The Gentleman instructed in the Conduct of a Virtuous and Happy Life, 2 vols. (London, R. Ware, 1755).

Gentleman of that City, *Modern Honour or the Barber Duellist, A comic opera in two acts* (London, J. Williams, 1775).

Goldsmith, Oliver, *The Life of Richard Nash* (London, J. Newberry, 1762).

[Grainger, Lydia] *Modern Amours* (London, 1733).

Gregory, George, *A Sermon on Suicide* [1785], 3rd ed. (London, J. Nichols, 1797).

Hanway, Jonas, *Observations on the Causes of the Dissoluteness Which Reigns Among the Lower Classes of the People* (London, J. & F. Rivington, 1772).

Hayes, Samuel, *Duelling, a poem* (Cambridge, J. Archdeacon, 1775).

Haywood, Eliza, *The History of Jemmy and Jenny Jessamy* (London, T. Gardner, 1753).

———, *The History of Miss Betsy Thoughtless* [1751], ed. Christine Blouch (Peterborough, Ont., Broadview Literary Texts, 1998).

Heath, Robert, "To one who was so impatient," in *Clarasella; together with Poems Occasional* (London, Humph. Moseley, 1650).

Henley, John, *Cato condemned, or the case and history of self-murder argu'd and displayed at large, on the principles of reason, justice, law, religion, fortitude, love of ourselves and our country, and example; occasioned by a gentleman of Gray's inn stabbing himself in the year 1730, A theological lecture, delivered at the Oratory* (London, J. Marshall, 1730).

Edward, Lord Herbert of Cherbury, *The Life of Edward, First Lord Herbert of Cherbury* (London, Oxford University Press, 1976).

Herries, John, *An Address to the Public on the frequent and enormous crime of suicide*, 2nd ed. (London, John Fielding, 1781).

Hey, Richard, *Three Dissertations; on the pernicious effects of gaming, on duelling, and on suicide* (Cambridge, 1812).

Hildrop, John [Timothy Hooker], *Essay on Honour* (London, R. Minors, 1741).

Hill, George Birkbeck, ed., *Boswell's Life of Johnson*, 6 vols. (Oxford, Clarendon, 1887).

A Hint on Duelling, in a letter to a friend (London, M. Sheepey, 1752).

Hobbes, Thomas, *The Elements of Law* [1650], edited by Ferdinand Tonnies (London, Simpkin, Marshall, 1889).

———, *Leviathan* [1651] (New York, Macmillan & Co., 1962).

Holbrook, Anthony, *Christian Essays upon the Immorality of Uncleanness and Duelling delivered in two Sermons preached at St. Paul's* (London, John Wyat, 1727).

Hume, David, "On the first Principles of Government," in *Essays and Treatises on Several Subjects* (London, A. Millar, 1758).

Hutcheson, Francis, *An Inquiry into the Original of Our Ideas of Beauty and Virtue* (London, J. Darby, A. Bettesworth, 1726).

Ingram, Rowland, *Reflections on Duelling* (London, J. Hatchard, 1804).

Jackson, William, *Thirty Letters on various subjects*, 2 vols. (London, T. Cadell, 1784).

Jeffery, John, *Felo de Se: or a Warning against the most Horrid and Unnatural Sin of Self-Murder in a Sermon* (Norwich, A. & J. Churchill, 1702).

Jephson, Alexander, *The heinous sins of* ADULTERY *and* FORNICATION, *considered and represented, in a* SERMON *lately preached in the . . . diocese of Durham* (London, J. and P. Knapton, 1754).

Johnson, Samuel, *Dictionary of the English Language*, 2nd ed., 2 vols. (London, W. Strahan, 1755–56).

Jones, Thomas, *A Sermon upon Dueling* (Cambridge, J. Archdeacon, 1792).

Junius, [*Letters*] (London, T. Bensley, 1797).

Kelly, John, *The Married Philosopher* (London, T. Worral, 1732).

Kenrick, William, *The Duellist* (London, T. Evans, 1773).

Knaggs, Thomas, *A Sermon against Self-murder* (London, H. Hills, 1708).

Kyte, Joshua, *Sermon*, "True Religion the only Foundation of true Courage" (London, B. Barker, 1758).

Leach, Stephen, *The Folly and Wickedness of Duelling* (Andover, 1822).

A Letter to Ball Hughes, Esq on Club House and Private Gaming (London, J. Evans, 1824).

Letters from Mrs. Elizabeth Carter to Mrs. Montague between the years 1755 and 1800 . . . ed. Rev. Montagu Pennington, 3 vols. (London, F. C. and J. Rivington, 1817).

Locke, John, *Two Treatises on Government*, ed. P. Laslett (New York, Mentor, 1963).

Mackqueen, John, *Two Essays: the first on courage, the other on honour* (London, John Morphew, 1711).

Mallet, David, *Mustapha* (London, A. Millar, 1739).

Mandeville, Bernard, *An Enquiry into the Origins of Honour and the Usefulness of Christianity in War* [1732], 2nd ed. with a new introduction by M. M. Goldsmith (London, Frank Cass, 1971).

———, *Fable of the Bees*, ed. F. B. Kaye (Oxford, Clarendon Press, 1924).

McDonnell, Thomas, *The Eighth Commandment considered in its full extent, and particularly as applicable to the present reigning spirit of gameing: a sermon* (Dublin, George Faulkner, 1760).

Member of Parliament, *Hints for a reform, particularly in the gambling clubs* (London, R. Baldwin, 1784).

Microcosm of London, or London in Minature [1809], 3 vols. (London, Methuen & Co., 1904).

A Modest Defence of Gaming (London, R. and J. Dodsley, 1754).

Moore, Charles, *A full inquiry into the Subject of Suicide to which are added (as being closely connected with the subject), Two Treatises on Duelling and Gambling* (London, J. F. & C. Rivington, 1790).

Moore, Edward, *The Gamester* (1753), introduced by Charles H. Peake (Los Angeles, Augustan Reprint Society, 1948), publication #14.

More, Hannah, *The Two Wealthy Farmers* (London, F. and C. Rivington, 1799).

[Maurice Morgann] *A Letter to My Lords the Bishops, on the occasion of the Present Bill for the Preventing of Adultery* (London, J. Dodsley, 1779).

Mumford, Erasmus, *A Letter to the Club at White's* (London, W. Owen, 1750).

Odell, Rev. William Butler, *Essay on Duelling, in which the subject is Morally and Historically Considered; and the practice deduced from the Earliest Times* (Cork, Odell and Laurent, 1814).

Oldmixon, John, *A Defence of Mr. Maccartney* (London, A. Baldwin, 1712).

Old Officer, *Cautions and Advices to Officers of the Army* (Edinburgh, Aeneas Mackay, 1777).

Parr, Samuel, *A Discourse on the late Fast* (London, J. Dodsley and H. Payne, 1781).

Pearce, Zachary, *A Sermon on Self-murder* [1736], 3rd edition (London, John Rivington, 1773).

Perceval, Thomas, *Moral and Literary Dissertations* (Warrington, W. Eyres, 1789), "True and False Honour."

The Periodical Press of Great Britain and Ireland: or an Inquiry into the State of the Public Journals, Chiefly as Regards their Moral and Political Influence (London, Hurst, Robinson & Co., 1824).

Person of Quality, *Marriage Promoted* (London, Richard Baldwin, 1690).

Philogamus, *Present state of matrimony: or the real causes of conjugal infidelity* (London, J. Buckland, 1739).

Pleasing reflections on life and manners with essays, characters, & poems, moral & entertaining, principally selected from fugitive publications (London, 1787).

Pollen, Thomas, *The fatal consequences of adultery, to monarchies as well as to private families, with a defence of the bill passed in the House of Lords in the year 1771* (London, T. Lowndes, 1772).

Popple, William, *The Double Deceit* (London, T. Woodward & J. Wallace, 1736).

Populousness with Oeconomy (London, C. Buckland, 1759).

Prince, John, *Self-Murder Asserted to be a Very Heinous Crime* (London, B. Bragge, 1709).

Public Characters of 1799–1800 (London, P. Alard, 1799).

Reflexions on Gaming (London, J. Barnes, 1750).

The Relapse, 2 vols. (London, T. Lowndes, 1780).

Reminiscences and Recollections of Captain Gronow 1810–1860, 2 vols. (London, John C. Nimmo, 1892).

Rennell, Thomas, "The Consequences of the Vice of Gaming, preached 1793," in *Discourses on Various Subjects* (London, F. and C. Rivington, 1801).

Richardson, Samuel, *Clarissa or the History of a Young Lady*, 8 vols. (London, S. Richardson, 1751).

———, *The History of Sir Charles Grandison* (London, S. Richardson, 1753–54).

Rowley, William, *A Treatise on Female . . . Diseases* (London, 1788).

Sedaine, M. J., *The Duel*, trans. William O'Brien (London, T. Davies, 1772).

Self-murther and duelling the effects of Cowardice and Atheism (London, R. Wilkin, 1728).

Shakespeare, William, "The Tragedy of Hamlet, Prince of Denmark," in *Shakespeare's Tragedies* (London, J. M. Dent, 1925).

A Short Treatise upon the Propriety and Necessity of Duelling (Bath, 1779).

Sketches of Modern Life, 2 vols. (London, W. Miller, 1799).

Smalbroke, Richard, *A Sermon to the Societies for the Reformation of Manners*, "Reformation Necessary to Prevent our Ruine" (London, Joseph Downing, 1728).

Stanton, Lieutenant Samuel, *The Principles of Duelling with Rules to be Observed in every particular respecting it* (London, T. Hookham, 1790).

Thornhill, Richard, *The Life and Noble Character of Richard Thornhill* (London, 1711).

Thoughts on Duelling (Cambridge, J. Archdeacon, 1773).

Thoughts on Gallantry, Love and Marriage (London, R. and J. Dodsley, 1754).

Thraliana, ed. Katherine C. Balderston (Oxford, Clarendon Press, 1942).

A Timely Advice, or Treatise of Play and Gaming (London, Th. Harper, 1640).

Trapp, Joseph, *Royal Sin, or Adultery Rebuk'd in a Great King, a sermon delivered at St. Martin's* (London, J. Higgonson, 1738).

Traveller, *The Art of Duelling* (London, Joseph Thomas, 1836).

The Trial of Captain Edward Clarke for the Murder of Captain Thomas Innes in a duel in Hyde park, March 12, 1749 (London, M. Cooper, 1750).

[Troussaint, Francois Vincent] *Manners*, trans. from the French (London, J. Payne & J. Boquet, 1749).

Voltaire, *Philosophical Letters* (1733) in *The Works of Voltaire*, vol. 10 of 25 (London, J. Newbery, 1761).

[Ward, Edward] *Adam and Eve Stript of their Furbelows: or the Fashionable Virtues and Vices of Both Sexes, Exposed* (London, J. Woodward, 1714).

Webster, William, *A Casuistical Essay on Anger and Forgiveness* (London, W. Owen, 1750).

Well-Wisher to both Peace and Honour, *Honours preservation without Blood* (London, Philip Brooksby, 1680).

Wesley, John, *The Works of the Rev. John Wesley*, 10 vols. (Philadelphia, D. & S. Neall, 1826–27).

Whole Art and Mystery of Modern Gaming fully exposed and detected (London, J. Roberts, 1726).

Wilberforce, William, *A Practical View of the Prevailing Religious System of Professed Christians* (London, T. Cadell jr. and W. Davies, 1797).

Wollstonecraft, Mary, *Vindication of the Rights of Women* in *The Vindication of the Rights of Men and the Vindication of the Rights of Women*, ed. Sylvana Tomaselli (Cambridge, Cambridge University Press, 1995).

Woman of Honour (London, T. Lowndes and W. Nicholl, 1768).

Wood, John, *An Essay towards a description of Bath* [1742], 2nd ed. (London, James Bettenhem, 1749).

[Woodward, Josiah], *Disswasive from Gaming* (London, Joseph Downing, 1726).

[Woodward, Josiah], *A Rebuke to the sin of uncleanliness* (London, Joseph Downing, 1720).

[Wray, Mary], *The Ladies Library*, 3rd ed. (London, Jacob Tonson, 1722).

Secondary Sources

Anderson, S. "Legislative Divorce: law for the aristocracy?" in G.R. Rubin & David Sugarman, eds., *Law, Economy and Society 1750–1914: Essays in the History of English Law* (Abingdon, Professional Books, 1984).

Andrew, D. T., *London Debating Societies, 1776–1779* (London, London Record Society, 1994).

Andrew, Donna T., " 'Adultery-A-La-Mode': Privilege, the Law and Attitudes to Adultery, 1770–1809," *History* (82) 1997.

Andrews, Alexander, *The History of British Journalism* (London, Richard Bentley, 1859).

Ashton, John, *The History of Gambling in England* (London, Duckworth & Co., 1898).

Asquith, Ivor, "The Structure, ownership and control of the press, 1780–1855," in George Boyce, ed., *Newspaper History from the 17th century to the present day* (London, Constable, 1978).

Banks, Stephen, *A Polite Exchange of Bullets* (London, Boydell & Brewer, 2010).

Barker, Hannah, *Newspapers, Politics and English Society 1695–1855* (Harlow, Longman, 2000).

Barrell, John, *Imagining the King's Death: Figurative Treason, Fantasies of Regicide, 1793–1796* (New York, Oxford University Press, 2000).

Beattie, J. M., *Crime and the Courts* (Princeton, Princeton University Press, 1986).

Beresford, Kathryn, "The 'hero of a thousand battles' betrays us! The Duke as hero and villain during the Emancipation crisis and after," in *Wellington Studies*, C. M. Woolgar, ed. (Southampton, University of Southampton Press) vol. 4, 2008.

Bernard, Sylvia M., *Viewing the Breathless Corpse* (Leeds, Words@Woodmere, 2001).

Binhammer, Katherine, "The Sex Panic of the 1790s," *Journal of the History of Sexuality*, January 1996.

Blanning, T. C. W., *The Culture of Power and the Power of Culture: Old Regime Europe 1660–1789* (Oxford, Oxford University Press, 2002).

Blyth, Henry, *Hell and Hazard, or William Crockford versus the Gentlemen of England* (London, Weidenfeld, 1969).

Bouwsma, William J., *A Usable Past: Essays in European Cultural History* (Berkeley, University of California Press, 1990).

Brewer, John, "The Most Polite Age and the Most Vicious," in *The Consumption of Culture, 1600–1800*, ed. Ann Bermingham and John Brewer (London, Routledge, 1995).

———, *Party Ideology and Popular Politics at the Accession of George III* (Cambridge, Cambridge University Press, 1976).

———, "This, that and the other: Public, social and private in the seventeenth and eighteenth centuries," in *Shifting the Boundaries: Transformation of the Languages of Public and Private in the Eighteenth Century*, ed. Dario Castiglione and Lesley Sharpe (Exeter, University of Exeter Press, 1995).

Bryson, Amanda, *From Courtesy to Civility* (Oxford, Clarendon, 1998).

Carter, Philip, *Men and the Emergence of Polite Society, 1660–1800* (Harlow, Longman, 2001).

Clarke, Bob, *From Grub Street to Fleet Street* (Aldershot, Ashgate Publishing, 2004).

Crump, Justine, "A Study of Gaming in Eighteenth Century English Novels" (Unpublished PhD thesis, Oxford University, 1997).

Dickinson, H. T., "The Mohun-Hamilton duel: personal feud or Whig plot?" *Durham University Journal* (1965).

Fletcher, Anthony, *Gender, Sex, and Subordination in England, 1500–1800* (New Haven, Yale University Press, 1995).

Franklin, Robert, "The Death of Lord Londonderry," *The Historian*, 96, 2007.

Fulford, Roger, *Samuel Whitbread, 1764–1815: A Study in Opposition* (London, Macmillan, 1967).

Gadd, David, *Georgian Summer* (Bath, Adam & Dart, 1971).

Gates, Barbara, *Victorian Suicide: Mad Crimes and Sad Histories* (Princeton, Princeton University Press, 1988).

Gattrell, V., *City of Laughter* (New York, Walter and Co., 2006).

George, M. Dorothy, *Catalogue of Political and Personal Satires* (London, 1978).

Gilbert, Arthur, "Law and honour among eighteenth-century British army officers," *Historical Journal*, 19, 1976.

Goodrich, Amanda, *Debating England's Aristocracy in the 1790s* (Rochester, N.Y., Boydell Press, 2005).

Glendinning, Victoria, *Trollope* (London, Hutchinson, 1992).

Haig, Robert Lewis, *The Gazetteer, 1735–1797* (Carbondale, Southern Illinois University Press, 1960).

Harris, Bob, *Politics and the Rise of the Press* (London, Routledge, 1996).

———, "Praising the Middling Sort? Social Identity in Eighteenth-Century British Newspapers," in *The Making of the British Middle Class?* ed. Alan Kidd and David Nicholls (Stroud, Sutton, 1998).

Havard, J. D. J., *The Detection of Secret Homicide* (London, Macmillan, 1980).

Hunt, Margaret R., *The Middling Sort, Commerce, Gender and the Family in England 1680–1780* (Berkeley, University of California Press, 1996).

Jones, Gareth Stedman, *The Languages of Class* (Cambridge, Cambridge University Press, 1983).

Kelly, James, *'That damn'd thing called honour': dueling in Ireland 1570–1860* (Cork, Cork University Press, 1995).

———, "The Decline of Dueling and the Emergence of the Middle Class in Ireland" in *Politics, Society and the Middle Class in Modern Ireland*, ed. Fintan Lane (Basingstoke: Palgrave Macmillan, 2010).

Klein, Lawrence, "Politeness and the Interpretation of the British Eighteenth Century," *The Historical Journal*, Volume 45, Number 4 (2002).

———, *Shaftesbury and the Culture of Politeness* (Cambridge, Cambridge University Press, 1994).

Langford, Paul, *A Polite and Commercial People 1727–1783* (Oxford, Oxford University Press, 1998).

Lieberman, David, *The Province of Legislation Determined; Legal theory in eighteenth-century Britain* (Cambridge, Cambridge University Press, 1989).

Lloyd, Sarah, "Amour in the Shrubbery: Reading the Detail of English Adultery Trial Publications of the 1780s," *Eighteenth-Century Studies*, 38(4) 2006.

Longford, Elizabeth, *Wellington*, 2 vols. (London, Weidenfeld & Nicholson, 1969).

MacDonald, Michael, and Terence Murphy, *Sleepless Souls* (Oxford, Clarendon, 1990).

McCord, James N., jr., "Politics and Honor in Early Nineteenth Century England: the Dukes' duel," *The Huntington Library Quarterly* 62, 1999.

McCreery, Cindy, "Breaking all the Rules: the Worsley Affair in Late Eighteenth-Century Britain," in *Orthodoxy and Heresy in the Long Eighteenth Century: 1660–1830*, ed. Pat Rogers and Regina Hewitt (Lewisburg, Pa., Bucknell University Press, 2002).

———, *The Satirical Gaze: Prints of Women in Late Eighteenth-Century England* (Oxford: Oxford University Press, 2004).

Michaelson, Patricia Howell, "Women in the Reading Circle," *Eighteenth-Century Life* 13 (1990).

Oldham, James, *English Common Law in the Age of Mansfield* (Chapel Hill, N.C., University of North Carolina Press, 2004).

Parlin, Hanson T., *A Study in Shirley's Comedies of London Life*, reprint from the *Bulletin of the University of Texas*, No. 371.

Peltonen, Markku, *The Duel in Early Modern England: Civility, Politeness and Honour* (Cambridge, Cambridge University Press, 2003).

———, "Politeness and Whiggism, 1688–1732," *Historical Journal* 48:2 (2005).

Roberts, M. J. D., *Making English Morals* (Cambridge, Cambridge University Press, 2004).

Russell, Gillian, "Faro's Daughters: Female Gamesters, Politics and the Discourse of Finance in 1790s Britain," *Eighteenth Century Studies*, 33, 4 (Summer 2000).

———, "The Theatre of Crim. Con.: Thomas Erskine, Adultery and Radical Politics in the 1790s," in *Unrespectable Radicals: Popular Politics in the Age of Reform*, ed. Michael T. Davis & Paul Pickering (Aldershot, Ashgate, 2008).

Sabine, Lorenzo, *Notes on Duels and Duelling* (Boston, Crosby, Nichols, 1855).

Sainsbury, John, " 'Cool Courage Should Always Mark Me': John Wilkes and Duelling," *Journal of the Canadian Historical Association*, 1997.

Savage, Gail, "Erotic Stories and Public Decency: Newspaper Reporting of Divorce Proceedings in England," *Historical Journal* 41, 2 (1998).

Scull, Andrew, *The Most Solitary of Afflictions: Madness and Society in Britain, 1700–1900* (New Haven, Yale University Press, 1993).

Simpson, Antony E., "Dandelions on the Field of Honour: Dueling, the Middle Classes, and the Law in Nineteenth-Century England," in *Criminal Justice History*, 1988.

Stater, Victor, *High Life, Low Morals: The Duel that Shook Stuart Society* (London, John Murray, 1999).

Staves, Susan, "Money for honour: damages for criminal conversation," in *Studies in Eighteenth-Century Culture*, 11, 1982.

Steinmetz, Andrew, *The Gaming Table: Its Votaries and Victims* [1870] (Montclair, N.J., Patterson Smith Reprint Series, 1969).

Stone, Lawrence, *The Road to Divorce: England 1530–1987* (Oxford, Oxford University Press, 1990).

Taylor, Antony, *Lords of Misrule* (Basingstoke, Palgrave Macmillan, 2004).

Thale, Mary, "London Debating Societies in the 1790s," *Historical Journal* 32:1 (1989).

———, "Women in London Debating Societies in 1780," *Gender & History* 7:1 (1995).

Thomas, Keith, "The Double Standard," *Journal of the History of Ideas* 20:2 (1959).

Thompson, E. P., "Eighteenth Century English Society: Class Struggle without Class," *Social History* (May 1978).

———, *The Making of the English Working Class* (Harmondsworth, Penguin Books, 1968).

Turner, David, *Fashioning Adultery* (Cambridge, UK, University of Cambridge, 2002).

Van Lennup, William, ed., *Index to the London Stage 1660–1800* (Carbondale, Southern Illinois University Press, 1979).

Wagner, Peter, "The Pornographer in the Courtroom," in *Sexuality in Eighteenth-Century Britain*, ed. Paul-Gabriel Boucé (Totowa, N.J., Manchester University Press, 1982).

Werkmeister, Lucyle, *The London Daily Press 1772–1792* (Lincoln, University of Nebraska Press, 1963).

Wilson, Ben, *Decency and Disorder* (London, Faber & Faber, 2007).

Wolfram, Sybil, "Divorce in England, 1700–1857," *Journal of Legal Studies*, 155, 1985.

The Yale Edition of Horace Walpole's Correspondence, ed. W. S. Lewis, 48 vols. (New Haven, Yale University Press, 1937–83).

Index